Mindset, Moral Choice and Sin in the Anthropology of John Chrysostom

Early Christian Studies 15

Mindset, Moral Choice and Sin in the Anthropology of John Chrysostom

by

Raymond Laird

SCD Press

Mindset, Moral Choice and Sin in the Anthropology of John Chrysostom
by Raymond Laird
© 2012

Republished 2017 by
SCD Press
PO Box 1882
Macquarie Centre NSW 2113 Australia http://
scd.edu.au/about/#scd-press

First published in Australia in 2012 by ST PAULS
PUBLICATIONS in association with the Centre for
Early Christian Studies Australian Catholic University

National Library of Australia Cataloguing-in-publication data:
Laird, Raymond
Mindset, moral choice and sin in the anthropology of John Chrysostom / Raymond
Laird. 9780980642834 (pbk.)
Series: Early Christian Studies ; v. 15
Notes: Includes bibliographical references and index.
Subjects: John Chrysostom, Saint, d. 407 / John Chrysostom, Saint, d. 407--Teachings.
/ Theology, Doctrinal. / Christian literature, Early.
Other Authors/Contributors: Australian Catholic University. Centre for Early Christian
Studies.
272.2

Printed and bound by:

Ingram Spark

ISBN   978 0 9806428 3 4 (pbk.)

TABLE OF CONTENTS

ABBREVIATIONS

Alexander of Aprhodisias (Alex. Aphr.)
De fato

Aristotle (Arist.)
EN   *Ethica Nicomachea*

Augustine
Contra Iulianum   *Contra Iulianum haeresis Pelagianae defensorem libre sex*

Demosthenes (Demos.)
Aristocr.   *In Aristocratem*
Cor.   *De Corona*
Cor. Trier.   *De Corona tierarchiae*
Callip. 2.   *Contra Callipum*
Epis.   *Epistulae*
Erot.   *Eroticus*
Exord.   *In Exordia*
Halon.   *De Halloneso*
Fals. Leg.   *De falsa Legatione*
Mid,   *In Midiam*
2 Olynth.   *Olynthiaca 2*
Sym.   *Peri ton Summorion*
Syntax.   *Peri Suntaxeos*
Tim.   *In Timocratem*
1 Philipp.   *Philippica 1*
2 Philipp.   *Philippica 2*

Diodore (Diod.)
Comm. Pss.   *Commentarii in Psalmos I-L*

Epictetus (Epict.)
Discourses   *Dissertationes ab Arriano digestae*
Enc.   *Enchiridion*

Gregory of Nyssa
Contra. Eun.   *Contra Eunomium*

Irenaeus
Adv. Haer.   *Adversus Haereses*

John Chrysostom (John Chrys.)

Ad eos scan.	*Ad eos qui scandalizati sunt*
Ad illum.	*Ad illuminandos catecheses 1-2*
Adv. Jud.	*Adversus Judaeos*
Adv. oppug.	*Adversus oppugnatores vitae monasticae*
Cat. 1-8	*Catecheses ad illuminandos 1-8* (series tertia)
Cat.	*Catecheses ad illuminandos* (series 1 and 2)
De decem.	*De decem millium talentorurm debitore*
De diabolo	*De diabolo tentatore*
De eleem.	*De eleemosyna*
De fato.	*De fato et providentia*
De mut. nom.	*De mutatione nominum*
De perf. car.	*De perfecta caritate*
De paen.	*De paenitentia*
De res. Mort.	*De resurrectione mortuorum*
De Sac.	*De Sacerdotio*
De sanc. mar.	*De sanctis martyribus*
Mart.	*Homilia in martyres*
In laud. concept.	*In laudem conceptionis sancti Joannis Baptistae*
In Matt.	*In Matthaeum*
In Joan.	*In Joannem*
In Acta	*In Acta apostolorum*
In Rom.	*In epistulam ad Romanos*
In 1 Cor.	*In epistula i ad Corinthios*
In 2 Cor.	*In epistulam ii ad Corinthios*
Comm. in Gal.	*In epistulam ad Galatas commentarius*
In Eph.	*In epistulam ad Ephesios*
In Phil.	*In epistulam ad Philippenses*
In Col.	*In epistulam ad Collessenses*
In 1 Thes.	*In epistulam i ad Thessalonicenses*
In 2 Thes.	*In epistulam ii ad Thessalonicenses*
In 1 Tim.	*In epistulam i ad Timotheum*
In 2 Tim.	*In epistulam ii ad Timotheum*
In Titum	*In epistulam ad Titum*
In Philm.	*In epistulam Philemonem*
In Heb.	*In epistulam ad Hebraeos*
In Gen.	*In Genesisim (homiliae 1-67)*
Non grat.	*Non esse gratian conconandum*
Non desp.	*Non esse desperandum*
Poss.	*In illud: Pater, si possible est, transeat*
Utinam	*In Illud: Utinam sustineretis modicum*

Justin Martyr
Trypho.   *Dialogus cum Tryphone*

Libanius
Auto.   *Autobiography and Selected Letters*
Or.   *Orationes*
Dec.   *Declimationes*
Epist.   *Epistulaes*

Theodoret (Thdt.)
Interp. in Psalmos   *Interpretatio in Psalmos*
Interp. Pauli   *Interpretatio in xiv epistulas sancti Pauli*

Theodore of Mopsuestia (Thdr. Mops.)
Ho.   *Hosea*
Abd.   *Obadiah*
Am.   *Amos*
Exp. Ps.   *Commentary on the Psalms*
Joan.   *Commentarii in Joannem (John)*
Nah.   *Nahum*
Mi.   *Micah*
Mal.   *Malachi*
Zach.   *Zechariah*

Reference Books, Monograph Series and Other Source Material

ACU   Australian Catholic University
ACW   Ancient Christian Writers
ANF   Ante-Nicene Fathers
CCSG   Corpus Christianorum Series Graeca
EB   *Estudios Biblicos*
ECF   The Early Christian Fathers
ECS   Early Christian Studies
FOTC   Fathers of the Church
GBWW   Great Books of the Western World
GRBS   *Greek, Roman, and Byzantine Studies*
HTR   *Harvard Theological Review*
ITQ   *Irish Theological Quarterly*
IVP   Intervarsity Press
JBL   *Journal of Biblical Literature*

Foreword

This volume situates itself at the forefront of a new wave of interest in John Chrysostom's contribution to the development of Christian thought from his perspective as an eastern theologian. Contrary to previous approaches that valued John as a preacher, yet denied him a more serious contribution by labelling him a "moral theologian", this study dives straight to the heart of John's anthropology to reveal the presence of a well-developed and carefully thought through understanding of the relationship between the human person, the soul, the mindset, and sin. John anticipates by some three centuries the systematisation within eastern Christian thought by Maximus the Confessor of the mindset as a major concept in the anthropology of fallen human beings. In this regard John is not alone. The contextualisation of John's thought within the rich Greek *paideia* within which he was educated and examination of its relationship to that of his fellow theologians of the Antiochene milieu further reveal that John's concept of the mindset builds firmly on a foundation of earlier Greek ethical philosophy and constitutes part of a common heritage among theologians linked to that part of the eastern Christian world. Both are important findings.

It is forty years ago that one of the great scholars of Chrysostom studies, Robert Carter S.J., at a symposium of Chrysostom scholars in Thessaloniki (1972), made a plea for renewal of the study of John's theology, an area which he considered to have been both undervalued and neglected. While a variety of studies of various aspects of John's theology have been published in the interim, few delve as deeply as this one or show so clearly that in this area, too, John had a serious contribution to make. It is to be hoped that this study will serve as a model for the future and that, on reading it, others will be inspired to look at John's theology in a new light.

Wendy Mayer
March 2012

Preface

It is twenty-three years since I first turned my mind to some serious study on John Chrysostom. As a lecturer who covered the wide scope of Church History with some concentrations here and there, I was familiar with the basic outline of his life and significance, but he was only an acquaintance. Now, I have the temerity to suggest that he has become a friend. I have endeavoured to dig into his mind to mine some of the theological treasure of this great scholar-communicator. I have thought for a very long time that the essence of good scholarship is the ability to make the difficult seem simple. Apart from his deep knowledge of the Bible, his expert understanding of his culture, and his appreciation of the vagaries of human nature, Chrysosotom's excellent rhetorical skill was the great asset that enabled him to communicate simply what is truly profound. I think I am much the richer for his companionship.

I am deeply grateful to those who supplied the initial sparks to embark on this journey. The late Professor Godfrey Tanner under whose expertise I first plunged into the world of post-graduate Patristic studies was a vital part of that impetus. Godfrey and I often had different interpretations of the Christian past, but his exceptional linguistic skills were to me a constant source of envy. Our discussions were lively, to say the least, and some of his searching questions still ring in my ears. If he were alive today, I would have to confess to him that he was more often right than I allowed at the time. He alerted me to threads and connections that I have since found cause to pursue to great advantage. The result of my work with Godfrey brought further fuel to the fire. Encouraging remarks from Sir Henry Chadwick and Dr Patrick Ryan on that work when submitted to them caused me to think that I should continue pursuing the path I had taken. Dr Robert Charles Hill was a rich source of encouragement, information and critique. I am deeply grateful that I have been privileged to benefit from the rich insights of his mature years before he passed away. Dr Bruce Harris brought his vast understanding of classical and early Christian thought to bear upon my work. I am thankful that he made me dig deep into my own classical studies, that had lain somewhat latent, and thus to enrich the quality of the final product. I am very thankful that another leading Chrysostom and Patristic scholar, Professor Pauline Allen, was prepared to see this project through to its completion. Her wealth of knowledge and her meticulous attention to detail ensured a better work than otherwise would have been the case. I have benefited also from the expert comments of Professor David Hunter and Professor Wendy Mayer. I have not accepted every bit of their critique or advice, but the work would be poorer without their wisdom. On the publication side, my thanks are due to the editorial skills of the faculty and staff at CECS, especially David Luckensmeyer and Dinah Joesoef with her expert composing skills. Their advice and patience have been much appreciated.

It would be extremely brutish of me to fail to give tribute to Valerie, my wife. She has always pursued my best interests and has done so with love and understanding. She has kept me to this task. She abhors waste in every realm of life, thus there was little chance, apart from the intervention of death, that this work would not be brought to completion. I am deeply grateful for her eagle eye and her expert computer skills in correcting the various drafts. Most of all I am indebted to her for all the encouragement she has contributed, not the least being the discipline to ensure that this journey would reach its destination.

Ray Laird.

CHAPTER 1

Introduction

In the Eastern Orthodox theological tradition there is no concept of original sin as understood in classical Western tradition.[1] Orthodoxy prefers to talk about the sin of the forebears and leave the individual free to progress and grow by struggling against mortality or death, the result of sin, as it impacts upon us in its various forms. In support of this view, appeal is made to St John Chrysostom who stands tall in Orthodox tradition. Some twelve years after Chrysostom's death, Julian of Eclanum in his dispute with Augustine went on record as being the first to claim Chrysostom as an authority for his own Pelagian views. In response, Augustine claimed that Chrysostom held to a doctrine of hereditary sin and guilt.[2] The debate continues, though many patristic scholars from the West prefer to acquit Chrysostom of any charge of Pelagianism on various grounds, including the assertion that this matter was not an issue during his ministry. Therefore, he had no cause to consider or include in his teaching the theological problems afterward raised.[3] Much of this debate has been conducted on a surface level, confined to a search for statements in Chrysostom's writings that aver or even infer what he thought about sin, grace, guilt and innocence, for example. As our Lord taught that sin is something that works deeply in the human psyche (Matt. 5:27-28; 15:18-20), it would seem more profitable to examine Chrysostom's anthropology, his understanding of the workings of the psyche, if we are to discern his concept of the nature of sin and its locus in the soul. My contention is that γνώμη, referring to

---

[1] J. Meyendorf, *Byzantine Theology: Historical Trends and Doctrinal Themes* (New York 1979²) 143-145. For a contrary or at least modified position, see P.C. Phan, *Grace and the Human Condition*, MFC 15 (Wilmington, DE 1988) 203.

[2] B. Altaner, "Augustinus und Johannes Chrysostomus. Quellenkritische Untersuchungen", *Kleine Patristiche Schriften herausgegeben von Günter Glockmann* (Berlin 1967) 302-311, repr. from *Zeitschrift für neutestamentliche Wissenschaft* 44 (1952-1953) 76-84.

[3] F.J. Thonnard, "Saint Jean Chrysostome et Saint Augustin dans la controverse pélagienne", *Revue des Études Byzantines* 25 (1967) 189-218; H. Rondet, *Original Sin: The Patristic and Theological Background*, trans. C. Finnegan (New York 1972) esp. 106-131; B. Collett, "A Benedictine scholar and Greek patristic thought in pre-Tridentine Italy: a monastic commentary of 1538 on Chrysostom", *JEH* 36 (1985) 66-81; R.C. Hill, "A Pelagian commentator on the Psalms", *ITQ* 63 (1988) 263-271; Phan, *Grace and the Human Condition*, 197-203; S. Donegan, "John Chrysostom's exegesis of Romans 5:12-21: does it support a doctrine of original sin?", *Diakonia* 22 (1988-1989) 5-14; R. Brändle, "Johannes Chrysostomus I", in E. von Dassman et al. (eds), *RAC* vol.17 (Stuttgart 1998) 471-472; R. Brändle, *Johannes Chrysostomus: Bischof – Reformer – Märtyr* (Stuttgart–Berlin–Cologne 1999) 52-53.

the mindset and its various aspects, is seen by Chrysostom to be the critical faculty of the soul in which sin works and in which it can find a permanent place of lodging. It is the faculty that Chrysostom perceived to be the citadel in the soul that needed release from its captivity to sin by the power of the Gospel. The γνώμη requires transformation by the willing cooperation of the individual with the ongoing work of the Holy Spirit. This may not solve the issue of the debate, but it does provide a more substantial base on which to conduct it. What this study does do is move the concentration away from the προαίρεσις (moral choice) to the controlling and motivating faculty behind it, the γνώμη.[4]

In attempting to discern Chrysostom's anthropology it must be noted that among the voluminous corpus Chrysostom left behind there is very little direct dogmatic discussion. Much of the material is homily or commentary. In the absence of any extended treatise on sin, in order to discern Chrysostom's mind on the subject we are forced to comb his corpus for incidental references and limited discussions on the matter. As the focus of this study is the issue of sin in relation to his anthropology, the procedure taken when thus endeavouring to gather his overall approach to the human situation is especially significant in relation to the validity of its conclusions.

In order to set the scene, it is relevant to note that in a homily on the parable of the sower in Matthew's Gospel, Chrysostom distinguishes between the basic nature of the land and something he calls the γνώμη. While he says, as does the parable, that the blame for the difference in crops is attributable to the distinctions in the nature of the land, he qualifies this by his comment, οὐ παρὰ τὴν φύσιν, ἀλλὰ παρὰ τὴν γνώμην ("it is not because of its nature, but because of its γνώμη").[5] The failure of the Word to become fruitful is attributed to τὴν γνώμην τὴν διεφθαρμένην ("the corrupt γνώμη").[6] The distinction between φύσις (nature) and γνώμη is important for understanding the basic elements of Chrysostom's anthropology. On first sight, this distinction appears to be moving the problem of original sin one step back from the essential nature of humankind but not removing it altogether. If the γνώμη is a fundamental element or faculty of human nature, or even if it is only the orientation of nature or some element within it, then, at least in experience, there seems little difference between a corrupt φύσις and a corrupt γνώμη. However, it is not fitting to make a judgment until the evidence has been presented. A number of questions must be answered before a

---

[4] I follow Aristotle in considering γνώμη to be a faculty or power of the soul. See *EN* 1143b 25-29 where he groups γνώμη with σύνεσις, φρόνησις, and νοῦς, as δυνάμεις, powers i.e. faculties or natural capacities.

[5] *In Matt. hom.* 44; PG 57,469 3.

[6] *In Matt. hom.* 44; PG 57,469 10-11.

verdict is pronounced. The chief among these are as follows: in Chrysostom's perception,

(a) What is the γνώμη that appears to be so critical to the acceptance or rejection of divine revelation?

(b) What relationship does it bear to the basic φύσις, the nature of the human being?

(c) What relationship does it bear to other faculties of the human psyche, especially the προαίρεσις which figures so centrally in many discussions of responsibility in patristic anthropology?

(d) To what extent is it the critical factor in Chrysostom's perception of the human situation?

(e) What responsibility is ascribed to it in the process of sin?

(f) Is it the locus of sin in the soul?

(g) Is it fixed or subject to change?

(h) If it is subject to change, how is it developed and conditioned to accept truth?

(i) If it is central to Chrysostom's anthropology, what sources and factors shaped his usage of this term?

I. Methodology

The main thrust of this study requires a detailed examination of numerous passages of the Greek text in a wide range of Chrysostom's homilies. This necessitates an appreciation of the contextual factors involved. First, there are the immediate and wider textual contexts of each of the passages examined. No term may be isolated from the text in which it appears or from its function in a particular text. This, at least, includes the immediate section of a homily, on occasion the whole homily, and in some instances a whole series of homilies. What must be avoided is proof-texting done without regard for contexts. With this in mind, examination of Chrysostom's usage of γνώμη will be done with due regard to the textual contexts.

Then there are the personal contexts of the preacher himself. For one thing, there are the exegetical and theological contexts, the general approaches in these regards of the Antiochene School of which Chrysostom was a notable member. E. Clark has provided a perceptive survey of the deconstruction of the traditional categories of the Antiochene and Alexandrian approaches to biblical exegesis.[7] It

---

[7] E.A. Clark, *Reading Renunciation: Asceticism and Scripture in Early Christianity* (Princeton, NJ 1999) 70-78. For various insights on the two traditions, see C. Schäublin, *Untersuchungen zu Methode und Herkunft der antiochenischen Exegese*, Theophaneia: Beiträge zur Religions-und-

appeared to be a well-established general principle that the Antiochenes were more historical, typological and literal in their approach to their exegetical work than the Alexandrian theologians who used a more allegorical method. Clark asserts that in regards to this divide of the ancient schools into allegorical and literal, "such categories shade into and conjoin each other in ways that ignore their alleged boundaries".[8] At a much earlier date L. Bouyer had questioned at least one element of the so-called division. He denied that the Alexandrians started on any other than a literal base and proposed that they went down a metaphysical and mystical road compared to the Antiochenes who, starting on the same base, took a historical, typological and moralistic path.[9] Underlying Bouyer's assertion is the reality that both schools accepted the biblical accounts as given fact.[10] What they

---

Kirchengeschichte des Altertums 23 (Cologne–Bonn 1974); P. Gorday, *Principles of Patristic Exegesis: Romans 9-11 in Origen, John Chrysostom and Augustine*, SBEC 4 (New York–Toronto 1983); F. Young, "Exegetical method and scriptural proof: the Bible in doctrinal debate", *SP* 19 (1989) 290-304; F. Young, "The rhetorical schools and their influence on patristic exegesis", in R. Williams (ed.), *The Making of Orthodoxy: Essays in Honour of Henry Chadwick* (Cambridge 1989) 182-199; A.S. McCormick, "John Chrysostom's Homily 50 as an example of the Antiochene exegetical tradition", *Patristic and Byzantine Review* 12 (1993) 65-82; M. Simonetti, *Biblical Interpretation in the Early Church: An Historical Introduction to Patristic Exegesis*, trans. J.A. Hughes (Edinburgh 1994); F. Young, *Biblical Exegesis and the Formation of Christian Culture* (Cambridge 1997); J.H. Barkhuizen, "John Chrysostom on the parables in the Gospel of Matthew: a study in Antiochean exegesis", *Ekklesiastikos Pharos* 80 (1998) 160-178; J.D. Cassel, "Key principles in Cyril of Alexandria's exegesis", *SP* 37 (2001) 411-420; H. Amirav, *Rhetoric and Tradition: John Chrysostom on Noah and the Flood*, TEG 12 (Leuven 2003) 33-38; R.C. Hill, *Reading the Old Testament in Antioch*, Bible in Ancient Christianity 5 (Leiden–Boston 2005) 135-165.

[8] Clark, *Reading Renunciation*, 71; Young, *Biblical Exegesis*, is of the same mind: "The traditional categories of 'literal', 'typological' and 'allegorical' are quite simply inadequate as descriptive tools, let alone analytical tools."; Cassel, "Key principles", 411-420, examines Cyril's use of allegory. His results seem to suggest that later Alexandrian interpreters may have moved away from the more fanciful allegorical applications of earlier periods to a more sober approach in their usage by the fourth century.

[9] L. Bouyer, *The Spirituality of the New Testament and the Fathers,* trans. M.P. Ryan, A History of Christian Spirituality (London 1963) 437-438.

[10] I hesitate to call Antiochene exegesis literal, as they were not always literalist in their approach, if those terms are used in certain narrow senses. R.C. Hill, "Chrysostom, interpreter of the Psalms", *EB* 56 (1998) 69, when discussing Chrysostom's "Attachment to the Literal Sense" writes, "Yet, while clearly preferring the literal sense of the text, he is not a literalist: he can appreciate the literary purpose of the Psalmist."; Hill, *Reading the Old Testament*, 102, where he later explains his position in a statement on Chrysostom's homilies on Genesis to the effect that they provided a literalist reading because the biblical text was taken as comprised of factual statements. Hill elaborates on this in the same place at 150-154, where he nuances the Antiochenes' literal approach to the text by saying, "their procedure was generally not literalist

ended up doing with the accounts is another thing. Early arguments proposed various reasons for the differences. H. Nash, in refuting the charge that Aristotelianism at Antioch was responsible for the rejection of allegory in exegesis there, ascribes that rejection of allegory to a reaction against Gnosticism in Syria.[11] T. Pollard traces the difference to the contrasting influences of Palestinian Judaism and Alexandrian Judaism.[12] F. Young traces the differences in approach to "the divide between the pagan schools of rhetoric and philosophy",[13] with Alexandria following the influence of philosophy and Antioch that of rhetoric. H. Amirav, in a very interesting study of exegetical models, concludes that traditional differences in theological understanding of critical issues such as the freedom of the will determined the respective exegetical approaches of the Alexandrians and the Antiochenes.[14] Even this brief survey suggests that perhaps the divide was a construct based on shaky grounds. This seems to be the case as the debate has shifted to the difficulty of distinguishing between allegory and typology in the patristic literature. Nevertheless, care needs to be taken not to dispense with the approach of some Fathers in searching for metaphysical principles, and that of others making a more direct theological application to pastoral needs.[15] Chrysostom clearly falls into the latter category. W. Mayer and P. Allen aptly describe Chrysostom's general approach as a "preference for directness".[16] The

---

or fundamentalist", because they did allow for such things as levels of meanings, for treasures concealed beneath the surface, and the need to search for the Spirit's meaning. They were not always consistent in this and sometimes fell into a simplistic approach. See also D.S. Wallace-Hadrill, *Christian Antioch: A Study of Early Christian Thought in the East* (Cambridge 1982) 32-33; for a contrary position, see Simonetti, *Biblical Interpretation*, 67-77, who ascribes an extreme literalist stance to Chrysostom.

[11] H.S. Nash, "The exegesis of the School of Antioch", *JBL* 11 (1892) 22-37.

[12] T.E. Pollard, "The origins of Christian exegesis", *JRH* 1 (1961) 138-147.

[13] F. Young, "The Rhetorical schools", 195; A. Attrep, "The teacher and his teachings: Chrysostom's homiletic approach as seen in the Commentaries on the Gospel of John", *St Vladimir's Theological Quarterly* 38 (1994) 293-301, on the contrary suggests a close resemblance in Chrysostom to Aristotle in their perspectives and themes.

[14] H. Amirav, "Exegetical models and Chrysostomian homiletics: the example of Gen. 6.2", *SP* 37 (1999) 311-325, esp. 318; Amirav, *Rhetoric and Tradition*, 6.

[15] Young, "The rhetorical schools", 192-193, illustrates the exegetical divide by the different treatments of the Matthew feeding story by Origen and Chrysostom.

[16] W. Mayer and P. Allen, *John Chrysostom*, ECF (London–New York 2000) 27. This point is significant, though these authors appear to maintain a wider divide between Alexandria and Antioch than other recent contributions suggest is defensible. D. Tyng, "Theodore of Mopsuestia as an interpreter of the Old Testament", *JBL* 50 (1931) 298-303, at 303 n. 5, gives a good demonstration of the Antiochene tradition of this preference for directness as represented by Chrysostom's colleague, Theodore: "In this connection there is an interesting contrast between Theodore's general method and, say, that of Cyril, which I may illustrate by the locusts

issue is not critical to the substance of this study; it suffices to note Chrysostom's preference for directness and to remember that, as Clark maintains, "there is no doubt that figurative reading was deemed essential by early Christian exegetes".[17] Chrysostom uses figurative language when it serves his purpose.

In relation to Chrysostom's exegesis, the influence of the *asketerion* of Diodore should not be overlooked. There, under a very able master, Chrysostom was brought in touch with exegetical tradition(s) of the past. As with his practice in other studies, it is evident that he drank deeply from those wells. Amirav makes a pertinent observation:

> Chrysostom is not the last in the line of Christian homilists and exegetes, but he is certainly not the first. He seems to owe his impressive output of writings to the exegetical teaching of his predecessors and colleagues, no less than to the teachings of his pagan professors.[18]

This suggests that aspects of the focus of this study would find substantial support in the writings of other Church Fathers. This is indeed the case. Whilst I have not given much attention to this in the detail of this dissertation, I have devoted a brief survey to it in Chapter 9.

More to the point is an observation by Hill who has translated a number of the works of Chrysostom and the other Antiochenes. He has discerned that Chrysostom differs from others in the Antiochene cohort in that whereas Diodore of Tarsus, Theodore of Mopsuestia and Theodoret of Cyrus produced desk commentaries and therefore could afford lengthy digression on theological topics, he was restrained by the discipline of the open text of the preacher's chair.[19] He would take time as a skilful preacher-pastor to apply the text to some moral evil. At times, he would engage in some theological subtlety elicited from the text and that addressed some current need, but rarely at length, and this was the exception rather than the rule. In any analytical research of Chrysostom's corpus, his focus upon pastoral needs should never be overlooked.

This raises a significant issue for this study, which is an attempt to discern Chrysostom's anthropology in relation to sin. As noted above, Chrysostom left very little in the vast corpus of his works that could be directly classified as

---

in Joel. Theodore finds the literal sense inadequate, so he takes locusts in the metaphorical-literal sense as a symbol of the ravaging Assyrian. Cyril has no difficulty with the literal sense, but jumps at once to the allegorical. The locusts symbolise the ravaging effects of sin. Again, they stand for the devouring heretic who leaves both mind and soul stripped and bare."

[17] Clark, *Reading Renunciation*, 77. She equates "figurative" with "spiritual" at 78.

[18] Amirav, *Rhetoric and Tradition*, 223.

[19] Hill, *Reading the Old Testament*, 169.

theological. The great majority fall under the category of expositional homilies that proceed through entire books of the Bible verse by verse. There are many others which are occasional homilies designed for particular events such as special times in the cycle of the Christian calendar, the instruction of catechumens or some notable event such as the death of a colleague or a crisis in the city.[20] Theological search under these circumstances, therefore, is both a delicate matter and a bold venture. In one exercise it deals with both the incidental and the substantial, gleaning scattered nuggets from material of a multi-purpose nature and not specifically designed as a theological treatise in the accepted sense of that term. This exercise is conducted with the recognition that great care must be taken in handling the material under examination. However, it is done with the following convictions:

(a) Chrysostom's homilies are theologically informed. No preacher of substance can prepare or deliver sermons that do not incorporate in some way their theological convictions and presuppositions.

(b) Those theological convictions and presuppositions will reveal themselves sooner or later in the course of a person's ministry. One cannot continually comment on Scripture and speak of God and divine-human relationships without exposing one's own understanding of these issues.

(c) Given the extent and intensity of Chrysostom's preaching ministry it is more than reasonable to think that many of his theological positions would be revealed in his homiletic material.

(d) It is wellnigh impossible to sit under someone's preaching ministry for a length of time without becoming aware not only of particular points of the preacher's theology but also of his/her general theological orientation. This applies more so to the reading of Chrysostom's homilies where time to absorb and analyse is far greater than attendance at the point of preaching. This is not to minimise what is lost thereby.

(e) Chrysostom's homilies were not created to entertain but to inform and motivate, to educate, and to stimulate application of truth to life. They were not mere calls to action but to action based upon biblical and theological understanding. Chrysostom was at great pains in his homilies to provide the theological motivations for actions.[21]

---

[20] Mayer and Allen, *John Chrysostom*, 29, mention six or seven categories but note that in practice they overlap.

[21] G. Fee, *To What End Exegesis? Essays Textual, Exegetical and Theological* (Grand Rapids, MI–Cambridge 2001) 280, asks a critical question about exegesis in relation to biblical texts, "to what end exegesis?" In answer he writes, "the ultimate aim of exegesis (as I perceive it) is to produce in our lives and in the lives of others true Spirituality, in which God's people live in

(f)   There is wide assent that Chrysostom, as with all of the church Fathers, treated the scriptures as divinely inspired.[22] In his mind there was no divorce of theology from scripture as often has become the case in more recent times. Thus the exposition of a biblical text was for him as much a theological enterprise as a pastoral exhortation. In this sense his homilies are theological documents. The comment of R. Wilken is appropriate:

> For most of the Church's history theology and Scriptural interpretation were one. Theology was called *sacra pagina* and the task of interpreting the Bible was a theological exercise. The Church's faith and life were seen as continuous with the Biblical narrative, and the Scriptures were interpreted within the context of a living theological and spiritual tradition.[23]

While this is my *apologia* for searching Chrysostom's homilies for his theological anthropology, the search must also take account of the historical, social, cultural and liturgical contexts that impinge upon the preacher and his audiences, especially as those factors play their part in determining the choice of images and vocabulary. Due regard will be given to those factors. Much has been written on these issues in recent times. The point here is that Chrysostom must be understood within the context of his own times. For example, it is not the intention here to apply our contemporary standards of exegetical practice to his handling of

---

faithful fellowship both with one another and with the eternal living God and thus in keeping with God's purpose in the world". Chrysostom would have been in full agreement. Though there might be differences in exegetical method, this is one issue in which fifteen hundred years makes no difference.

[22] F. Young, *From Nicaea to Chalcedon: A Guide to its Literature and its Background* (London 1983) 156, observes: "Chrysostom's perspective is that of a fourth-century churchman regarding the scriptural text as divine oracles, miraculously delivered to men in spite of their barbarity, in spite of the poverty of the writer's intellect – after all, Paul was a mere tent-maker!"; R.C. Hill, "Chrysostom's terminology for the inspired Word", *EB* 41 (1983) 367-373, at 367 begins his article with the sentence: "St John Chrysostom, like the Fathers generally, is deeply convinced of the fact of the inspiration of Scripture." See also his *Reading the Old Testament*, 27-45, for a discussion pertinent to this issue.

[23] R.L. Wilken, "Defence of allegory", *Modern Theology* 14 (1998) 198-212, at 210; see also H. Reuling, *After Eden: Church Fathers and Rabbis on Genesis 3:16-21* (Leiden 2006) 115-157, esp. 115 n. 3, the remark: "It has been noted that Chrysostom's works are of limited theological originality, and that his moral orientation makes him less interesting from a technical-exegetical view-point...Accurate as these observations may be, they are not very productive. It seems to me that Chrysostom's originality is to be found exactly in the homiletic adaptation of Antiochene thought." Also at 116 n. 5, "Yet far from being the moralist he is sometimes held to be, Chrysostom preaches from a profound understanding of the Christian faith which is rooted in the ideal of perfect spiritual life."

the biblical text. The aim is to determine what he thought about the motions of the soul in regard to sin and response. Here it is not for us to say whether his particular interpretation of a Biblical text is correct or otherwise. At times one's heart might be caused to sing, at others one's eyebrows might be raised in doubt; some light might be shed, some scepticism might be stirred, but all that is incidental and must not be allowed to deflect from the task in hand, that is to discern his thinking on the issue in question.

Needing special mention is the rhetorical context. Although this is a part of the social and cultural context, it is worthy of separate recognition and treatment. The reason for this is the fact that, for the main part, Chrysostom's corpus is a compilation of sermons delivered by a rhetor *par excellence* that knew well all the arts of his trade and did not refrain from using them when he felt that his purpose could be better accomplished by their use.[24] As M. Mitchell has presented an excellent survey of previous scholarship on this issue together with extensive bibliographic material, it is not intended here to repeat that exercise.[25] There is only the need to make the following observations:

(a) T. Ameringer appears to have established the intense rhetorical nature of Chrysostom's homilies. He thinks that Chrysostom overdid it and "is not free from the bad taste and the mannerisms of the sophistic rhetoric".[26] Although, in my opinion, he is somewhat unjustified in this judgement, there is no doubting the value of his seminal work in demonstrating Chrysostom's wide-ranging use of the skills he learnt in his education, especially at the feet of Antioch's premier rhetor,

---

[24] Mayer and Allen, *John Chrysostom*, 27: "The traces of John's rhetorical education can be seen in every aspect of his sermons' structure, content and delivery...The full range of the rhetorical tricks at the disposal of the well-trained orator are to be observed throughout John's sermons."

[25] M.M. Mitchell, *The Heavenly Trumpet: John Chrysostom and the Art of Pauline Interpretation* (Louisville, KY–Westminster, MD 2002) 22-28.

[26] T.E. Ameringer, *A Study in Greek Rhetoric: The Stylistic Influence of the Second Sophistic on the Panegyrical Sermons of St John Chrysostom*, Patristic Studies of the CUA 5 (Washington, DC 1921) 102. This is reminiscent of J. Locke, *An Essay Concerning Human Understanding*, GBWW 35 (Chicago–London–Toronto–Geneva 1952), the 17th-century political and educational philosopher, who laid the epistemological foundations of modern science. He made this assessment of the use of rhetorical figures at 299: "But yet if we would speak of things as they are, we must allow that the art of rhetoric, besides order and clearness; all the artificial and figurative application of words eloquence has invented, are nothing else but to insinuate wrong ideas, move the passions, and thereby mislead the judgement; and so indeed are perfect cheats; and therefore, however laudable or allowable oratory may render them in harangues and popular addresses, they are certainly, in all discourses that pretend to inform or instruct, wholly to be avoided; and where truth and knowledge are concerned, cannot but be thought a great fault, either of the language or person that makes use of them."

Libanius. Ameringer, in his introduction to his dissertation, writes against those scholars who minimised the influence of the sophists on Chrysostom when he says,

> If these statements were correct, we argued, then the sermons of Chrysostom presented a psychological phenomenon that was indeed remarkable. It seemed strange to us that Chrysostom should be detached to such an extent from the rhetoric in which he was trained from his early youth, and which, prior to his ordination, claimed him as one of its ablest exponents.[27]

(b) In addition to the scholarship since Ameringer which has confirmed and expanded upon his basic thesis, recent contributions made by those who have focused on the study of ancient rhetoric and its application to early Christianity have unearthed some interesting material. M. Heath has observed that rhetorical training in late antiquity was focused on judicial and deliberative oratory in order to meet the need of the times and that Chrysostom's exegetical works reflects the techniques of that focus.[28] L. Thurén, in asserting that Chrysostom's rhetorical education was somewhat broader than the judicial and deliberative focus, remarks that as a rhetorician, "He represents a dynamic understanding of the text: it is not seen as displaying static dogmatic ideas, but as a means of persuading the addressees."[29] Their different perspectives do not diminish the fact that both Heath and Thurén are acknowledging the intense persuasive element of Chrysostom's preaching. This points to his convictions of the necessity of scripture for life and salvation, its applicability to all and not to just a favoured elite, and his justification of the use of the rhetorical skills that were a significant part of his education. J. Maxwell, referring to the Second Sophistic, has weighed in with the remark that "One of the defining characteristics of this movement was its double focus on philosophical content and rhetorical form."[30] She points out that this constitutes a difficulty in drawing a definitive line between the philosophers and

---

[27] Ameringer, *A Study in Greek Rhetoric*, 10.

[28] M. Heath, "John Chrysostom, rhetoric and Galatians", *Biblical Interpretation* 12 (2004) 369-400, at 371-372.

[29] L. Thurén, "John Chrysostom as a rhetorical critic: the hermeneutics of an early Father", *Biblical Interpretation* 9 (2001) 180-218, at 213.

[30] J.L. Maxwell, *Christianization and Communication in Late Antiquity: John Chrysostom and His Congregation in Antioch* (Cambridge 2006) 12. Maxwell provides a perceptive study of the social framework that bridged the gap between the educated elite and the general populace in Chapter 1, "Philosophical preaching in the Roman world", 11-41. The case-study on Amphilochius, 36-39, is particularly helpful.

the sophists of late antiquity.[31] Add to this the influence of the Cynics on ethics, the common schooling of the Greek παιδεία, the shared rhetorical training of pagans and Christians under noted pagan rhetors, the affectionate relationships which often existed between the pagan teachers and their Christian students, and indeed, between the students themselves. With those considerations in mind, the drawing of the line between these groups and the Christian preachers would be difficult to define were it not for the preachers' Christian faith. Among other things, this move to the enriching of rhetorical content with philosophical ideas and forcing philosophers to be more public in their teaching made philosophy more accessible to ordinary people. For the purpose of this study, this combination of factors ensures that we are on safe ground in accepting Chrysostom's familiarity with the philosophical literature of the Greeks even though at times he expresses disdain for them. Furthermore, it suggests why it was that Chrysostom had no hesitation in integrating his rhetorical skills with his Christian understanding and knowledge of the scriptures. Integration in this fashion had been inculcated through his rhetorical training until it had become spontaneous practice.[32] Substitution of the content of Classical pagan literature, but not necessarily many of its images and much of its vocabulary, by that of the Christian scriptures would have been somewhat automatic. It must be said, however, that like many then and since, Chrysostom was caught in the tension between revelation, as understood as needing no education for cognition, and reason, which requires the best training possible. The simple fishermen, Peter and John, and the educated Saul of Tarsus were alike apostles of the Lord Jesus. Hence, we meet Chrysostom's ostensible ambivalence, at times exalting the simple, at others commending the wisdom of the wise. It is interesting to note that Mitchell has discerned his main archetypal image as Paul: "In my reading in Chrysostom's writings I soon was able to articulate what is *the* interpretive key to John's

---

[31] Maxwell, *Christianization and Communication*, 12; See also G. Anderson, *The Second Sophistic: A Cultural Phenomenon in the Roman Empire* (New York 1993) 9: "We should also note that rhetoric and literature were, if not totally inseparable, certainly convergent".

[32] A. Olivar, "Reflections on problems raised by early Christian preaching", trans. J. Munitiz, in M.B. Cunningham and P. Allen (eds), *Preacher and Audience: Studies in Early Christian and Byzantine Homiletics*, A New History of the Sermon 1 (Leiden–Boston–Cologne 1998) 21-32, at 22 sums up the general situation precisely: "However, if the message to be preached by the early Fathers of the church held something new in the history of oratory, in so far as it dealt primarily with explanations of the Christian creed, scripture and sacraments, the formal aspect of this preaching owed an incalculable debt from its beginning to the art of rhetoric that was pre-Christian. It was in the technique, the rules and the practice of established oratory that most ancient preachers were trained."

exegesis: his author-centered devotion to the person of Paul".[33] It appears that reason won the day, although that did not stop him from depicting Paul at times as the simple tent-maker.[34] W. Kinzig, in discussing the adoption of rhetorical techniques by many of the later Greek Fathers for proclaiming the Christian message, refers to Chrysostom's ambivalence towards this practice and shows how he overcame his hesitations:

> They maintained that, in principle, Christians could use all literary genres and styles as long as they were appropriate (πρέπον, οἰκεῖον, and πρόσφερον) to the subject. In addition the listener had to profit from it. John Chrysostom, somewhat at variance with his predilection for simplicity just mentioned, expressed this latter principle in another work like this: 'When we have the care of the sick, we must not set before them a meal prepared haphazard, but a variety of dishes, so that the patient may choose what suits his taste.[...] Thus we should proceed in spiritual repasts. Since we are weak, the sermon must be varied and embellished; it must contain comparisons, examples, elaborate periods, and the like, so that we may select what will profit our soul.' (*Proph. obscurit.* 1.1; PG 56,165). As regards rhetorical theory, therefore, the Christian orators did not hesitate to adopt the pagan theorems and ideas, as long as they suited their needs and were regarded as useful (χρήσιμος) and these needs differed markedly from those of their pagan predecessors and contemporaries in that they consisted in proclaiming the message of salvation in Christ.[35]

(c) The linguistic revolution of the last half-century or so has witnessed a remarkable recovery of the value of metaphorical language in the communication of ideas, especially in relation to what has been called god-talk. Indeed, metaphors and associated tropes are now seen as a cognitive necessity for effective holistic perception.[36] Proper cognitive functioning is impossible without emotive

---

[33] Mitchell, *The Heavenly Trumpet*, xvii, also 43 and n. 41.

[34] Anderson, *The Second Sophistic*, 206, has made a general observation along these lines: "At the end of antiquity we can still see the two cultural pressures at work within Christianity: on the one hand we find in the age of Constantine an illiterate St Antony in the Egyptian desert, exercising spiritual authority over men and demons alike without any benefit of a formal education. Or, on the other hand, a century later we can find Augustine drawing on the Biblical past as a justification for exploring the pagan classics in education: as the Israelites spoiled the Egyptians before the flight from Egypt, so the Christians are entitled to take what is valuable from the heritage of paganism. In short the arguments were available to allow anyone with serious educational aspirations to import these in to their Christianity, and in the event this was clearly done."

[35] W. Kinzig, "The Greek Christian writers", in S.E. Porter (ed.), *Handbook of Classical Rhetoric in the Hellenistic Period: 330 BC–AD 400* (Boston–Leiden 2001) 633-670 at 639-640.

[36] There is a vast literature on this issue which is beyond the scope of this study even to survey, let alone analyse. A small representative sampling of literature which I have found helpful could

elements. This is why metaphor is being recognised by many scholars across the disciplines as indigenous to all learning. In reference to this recognition, of particular relevance for this study is a comment by S. McFague: "All metaphors...have a strong attitudinal component, for we respond at an affective level to metaphors which have significant associations for us."[37] This is significant for Chrysostom studies because attitude is an endemic feature of the mindset (γνώμη), a concept crucial to the rhetor who is embarked upon the vocation of persuasion. Rhetorical language, therefore, should not be treated *à la* John Locke as "perfect cheats",[38] but as genuine attempts to communicate effectively. Exception to this might be made in the case of certain members of the sophistic movements of Greek antiquity who set out merely to entertain rather than to instruct, but in the hands of the Christian preachers who saw their vocation in the terms of ultimate concerns, rhetoric as a vehicle employed in the task of changing attitudes or mindsets is to be viewed as both legitimate and sincere. This does not mean that hyperbole or other exaggerative language should be ignored; it should be allowed for in its normal use of speaking to the heart as well as to the mind, and not as something unusual or deceptive.[39]

Thus, the rhetorical context is critical to this study. This does not mean that Chrysostom's homilies are the less reliable for discerning his theology. Perhaps they are even more valuable because they are persuasion literature, representing the attempt to change the mindset of his congregations to his own thinking on the ultimate issues of life.[40] They represent convictions that are strongly held, convictions that as far as he is concerned, are biblically based and are an essential

---

include: G. Lakoff and M. Johnson, *Metaphors We Live By* (Chicago-London 1980); S. McFague, *Metaphorical Theology: Models of God in Religious Language* (London 1982); N. Murphy, *Beyond Liberalism and Fundamentalism: How Modern and Postmodern Philosophy Set the Theological Agenda* (Valley Forge, PA 1996); J. Soskice, *Metaphor and Religious Language* (Oxford 1985); J. Wood, *Epistemology: Becoming Intellectually Virtuous* (Leicester 1998); D.R. Stiver, *Theology after Ricoeur: New Directions in Hermeneutical Theology* (Louisville, KY 2001) esp. 105-124. All that is intended here is to point to a significant finding, probably the central one, of this movement as I have précised it here.

[37] McFague, *Metaphorical Theology*, 41.

[38] Locke, *An Essay Concerning Human Understanding*, 299.

[39] Olivar, "Reflections on problems", 23, comments: "In my opinion, historians who consider formal aspects of early preaching must bear in mind the pastoral intent of this form of communication, especially as this brings to light its human interest".

[40] D. Rylaarsdam, "Painful preaching: John Chrysostom and the philosophical tradition of feeding souls", *SP* 41 (2006) 463-468, esp. 463 discusses Chrysostom's use of psychagogy, persuasion, which he defines as spiritual guidance: "Certain features of classical psychagogy such as harsh rhetoric in guiding souls shape John Chrysostom's exegesis and homiletical methods."

part of the guiding principles of life and salvation. If the observations of scholars on the insincerity of the ancient orators have any foundation, then Chrysostom is not to be numbered among them.[41] His preaching was of the utmost sincerity as, in his mind, so much depended upon adequate response.[42] One result of this understanding of Chrysostom is that when I use "comment" in relation to him in a particular homily, this does not mean that I understand his homilies as pure exegetical commentaries. I am aware that these are rhetorical constructions aimed at persuasion and directed towards addressing concrete situations in his congregations. This does not mean that I think he plays deceitfully with the text – far from it. Rather, his chief concern is to apply the text. In doing so he marshals all the skills he has to hand, his rhetorical genius being by no means the least of them. Nevertheless, as Thurén suggests, "The theology must be sought through comprehension of the devices and tactics".[43]

Due to the nature of this study, Chrysostom's linguistic context, though also a part of the cultural context, requires special treatment. It has been observed that Chrysostom composed and presumably delivered his homilies in the elevated style of a rhetor in Attic Greek. This raises the question of the suitability of this form of language to communicate effectively with the various classes in his congregations, many of whom, one would think, would not normally be familiar with something other than ordinary everyday language. In a well-supported study, Maxwell answers this question by reference to the nature of the urban culture that featured a number of contexts of public oratory. She makes the point that

> …in all of these contexts, the inclination to listen and to value eloquence was not limited to the upper-class men who studied how to produce eloquence. For pagans and Christians alike, the appreciation of rhetoric depended more upon access to a lively urban culture than upon social class.[44]

---

[41] M. Gargarin, "Probability and persuasion: Plato and early Greek rhetoric", in I. Worthington (ed.), *Persuasion: Greek Rhetoric in Action* (New York 1994) 46-68, has disputed the general negative view of early Sophistic as portrayed by Plato. He ascribes to the movement a positive philosophic contribution. This is similar to Maxwell for the Second Sophistic as already noted above. No doubt, there were both the genuine and the fraudulent at all times.

[42] Maxwell, *Christianization and Communication*, 36, comments that the issue of salvation for themselves as well as for their listeners provided the motivation for the patristic preachers to use their rhetorical skills: "It is important to remember that these men had strong motivations compelling them to speak to ordinary people in an accessible way".

[43] Thurén, "John Chrysostom as rhetorical critic", 213.

[44] Maxwell, *Christianization and Communication*, 63; C. Fabricius, *Zu den Jugendschriften des Johannes Chrysostomos: Untersuchungen zum Klassizismus des vierten Jahrhunderts* (Lund 1962) 117, claims that no more than 0.5 percent of Chrysostom's vocabulary was unintelligible to his audience.

Maxwell's chapter on the make-up of Chrysostom's congregation in Antioch, together with her following chapter on his pedagogy, significantly strengthen her case that the audience was far wider than an all-male educated elite and that it was able, for the most part, to comprehend his sermons.[45] Sandwell goes a step further to underline the positive nature of the use of rhetoric in communicating the Christian faith: "The very fact that they used a rhetorical form of public display that was popular as well as common in the ancient world helped them to spread their Christian message rather than hindered them in any way".[46]

A related issue is whether or not some, at least, of the exegetical homilies were preached at all. Neither of these issues materially affects this study which is concerned with Chrysostom's thought. As it is clear that his homilies were published, whether or not they were refined for that purpose is of no great consequence for this exercise. We have his texts, indeed a super-abundance of them. His thought is preserved in them. It is his thought that is the concern of this exercise.[47] There may be problems of faithfulness in recording and editing for publication but all that is virtually unknown. The popularity and prestige of Chrysostom probably meant that loyal scribes protected his work from unwanted distortion.

One thing that the linguistic context raises as a matter for discussion is the source of Chrysostom's usage of the key term γνώμη. There are a number of possibilities. For one, the Greek παιδεία ensured his familiarity with the literature

---

[45] Maxwell, *Christianization and Communication*, 65-87. There is a growing literature on this issue, the more recent thereof disputing earlier claims of the narrow nature of audiences as consisting only of educated elites. See W. Mayer, "John Chrysostom: extraordinary preacher, ordinary audience", in Cunningham and Allen (eds), *Preacher and Audience*, 105-137; Maxwell, *Christianization and Communication*, 66 n. 1-3, who gives a fuller list, and also a list of those who hold contrary positions; see also A. Quiroga, "From Sophistopolis to Episcopolis. The case for a Third Sophistic", *Journal for Late Antique Religion and Culture* 1 (2007) 31-42, who proposes a third wave of sophistic development in the fourth century, in which Christians played a significant part, and which contributed to the popularity of rhetoric.

[46] I. Sandwell, *Religious Identity in Late Antiquity: Greeks, Jews and Christians in Antioch* (Cambridge 2007) 57.

[47] Mayer and Allen, *John Chrysostom*, 30-31, briefly address the questions of composition and publication; J.N.D. Kelly, *Golden Mouth: The Story of John Chrysostom – Ascetic, Preacher, Bishop* (New York 1995) 92-94, in refuting Baur's claim that more of Chrysostom's sermon-commentaries were written than preached, has made a good case for accepting most of them as being preached. See C. Baur, *John Chrysostom and His Time*, vol. 1, trans. M. Gonzaga (London–Glasgow 1959²) 299.

of the Classical era.[48] As the literature of the sixth to the fourth centuries BC formed the basis of education, it is necessary to survey the usage in the formative period with special attention to what appears to be the more influential sources. This survey is the substance of Chapter 8. Then four years under the instruction of the rhetorical school of Libanius not only reinforced the Greek literary heritage of his previous schooling, but also left the imprint of his teacher upon him. It will be seen that Libanius' influence is probably critical, and the analysis of Libanius' usage of γνώμη comprises the content of Chapter 7. Chrysostom's early penchant for legal studies with eyes on a career in the civil service may also have played a part as the term is frequently found in the contractual and political documents of the time.[49] There may have been a useful legacy from this experience, but other factors appear to have loomed larger in his life and thus make this a less fruitful path to explore. The *asketerion* of Diodore brought Chrysostom in touch with an exegetical methodology, but there is reason to think that under the training of this Christian scholar he also absorbed the skill of adapting the vocabulary of the classical Greek παιδεία to biblical exegesis. This issue is discussed in Chapter 9. Then the years of ascetic discipline wherein he learnt the New Testament by heart are another possibility.[50] However, our term, γνώμη, appears only nine times in the New Testament.[51] Thus, while it is useful to examine those, especially from the aspect of how he understood the term in his exegesis of the passages in the New Testament where γνώμη appears, and upon which he made comments, it seems clear that this source could not have provided the impetus for the use that Chrysostom made of γνώμη.

The ascetic context probably influenced Chrysostom in another way. This experience not only carried forward the effects of the years he spent as a monk, but also confirmed to him the general exaltation of asceticism as being next to martyrdom as the highest form of Christian spirituality in Christian thought and practice of late antiquity. E. Clark, in her study of the patristic "axiology of abstinence",[52] has shown convincingly the effect of this ascetic ethos upon

---

[48] See W. Jaeger, *Early Christianity and the Greek Paideia* (Cambridge, MA 1965) 140 n. 1, where he speaks of the "unbroken strength of that great ideal, which has upheld the classical Greek tradition even at times when new spiritual sources, such as the Christian religion seemed to be transforming everything in man's inner life".

[49] See J.H. Moulton and G. Milligan, *The Vocabulary of the Greek New Testament: Illustrated from the Papyri and Other Non-Literary Sources* (Grand Rapids, MI 1930; repr. 1980) 129, for examples of usage of γνώμη in marriage contracts, government decrees, policy decisions and court cases.

[50] Kelly, *Golden Mouth*, 32.

[51] Acts 20:3, 1 Cor 1:10, 7:25, 7:40, 2 Cor 8:10, Phil 14, Rev 17:13, 17:17 (2).

[52] Clark, *Reading Renunciation*, 13.

Chrysostom's exegetical practice in relation to certain issues. In this there does not appear to be any direct link to his anthropologic understanding as far as the γνώμη is concerned, except that he had become acutely aware of how to mould the γνώμη, a legacy of the stern discipline of those years. The moulding and development of the γνώμη is discussed in Chapter 6.

There is no doubt that his ascetic experience had a significant effect upon his own being. There is no doubting Chrysostom's discipline. That had become a firm habit of life. For that reason, I am not convinced that his homilies are as lacking in structure as some like to say. Any good preacher is well aware of the need of careful planning in the composition of sermons and Chrysostom was among the best. Also his rhetorical training, which preceded his ascetic years, through the discipline and habit therein inculcated, made preparation and structuring of his orations a fixed habit of life.[53] It is true, that in delivery, for one reason or another, he might run out of time, or sometimes spontaneously move away from his theme for a time, but there is little doubt that he knew where he was heading and what he intended to say. As far as his exegetical homilies are concerned, he was constrained in form by the text before him.[54] Nevertheless, he had definite goals in mind and his homilies exhibit the features belonging to those goals. These may be summed up as (a) to instruct in doctrine, (b) to produce Christian φιλοσοφία (philosophy),[55] and (c) to attain final salvation. The very first homily on Matthew is an introduction to the series. Here we find these aims. Both Old and New Testament saints were meant to live by the grace of the Spirit without the aid of the Scriptures and, in the event, failed to do so, but in time were shipwrecked, so there existed the necessity for them to be assisted in remembrance by the

---

[53] Brändle, *Johannes Chrysostomus: Bischof*, 42, referring to Homily 6 of the homilies on Matthew, notes Chrysostom's careful sermon preparation and writes that Chrysostom knew well the necessity of "strenuous study and much prayer in order to comprehend the meaning of the text in question". See *In Matt. hom.* 6; PG 57,61 43-44.

[54] Mayer and Allen, *John Chrysostom*, 30, note the difficulty in determining the relevance to each other of the various sections of his homilies, especially those of the exegetical series. Young, *From Nicaea to Chalcedon*, 155-156, suggests some possible reasons for this apparent lack of structure and relevance, includes *In Joan. hom.* 23; PG 59,137 from Chrysostom to indicate the pastoral priorities that were incorporated into his sermons.

[55] A-M. Malingrey, *"Philosophia"*: *Étude d'un groupe de mots dans la littérature grecque, des Présocratiques au IVe siècle après J.-C.*, Études et Commentaires 40 (Paris 1961) 263-288, has given a perceptive survey of Chrysostom's usage of φιλοσοφία, esp. the definition at 268: "la foi chrétienne authentiquement vécue au milieu du monde". (Christian life authentically lived in the world). In the first *Matthew* homily Chrysostom contrasts the Christian φιλοσοφία with that of the pagan philosophers, tracing the weakness of pagan φιλοσοφία not only to their contradictory teachings, but also to their moral failure. In particular, this moral failure was unflattering of the classic παιδεία pointing, in Chrysostom's opinion to its great weakness.

Scriptures.[56] Preaching was intended to explain from the written word the all-embracing vision of the heavenly city embedded in the inspired texts.[57] It was designed to enable those who listen in μετὰ σιγῆς μυστικῆς ("with mystical silence")[58] to see the gates of the city ἀναπετασθείσας ("thrown wide open").[59] Using this latter image, no doubt from Revelation 21:25, but also familiar from his Greek παιδεία, Chrysostom describes this task as ἡ τῶν ζητημάτων λύσις ("the resolution of the difficulties").[60] These were the issues he would raise from the text and try to resolve only if the congregation was διεγερθέντας καὶ ἐπιθυμοῦντας μαθεῖν ("aroused and eager to learn").[61] His preaching was the vehicle whereby their lives could be adjusted and brought to perfection as a fit citizen of that city and ultimately, πρὸς αὐτὸν ἥξομεν τὸν θρόνον τὸν βασιλικὸν ("we will come to the same royal throne").[62] There is no doubt as to how Chrysostom viewed his vocation. Matthew, the tax-collector, may be the ἄριστον χειραγωγὸν ("best guide"),[63] but Chrysostom is the interpreter of the guidebook to ensure his people reach the desired destination. Thus, Chrysostom's homilies are always pastorally applied. Words without deeds he saw as vain; professed belief without virtuous and compassionate conduct as hypocrisy; and even baptism without a subsequent striving for perfection as endangering final salvation. Exhortation to moral application of the text was a necessary component of his homilies as it was a vital element of his pastoral theology.[64] In the first homily on the large Genesis series,

---

[56] *In Matt. hom.* 1; PG 57,13-14.

[57] *In Matt. hom.* 1; PG 57,23-24. The πόλις, πολιτεία image starts much earlier in this homily as a contrast to the "absurd city-state", τὴν καταγέλαστον πολιτείαν of Plato, PG 57,18 57-58.

[58] *In Matt. hom.* 1; PG 57,24 15.

[59] *In Matt. hom.* 1; PG 57,24 2.

[60] *In Matt. hom.* 1; PG 57,24 2-3.

[61] *In Matt. hom.* 1; PG 57,22 10-11.

[62] *In Matt. hom.* 1; PG 57,24 24; See Mitchell, *The Heavenly Trumpet*, 78-79, and ns 56 and 58, observes that this heavenly citizen image is common with Chrysostom, who applies it to monks, martyrs, Paul, John the Baptist and all the saints; see *De paenit. hom.* 2; PG 49,290 60; *In Matt. hom.* 36; PG 57,413 47; *De res. mort.*; PG 50,428 51-54.

[63] *In Matt. hom.* 1; PG 57,23 18.

[64] J.H.W.G. Liebescheutz, *Barbarians and Bishops: Army, Church, and State in the Age of Arcadius and Chrysostom* (Oxford–New York 1991) esp.177-178. In this survey of Chrysostom's preaching, Liebescheutz describes it as morally focused. Following R.L. Fox and P. Brown, he makes the observation that Christian sermons generally included moral teaching as an integral part of Christian worship. See also: Young, *From Nicaea to Chalcedon*, 145-148; Young, "The rhetorical schools", 192-193; J. Maxwell, "Lay piety in the sermons of John Chrysostom", in D. Krueger (ed.), *Byzantine Christianity*, A People's History of Christianity 3 (Minneapolis, MN 2006) 19-38.

he calls the Church the "medical clinic of the spirit",[65] where the people ought to receive appropriate medicines and apply them to their wounds before they left. It could be said that this pastoral concern was the main structural element of his homilies.[66] They vibrate with it, and should be read with that concern to the fore. It serves as an interpretive tool for understanding his theology. If that is done, the structural unity will be seen. In the course of this study, I will take one homily that is relevant to my theme and from it demonstrate this structure. This will indicate the planning that Chrysostom developed to secure the definite outcome he had in view. This will also demonstrate how the structure, as a contextual principle, gives meaning to the terms used.

One other issue relating to language is that of translation. Unless otherwise noted all translations are mine. With regard to these, as I am dealing with the significance of words and their nuances in order to discern Chrysostom's anthropology, I am striving for precision (Chrysostom's ἀκρίβεια) rather than elegance, thus sometimes needing to coin terms for the occasion, and to use terms and constructions that would be replaced with something less stilted or ungainly in normal free-flowing English. Nevertheless, I have made the translations as stylish as possible while adhering to the afore-mentioned principle. In particular, I have used "mindset" throughout as the translation of γνώμη. At times it sounds awkward, but I did not want it to be lost in the process of translation into an English word that gives the sense but obscures the source. Sometimes it sounds

---

[65] *In Gen. hom.* 1; PG 53,22 9-12. Ἰατρεῖον γάρ ἐστι πνευματικὸν ἡ ἐκκλησία.

[66] In discussing the formal defects of Chrysostom's homilies this feature caused P.W. Harkins (trans.), *St John Chrysostom, Baptismal Instructions*, ACW 31 (Westminster, MD-London 1963) 5, to comment on the "spiritual unity" of Chrysostom's homilies. He writes: "Yet his homilies, which often lack structural unity, always have an interior, a spiritual unity. There is never a digression, never a detail which swerves from the end he set for himself: the confirmation of his hearer's faith and the correction of their lives." He repeats this information in S*aint John Chrysostom: Discourses Against Judaizing Christians*, FOTC 68 (Washington, DC 1979) xxii; G. Downey, *Antioch in the Age of Theodosius the Great*, The Centers of Civilization Series (Norman, OK 1962) 105, remarks: "John Chrysostom felt, and rightly, that his true vocation was but a pastor of souls – and it was as such that people flocked to hear him."; See also Mayer and Allen, *John Chrysostom*, 43, who speak of "the genuine concern for the souls of his listeners, that permeates and prompts virtually every word..."; see also B. Nassif, "The 'spiritual exegesis' of Scripture: the school of Antioch revisited", *Anglican Theological Review* 75 (1993) 437-470, suggests θεωρία as another element of Antiochene exegesis, in a discussion of the history of scholarship on a principle that generally has been bypassed, but which may provide a valuable addition to the search for a richer perception of their approach; for a shorter and more focused essay on this theme by this author, see B. Nassif, "Antiochene in John Chrysostom's exegesis", in K. Tanner and C.A. Hall (eds), *Ancient Modern Christianity* (Downers Grove, IL 2002) 23-37.

too rational or intellectual and does not do justice to the emotional elements that are embodied in it. Nevertheless, I think that in our contemporary society we understand that a person's mindset can be extremely emotional.

II. Sources

On embarking on this study, I had it in mind to survey the usage of γνώμη in most if not all of Chrysostom's corpus. In hindsight that was an impractical task to set and one that was not necessary to do justice to the focus of this study. Faced with Chrysostom's enormous corpus, a preliminary survey revealed the vast number of references to the key term, γνώμη. The choice was either to attempt a total coverage or to cover all the issues involved. In the event I chose the latter and have had to be content with detailed surveys of all the Genesis homilies, both the larger and smaller series, those on Matthew, those on Paul's letters (including Hebrews), a number of the occasional homilies such as *Adversus Judaeos, Catechesis de Illuminandos* and *De Fato,* and less detailed, yet sufficient, surveys of Acts and John. This compasses over 500 homilies plus the commentary material on Galatians and the treatise on *The Priesthood.* This provides not only an adequate basis for the research, but also the confidence that the conclusions drawn actually represent Chrysostom's thought. For ease of access I have worked from the online TLG and thus in a number of texts have worked with the most up-to-date editions available. Another consequence is that for the homilies on Matthew, John and the Pauline texts I have worked from the Migne texts. I have checked with the Field editions where possible, but must confess that there are no guarantees that one has been working with the *ipsissima verba* of Chrysostom. When possible, for comparative verification of my translations of the text I have used those English and French translations that are available.[67]

As this research necessitated a survey of the use of γνώμη over an extended period, the TLG has been the base for other church Fathers and the non-Christian writers of the Greeks from the formative period through the Classical and Hellenistic periods up until the seventh century. This includes Libanius where I have also used the Loeb editions for those works that appear in that series.

---

[67] As included in the Primary Sources Bibliography.

III. Literature Review[68]

Previous scholarship on the focus of this dissertation as contained in the term γνώμη is sparse and scattered. Indeed, most of the literature directly bearing upon the issue is post-Chrysostom in its source orientation, referring back in the main to the seventh-century theologian, Maximus the Confessor. There are claims made that the subsequent anthropology embraced by the Eastern churches is based on earlier Fathers, including Origen, whose ideas become greatly modified in the hands of later writers, and particularly the Cappadocians. While reference is made to these, it is with Maximus, through whom the contributions of these Fathers undergo significant classification and development that the anthropology of the eastern tradition comes to first bloom. In his work, γνώμη comes to the fore as a major concept in the anthropology of fallen human beings. Thus, it is no surprise to find that L. Thunberg attributes to Maximus the leading role in giving γνώμη a dominant position and a fixed use for later Byzantine theological anthropology.[69]

It is interesting to note that in Thunberg's brief survey of Maximus' use of γνώμη there is no mention of Chrysostom, even though, as this study will show, γνώμη is a major concept that, along with other aspects of his anthropology, anticipates in his rhetorical exegesis much of what Maximus had to say in treatise form. The consequence of this is that the most useful modern discussions of γνώμη are found in the commentators on Maximus, viz., P. Sherwood, L. Thunberg, A. Louth, A. Nichols and P. Christou.[70] As Chrysostom does not figure in these discussions, and the gap to Maximus is over two centuries, their value for this study would appear to be tangential and minimal. However, some of the insights, such as a prototypical definition of γνώμη, are similar to what I had discerned in Chrysostom previous to following research through to Maximus and these authors.

---

[68] Fuller bibliographies than noted here are provided for each chapter.

[69] L. Thunberg, *Microcosm and Mediator: The Theological Anthropology of Maximus the Confessor*, trans. A.M. Allchin (Chicago 1995[2]) 226.

[70] P. Sherwood (trans.), *St Maximus the Confessor: The Ascetic Life; The Four Centuries on Charity*, ACW 21 (New York–Ramsey NJ 1955) 55-63; P. Christou, "Maximos the Confessor on the infinity of man", in F. Heinzer and C. Scönborn (eds), *Actes du Symposium sur Maxime le Confeseur* (Fribourg 1982) 261-271; L. Thunberg, *Microcosm and Mediator*, 220-243; Thunberg, *Man and the Cosmos: The Vision of St Maximus the Confessor* (Crestwood, NY 1985) 95, 224-231, 264-265, esp. 226-227; A. Nichols, *Byzantine Gospel: Maximus the Confessor in Modern Scholarship* (Edinburgh 1993) 158-195, esp. 173-176; A. Louth, "Dogma and spirituality in St Maximus the Confessor", in P. Allen et al. (eds), *Prayer and Spirituality in the Early Church*, vol. 1 (Everton Park 1998) 197-208, esp. 205-206; A. Louth, *Maximus the Confessor*, ECF (London–New York 1996) 59-62, 86-90, 197. See Chapter 9 below for further and more recent texts, especially the contributions of P. Allen and B. Neil.

This, at least, may be considered confirmatory of my understanding of Chrysostom's usage.[71] Other modern discussions of γνώμη which draw heavily upon Maximus are represented by Orthodox scholars such as V. Lossky and J. Meyendorf.[72] These are articulating a fully evolved Orthodox doctrine, and as their discussion of γνώμη falls within that larger canvas their treatment is brief and adds little if anything to the specialist commentators on Maximus.

Few studies exist on Chrysostom that contain discussions of γνώμη. P. Yazigi is one Eastern Orthodox scholar who is an exception to this. He has focused on aspects of Chrysostom's anthropology in which some treatment of γνώμη is given.[73] Patristic scholars have to a large degree followed the crowd in giving προαίρεσις, the exercise of moral choice, the central place in their understanding of the anthropology of the Fathers. In so doing they have, to a large extent, overlooked or not fully appreciated the role of the γνώμη. Typical is E. Nowak whose work has formed something of a benchmark for subsequent discussions, with most, if not all, patristic scholars following his lead.[74] This is true of C. Hall in his treatise on Chrysostom's treatment of providence. Although he acknowledges the import of γνώμη, he gives the pre-eminence to προαίρεσις throughout his dissertation:

> Key to our discussion of disposition will be Chrysostom's understanding of προαίρεσις, for although this particular word only occurs in *On Providence* one time, the theology underpinning its meaning is present throughout the work.[75]

This is curious, because against this one occurrence of προαίρεσις, γνώμη and its cognates, εὐγνωμόνος and ἀγνωμόνος occur twenty-three times. Perhaps Hall

---

[71] It also raises the questions of (a) the possible familiarity of Maximus with Chrysostom's work and some form of dependence upon him, and/or (b) a common heritage from which both drew, both of which issues are beyond the scope of this study.

[72] V. Lossky, *The Mystical Theology of the Eastern Church* (Crestwood, NY 1976) 114-134; Meyendorff, *Byzantine Theology*, 138-146.

[73] P. I. Yazigi, "Human freedom and eschatology: freedom and fall", and "The eschatological pedagogy (παιδεία): the 'Good'", Cambridge University Institute of Orthodox Christian Studies, November 2006; Yazigi, "Fleshy, psychic and spiritual man: flesh's and souls' warfare according to the Apostle Paul and St John Chrysostom", Cambridge Lecture 2002; all papers available at www.alepporthodox.org, in the *Annals* of St. John of Damascus Institute of Theology, University of Balamand.

[74] E. Nowak, *Le Chrétien devant la souffrance. Étude sur la pensée de Jean Chrysostome*, Théologie Historique 19 (Paris 1972) 57-73. This is not to undervalue Nowak's many constructive insights.

[75] C.A. Hall, "John Chrysostom's 'On Providence': a translation and theological interpretation", diss., Drew University 1991, 16.

includes γνώμη in "the theology underpinning its [προαίρεσις] meaning", which serves to highlight the neglect of scholarly discussions on γνώμη in Chrysostom and other early Fathers. D. Trakatellis goes down a similar path. He has noted the importance of the προαίρεσις in Chrysostom's exegesis of Romans from which he demonstrates its value in Chrysostom's thinking. However, he completely overlooks the even more critical role of the γνώμη, even though it figures in the most significant passage used by him to support his case.[76] Two things emerge from this as significant for this study. There is obvious need to discern Chrysostom's comparative usage of these two terms and to determine his understanding of their relationship. Is γνώμη merely an aspect of προαίρεσις as Nowak suggests?[77] Or, contrary to Nowak, is it the case that προαίρεσις is a function of the γνώμη or, at least, dependent upon and determined by it? Then there is need to give thought to the general focus on προαίρεσις to the neglect of γνώμη in patristic scholarship.[78]

In view of this sparse treatment of γνώμη by patristic scholars, turning attention to classical scholarship finds a more fruitful field where some specialist studies on this term is to be found.[79] What applies in the sphere of patristic scholarship is similar in general scholarship relating to Hellenic studies of the Roman imperial period. While προαίρεσις is given much attention, especially by commentators on Stoic philosophers, γνώμη gets little attention apart from some scattered notes in the commentaries on the works of various ancient authors. R. Sorabji's discussions of will are invaluable, especially in relation to προαίρεσις, but only highlight the problem.[80]

---

[76] D. Trakatellis, "Being transformed: Chrysostom's exegesis of the Epistle to the Romans", *Greek Orthodox Theological Review* 36 (1991) 216.

[77] Nowak, *Le Chrétien devant la souffrance*, 62: "C'est ici qu'apparaît le mot γνώμη, employé à côté de προαίρεσις."

[78] These issues are wider than Hall and Trakatellis, but to be fair to them, there is need to interact more precisely with their work, which is done below in Chapter 5.

[79] P. Huart, *Le Vocabulaire de l'analyse psychologique dans l'œuvre de Thucydide*, Études et Commentaires 69 (Paris 1968); P. Huart, *Γνώμη chez Thucydide et ses Contemporains, (Sophocle – Euripide – Antiphon – Andocide –Aristophane)*, Études et Commentaires 81 (Paris 1973); P. Karavites, "*Gnome*'s nuances: from its beginning to the end of the fifth century", Classical Bulletin 66 (1990) 9-34. These three works are invaluable. They are supplemented with other recent studies below.

[80] R. Sorabji, *Emotion and Peace of Mind: From Stoic Agitation to Christian Temptation* (Oxford–New York 2000); R. Sorabji, "The concept of will from Plato to Maximus the Confessor", in T. Pink and M.W.F. Stone (eds), *The Will and Human Action: From Antiquity to the Present Day* (New York 2003) 6-28. There is a large body of modern literature on the will in Classical and Hellenistic thought, some of which is relevant to this study. Reference will be made to particular works I have examined at relevant points.

IV. Structure

With all the above considerations of researching Chrysostom's anthropology in mind, the study will be presented in three parts: (a) exegetical texts, which will cover the basic unfolding of the meaning, attributes, functions and significance of γνώμη from examination and analysis of various texts where this term occurs; (b) comparative material, which examines possible sources for Chrysostom's use of this term, and (c) conclusions, which explore the role of the γνώμη in the crucial issue of the operation of sin in the psyche, and a final chapter which will encapsulate the findings of this research. It is to the first of these tasks that we now turn.

CHAPTER 2

Discerning the Γνώμη: A Theologian of the Mindset
ὁ Θέος σκοπεῖ ἀλλὰ τὴν γνώμην; but God inspects the mindset.

As an introduction to the exploration of the meaning and significance of the γνώμη (mindset) in Chrysostom's anthropology, one can do little better than turn to a statement in one of his homilies on Matthew where he speaks to a section of the Sermon on the Mount. There he says that when God is approached in prayer, God does not look at things like reputation or standing or the seeming worth of a person but at that person's γνώμη. In this part of the homily, Chrysostom is pressing home the value of earnestness in prayer. External circumstances, he claims, are immaterial to the efficacy of prayer. Whether one is a Phoenician, a Gentile dog, a Jew or an excessive sinner is of no consequence. Neither race nor sins bar the way to God. Things that give or deny people worth in the eyes of others do not give or deny access to the ear of God. No, Chrysostom argues, οὐ γὰρ τὴν ἀξίαν ὁ Θέος σκοπεῖ, ἀλλὰ τὴν γνώμην ("For God does not inspect a person's [apparent] worth, but their mindset").[1] A number of issues are raised by this comment on the text: (a) It shifts the focus from external matters such as race, reputation, actions and surroundings to the condition of the inner being. The γνώμη is revealed as the critical faculty of the soul in divine-human relationships. (b) Secondly, it suggests that in order to discover the real person, and also to understand the distortions of human experience, it is necessary to turn attention to the functions of the γνώμη in the workings of the psyche. (c) Then, in the issue of responsibility before God, the γνώμη is seen to be the faculty of the soul which is under constant appraisal. (d) The last of the issues relates to response to God. The γνώμη becomes apparent as the critical faculty in acceptance or rejection of the overtures of grace and truth. These issues will be investigated in what follows. Some comprehension of Chrysostom's perception of γνώμη will emerge in the course of the discussion. Also, as the issues are integrated in Chrysostom's presentations, it is unavoidable that though they be dealt with in the order proposed, there will be some overlap. Inevitably, the underlying principle that God inspects the γνώμη will be a rather constant refrain.

---

[1] In Matt. hom. 22; PG 57,306 27-29.

I. From external to internal: γνώμη as the critical faculty in divine-human relationships.

Chrysostom has been classified as typical of the so-called Antioch school in emphasising moral teaching rather than the more mystical or dogmatic approaches of the Alexandrian exegetes.[2] It is true, as many have claimed, that Chrysostom was very practical in his preaching. His moral emphasis has been noted by many scholars.[3] It would be a mistake, however, to think that he dealt merely with external forms and practices. Whilst he would insist that faith without works is dead, he often turns our attention from the external expression to the internal motivation.

This shift in focus from external action to inner motivation as exemplified in the above homily reminds us that Chrysostom was very much a theologian of the heart, or more precisely, of the γνώμη, the mindset. Those who dismiss him as being superficial and purely moralistic have grasped neither his spirit nor his use of words. He might have prescribed various acts and deeds as would any careful teacher who, leaving nothing to chance, would rigorously apply the text, but to him the inner motivation was of prime importance. Because of his skill in rhetoric and his use of examples and illustrations from everyday life, he may seem to have been rather earthy, but he was ever pointing to the heavenly and had the capacity to lift the souls of his hearers to higher things and to consideration of the cosmos of the inner life. This ability to penetrate below the surface and to carry his hearers to the core of being is amply illustrated in a number of places where he discounted external appurtenances to turn attention to the motivating springs of human life.

---

[2] Bouyer, *Spirituality of the New Testament*, 438.

[3] L. Meyer, "Liberté et moralisme chrétien dans la doctrine spirituelle de Saint Jean Chrysostome", *Recherches de science religieuse*, 23 (1933) 283-305, at 283; F.X. Murphy, "The moral doctrine of St John Chrysostom", *SP* 11/2 (1967) 52-64; Young, *From Nicaea to Chalcedon*, 147-159, at 149, comments that although Chrysostom's demands in this regard are rigorous, "yet at the same time, he admits the need for lightheartedness, for an appreciation of beauty, and for genuine relationships resting on respect even for a younger brother or indeed a servant".; E. Mühlenberg, "From early Christian morality to theological ethics", *SP* 19 (1987) 203-215; Young, "The rhetorical schools", 192-193; Liebescheutz, *Barbarians and Bishops*, 172, 177-178; B. Aland, "Trustworthy preaching: reflections on John Chrysostom's interpretation of Romans 8", in S.K. Soderlund and N.T. Wright (eds), *Romans and the People of God: Essays in Honor of Gordon D. Fee on the Occasion of his 65th Birthday* (Grand Rapids, MI–Cambridge 1999) 271-280 at 273; Hill, *Reading the Old Testament*, 178, observes that the Antiochene theologians' insistence on moral accountability was not applied with Novatian rigour.

The passage under consideration is a shining example where, as noted above, race, reputation and, somewhat surprisingly for a perceived moralistic preacher, external acts of sin are selected as being among those things which do not stand in the way of earnest calling upon God. The focus is emphatically turned away from purely external considerations.

As already observed, Chrysostom asserts that God inspects the γνώμη. From this context, it is evident that the γνώμη is to do with the inner being. In fact, one is very tempted to translate the above text into our usual English idiom, "but God inspects the heart", for it does not seem too much to say that in γνώμη we approach the very core of the human psyche. Something basic and fundamental to the person's being, character and attitude is in view. In this section on approaching God in prayer, Chrysostom indicates that the desirable γνώμη that God seeks is one which is earnest in the extreme, as indeed was the entreaty of the Phoenician woman.[4] Chrysostom indicates the intensity of the woman's feeling that prevailed to obtain her request by his metaphor of a siege, ἐπειδὴ σφοδρῶς ἐπετέθη ("since she violently attacked").[5] The image continues with the use of προσεδρεία ("blockade"),[6] and states that it was on account of this approach that the request was granted.[7] It is at this point that Chrysostom speaks of the γνώμη as being the focus of God's attention, and that he puts great value upon a γνώμη that is noteworthy for its persistence or importunity, so much so that: πολλῷ μᾶλλον τὸν ἀγαθὸν ἐπισπάσεται ἡ συνεχὴς ἔντευξις ("much more will continuous intercession draw in the good thing").[8] This points to a dominant attitude in the γνώμη, to an outstanding characteristic of this personality that belongs to the basic orientation of the person's being. Here is no momentary enthusiasm, no passing flash of piety, no transitory desire to pray, but, as in the examples referred to by Chrysostom, the friend at midnight, the woman appealing to the unjust judge, and the Syrophonecian woman, a constant, fixed determination to hold onto God.

Chrysostom's focus on the inner being is seen in his attitude to human ancestry. This is taken up in the third homily on Matthew where he speaks from the genealogy of the Lord Jesus against pride in ancestry. There he expresses the view that parentage is totally irrelevant in regard to one's relationship with God.[9] It matters not, he thinks, whether one has for a mother a prostitute like Tamar or Rahab, an alien like Ruth, a slave, a free woman or a woman of noble birth. The

---

[4] *In Matt. hom.* 22; PG 57,305 58, 306 9, 16:σφοδρῶς (violently), 306 12:σφοδρά (violent).
[5] *In Matt. hom.* 22; PG 57,306 16, LSJ 666 B.III.2 *s.v.*
[6] *In Matt. hom.* 22; PG 57,306 18, 19, 21, 24: προσεδρεία (2), προσεδρεύων, προσεδρεύειν.
[7] *In Matt. hom.* 22; PG 57,306 24: διὰ τὸ προσεδρεύειν.
[8] *In Matt. hom.* 22; PG 57,306 32.
[9] *In Matt. hom.* 3; PG 57,33 48-50.

same applies to a father, Judah and David being exposed as sinners yet blessed of God. All of these appear in the lineage of Jesus. In the thing that matters most, lineage adds nothing to or subtracts nothing from the person. We should note the range of ancestry mentioned in his examples, obviously intended to encompass the totality of possibilities. The focus is turned away from human ancestry, something valued in antiquity but over which the person had no control, to the condition of the soul. What does matter, says Chrysostom, is the person's γνώμη: the issue is, he says, ἀλλ' ἕν ἐστι τὸ ζετούμενον, ἡ γνώμη καὶ ὁ τῆς ψυχῆς τρόπος ("but one thing is to be sought, namely the mindset, and the way of the soul").[10] Here is further evidence of the primary underlying place that the γνώμη played in Chrysostom's understanding of the human situation. Here γνώμη is viewed as the essential determining faculty of persons in their relationships with God. External criteria, such as ancestry, do not express the reality of those relationships. This province belongs to the γνώμη, the mindset.

This same passage gives further elucidation to the content of Chrysostom's anthropology in regards to the role of the γνώμη. Here γνώμη is found in association with ὁ τῆς ψυχῆς τρόπος, the way (direction, habit, temper, character, manner) of the soul. The construction looks very much like a hendiadys, the καὶ not indicating two different things but two descriptions of the one thing, the ἕν with which both γνώμη and τρόπος are in apposition pointing to this. "Even" or "that is" would be suitable and proper translations here: "but one thing alone is being sought: the mindset (γνώμη), that is the set habit of the soul". We have before us something of a definition of γνώμη: it is equivalent to the way in which the psyche is habitually inclined. This is very helpful in assisting us to comprehend the place and function of the γνώμη both in regard to sin and also in respect to response to God. The γνώμη controls the way in which the soul is disposed.[11] The soul is shaped by various factors including education and experience and reaches a certain orientation which determines its responses and reactions. In Chrysostom's perception of the workings of the psyche, this orientation or inclination of the soul was the γνώμη, the basic mindset of the person. As such, it refers to the fundamental character of the individual.

In Homily 43 on Matthew we come upon Chrysostom's insistence on the one thing that is needful in the pursuit of a virtuous life that will effectively witness to the blessings of the kingdom of God. In bringing this sermon to its conclusion, Chrysostom urges upon his hearers the inadmissibility of excuses relating to the circumstances of life. Once more we are directed to the inner life:

---

[10] *In Matt. hom.* 3; PG 57,34 44-46.

[11] *John Chrys., Matthew*; trans. G. Prevost, in P. Schaff (ed.), NPNF Series 1, vol. 10,16, translates τρόπος as "disposition" here.

For one thing is being sought, the preparation of a noble mindset; and neither age, nor poverty, nor wealth, nor surrounding circumstances, nor any other thing is able to impede this; for both the old and the young, the married, those rearing children, those practising trades, and those serving as soldiers, successfully accomplished the duties asked of them. For David was young, Joseph was slave, Aquilla was a tradesman, and a dealer in purple had managed a factory, and another was a gaoler, another a Centurion like Cornelius, another sickly like Timothy, and another was a runaway like Onesimus; but none of these had found anything to be an impediment, but all of them, were honoured, both men and women, old and young, slaves and free, and soldiers and civilians. Therefore, do not let us make extraordinary excuses, but let us prepare a noble mindset.[12]

One thing matters, and no state of life or station in life is an impediment to its attainment. The only requirement is the preparation of a noble or high-born (γενναία) γνώμη. This is open to all who seek to be γενναία, "true to one's birth".[13] The underlying axiom of this term is: a noble birth leads to a noble character, although this expectation was not always met in the realities and exigencies of life. Within the Christian community this expectation was intensified on at least two grounds, one of which was the transforming power of the new birth of the Spirit, and the other the shift of the focus from the outer circumstance to the inner life. Thus, as Chrysostom suggested, the tradesman may have a noble mindset though he lacks the noble birth of the aristocratic class. Such a person possesses a noble birth of another dimension. Chrysostom insisted that nobility was a matter of the spirit, of character, not of one's station in life. Indeed, the implication here, if not the explicit assertion, is that a noble mindset is a noble birth. It is not surprising therefore to find Chrysostom concluding his sermon – apart from the doxology – exhorting his people to prepare the best or noblest γνώμη. The epithet, ἀρίστη is used, meaning in its primary sense "best by birth or

---

[12] *In Matt. hom.* 43; PG 57,464 25-40: Ἕν γάρ ἐστι τὸ ζητούμενον, γνώμης γενναίας παρασκευή· καὶ οὔτε ἡλικία, οὔτε πενία, οὐ πλοῦτος, οὐ πραγμάτων περίστασις, οὐκ ἄλλο οὐδὲν, ἐμποδίσαι δυνήσεται. Καὶ γὰρ καὶ γέροντες καὶ νέοι, καὶ γυναῖκας ἔχοντες, καὶ παῖδας τρέφοντες, καὶ τέχνας μεταχειριζόμενοι, καὶ στρατευόμενοι, κατώρθωσαν τὰ ἐπιταχθέντα ἅπαντα. Καὶ γὰρ ὁ Δανιὴλ νέος ἦν, καὶ ὁ Ἰωσὴφ δοῦλος ἦν, καὶ ὁ Ἀκύλας τέχνην μετεχειρίζετο, καὶ ἡ πορφυρόπωλις ἐργαστηρίου προειστήκει, καὶ ἄλλος δεσμοφύλαξ ἦν, καὶ ἄλλος ἑκατοντάρχης, ὡς ὁ Κορνήλιος, καὶ ἕτερος ἀσθενὴς, ὡς ὁ Τιμόθεος, καὶ ἄλλος δραπέτης, ὡς Ὀνήσιμος· ἀλλ' οὐδὲν οὐδενὶ τούτων γέγονε κώλυμα, ἀλλὰ πάντες εὐδοκίμησαν, καὶ ἄνδρες καὶ γυναῖκες, καὶ νέοι καὶ γέροντες, καὶ δοῦλοι καὶ ἐλεύθεροι, καὶ στρατιῶται καὶ ἰδιῶται. Μὴ τοίνυν περιττὰ σκηπτώμεθα, ἀλλὰ γνώμην παρασκευάσωμεν ἀρίστην.

[13] LSJ, 344 *s.v.*

rank",[14] i.e. noblest. It links up nicely with γενναῖα, augmenting the focus upon the inner being and substantiating the vital role of the γνώμη in personal relationships with God.

If it was held that the general circumstances of life are not of critical account, it is no cause of wonder to find that Chrysostom viewed the immediate personal environment in this same way. In a surprisingly positive assessment of Lot, Chrysostom draws a lesson for those living in the city. There is no need, he asserts, to withdraw to the desert or to the mountains to live a life of virtue. Lot (not a particularly good example one might think) demonstrated that the city-dweller is quite able to do this. Neither desert nor city affects the outcome for better or for worse. It is not the external environment but the inner orientation that determines the result. Again, as Chrysostom points to the inner being, it is the γνώμη together with the τρόπος that he distinguishes as the significant factors in this regard: οὐδὲ γὰρ ὁ τόπος ἐστὶν ὁ τὴν ἀρετὴν κατορθῶν, ἀλλ' ἡ γνώμη καὶ ὁ τρόπος ("It is not the place that brings success in virtue, but the mindset and the manner").[15] This passage is of particular note given the veneration afforded to the monastic life in the ancient church. Chrysostom, though he had experience and appreciation of the ascetic discipline, generally insisted that the ordinary person is called to the life of virtue just as much as the monk. With him there was no distinction between the counsels of perfection, which were generally thought to be attainable only by the solitary, and the normal standard required of the rest. The thing that matters is not place, position or task, but inner disposition of the mindset, something that is not only open to all but also required of all.[16]

Chrysostom is thus seen to have been adamant that neither status, nor reputation, nor ancestry, nor circumstances, nor environment are critical to the ultimate issues of life. To this list he adds signs. In a homily based on Matthew 12:38-39 where Jesus answered the demand of some Scribes and Pharisees for signs as a basis for belief, Chrysostom indicated that nothing else but the right disposition of the γνώμη is of significance as far as salvation is concerned. In particular, external signs are of no profit. What is required is what Chrysostom

---

[14] LSJ, 241 s.v.

[15] *In Gen. hom.* 42; PG 54,396 48-49.

[16] Bouyer, *The Spirituality of the New Testament*, 447, writes: "All his public preaching insisted on the fact that perfection, in the final analysis, is proposed to all, those who are monks and those who are living in the world, and that all can attain it in the world if they attain fullness of charity."; Malingrey, *Philosophia*, 277-278, asserts that Chrysostom came to use φιλοσοφία to denote authentic incarnational Christian living in the milieu of the world.

called a "well-*gnomed*" γνώμη.[17] Here is an interesting word and combination of words: γνώμης ...εὐγνώμονος, a well-disposed mindset, a rightminded, candid, honest γνώμη. Lampe's basic choice of meaning of εὐγνώμονος is, "rightminded, having right feelings or right judgement".[18] I would agree that both feelings and critical thought are involved in the term. What is at stake here is that there needs to be a right orientation of the inner being or some faculty of the inner being. Chrysostom insisted that signs do not produce that orientation and that such orientation is independent of the presence or absence of signs. He asserted that one must feel well towards and think well of the truth. The essential need to which one must devote one's time and energy is that of the attainment of a rightly disposed γνώμη. External phenomena are not the critical issue; in his opinion inner condition as expressed in the state of the γνώμη most certainly is the thing required.

In all of these instances Chrysostom has turned his listeners' attention from the outer to the inner. It follows that in order to understand divine-human relationships truly, an examination must be made of the psyche. This he does by pointing in each instance to the γνώμη. It appears that he saw the γνώμη as critical both in our relationship with God and with our actions in the world.

II. The γνώμη as the real person: observing the functions of the inner being.

When Chrysostom used γνώμη he often, if not always, had in mind the deep desires of a person's being. A vivid example of this is found in Homily 6 on 1 Thessalonians. Chrysostom urged the women in the congregation to love God more than their husbands. If that is the case then widowhood will be no great burden. In making his point he illustrates by comparison with the loss of a child. He commences the illustration with the question in which he lists the qualities of the ideal husband. At the head of that list we find reference to the γνώμη: Εἰπέ μοι, εἰ ἄνδρα ἔχεις κατὰ γνώμην σοι πάντα πράττοντα ("Tell me, if you have a husband who does all things for you according to your mindset").[19] The perfect husband does just what his wife wishes in the depths of her being. A translation that gathers up our English idiom would be "according to your heart's desires". My own

---

[17] *In Matt. hom.* 43; PG 57,461 9-10: Ποῦ νῦν εἰσιν οἱ τὰ σημεῖα ζητοῦντες; Ἀκουέτωσαν ὅτι γνώμης χρεία εὐγνώμονος ("Where now in our case are the signs for us to seek? Let us take note that the need is of a rightminded mindset.")

[18] LPGL, 561 *s.v.*; LSJ, 708 *s.v.*: "of good feeling, considerate, reasonable".

[19] *In 1 Thes. hom.* 6; PG 62,432 10-11.

preferred translation of γνώμη, "according to your mindset" is somewhat less romantic, but it indicates the deliberated set orientation of the being which is involved. This is the thrust of Chrysostom's words: what the husband does is in tune with the real hopes and dreams of the wife, what she thinks and feels in her inner being. Γνώμη here clearly gathers up the deep desires of the soul.

Another example of this also comes from the domestic scene. In a homily in Ephesians where Chrysostom speaks against the ostentatious use of wealth, a favourite theme in his preaching, he encourages husbands to instruct their wives, in a gentle manner, against the use of finery and jewellery. Three results, he alleges, will ensue, the third being that the husband ἐνδείξεται τὴν αὐτοῦ γνώμην ("will be showing his mindset").[20] He will be revealing the orientation of his inner being, the desires of his heart, his real thought on the matter. Chrysostom expands on this and from a somewhat austere perspective teaches that the γνώμη that God approves is one which has no pleasure in finery. This γνώμη is a stance of the inner being that condemns all kinds of things of that nature including dances and indecent songs. He points out: ἀλλὰ ταῦτα ἀφεὶς τοῖς ἐπὶ τῆς σκηνῆς ("But these things belong to the people of the stage"),[21] which was not known as a morally healthy occupation in those times.[22] It appears from this that the γνώμη is what a person thinks, feels and determines in their inner being. Also, it is evident from these texts that Chrysostom recognised that the state of the psyche is crucial in human relationships.

Compelling evidence of this latter perspective is seen when he addresses the issue of friendship and love among friends in a homily on 1 Timothy. In his explanation of the text, he makes a distinction between a love that is τὴν μέχρι ῥημάτων ("merely in words") and one which has its source in the τὴν ἀπὸ διαθέσεως καὶ γνώμης καὶ τοῦ συναλγεῖν.[23] Here γνώμη is grouped with two words which speak of the settled depths of the being: διάθεσις (disposition), which bears the nuance of the fixed arrangement of the inner being, and συναλγέω (sympathise), which carries the idea of feeling with someone in the sense of sharing in their suffering. It would be safe to assume that γνώμη shares with these terms the same reference to the established state of the psyche. In other words, although there are distinctions between the terms, there is quite an overlap. The full text could be translated as: "That [love] which is sincere is not merely in

---

[20] *In Eph. hom.* 20; PG 62,145 26-31.

[21] *In Eph. hom.* 20; PG 62,145 17-18.

[22] See *In Joan. hom.* 1; PG 59,28 for a typical offensive by Chrysostom against Christians attending the theatre, which he called a Satanic parade.

[23] *In 1 Tim. hom.* 2; PG 62,509 42-46: Ἀγάπην δὲ ποίαν φησί; Τὴν εἰλικρινῆ, ἀλλὰ τὴν ἀπὸ διαθέσεως, καὶ γνώμης καὶ τοῦ συναλγεῖν, Ἐκ καθαρᾶς, θησί, καρδίας.

words, but arises from the disposition, the mindset, and fellow-feeling". It seems clear that γνώμη is descriptive of something that belongs to the depths of one's being and its orientation. It is to be noted that Chrysostom was using these words to explain the Apostle Paul's "from a pure heart" (καρδία).[24] Along with the other terms, γνώμη is referring to the core of one's being. It speaks with them of both depth and permanence, of how that core is disposed or oriented.

Another aspect of this focus upon internal motivation by Chrysostom is seen when he deals with the issue of consecration. Separation from the world, he asserts, is something that has been decided in the inner being before it finds expression in daily life. This separation is attributed to the γνώμη in a homily on 2 Timothy. In commenting rather enthusiastically upon two women in the church who were διάπυροι περὶ τὴν πίστιν καὶ θερμαί ("red-hot about their faith and fervent"),[25] he describes them as ἔδη ἐσταυρωμέναι ("already having been crucified"),[26] and ἔδη παρατεταγμέναι ("already having stood side by side in battle").[27] Chrysostom thought that Priscilla and Claudia had been specifically mentioned in this regard by Paul ὡς ἐκβεβηκότων ἤδη τῇ γνώμῃ τῶν κοσμικῶν πραγμάτων ("because they had already been separated in their mindset from the things of the world").[28] It is clear that in Chrysostom's estimation the separation in the γνώμη had occurred prior to any external expression of their zeal and their crucified lives. There is no doubt that by the use of the term γνώμη, Chrysostom has brought us in touch with the intentions of the heart. He would have his hearers understand that the inner being must be set in its direction towards the pathway of the Cross in an inner detachment from worldly values and affairs. A similar example of this focus upon inner consecration is found in an exhortation to give no place to idolatry. Chrysostom cites the example of a mother who did not allow amulets to be used on her sick child. She had acted as a martyr, he said, because εἵλετο μᾶλλον νεκρὸν τὸ παιδίον ἰδεῖν, ἢ εἰδωλολατρείας ἀνασχέσθαι ("she chose rather to see her child dead than to endure idolatry").[29] Whatever might happen to the child, κατέθυσε γὰρ τὸν υἱὸν τῇ γνώμῃ ("...she sacrificed him in her mindset").[30] This translation, using my preferred term, mindset, points to her resolute dedication.[31] Again there is little doubt that we are looking at what

---

[24] 1 Tim. 2:22.
[25] *In 2 Tim. hom.* 10; PG 62,659 26-27.
[26] *In 2 Tim. hom.* 10; PG 62,659 27.
[27] *In 2 Tim. hom.* 10; PG 62,659 28.
[28] *In 2 Tim. hom.* 10; PG 62,659 31.
[29] *In Col. hom.* 8; PG 62,357 57-58.
[30] *In Col. hom.* 8; PG 62,357 54-55.
[31] *John Chrys., Colossians*; trans. J. Tweed, in P. Schaff (ed.), NPNF Series 1, vol. 13,298, uses "resolve" to translate γνώμη here.

Chrysostom perceives as the citadel of motivation, what appears to be operating as the controlling faculty of our inner beings. Once more we are put in touch with the motivating mindset of the soul.

Further confirmation that γνώμη as used by Chrysostom refers to the secret motivation of the soul is presented in a striking example from the Old Testament. In a homily on Philippians, reference is made to Nabal and the Ziphites. They were used by Chrysostom to demonstrate that flattery is as evil as audacity. Nabal rebuked, the Ziphites flattered, but both were betraying David. In pointing to their betrayal, Chrysostom moved his focus from the outward expression to the inner being. Rebuke or flattery may be uttered, οἱ δὲ προδεδώκασι τῇ γνώμῃ τὸν Δαυίδ ("but in their mindset they were set on betraying David").[32] Again it is very tempting to translate τῇ γνώμῃ here as "in their heart". That certainly gives the sense of Chrysostom. J. Broadus gives "purpose",[33] which is to the point, but is more narrow than required. Γνώμη, I suggest, is wider, referring to the totality of which purpose is but a part or perhaps but one expression of the whole. With this term we are brought in contact with the motivating springs of human action.

That γνώμη is the source from which action springs and which gives meaning to actions is clearly seen in comments on Paul's dispute with Peter in Antioch. Chrysostom defends Peter and suggests that in changing his behaviour when some Jews arrived from Jerusalem he was secretly giving Paul the opportunity to rebuke him. Paul, Chrysostom proposes, knew all the facts: γὰρ ᾔδει τὴν γνώμην μεθ' ἧς ἐγίνετο ταῦτα ("for he knew the mindset with which he [Peter] did these things").[34] Whatever we might think of Chrysostom's interpretation and exegesis, we have an excellent pointer here to the meaning of γνώμη in his usage. The distinction between the external actions and the inner motivation which we have noted already is vividly drawn. Peter's actions have a secret motive, his γνώμη, which, in appearance, differed markedly from his external actions. Paul, it is claimed, knew Peter's γνώμη and thus interpreted his actions accordingly. Paul's rebuke, Chrysostom suggests, was a screen by which he actually revealed Peter's γνώμη.[35]

This ability of Chrysostom to penetrate below the surface and to carry his hearers to the core of being is amply illustrated in a homily on the Lord's words in

---

[32] *In Phil. hom.* 5; PG 62,218 6-7.

[33] *John Chrys., Philippians*; trans. C.W. Cotton, P. Schaff (ed.), NPNF Series 1, vol. 13,205.

[34] *Comm. in Gal.*; PG 61,641 9.

[35] *Comm. in Gal.*; PG 61,642 31-33: Ἀλλ' οὕτω μὲν οὐ λέγει· οὐ γὰρ ἂν ἐδέξαντο τὴν παραίνεσιν· προσχήματι δὲ ἐπιτιμήσεως τῆς ὑπὲρ τῶν ἐθνῶν ἐκκαλύπτει τοῦ Πέτρου τὴν γνώμην ("But he does not mean this, for they would not have received this exhortation; but by this screen of criticism for the sake of the Gentiles he reveals the mindset of Peter").

the Garden of Gethsemane, "If it be possible..." (Matt. 26:39). In speaking of the unity of the Son with the Father in the Cross, Chrysostom remarks that: Ἡ γὰρ ἀγάπη τῶν κατὰ γνώμην ἐστί ("Love is of those who are united in mindset").[36] The γνώμη is the faculty base of true love: ἀγάπη, in its fully developed Christian sense, flows from those who, like the Father and the Son, share a common γνώμη, that is, they think and feel the same in their mindsets. Commitment in love is made in the γνώμη. This is in harmony with the established Christian usage of ἀγάπη as the deliberate policy of the being to give oneself to others. The use of γνώμη here implies this characteristic of commitment, this attribute of deliberate devoted love. Here again we come face to face with the motivating core of the person. Furthermore the γνώμη is the critical factor in true love. Chrysostom has stated that true love is κατὰ γνώμην. The converse is that true love cannot exist unless it is κατὰ γνώμην. The γνώμη must be involved for true love to occur. It is the critical factor as to whether or not love is present. Whatever is said or happens on the surface, if the harmony of mindsets of persons is not achieved, then true love cannot exist.

The harmony of the γνώμη is mentioned again in this homily, when Chrysostom discusses what to many was the unfathomable problem of the opposition of wills of the Father and the Son suggested in the Gethsemane prayer. Chrysostom moves the issue away from will or desire (βούλομαι) by pointing to the σύμφωνος of the γνώμη of Son and of Father:

> And yet everywhere we see him (the Son) willing the same things as the Father, and choosing the same things. For when he says 'Give to them that, as You and I are one, they also may be one in us', this means nothing if not that the mindset of the Father and the Son are one. And when he says, 'The words that I speak, I do not myself speak, but the Father who dwells in me, he himself does these works', he points to this [mindset]. And when he says, 'I have not come on my own initiative', and 'I can do nothing from myself', it is clear that this does not mean that he has been robbed of his authority, either of speaking or acting, (away with that!) but that he was wishing to show with precision that his mindset was harmonious with the Father, both in words and deeds, and in all the arrangements of the divine economy was one and the same in relation to the Father, even as we [Chrysostom *et al*] have often already displayed.[37]

---

[36] *Poss.*; PG 51,34 59. A less stilted translation in our idiom would be: "For love is between those who are one in heart".

[37] *Poss.*; PG 51,36 35-46: Καίτοι γε πανταχοῦ ὁρῶμεν αὐτὸν τὰ αὐτὰ τῷ Πατρὶ βουλόμενον, τὰ αὐτὰ προαιρούμενον. Καὶ γὰρ ὅταν λέγῃ, 'Δὸς αὐτοῖς, καθὼς ἐγὼ καὶ σὺ ἕν ἐσμεν, ἵνα καὶ αὐτοὶ ἐν ἡμῖν ἓν ὦσιν', οὐδὲν ἄλλο λέγει, εἰ μὴ τὸ μίαν εἶναι γνώμην Πατρὸς καὶ Υἱοῦ. Καὶ ὅταν λέγῃ, 'Τὰ ῥήματα, ἃ ἐγὼ λαλῶ, οὐ λαλῶ ἐγὼ, ἀλλ' ὁ Πατὴρ ὁ ἐν ἐμοὶ μένων, αὐτὸς ποιεῖ τὰ ἔργα ταῦτα', τοῦτο ἐνδείκνυται. Καὶ ὅταν λέγῃ, ' Ἀπ' ἐμαυτοῦ οὐκ ἐλήλυθα, καὶ, Οὐ δύναμαι ἀπ' ἐμαυτοῦ ποιεῖν οὐδέν', οὐ τοῦτο δηλῶν λέγει, ὅτι ἐξουσίας ἀπεστέρηται ἢ τοῦ λαλεῖν ἢ τοῦ

This inner symphony of the γνώμη was expressed in such a harmony of speech, action and conformity to the will of the Father that it is described as μίαν καὶ τὴν αὐτὴν οὖσαν ("being one and the same").[38] It is interesting to find how, in this way, Chrysostom resolves the opposition of the two wills. Though desires or wills may be different because of particular circumstances, two mindsets (γνώμη) that are in harmony will cause the final choices (προαίρεσις) in those circumstances to be the same.[39] This highlights the emphasis Chrysostom placed upon inner motivation and internal harmony rather than upon a superficial analysis of bare externals. On the surface, in the words there is apparent opposition; in the inner depths of the psyche there is total agreement. Discernment of the γνώμη is critical for a true understanding of a person and their words and actions. On the other hand Chrysostom suggests that a comprehensive inspection of all the words and actions, not merely the isolated few, would reveal the inner unity.

This harmony of the γνώμη, Chrysostom insists, is vital for relationships within the church, especially between the leadership and the rest of the flock. Chrysostom contrasts the rule of a leader in the church with one in secular society. Outside it may be legitimate for a ruler not to consult the γνώμη of those he rules. For one thing he is restrained by law; for another he rules by force. According to Chrysostom, in the church the leader who, ὡς ἀπὸ τῆς οἰκείας γνώμης μόνον πάντα ποιεῖν ("does everything only from his own mindset")[40] is nothing less than a tyrant. This is not acceptable in the Church where rule must be something willingly accepted. The γνώμη of the ruled and that of the ruler must not be placed against each other. Oneness of mind and heart must be the order of the day. Γνώμη, as used by Chrysostom, indicates that kind of depth: it is the faculty of being where the issues of life are resolved and from which expressions of life emanate.

Chrysostom's explanation of the division in the Corinthian church as addressed in Paul's letter demonstrates the nature of this harmony of γνώμη. In a homily on 1:10, he distinguishes clearly between νοῦς and γνώμη.[41] Indeed, he places the one over against the other, with νοῦς and its cognates, διάνοια, νόημα and νοέω applying to the thought process, and γνώμη to an inner orientation that

---

ποιεῖν, (ἄπαγε!) ἀλλὰ μετὰ ἀκριβείας δεῖξαι βουλόμενος σύμφωνον αὐτοῦ τὴν γνώμην, καὶ τὴν ἐνρήμασι, καὶ τὴν ἐν πράγμασι, καὶ τὴν ἐν πάσαις οἰκονομίαις πρὸς τὸν Πατέρα μίαν καὶ τὴν αὐτὴν οὖσαν, καθὼς καὶ ἤδη πολλάκις ἀπεδείξαμεν.

[38] *Poss.*; PG 51,36 45.

[39] Γνώμη is ascribed to God by Chrysostom in many places, e.g. *In Gen. hom.* 8; PG 53,71 46; *hom.* 53; PG 54,466 58, 467 9, 468 12, 470 1, *hom.* 57; PG 54,499 13.

[40] *In Tit. hom.* 2; PG 62,672 29-30.

[41] *In 1 Cor. hom.* 3; PG 61,23 7-28.

goes deeper. At first, he asserts that Paul was looking for harmony of thought (διάνοια) and not merely harmony of words.[42] Then he goes a step further indicating that it is possible to have harmony of mind or thought (διάνοια) on some things but still lack it in others, thus falling short of true concord (ὁμοφροσύνη).[43] That is not all, for the next step Chrysostom takes is to assert that there may be harmony of thoughts or ideas (νοήματα), but not as yet harmony of γνώμη.[44] To illustrate, he points to the case where there is unity in faith (πίστις) but not in love (ἀγάπη),[45] which he explains as: Οὕτω γὰρ κατὰ μὲν τὰ νοήματα ἠνώμεθα (τὰ γὰρ αὐτὰ νοοῦμεν), κατὰ δὲ τὴν γνμώην οὐκέτι ("Thus there is a concord of ideas, (for we think the same things), but that is not as far as a concord of mindset").[46] Two things appear clear: one is that he understands νοῦς, διάνοια and νοήμα as referring to perception or thought, that is mind in the sense of its function of rational discernment and the shaping of ideas; the other, that γνώμη is understood as referring to something extra and deeper, to an orientation of the being, to an attitude of heart, to a disposition of the soul. Thus faith in its sense of understanding of and intellectual commitment to a body of truth is traced back to the νοῦς, whereas love belongs to the realm of the γνώμη. It is significant that he concludes by laying the blame for the schisms at Corinth to the division in the γνώμη and not to differences of faith, that is of the understanding. This division in γνώμη, he charges, comes from the human love of rivalry and contention (ἀνθρωπίνην φιλονεικίαν).[47] Chrysostom sees the issue as one of disposition and attitudes, that is, of mindset and not of intellect and doctrine. It is not enough to

---

[42] *In 1 Cor. hom.* 3; PG 61,23 11-13: Μὴ νομίσητε, φησὶν, ὅτι μέχρι ῥημάτων εἶπον εἶναι τὴν ὁμόνοιαν· τὴν γὰρ ἀπὸ διανοίας συμφωνίαν ἐπιζητῶ ("Do not assume, he says, that I said that agreement should only extend as far as words, for I seek the harmony that sources from the intellect").

[43] *In 1 Cor. hom.* 3; PG 61,23 16-18: Ὁ γὰρ ἡνωμένος ἔν τινι, ἔν τινι δὲ διχονοῶν, οὐκέτι κατήρτισται, οὐδὲ ἀπήρτισται εἰς ὁμοφροσύνην ("For the person who is in agreement in one thing but dissenting in another is no further restored to or made ready for harmony of mind and feeling").

[44] *In 1 Cor. hom.* 3; PG 61,23 18-19: Ἔστι δὲ καὶ τοῖς νοήμασι συμφωνοῦντα, μηδέπω καὶ τῇ γνώμη συμφωνεῖν ("It is also possible to be in harmony in ideas, and not yet to be harmonious in mindset").

[45] *In 1 Cor. hom.* 3; PG 61,23 19-21: οἷον, ὅταν τὴν αὐτὴν πίστιν ἔχοντες, μὴ ὦμεν συνημμένοι κατὰ τὴν ἀγάπην ("such as, while having the same faith we might not be agreeing together according to love").

[46] *In 1 Cor. hom.* 3; PG 61,23 21-23.

[47] *In 1 Cor. hom.* 3; PG 61,23 25-28: Οὐδὲ γὰρ ἀπὸ τοῦ διεστάναι κατὰ τὴν πίστιν τὰ σχίσματα ἐγίνετο, ἀλλὰ ἀπὸ τοῦ τὴν γνώμην διῃρῆσθαι κατὰ ἀνθρωπίνην φιλονεικίαν ("For the schisms did not happen from their being at variance about the faith, but from the tearing apart of their mindset by the human love of strife").

agree to a form of words. Only when unity of γνώμη is attained can it be said that true heartfelt harmony is present.

As suggested above, Chrysostom placed so much emphasis upon the inner life that he would have us believe that a person is not truly known until his or her γνώμη is discerned. This is brought out in his observations upon the appointment of leaders in the Church. In commenting on 1 Timothy 3:8 he illustrates, by reference to common household practice, Paul's point about not appointing a novice to leadership. No one, he asserts, would think of entrusting anything of prime value in a household to a novice slave until that slave had been well and truly tested. Such an appointment would be ἄτοπον...πρὶν ἂν διὰ πολλῆς τῆς πείρας τῆς αὐτοῦ γνώμης πολλὰ τεκμήρια δῷ ("ridiculous...before he gives positive proof of his mindset through many trials").[48] Thus, it would be equally ridiculous to appoint immediately to leadership in the Church someone recently coming in from pagan society. The point is that sufficient time should be allowed for the γνώμη, the mindset of the inner being of such a person to be revealed. The revised Schaff translation here gives γνώμη as "character", a quite useful translation in this context.[49] It is the revelation of the person's inner being and their constant mindset that is required. This can only be done over a lengthy period. Note also Chrysostom's reference to many trials; only through such tests is true character, the real mindset, revealed. The time factor and the trials allow for the real person to emerge. They make room for the true direction of a person's life to be seen. The γνώμη is this direction, is this constancy of character. It is the faculty of the inner life that rules the external expressions.

Something similar is found in a passage commenting on Abraham's offering of Isaac. Chrysostom compares Abraham to a champion soldier who triumphs over the enemy for his general, a victory attained by the soldier by means of the way he handles his weapons, his stance, and his strength. As for Abraham, he too was adequately equipped: with his mindset, his inner stance, and character shape, which in the hands of God terrified the devil and put him to flight.[50] Γνώμη here is linked with σχῆμα, character, and στάσις, the static inner state of the soul, the state of the soul at rest, the mien of the centre of the being. In the true champion, it is

---

[48] *In 1 Tim. hom.* 11; PG 62,553 38-43.

[49] *John Chrys., Titus*; trans. J. Tweed, in P. Schaff (ed.), NPNF Series 1, vol. 13,441.

[50] *In 2 Cor. hom.* 3; PG 61,415 9-15: Καὶ γὰρ ὥσπερ ἂν εἴ τις στρατηγὸς ἄριστον ἔχων στρατιώτην, ἀπὸ τῆς ὁπλοδεξιᾶς, ἀπὸ τῆς στάσεως, ἀπὸ τῆς ῥώμης καταπλήξειε τὸν ἀντίδικον· οὕτω καὶ ὁ Θεὸς, ἀπὸ τῆς γνώμης, ἀπὸ τοῦ σχήματος, ἀπὸ τῆς στάσεως μόνης τοῦ δικαίου τὸν κοινὸν ἁπάντων ἡμῶν ἐχθρὸν διάβολον κατέπληξε καὶ ἐφυγάδευσε ("For, just as if some commander who has a first-rate soldier whose skill with his weapons, his stance and his strength would terrify his opponent, so also God, by the mindset, character and inner stance of this righteous man alone terrified and banished the devil, the common enemy of us all").

this which comes to the fore in the heat of battle and in the face of challenge. Indeed, in any crisis the real person tends to be revealed. This linkage again points unmistakably to the orientation of the inner being where the shape of the real person is to be found. The γνώμη was seen by Chrysostom to be a critical element of that shape.

Further indication in this direction is found in the tenth homily of the Matthew material. In speaking of the universal proclamation and application of the Gospel, Chrysostom takes the words of Isaiah 11:6 to show the effect of the Gospel upon people everywhere. Reception of the Gospel would mean that the human race would be changed, he suggests: ἀπὸ θηριώδους τρόπου καὶ σκληρότητος γνώμης εἰς ἡμερότητα πολλὴν καὶ ἀπαλότητα μεταβάλλουσα τῶν ἀνθρώπων τὸ γένος ("converting the human race from brutishness of manner and harshness of mindset to much gentleness and tenderness").[51] The change is clearly a change in demeanour in the basic attitude of the psyche from a wild people to a gentle people. Once again we are encountering the set habit of the soul. There seems little doubt that the γνώμη represents the fundamental mindset of the human person.

According to Chrysostom, the γνώμη has ruling significance in the soul. This may be demonstrated from various texts where he refers the functions of judgement and decision to the γνώμη. For instance, the crucial role of the γνώμη in judging and ratifying ideas is seen in the commentary on Galatians where the γνώμη is referred to as the final arbiter. Chrysostom refers to the same words being repeated to show that they were not spoken in anger or rashly or with exaggeration, but in a cooler critical manner:

> When the same words are spoken a second time, it demonstrates that he spoke because he had judged this way, and he thus produced that which was spoken because he had previously ratified it in his mindset.[52]

The structure of the sentence here employed by Chrysostom is informative and bears analysis. Two dependent clauses follow the main verb δείκνυσιν and its ὅτι: (a) κρίνας οὕτως εἶπε ("having judged thus he spoke"), and (b) καὶ πρότερον ἐν τῇ γνώμῃ κυρώσας, οὕτως ἐξήνεγκε τὸ λεχθέν ("...having previously ratified it in his mindset, he produced what was spoken"). There is a reference to speaking in each clause, and in each, a critical sifting occurred prior to the speaking. As the speaking activities are identical, it is reasonable to conclude that the two critical

---

[51] *In Matt. hom.* 10; PG 57,188.4-10.
[52] *Comm. in Gal.*; PG 61,624 31-33. ὁ δὲ δεύτερον τὰ αὐτὰ λέγων, δείκνυσιν ὅτι κρίνας οὕτως εἶπε, καὶ πρότερον ἐν τῇ γνώμῃ κυρώσας, οὕτως ἐξήνεγκε τὸ λεχθέν.

activities to which he refers are identical also. Thus κρίνας here parallels and thus appears equivalent to the ἐν τῇ γνώμῃ κυρώσας. The γνώμη is equated to that faculty of the psyche which makes critical judgements. Here, in the individual, is where an idea is stamped for that person with legitimacy or otherwise. If the γνώμη has the capacity to make such judgements it must include the reasoning faculty or, at least, be closely associated with it. Also, the term κυρόω, to make valid or ratify, contains a nuance that suggests a final arbitration role for the γνώμη. The matter had to be referred to the γνώμη for its approval. This means that the γνώμη was allied to the intellect and occupied a position of authority within the human psyche as far as Chrysostom was concerned.

This ruling significance of the γνώμη is highlighted in a comment by Chrysostom on Paul's uncertainty about his travels. This uncertainty is ascribed to the fact that Paul was Ἐπειδὴ γὰρ πνεύματι ἤγενετο ("for he was led by the Spirit").[53] Thus Chrysostom proposes that Paul οὐκ οἰκείᾳ γνώμῃ ἔπραττεν ἅπερ ἔπαττε ("did not do what he did by his own mindset").[54] It is implied here that normally a person would act from their γνώμη. The γνώμη was the spring of action, the governing faculty behind the deed. In Paul's case the γνώμη in this function is placed in submission to the leading of the Spirit of God, hence the uncertainty about the future. We are not told how this leading operated or what this meant as far as the reasoning faculty or the intuition or anything else was concerned. Nevertheless, that in the normal course of events the γνώμη assumed the role of setting the agendas of life seems clear enough.

This agenda-setting feature of the γνώμη is brought out in a discussion on the need to accept sorrow and evils as a normal part of life. No one can expect to be exempt from them. Chrysostom illustrates from the experience of a king that none of us are able to live as we would like, that is, free from all constraints. The king also, he says, αὐτὸς ὑπὸ πολλῶν κρατεῖται, καὶ οὐ πάντα κατὰ γνώμην πράττει ("is ruled by many and cannot do everything according to his mindset").[55] He has to grant many favours contrary to what he himself thinks. Chrysostom adds that on the contrary, as king καὶ μάλιστα πάντων ἐκεῖνός ἐστιν ὁ πάντα πράττων ἃ μὴ θέλει ("more than all persons he has to do many things that he does not wish to do").[56] Γνώμη is seen here to be the natural ruling faculty in the individual. If all things were equal and he was free from all external constraints this is how he would act, κατὰ γνώμην, according to his mindset. However, all things are not equal, constraints do exist and the king cannot act κατὰ γνώμην. He is obliged to

---

[53] *In 1 Tim. hom.* 11; PG 62,554 25-26.
[54] *In 1 Tim. hom.* 11; PG 62,554 27.
[55] *In 2 Tim. hom.* 1; PG 62,604 23-25.
[56] *In 2 Tim. hom.* 1; PG 62,604 25-27.

do otherwise. It is of note that not acting κατὰ γνώμην is here equated with παρὰ τὸ δοκοῦν ("contrary to what he thinks or purposes"), and with ἃ μὴ θέλει ("which he does not will"). To act κατὰ γνώμην, then, is to do what one would normally expect to do and in accord with one's settled desires. All things being equal, this is where the agendas of life are set. However, all things are not equal, and thus the king is forced by the demands of office to act differently to κατὰ γνώμην, against the real intent and mindset of his being.

Much more could be produced along similar lines to the above. Sufficient has been brought forward to demonstrate that Chrysostom viewed the internal state of the human person as being of ultimate significance for life. A constant note has been struck in many of the texts thus far examined here that this inner focus is best expressed in the words, God inspects the γνώμη.[57] The γνώμη was considered by Chrysostom to be the motivating core of a person's being. It represents the deep desires and intentions of the heart. It is what one thinks or feels in one's inner being. It is the citadel of motivation, the motivating spring of action, the motivating mindset of the psyche. It is the place of commitment, the governing principle, the normal ruling faculty of the soul. While its significance in Divine-human relationships has been noted in this discussion, its function in this regard requires some filling out.

III. The responsible γνώμη: the object of God's evaluation.

In a comment on the offering of Abel in homily 18 on Genesis, Chrysostom reminds us "that our Lord does not acknowledge distinction of persons (differences in external appearances), but that from scrutinising the moral choice, he rewards the mindset".[58] Here it is the προαίρεσις (faculty of choice) and the γνώμη that are the faculties subject to appraisal. More precisely, God scrutinises the προαίρεσις as his ground for judgment. However, the reward goes to the γηώμη. The προαίρεσις, the faculty of choice, may be disposed in a certain direction. This disposition of the προαίρεσις is determined by the γνώμη which

---

[57] *In Matt. hom.* 22; PG 57,306 27-29.

[58] *In Gen. hom.* 18; PG 53,154 37-40: ὅτι διαφορὰν προσώπων οὐκ οἶδεν ὁ Δεσπότης ὁ ἡμέτερος, ἀλλὰ ἐκ προαιρέσεως ἐξετάζων τὴν γνώμην στεφανοῖ. There is some difficulty with the translation here, but ἐκ with the genitive carries the sense of a ground for judgement. As no other use of ἐκ with the genitive can apply, the text must read: "but from scrutinising the choice (προαιρέσεως) (as the ground for judgement) he rewards the mindset (γνώμην)". Later in this homily, PG 53,155 39-40, Chrysostom states that the προαίρεσις was also crowned, which demonstrates the close relationship between προαίρεσις and γνώμη, a reality that has led to some confusion as to the nature of that relationship in much patristic scholarship.

receives the reward. The importance of the γνώμη in this regard is underlined in a comment that it was the difference in the γνώμη that determined the acceptance or otherwise of the brothers' offerings.[59] There, the text indicates that in the case of Cain the disposition of the γνώμη issued in indifference or carelessness in the faculty of choice. As far as Chrysostom was concerned, ῥαθυμία (indifference /carelessness/apathy) was always an imminent danger and almost the ultimate sin.[60] In this passage, salvation itself is betrayed and punishment merited by such an attitude. The γνώμη is critical in the assessment. In fact, Chrysostom sums up what is meant by God taking notice as consisting of his acceptance and applause of the γνώμη.[61] He elaborates on this theme, twice mentioning the state of the γνώμη as the reason for God's interest in both the offerer and offerings:

> Therefore God looked upon him because he made his offering with a healthy mindset, and upon the gifts that were offered, not only because they were spotless, but because in every way they were obviously highly valuable, both from the mindset of the offerer, and from being of the firstborn...[62]

---

[59] *In Gen. hom.* 18; PG 53,155 28: ἀλλ' ἡ διαφορὰ τῆς γνώμης λοιπὸν καὶ τῆς προαιρέσεως ἡ ῥαθυμία τοῦ μὲν εὐπρόσδεκτον ἐποίησε τὴν προσαγωγήν, τοῦ δὲ ἀπόβλητον ("but finally the difference in the mindset and the apathy of the choice made the offering of one cherished, and of the other despised").

[60] Chrysostom's usage of ῥαθυμία is so extensive and critical a concept in his theology that it merits a study in itself. For example, *In Rom. hom.*13; PG 60,507 48-50, sin is produced by it; *In Gen. hom.* 24; PG 53,207 62, wickedness surfaced in the whole human race on account of it; *In Matt. hom.* 44; PG 57,468 45-46, it is classed along with vulgar and contemptuous as the attitudes that makes the seed by the wayside unfruitful; *In Gen. hom.* 23; PG 53,202 14 it seduces people to bestial passions. In an extended passage in this latter homily on Genesis, the forfeiture of salvation is attributed to it: PG 53,204 35, 37, 45; 205 8, 25; and 206 2 all name ῥαθυμία; see esp. PG 53,205 8: μηδέποτε τὸν διάβολον αἰτιᾶσθαι, ἀλλὰ τὴν ῥάθυμον ἡμῶν γνώμην ("...never blame the devil, but our own apathetic mindset"). See also *In Matt. hom.* 6; PG 57,67 46-68 1-2; See R.C. Hill (trans.), *St. John Chrysostom: Eight Sermons on the Book of Genesis* (Boston, MA 2004) 18, in the Introduction asserts: "The root cause of the Fall, as of all our sins, he [Chrysostom] diagnoses as usual as ῥαθυμία, indifference, negligence, as he will conclude also in these homilies."; See also R.C. Hill, "Chrysostom as Old Testament commentator", *EB* 46 (1988) 74-75; Hill, *Reading the Old Testament*, 180.

[61] *In Gen. hom.* 18; PG 53,155 38-40: ἀπεδέξατο, ἐπήνεσε τὴν γνώμην, ἐστεφάνωσε τὴν προαίρεσιν ("he accepted, he applauded the mindset, he crowned the choice"). Chrysostom's imagery of a great celebration is as inspiring as it is instructive.

[62] *In Gen. hom.* 18; PG 53,155 48-51: Ἐπεῖδε τοίνυν ἐπ' αὐτὸν, ὅτι ὑγιεῖ γνώμη τὴν προσαγωγὴν ἐποιήσατο, καὶ ἐπὶ τὰ δῶρα τὰ προσενεχθέντα, οὐχ ὅτι ἀκηλίδωτα μόνον, ἀλλ' ὅτι πανταχόθεν τίμια φαινόμενα, ἀπό τε τῆς γνώμης τοῦ προσάγοντος, ἀπό τε τοῦ πρωτότοκα εἶναι...

It is a healthy γνώμη (ὑγιεῖ γνώγ) that captures God's interest and approval. Chrysostom continues with an impressive list as to things that gave such value to the offering, but it should be noted that this healthy γνώμη heads the list. Chrysostom, the model rhetor, is not satisfied with a passing reference. Rather he re-states his point again and again. Thus we find him pressing home his theme, this time referring to Abel as having an ὀρθῆ γνώμη (a morally upright mindset), along with a εἰλικρινεῖ διανοίᾳ (pure intention).[63] Then again, sacred scripture, Chrysostom asserts, teaches us that: ...ζητεῖται παρὰ τῷ Δεσπότῃ, ἀλλ᾽ ἡ τῆς γνώμης διάθεσις μόνον ("the disposition of the mindset is the only thing for which the Lord seeks").[64] Chrysostom then has God addressing Cain telling him the same thing: οὐκ ᾔδεις ὅτι οὐχὶ τῶν προσαγομένων ἐδεόμην, ἀλλὰ τῆς τῶν προσαγόντων ὑγιοῦς γνώμης; ("Do you not see that I was in no need of the offerings, but of the healthy mindset of the offerers?")[65] In true rhetorical form, re-enacting and interpreting this conversation between God and Cain, in which God points to their respective mindsets (γνώμη) as holding the key to divine acceptance or rejection, he specifies the particular function of their mindsets that was under examination. Cain's γνώμη failed to calculate the difference in the offerings to be made, whereas Abel's γνώμη demonstrated great precision in making the distinction. Chrysostom uses an image from archery to describe Abel's γνώμη: ὀρθή τε τυγχάνουσα ("straight and hitting the mark").[66] Here, in Abel's mindset, was an instrument that was finely shaped and balanced to its task of discrimination. On the contrary, Cain's γνώμη was, by inference, out of true and missing the mark. Cain is rejected because his γνώμη is not truly shaped; it was not ὀρθή, righteous.[67] In praising Abel, it was noted above that Chrysostom states that God honoured the γνώμη of Abel by calling his offerings gifts. As it was the γνώμη that was so honoured, we are in touch with the determining faculty of the person. It is evident from the examination of this homily that Chrysostom viewed the γνώμη as critical

---

[63] *In Gen. hom.* 18; PG 53,155 56-59: Ἐπειδὴ ὀρθῇ γνώμῃ καὶ εἰλικρινεῖ διανοίᾳ προσήνεγκεν ὁ Ἄβελ, Ἐπεῖδε, φησὶν, ὁ Θεός, τουτέστιν, ἐδέξατο, ἠρέσθη, ἐπήνεσε· δῶρα δὲ ἐκάλεσε τὰ προσενεχθέντα, τιμῶν καὶ διὰ τούτου τοῦ προσενέγκαντος τὴν γνώμην ("Since Abel offered with a righteous mindset and pure thought, 'God took interest', meaning that he accepted, he was pleased, he applauded; he called the offerings gifts, by this honouring the mindset of the offerer").

[64] *In Gen. hom.* 18; PG 53,156 13: This assertion is repeated in relation to Noah in *hom.* 27; PG 53,242 21-22.

[65] *In Gen. hom.* 18; PG 53,157 1-4.

[66] *In Gen. hom.* 18; PG 53,157 15-17.

[67] *In Gen. hom.* 18; PG 53,157 43-44: Μὴ νομίσῃς, φησὶν, εἰ καὶ ἀπεστράφην σου τὴν θυσίαν διὰ τὴν οὐκ ὀρθὴν γνώμην... ("Do not suppose, he means, that even if your offering was turned away because there was no upright mindset...").

in divine-human relationships. He saw it functioning as the faculty of the psyche responsible for discernment and for directing the crucial choices of life. As such it comes under the sifting gaze of the Almighty who praises or condemns these internal dispositions of humankind.

Chrysostom is adamant that all judgement, whether made by God or by humans, is to be made on the basis of the γνώμη. In what R. Hill has observed as "recourse to rationalizing",[68] Chrysostom explains Jacob's deceit of his father to be of the same ilk as that of Abraham's intended infanticide and the slaughter of offending Israelites by Phineas. In view of the immensity of the ethical issues raised by these events, this comparison is especially significant for an adequate grasp of the importance of γνώμη:

> If, therefore, bloodshed and infanticide were held in esteem in those instances because they happened according to the mindset of God, and if we focus, not on the actual deeds but upon the aim of the doers and the mindset of the perpetrators, much more would we reckon them necessary.[69]

All of these deeds are to be judged on the basis of God's γνώμη, and the σκοπός and γνώμη of the perpetrators. To focus on the deeds in themselves is to miss the point. They did what they did because they were convinced in their γνώμη that they were acting according to God's γνώμη. Thus what may appear to us to be evil in itself, takes on a halo of reverence and holiness when viewed from the aspect of the γνώμη. Irrespective of our assessment of the rightness or wrongness of Chrysostom's exegesis, the weight he placed upon the role of the γνώμη in regard to motivation and therefore to judgement is clear. This is all the more remarkable because, in using the example of Abraham, Chrysostom has taken us a step further than the matter of discerning the γνώμη behind the committed deed. Abraham's aim in reference to Isaac was never completed, as discussed below in this paragraph. In another of the Genesis homilies this same remarkable assertion concerning the γνώμη is made in discussing an offering of Noah. Chrysostom avers that it is possible to be rewarded merely on the basis of the γνώμη even though the thing done seems small, or the work contemplated has not been completed, or not even done at all.[70] Two examples of this are given in Homily 42.

---

[68] R.C. Hill (trans.), *St John Chrysostom, Homilies on Genesis, 46-67*, FOTC 87 (Washington DC 1992) 83 n. 12.

[69] *In Gen. hom.* 53; PG 54,466 58-60: Εἰ τοίνυν φόνος εὐδοκίμησε καὶ παιδοκτονία ἐν ἐκείνοις, ἐπειδὴ κατὰ Θεοῦ γνώμην ἐγένετο, καὶ οὐ τοῖς γεγονόσι προσέχομεν, ἀλλὰ τῷ σκοπῷ τῶν γινομένων, καὶ τῇ τῶν πεποιηκότων γνώμῃ, πολλῷ μᾶλλον καὶ ἐνταῦθα τοῦτο λογίζεσθαι χρή.

[70] *In Gen. hom.* 27; PG 53,243 50-52. This passage and the portions of the surrounding context will be translated and discussed in Chapter 3 when analysing Homily 27.

The widow of Zarepthah is presented as a model of God's response to the disposition of the γνώμη rather than to the size of the offering.[71] Likewise the widow in the Gospel who put in two small coins is seen as a paragon of liberality.[72] In both cases it is the condition of the γνώμη that is the decisive factor in the Lord's evaluation. This same point is made clear in homily 3 on 2 Corinthians in which Chrysostom becomes rather excited in his dramatisation when considering the incident of Abraham's offering up of Isaac. Although God held back the hand that was about to thrust the knife into the throat of Isaac, Chrysostom, in a very vivid rhetorical presentation, asserts that the stroke was accomplished in the γνώμη of the righteous Abraham.[73] No blood was shed but once again the decisive deliberation of the γνώμη was as effective as the deed. This is striking for a preacher who was so practical in his application, who, for example, defended his daily habit of discoursing on almsgiving on the grounds that his preaching appeared to have made little difference to their practice.[74] Chrysostom, for all his appeal to action, was essentially concerned with inner motivation. He was eminently aware that God inspected the γνώμη.

In a passage in Genesis homily 20 we again find that the γνώμη is the basis for reward (στεφανοῖ) and/or condemnation (κατακρίνει).[75] Chrysostom claims that the knowledge of what and what not to do is innate (ἔγκειται) in our natures. This together with the fact that God has made us self-authoritative (αὐτεξουσίους)

---

[71] *In Gen. hom.* 42; PG 54,394 43-44: Ἀλλ' ὁ Δεσπότης ὁ ἡμέτερος οὐ τῇ ποσότητι προσέχειν εἴωθεν, ἀλλὰ τῇ δαψιλείᾳ τῆς γνώμης ("...but our Lord has not been accustomed to be devoted to the amount, but to the liberality of the mindset").

[72] *In Gen. hom.* 42; PG 54,394 49-50: οὐκ ἐπειδὴ πλείονα τῶν ἄλλων ἔβαλεν, ἀλλ' ὅτι δαψιλῆ τὴν γνώμην ἐπεδείξατο ("not because she threw in more than others, but because she exhibited the liberality of her mindset"). For further reference to this widow, see *In Gen. hom.* 55; PG 54,484 46.

[73] *In 2 Cor. hom.* 3; PG 61,414 50-52: Καὶ γὰρ οὐχ ὁ Ἀβραὰμ αὐτὴν κατεῖχε μόνον, ἀλλὰ καὶ ὁ Θεός· καὶ ὁ μὲν ὤθει διὰ τῆς γνώμης, ὁ δὲ Θεὸς ἀνέστελλε διὰ τῆς φωνῆς ("For Abraham alone did not himself hold back, but God also: he, in his mindset, thrust through [with the knife], but God repulsed it with his voice").

[74] *In Matt. hom.* 88; PG 58,779 14-15: Even allowing for a certain amount of hyperbole there is little doubt that almsgiving was a frequently visited theme.

[75] *In Gen. hom.* 20; PG 53,166 40-44: Ἴιστε γὰρ...ὡς ἔγκειται τῇ ἡμετέρᾳ φύσει ἡ γνῶσις τῶν πρακτέων καὶ τῶν μὴ πρακτέων, καὶ ὅτι αὐτεξουσίους ἡμᾶς εἰργάσατο ὁ τῶν ἁπάντων δημιουργός, καὶ πανταχοῦ ἀπὸ τῆς γνώμης τῆς ἡμετέρας ἢ κατακρίνει, ἢ στεφανοῖ... ("For you know... how the knowledge of what to do and what not to do lies in our nature, and that the Creator of all built independence into us, and in all things he either condemns or crowns us on the basis of our mindset").

means that what is done or not done depends upon some power in us. In another place in this homily, Chrysostom states that power to be the γνώμη.[76]

Perhaps the most outstanding image that Chrysostom employed relevant to this issue is presented in homily 23 on Genesis in a passage evaluating the life and work of Noah. This superior man, Chrysostom argues, though quite unpopular with his generation, found grace (χάριν) in the estimation of "the one who haunts (ἐμβατεύοντα) the heart".[77] In Classical Greek literature ἐμβατεύω was used of the activity or presence of the tutelary gods.[78] The allusion refers to these deities frequenting the home as those who own it and who receive the devotion and allegiance of the members of the household. God is engaged in similar activity: he frequents the heart of the person as its sacred owner. He does so, asserts Chrysostom, to ascertain the γνώμη. In Noah's case he finds it acceptable. We might note from this reference that καρδία is closely linked with γνώμη, the latter being the more specialised term for a power or faculty of the psyche than the former more general term which refers to the inner core of personal being. It is not out of place to label Chrysostom a theologian of the mindset and the heart due to his obvious conviction that God's main interest with humankind is the condition of the inner being.

IV. The γνώμη as the faculty of response.

If the γνώμη plays such a critical role as argued above, it is credible that it would be presented as having the key function in the issue of human response to God and the overtures of his grace. This is indeed the case. In Chrysostom's understanding of the human situation, there is little doubt that he viewed the condition of the γνώμη as the critical factor in the individual's rejection or acceptance of the Gospel. In a comment on John the Baptist, Chrysostom points to the Pharisees as possessing a particular γνώμη and the people as possessing another which was quite different.[79] The people, from their γνώμη, confessed their sins, whereas the γνώμη of the Pharisees was hardened and they were condemned for their rejection.

---

[76] *In Gen. hom.* 20; PG 53,169 57: Ὁρᾷς, ἀγαπητέ, πῶς αὐτεξούσιον ἡμῶν τὴν γνώμην ὁ Θεὸς ἐδημιούργησε ("Do you see, beloved, how God has created our mindset self-authoritative").

[77] *In Gen. hom.* 23; PG 53,200 7-9: ἀλλὰ πρὸς ἐκεῖνον τὸν τὰς καρδίας ἐμβατεύοντα χάριν εὗρε, καὶ ἐκεῖνος αὐτοῦ τὴν γνώμην ἀπεδέξατο. Hill, *Homilies on Genesis 18-45*, 93, translates this as "...nevertheless he found favour in the eyes of the one who haunts the heart, and to him his attitude was acceptable".

[78] LSJ, 539 *s.v.*

[79] *In Matt. hom.* 11; PG 57,193 11-12: Καὶ ἵνα μάθῃς ὅτι ἑτέρα μὲν οἱ Φαρισαῖοι, ἑτέρα δὲ ὁ δῆμος παρεγένοντο γνώμῃ...

Earlier in the same passage the multitudes are described as possessing an ἀπλάστου γνώμη ("unaffected mindset").[80] Here is a lack of pretence, an openness that, in contrast to the Pharisees, elicits commendation. Such a condition in the γνώμη makes way for the truth to lodge in the heart.

In a section of homily 1 on Matthew, Chrysostom, employing the analogy of distance, observes that the stance of the γνώμη is critical because it determines our closeness or otherwise to heaven. The γνώμη is presented as the direction in which our way of life is set. Chrysostom gives two alternatives, one that takes us further away: ἐὰν ἀμελῶμεν ("if we are negligent/careless"), and the other that brings us in a moment of time to its gates: ἐὰν σπουδαζῶμεν ("if we are diligent").[81] His summary conclusion is: Οὐ γὰρ μήκει τόπων, ἀλλὰ γνώμῃ τρόπων τὰ διαστήματα ταῦτα ὥρισται ("It is not by the distance of positions, but by the mindset with its dispositions that these spaces are determined").[82] It is evident that in his thinking the γνώμη plays a crucial role in our relationship with God. It has the capacity to accept or reject the overtures of grace and to determine our destiny.

In another homily on Matthew, Chrysostom speaks to the ministry of John the Baptist and applies lessons from it. Chrysostom makes much of the threatening context but, to allay any feelings of despair, he hastens to reassure his hearers of the ease with which one may bring forth fruit unto salvation. He points to the only thing that is required, and that is "the mindset alone is necessary".[83] He does add faith to this, but the emphasis is upon something which he thinks is easily within reach of all. His point is that God is not asking for great deeds, works, labours or toils. Rather, he seeks only our γνώμη. Although no epithet is used with γνώμη, the context indicates a γνώμη disposed toward faith. This strengthens the force of the γνώμης μόνον; fruit-bearing is something that flows only from the disposition of our inner beings, from the mindset focused on trust in God.

Turning from the positive to the negative aspect, we find elsewhere in his Matthew homilies that Chrysostom explains why Jerusalem as well as Herod was troubled by the news of the impending birth of the Messianic king. He ascribes their anxiety to the same rebellious γνώμη which had been distinctive of their history. It was that γνώμη which was the source of the rebellion of the ancient Israelites when God was their benefactor in the wilderness and the one who had

---

[80] *In Matt. hom.* 11; PG 57,193 2-3: Ἀλλ' οἱ μὲν ὄχλοι ἀπὸ γνώμης ἀπλάστου τοῦτο ὑπώπτευον· οἱ δὲ Φαρισαῖοι, ἐπιλαβέσθαι βουλόμενοι.

[81] *In Matt. hom.* 1; PG 57,22 53-54

[82] *In Matt. hom.* 1; PG 57,22 56. This is a rhetorical *parachesis*, featuring two phrases with similarity of sound but difference of roots in the main terms τόπων and τρόπων. I have attempted to replicate this in translation.

[83] *In Matt. hom.* 11; PG 57,196 29-31: διὰ τούτων δεικνὺς, ὅτι γνώμης μόνον δεῖται καὶ πίστεως, οὐ πόνων καὶ ἱδρώτων·

given them freedom from their Egyptian slavery.[84] This γνώμη he describes as
φιλονεικία ("contentious"), ῥαθυμία μάλιστα πάντων ("apathetic most of all"),
marked by νωθεία ("dullness/sloth"), and βασκανία ("envy").[85] These are attitudes
that had found a home in their thinking (διάνοια) and needed to be rooted out with
rigid discipline and severity.[86] The γνώμη is the source of the problem. Prevost's
"feeling"[87] is somewhat weak for a translation of γνώμη in this context where
γνώμη is linked with διάνοια. What Chrysostom speaks of is a determined policy
of life, not some mere evanescent passion of the moment. Here is something that
is planted deep within the mindset and the thinking process, indicating that chosen
policy is in view. The deliberate nature of the position adopted is seen in the
parallel Chrysostom draws with the Israelites of old. They turned back from God
in the face of all the benefits of the grace of God that they had been experiencing.
It is this deliberate stance of the γνώμη that Chrysostom found so dangerous and
against which he so often warned. It is but a small step from ῥαθυμία
(carelessness/apathy) to φιλονεικία (contention), νωθεία (sloth), and βασκανία
(envy). Thus ῥαθυμία is seen as the great enemy of a well-disposed γνώμη. Again
it is the condition of the γνώμη that determines human destiny.

Further evidence of the weight placed upon the role of the γνώμη in
responding to God is found in homily 19 on Genesis. This homily opens with a
discussion under the image of the incurable wounds of the soul affected by sin.
The problem, Chrysostom claims, is οὐκ ἐπειδὴ μὴ δύναται, ἀλλ' ἐπειδὴ μὴ
βούλεται ("not lack of ability but lack of desire").[88] The faculty of deliberate
choice (προαίρεσις) is not stationary but can change because God has endowed
our nature with independence or freewill (αὐτεξούσιον).[89] God, knowing the
stirrings in the depth of our thought (διάνοια), provides great blessings for us and

---

[84] *In Matt. hom.* 6; PG 57,67 45-49: Τίνος οὖν ἕνεκεν ἐταράχθησαν; Ἀπὸ τῆς αὐτῆς γνώμης, ἀφ'
ἧς καὶ ἔμπροσθεν τὸν Θεὸν εὐεργετοῦντα ἀπεστρέφοντο, καὶ τῶν Αἰγυπτιακῶν ἐμέμνηντο κρεῶν,
τοσαύτης ἀπολαύοντες ἐλευθερίας (" For what reason were they troubled? From the same
mindset as before, by which they abandoned God who was showing them kindness, and that
reminded them of the flesh pots of the Egyptians when they were enjoying so much freedom").
[85] *In Matt. hom.* 6; PG 57,68 1, 2, 16, 17.
[86] *In Matt. hom.* 6; PG 57,68 16-17: ἅπερ ἀμφότερα δεῖ μετὰ ἀκριβείας ἐξορίζειν τῆς ἡμετέρας
διανοίας, καὶ πυρὸς εἶναι σφοδρότερον τὸν μέλλοντα ἐπὶ τῆς τοιαύτης παρατάξεως ἵστασθαι
("[sloth and envy] ...both the very things that with exactitude must be banished from our
thinking, and one who is going to stand in place in such a line of battle must be as fervent as
fire").
[87] *John Chrys., Matthew*; trans. G. Prevost, in P. Schaff (ed.), NPNF Series 1, vol. 10, 40.
[88] *In Gen. hom.* 19; PG 53,158 51.
[89] *In Gen. hom.* 19; PG 53,158 58-59: Ἐπεὶ οὖν αὐτεξούσιον ἡμῶν τὴν φύσιν εἰργάσατο ὁ τῶν
ὅλων Θεός·

exhorts, advises and even checks the attack of evil,[90] but it is the γνώμη which is the determining factor: ἀλλὰ τὰ φάρμακα κατάλληλα ἐπιθείς, ἀφίησιν ἐν τῇ γνώμῃ τοῦ κάμνοντος κεῖσθαι τὸ πᾶν ("But having contributed the appropriate drugs, he [God] allows everything to rest on the mindset of the one who is ill").[91] God applies all the appropriate remedies but, having done all, he then leaves the patient to dispose his/her γνώμη to respond to the treatment so graciously offered. We find that the great danger to the patient once again is ῥαθυμία, a state of the γνώμη which is life-threatening. It is imperative that the γνώμη be properly inclined. The image is applied powerfully to Cain who murdered his brother and whose γνώμη is presented as something to be avoided, a cautionary figure teaching self-control to generations to come.[92] Therefore, it is not the deed by itself, but rather the γνώμη behind it that should attract the condemnation.[93]

If the γνώμη plays such a key role in divine-human relationships then it must, in Chrysostom's thinking, be the citadel that needs to be taken if the person is to be taken captive by the truth. This is so: in his commentary on Paul's letter to the Galatians, Chrysostom asserts that the point of preaching and teaching is to persuade and grasp the γνώμη of the hearers.[94] The comment refers to the work of false teachers who wished to persuade people with deceit and falsehood. Nevertheless the point is that the place where persuasion is effected is the γνώμη. If one is able to persuade the γνώμη one has taken the person captive.

More could be said but sufficient has been provided to demonstrate the critical importance of the γνώμη in Chrysostom's theology of human persons. The following points have emerged in this discussion which provide an introduction to Chrysostom's usage of γνώμη and to his anthropology. In regard to divine human relationships:

---

[90] *In Gen. hom.* 19; PG 53,158 61-159 2: …καὶ τὰ ἀπόρρητα καὶ τὰ ἐν τῷ βάθει τῆς διανοίας κινούμενα ἐπιστάμενος παραινεῖ, συμβουλεύει, προαναστέλλει τῆς κακῆς ἐπιχειρήσεως ("…and [God] being acquainted with our forbidden secret things, even those stirring in the depths of our intellect, exhorts, counsels and checks beforehand the attack of evil").

[91] *In Gen. hom.* 19; PG 53,159 4.

[92] *In Gen. hom.* 19; PG 53,164 1: καὶ διδάσκαλον καταλείψω ταῖς εἰς τὸ ἑξῆς γενεαῖς, ἵνα ἡ σὴ θέα σωφρονισμὸς αὐτοῖς γένηται, καὶ μηδεὶς τῇ σῇ γνώμῃ κατακολουθήσῃ ("I will leave you as a lesson to succeeding generations, so that your spectacle might be to them about self control, and that no-one might emulate your mindset").

[93] *In Gen. hom.* 19; PG 53,160 7-11. This passage is translated and examined in Chapter 10 below.

[94] *Comm. in Gal.*: PG 61,625 39: Ὁ μὲν γὰρ ἀνθρώπους θέλων πεῖσαι, πολλὰ ὕπουλα ποιεῖ καὶ διεστραμμένα, καὶ ἀπάτῃ κέχρηται καὶ ψεύδει, ὥστε πεῖσαι καὶ ἑλεῖν τὴν τῶν ἀκουόντων γνώμην ("For the one who wishes to persuade people makes many twists and turns, and by deceit delivers oracles and beguiles with falsehoods, in order to persuade and win the mindset of the hearers").

It is a critical faculty of the soul.
1. Whether or not God listens to our prayers or accepts our offerings depends upon its state.
2. It is the set habit of the soul.
3. It has intellectual and emotional elements.

It is the seat of individual personality.
4. It is the motivating core of being that is the spring of action.
5. It is the place of commitment, consecration and love. Love is real only when it is κατὰ γνώμην.
6. It is the governing principle or ruling faculty of the soul.
7. It is the agenda-setting faculty, the place of deep settled desires and intentions.
8. It is the store of determined policy of life and action.
9. It is the faculty of discernment and evaluation. It determines whether or not truth is to be accepted, having the function of stamping ideas with legitimacy or otherwise.
10. It is the determining faculty of decision and choice.

It is responsible to God.
11. It is the faculty he evaluates – God inspects the γνώμη.
12. It is the basis of rewards and condemnation rather than the deeds dissociated in isolation from their source.
13. It is the basis for reward when deeds are beyond a person's capacity to perform.
14. It determines our nearness to or distance from heaven.
15. It is responsible because it is the locus of personal autonomy.
16. It is the source of rebellion and the key to a virtuous life.
17. Its disposition is crucial; everything rests on it, acceptance or rejection of God.
18. It is the citadel to be taken for real change to occur.

Without doubt the γνώμη was of great significance in Chrysostom's anthropology. From what has been discussed here, there is no hesitation in describing Chrysostom as the theologian of the mindset. There is need to fill out the picture presented above, to confirm it, perhaps to adjust it upon further investigation, and to discuss the issues arising from it. First, it is needful to demonstrate further the critical place γνώμη possessed for divine-human relationships in Chrysostom's anthropology (Chapter 3). This is clearly seen in his Homily 27 on Genesis, where two contrasting mindsets are presented in the form of the characters he chose from various parts of the sacred text. This is followed by a discussion of the authoritative place in the psyche that Chrysostom perceived it to possess (Chapter

4), an authority to a large extent based upon the autonomy given to the γνώμη by God in his creative genius (Chapter 5). Attention is then turned to a significant feature of the γνώμη, for although it is seen by Chrysostom as a created power in the soul, he also sees it as subject to development that is the personal responsibility of human agency. As a true pastor, from a Christian perspective he discusses the instruments available to the Christian for this task of shaping the γνώμη in accord with our destiny (Chapter 6).

CHAPTER 3

Genesis Homily 27: Contrasting Mindsets (Γνῶμαι)

A rich vein for this study is found in Homily 27 of the long series of Chrysostom's Genesis homilies. Not only does it confirm much of what already has been discussed as to the critical importance of the γνώμη in his understanding of divine-human relationships, but also provides some further insights into its role and functions. This homily gives some noteworthy clues to Chrysostom's ideas of the workings of the psyche, particularly in regard to the relationship of the γνώμη to some other faculties of the psyche, the διάνοια and προαίρεσις. Furthermore, it provides a fuller understanding of the significance of the concept by means of a vivid contrast between two biblical characters. An examination of the broad structure of the homily will be followed by an explanation of each use of γνώμη and its cognates.

I. Structure[1]

The homily commences with a focus on Noah as a model of response to God that elicits greater favour from him.[2] Thus it is, in substance, an exhortation to live a life thankful for all God's blessings in all the varied circumstances of life, a life that is characterised by a certain kind of attitude or mindset (γνώμη). Chrysostom, conversely, was not content to present only the positive side. As already noted, his haunting fear was ever the threat of ῥαθυμία (indifference/apathy) in his people, so it is not at all surprising that he would turn to the parable of the wicked servant to

---

[1] This homily is an example of a carefully crafted sermon that has a vital pastoral aim, discussed below, as a moral aim. This pastoral aim serves as a hermeneutical tool in understanding his work. This does not negate Chrysostom's rhetorical skills, but asserts that he employed them in the service of the task before him. See the discussion in my Introduction above.

[2] *In Gen. hom.* 27; PG 53,239 60-63: Μάθωμεν σήμερον τοῦ Νῶε τὴν εὐγνωμοσύνην, καὶ τὴν εὐχάριστον ψυχὴν, δι' ἧς πάλιν πλείονα καὶ πολλῷ μείζονα ἐξεκαλέσατο τοῦ Θεοῦ τὴν περὶ αὐτὸν εὔνοιαν ("Let us learn today of the rightmindedness of Noah and his grateful soul, through which he elicited back again from God more and a much greater degree of the favour that surrounds him"). I have been unable to track down any recent discussions of this homily. Amirav, *Rhetoric and Tradition*, has analysed homilies 22, 23, and 24; at 58-62 there is excellent coverage of relevant source material relating to patristic Genesis commentary, of which extant material is sparse and mainly in Syriac. In addition, the focus appears to be upon the creation accounts.

paint a vivid picture of the consequences of succumbing to this ever-present danger.[3] Thus, the homily is balanced by these two figures: Noah, the model of zeal in the pursuit of grace; and the wicked servant, the depiction of indifference to the same generosity so prized by Noah. This is not all, for Chrysostom had something specific in mind in placing these two figures side by side in his sermon: he was ardently concerned that anyone in his congregation who was at enmity with another would be urgent in seeking reconciliation.[4] This was not an issue to be treated with indifference; rather, it was to be attended to with ardour. God, he asserted, hates and abhors nothing more than the person who holds a grudge against a neighbour.[5] The imagery in the term used by Chrysostom speaks of his rhetorical skill in conveying the gravity of this sin: διηνεκῶς θυλάττοντα ("continually guarding") hatred in his soul, a picture of the deliberate cultivation of a passion that in the passage of time might otherwise fade. Such indifference to the moral values elicits the Lord's anger, whereas, on the positive side, he was definite that reconciliation pursued with σπουδή (eagerness) secures favour from God.[6]

Another significant feature of the structure of this homily is the use by Chrysostom of two terms of interest to this study regarding the place of γνώμη in his theological anthropology, two terms in which he gathers up the contrasted frames of mind or dispositions of Noah and the wicked servant. To Noah he attributes εὐγνωμοσύνη,[7] and to the wicked servant ἀγνωμοσύνη.[8] Both words contain the γνώμη stem, thus indicating that a state of a faculty of the psyche is in

---

[3] See in this homily, PG 53,240 23; 242 50; 248 8; 250 63; 251 26.

[4] *In Gen. hom.* 27; PG 53,251 8-1: ἵνα, ὡς ἔτι καιρὸς, ἕκαστος ἡμῶν, εἴ τινα ἔχοι ἐχθρωδῶς πρὸς αὐτὸν διακείμενον, σπουδὴν ποιήσηται διὰ τῆς πολλῆς θεραπείας καταλλάξαι αὐτὸν ἑαυτῷ ("...so that, as there is yet time, each one of us, if he/she holds anyone in a hostile manner, having been disposed in this way toward the same, he/she should make an effort through many cures to reconcile her/him to him/herself").

[5] *In Gen. hom.* 27; PG 53,248 19-22: Οὐδὲν γὰρ, οὐδὲν οὕτως ὁ Θεὸς μισεῖ καὶ ἀποστρέφεται, ὡς τὸν μνησικακοῦντα ἄνθρωπον καὶ τὴν ἔχθραν τὴν πρὸς τὸν πλησίον ἐπὶ τῆς ψυχῆς διηνεκῶς φυλάττοντα ("For there is nothing God hates and turns his face away from as much as the person who remembers past injuries and continually guards hatred toward his neighbour in his soul").

[6] *In Gen. hom.* 27; PG 53,251 15-19: Εἰς ἡμᾶς διαβαίνει τὰ τῆς εὐεργεσίας· τοῦ Θεοῦ τὴν εὔνοιαν ἐπισπώμεθα, τῶν ἁμαρτημάτων τὴν συγχώρησιν ἑαυτοῖς προαποτιθέμεθα, παρρησίαν πολλὴν πρὸς τὸν Δεσπότην ἐκ τούτου λαμβάνομεν ("These [gifts and prizes] come home to us: we draw in the goodwill of God; we provide beforehand for ourselves the remission of sins; out of this we receive much boldness towards the Lord").

[7] *In Gen. hom.* 27; PG 53,239 60.

[8] *In Gen. hom.* 27; PG 53,249 4.

view. Both relate not to some passing attitude but to a person's settled mindset. Also it seems obvious that these terms are intended as antonyms.[9]

For εὐγνωμοσύνη Lampe gives the basic meanings as "rightmindedness, right feeling, right judgement", making the observation that the "fundamental meaning seems to imply an honest acknowledgement of facts", and also that it has a wide semantic range dependent upon the context in which it is used, such as "candour, frankness, honesty, gratitude, loyalty, fidelity, generosity, liberality, affection" and "good conduct".[10] Liddell and Scott, after defining the root verb εὐγνωμονέω as "having good sense or feeling", give for εὐγνωμοσύνη "considerateness, courtesy, a reasonable spirit", and "prudence".[11] R. Hill, in his translation of this homily, has chosen "gratitude",[12] a good choice in the context as it is within the semantic range of this word. Its first use in this homily is in association with τὴν εὐχάριστον ψυχὴν ("his thankful soul"),[13] within what might be a rhetorical hendiadys, or more probably simply an appropriate expression of rightmindedness in this context. The right mindset or feeling in the context of God's generous giving most certainly is gratitude. The homily, as we have noted, begins with the exhortation to learn about Noah's rightmindedness that expressed itself in thanksgiving to God. Taking all this into consideration, the basic meaning and semantic usage indicates that it is a relationship term which acknowledges one's place in the scheme of things thus giving others due respect and, above all, recognises one's dependence

---

[9] W.W. How and J. Wells, *A Commentary on Herodotus*, vol. 2 (Oxford 1928) 5.83 1, assert that ἀγνωμοσύνη is the opposite of σωφροσύνη. This is pertinent, as the basic meaning of σωφροσύνη is "soundness of mind", LSJ, 1751 *s.v.* But εὐγνωμοσύνη, not used at all by Herodotus, is the more appropriate basic antonym for a rhetorician like Chrysostom with an artistic appreciation of the power of words. M.A. Shatkin, *John Chrysostom as Apologist, with Special Reference to De incomprehensibili, Quod nemo laeditur, Ad eos qui scandalizati sunt, and Adversus oppugantores vitae monasticae*, Analecta Vlatadon 50 (Thessaloniki 1987) 31 n. 80, remarks on Chrysostom's point that virtue is better than apologetics: "This brings up the need for εὐγνωμοσύνη, i.e., rightmindedness, on the part of the opponent in apologetics. The opponent to whom the apology is addressed must be εὐγνωμονων, i.e. willing honestly to acknowledge facts. The opposite quality is ἀγνωμοσύνη."

[10] LPGL, 561 *s.v.*

[11] LSJ, 708 *s.v.*

[12] Hill, *Chrysostom, Homilies on Genesis 18-45*, 162. There are 129 instances of εὐγνωμοσύνη in Chrysostom's Genesis homilies (long series). The term is used in different contexts and "gratitude" would not be an appropriate translation in quite a number of these. It is often used of human relationships where different nuances are intended, for example in homily 48, where speaking about Abraham's servant, Hill translates it at PG 54,437 27 in *Homilies on Genesis 46-67*, 30 as "sense of duty", at 438 27 in 32 as "dutifulness", and twice concerning Rebecca, at 439 54 in 34, and at 440 11 in 3 as "candour". In view in each of these is the issue of whatever is the right γνώμη (mindset) in the particular circumstance.

[13] *In Gen. hom.* 27; PG 53,239 60-61.

55

upon God. This fits the context of this homily with its aims to encourage thanksgiving to God for his gifts, to foster a forgiving spirit and prevent people from bearing grudges. Pertinent to this is that Chrysostom, commenting on the prohibition of shedding human blood in Genesis 9:6, lists those things that a murderer might brush aside in the performance of the deed. First, in an obvious reference to Cain, kinship, community of nature and brotherly empathy are listed. Then he turns to what he sees as weightier considerations: the creation of human beings in God's image, by how much they were deemed worthy by God of pre-eminence, and the fact that they received authority over all creation. Rightly considered, he says, these facts should divert people from their μοχθηρᾶς γνώμης ("depraved mindset").[14] The full sense of εὐγνωμοσύνη is seen against this background of responsibility in personal relationships involving both God and those created in God's image. On one hand εὐγνωμοσύνη (rightmindedness) will result in rendering thanksgiving to God; on the other it will issue in treating fellow-humans with dignity and respect. For the purposes of this discussion, in order to keep the basic meaning of εὐγνωμοσύνη to the fore, I will use "rightmindedness" in translation, noting that it is used for this study and would be replaced with something less stilted or ungainly in normal free-flowing English.

Turning to a consideration of ἀγνωμοσύνη we find that Liddell and Scott give (a) "want of acquaintance with", (b) "want of sense, folly, senseless pride, arrogance", and (c) "want of feeling, unkindness".[15] Just as εὐγνωμοσύνη basically points to an honest acknowledgement of facts, so ἀγνωμοσύνη points to a conceited disdain of facts. Lampe gives as basic, "want of sense or feeling", but contributes an additional element in the nuances of "ingratitude, sinfulness and wilful misunderstanding".[16] This indicates that the want of acquaintance or sense of feeling involved is a determined disregard of facts and a deliberate disdain for others. One of the texts with which Chrysostom had become familiar in his education in the Greek παιδεία was Herodotus' *The Histories*.[17] How and Wells in their commentary on Herodotus suggest that ἀγνωμοσύνη signifies: (a) "overweening self-confidence" at 5.83 1, (b) "obstinacy" at 6.10 4, (c) "conceit" at 9.3.1, and (d) "want of sense" at 2.172 2.[18] G. Rawlinson translates in these

---

[14] *In Gen. hom.* 27; PG 53,246 34-41, at 41.

[15] LSJ, 12 *s.v.*

[16] LPGL, 22 *s.v.*

[17] Harkins, *Saint John Chrysostom: Discourses Against Judaizing Christians*, xxv n. 18, asserts: "…that the educational system was still basically the Greek *paideia,* and brilliant pagan teachers such as Libanius and Themistius fought hard to retain it."; Kelly, *Golden Mouth*, 8; Jaeger, *Early Christianity and the Greek Paideia*, 140 n. 1. The Greek *paideia* is discussed below in Chapter 8.

[18] How and Wells, *A Commentary on Herodotus.*

references an assortment of "proud, obstinately, obstinacy, staunch, stubbornness, inborn stubbornness", and "severity".[19] R. Macan, in a note to 9.3 1, explains the term as "vanity, arrogancy, obstinacy".[20] The weight appears to come down on the note of ὕβρις, insolence, that egotistical arrogance that rides roughshod over the reasonable claims of fellow-humans and even at times of the gods, indeed over the claims of reason itself.[21] This certainly fits the mindset of the wicked servant of the parable as Chrysostom presents it in this homily. Just as εὐγνωμοσύνη is a term referring to relationships, so also is ἀγνωμοσύνη, the difference being that whereas the former acknowledges one's place in the scheme of things, the latter does not. Indeed, it takes a stance against this, giving no respect to others be they human or divine. This is akin to E. Brunner's perceptive definition of sin: "the spiritual defiance of one who understands freedom as independence".[22] This is the wicked servant of the parable who acted as if free of any obligation to his master or to his fellowservant. Thus ἀγνωμοσύνη is quite clearly the antonym of εὐγνωμοσύνη, both having reference to fundamental mindsets that dictate choices and actions in the varying relationships of life. I shall use "insolence" for the translation of ἀγνωμοσύνη in this discussion in order to capture the essence of the term as used here by Chrysostom.

II. Detailed Explanation of Usage

The detailed examination of the usage of γνώμη and its cognates in this homily will follow the order of first, εὐγνωμοσύνη, second, ἀγνωμοσύνη and ἀγνωμόνων, and finally γνώμη itself.

---

[19] G. Rawlinson (trans.), *The History of Herodotus*, GBWW 6 (Chicago 1952) 86, 140, 187, 288, 289, 297.

[20] R. Macan (trans.), *Herodotus: The Seventh, Eighth, and Ninth Books with Introduction and Commentary*, vol. 2 (Edinburgh 1907) 9.3.1.

[21] A perceptive discussion of ὕβρις is found in N.R.E. Fisher, "*Hybris* and dishonour: I", *Greece and Rome* 23 (1976) 177-193, and "*Hybris* and dishonour: II", *Greece and Rome* 26 (1979) 32-47, at 45 where Fisher sums up his findings in three conclusions, the first being: "...*hybris* remains in all classical authors a term of strong moral force, whose main use is to condemn behaviour that causes dishonour to individuals, to groups, or to values that hold a society together". Thus Fisher, basing his opinion on Aristotle's *Rhetoric*, places *hubris* in the honour-shame nexus of the mores of classical society, pointing to the blatant grasp for power over others, the brazen claim of superiority, and the pleasurable exaltation of self at the expense of others that is thoroughly explored and condemned in Greek literature from Homer onwards.

[22] E. Brunner, *The Christian Doctrine of Creation and Redemption: Dogmatics*, vol. 2, trans. O. Wyon (London 1952) 93.

A. Εὐγνωμοσύνη

Three features of εὐγνωμόσυνη come to the fore in this homily: its benefits or results, its mode of expression, and its importance in a person's relationship with God.

It was noted above that Chrysostom, when focusing in on εὐγνωμόσυνη at the beginning of the homily as being the lesson for the day, immediately points to it as the means by which Noah called forth more and greater goodwill to himself from God. Noah demonstrated his rightmindedness by building an altar to God in thankfulness for blessings received. This, claims Chrysostom, elicited more goodwill from God in the form of plans and promises which he subsequently implemented through Noah and his descendants.[23] Indeed, Chrysostom understands that this is the very nature of God: whenever he sees the response of εὐγνωμόσυνη for previous gifts, he lavishes out more gifts from himself.[24] A little later in this homily, Chrysostom, the skilful preacher, again asserts that Noah's εὐγνωμόσυνη for previous blessings was the reason why he enjoyed goodwill and honour from on high.[25] Yet once more Chrysostom will press home this argument when he points to the promise of the succession of seasons as being a great reward for Noah's rightmindedness.[26] There is little doubt that he saw many gifts and blessings resulting from εὐγνωμόσυνη.

Another benefit that Chrysostom sees as arising from the practice of εὐγνωμόσυνη is security.[27] This is an interesting turn of phrase which is a rhetorical metonymy, in this instance the effect being put for the cause; one cannot directly practise or produce this security, one practises rightmindedness and

---

[23] John Chrys., *In Gen. hom.* 27; PG 53,240.

[24] John Chrys., *In Gen. hom.* 27; PG 53,239 63-240 1: Καὶ γὰρ τοιοῦτος ὁ Θεός· ἐπειδὰν ἤδη ἐπὶ τοῖς φθάσασιν εὐγνώμονας γεγενημένους, ἐπιδαψιλεύεται τὰς παρ᾽ ἑαυτοῦ δωρεάς ("For such is God: whenever he sees those who initially have become rightminded, he lavishes gifts from himself upon them").

[25] John Chrys., *In Gen. hom.* 27; PG 53,241 54-57: Ἐντεῦθεν γὰρ καὶ ὁ δίκαιος οὗτος τοσαύτης ἀπήλαυσε τῆς ἄνωθεν εὐνοίας καὶ τῆς τιμῆς, ἐπειδὴ πολλὴν ὑπὲρ τῶν φθασάντων τὴν εὐγνωμοσύνην ἐπεδείξατο ("Henceforth this righteous man enjoyed so much of the favour and honour from above, because over the previous time he had displayed much rightmindedness").

[26] John Chrys., *In Gen. hom.* 27; PG 53,245 26-29: εἶδες τῆς εὐγνωμοσύνης οἵαν δέχεται τὴν ἀμοιβήν; ("Do you see what reward he receives for his rightmindedness?")

[27] John Chrys., *In Gen. hom.* 27; PG 53,245 5: Ἀλλ᾽ ἀναγκαῖον γοῦν ταῦτα κινεῖν ἐπὶ τῆς ὑμετέρας ἀγάπης, ἵνα τούτων τὴν ἀκρίβειαν εἰδότες πολλὴν τῆς εὐγνωμοσύνης ποιῆσθε τὴν ἀσφάλειαν ("But at least then it is a necessity for these things to stir up your love, so that knowing the great precision of these things you may produce the security that comes from rightmindedness").

security is the effect. As always with Chrysostom, knowledge is not enough; only practice of this mindset issuing from knowledge is efficacious. This could relate to salvation but the context is more suggestive of the security of any rewards that might be gained. Chrysostom has been arguing for attention to inner motive when performing spiritual acts so as to avoid loss of the rewards attendant upon them.[28] Rightmindedness in approaching the performance of these acts will secure the expected blessings.

Regarding the mode of expression, Chrysostom would have us believe that rightmindedness is displayed in the choices we make. Noah is described as acting with great wisdom in the whole process of building an altar and offering suitable sacrifices. Chrysostom places this offering in the context of his contention that God as Creator has implanted in our human nature "the precise knowledge of virtue".[29] This is applied to the choice of offerings that are presented to God. Thus Noah is depicted as having presented his offerings in the same way as Abel, μετὰ πολλῆς τῆς ἀκριβείας ("with great precision").[30] He chose clean cattle and clean birds for his sacrifices, thus demonstrating, says Chrysostom, τῆς οἰκείας προαιρέσεως τὴν εὐγνωμοσύνην ἐπεδείξατο ("the rightmindedness of his own choice").[31] The choice revealed the mindset of Noah, showing it to be in accord with that precise knowledge of virtue implanted within us and expressed κατὰ τὴν ἀνθρωπίνην δύναμιν ("in keeping with our human capacity").[32]

Chrysostom pursues the issue of human capacity in terms of God's loving adjustment to human weakness. He states that though in some instances the expressions of sacred scripture may seem to be offensive, they are a manifestation of God's συγκατάβασις, his "considerateness of our limitations".[33] Likewise, the

---

[28] *In Gen. hom.* 27; PG 53,243 38-55.
[29] *In Gen. hom.* 27; PG 53,242 9-11: Σκόπει μετὰ ἀκριβείας, ἀγαπητέ, ἐκ τῶν νῦν ῥημάτων πάλιν, πῶς ἐν αὐτῇ τῇ φύσει ὁ τῶν ἁπάντων δημιουργὸς ἐναπέθετο τὴν γνῶσιν ἡμῖν ἀκριβῆ τῆς ἀρετῆς ("Consider with precision, beloved, now once more from the words, how in our nature itself the Creator of all embedded the precise knowledge of virtue").
[30] *In Gen. hom.* 27; PG 53,242 15. See also *hom.* 18; PG 53,157 5-22, for a fuller presentation of this point.
[31] *In Gen. hom.* 27; PG 53,242 26-27.
[32] *In Gen. hom.* 27; PG 53,242 17.
[33] *In Gen. hom.* 27; PG 53,242 38-41. Συνκατάβασις, the concept of divine accommodation, has long been recognised as an important feature of Chrysostom's theology. R.C. Hill, *Saint John Chrysostom: Homilies on Genesis 1-17*, FOTC 74 (Washington 1985) 96 n.11, in an editorial note to his English translation of homily 7, includes συνκατάβασις among the four basic principles of Scripture that marked Chrysostom's methodology, the others being θεόπνευστος/ἐνηχεῖν, inspiration, φιλανθρωπία, God's generous love, and ἀκρίβεια, precision. Thus it may be said that the essence of συγκατάβασις is the loving generosity of God that accommodates his revelation to human limitations by using familiar words and images without

whole Old Testament sacrificial system is to be viewed in this light. It was permitted on the basis of God's loving adjustment to humankind which had gone astray and was likely to be found offering sacrifices to self-invented deities.[34] Jewish circumcision is another example of this principle, being provided as δεῖγμα τῆς οἰκείας εὐγνωμοσύνης ("evidence of their own rightmindedness"),[35] and not as a power to salvation. Chrysostom explains all these institutions as having been

---

losing the precision of a genuine communication of the divine realities. See Hill, "Chrysostom, interpreter of the Psalms", 61-74, and Hill, *Reading the Old Testament*, 7-43 where additional principles are discussed. Of special note is Hill, "Chrysostom, interpreter of the Psalms", 68 and "Chrysostom's terminology for the inspired Word", 367 and n. 1, where he is emphatic that any thought of "patronising behaviour" in the use of συνκατάβασις is foreign to the usage of Chrysostom; hence his rejection of 'condescension' as a translation of this term and his preference for 'considerateness'. Its importance in Chrysostom's theology is demonstrated by R.C. Hill, "The Spirituality of Chrysostom's *Commentary on the Psalms*", *JECS* 5 (1997) 569-579 at 576 where he notes that Chrysostom viewed συνκατάβασις as "the principle of incarnation, in both scriptural interpretation and spiritual direction". The concept is recognised as of considerable significance in Antiochene theology of late antiquity and foundational to the expositions of scripture that issued from those individuals associated with the ἀσκητήριον of Diodore. It has been subject to much scholarly discussion: Hill has written extensively on it and on related concepts. For a listing of his writings see the bibliography attached to his *Reading the Old Testament*, 203-209 at 205-206. See also F.H. Chase, *Chrysostom, A Study in the History of Biblical Interpretation* (Cambridge 1887); F. Fabbi, "La 'condiscendenza divina nell' inspirazione biblica secondo s. Giovanni Crisostomo", *Biblica* 14 (1933) 330-347; M.H. Flanagan, *St. John Chrysostom's Doctrine of Condescension and Accuracy in the Scriptures: Being an Extract from an Essay having the above title which was Presented to the Theological Faculty of St. Patrick's College, Maynooth, as a Thesis for the Degree of Doctor*. Napier N.Z. 1948; R.C. Hill, "On looking again at *synkatabasis*", *Prudentia* 13 (1981) 3-11; S.D. Benin, "Sacrifice as education in Augustine and Chrysostom", *Church History* 52 (1982) 7-20; S.D. Benin, "The 'cunning of God' and divine accommodation", *Journal of the History of Ideas* 45 (1984) 179-191; S.D. Benin, *The Footprints of God: Divine Accommodation in Jewish and Christian Thought* (Albany NY 1993); R. Brändle, "*Sunkatabasis* als hermeneutisches und ethisches Prinzip in der Paulusauslegung des Johannes Chrysostomus", in G. Schöllgen and C. Schölten (eds), *Stimuli: Exegese und ihre Hermeneutik in Antike und Christentum, Festschrift für Ernst Dassmann* (Münster 1996) 297-307; D. Rylaarsdam, "The adaptability of divine pedagogy: *Sunkatabasis* in the theology and rhetoric of John Chrysostom", diss., University of Notre Dame 1999; M.W. Tse, "Synkatabasis and akribeia – the warp and woof of Chrysostom's hermeneutic: a study based on Chrysostom's Genesis homilies", *Jian Dao* 15 (2001) 1-17; S. Muto, "The Syrian origin of the divine condescension as the key to biblical interpretation", *The Harp* 20 (2006) 249-261; D. Rylaarsdam, "Painful preaching", 463-468; Reuling, *After Eden*, 151 n. 78, suggests that "adaptation" might be even a better translation.
[34] *In Gen. hom.* 27; PG 53,242 48-54.
[35] *In Gen. hom.* 27; PG 53,242 59-60.

temporary measures to encourage rightmindedness and to provide some acceptable outward expression for it in the choices that were made.[36]

Chrysostom leaves us in no doubt that εὐγνωμοσύνη (rightmindedness) is important in a person's relationship with God for at least three reasons: God's desire for it to be taught, his wanting it practised, and by drawing attention to the ways God encourages it. God wants εὐγνωμοσύνη taught to us. The building of the altar and offering of sacrifices by Noah are recorded for that very reason.[37] It has already been noted that the homily opens with the exhortation to learn about Noah's εὐγνωμοσύνη.[38] Rightmindedness is something God expects us to practise or produce. Chrysostom is clear on this point. If we want to gain and keep further benefits from God we need to practise rightmindedness. This is the pathway of security. As seen above God encourages rightmindedness. He permitted practices and signs such as circumcision and sacrifices that served the function of encouraging rightmindedness. Though those particular things have passed away or have been superseded in the New Covenant, Chrysostom saw other material objects such as the tombs or relics of the martyrs fulfilling that same function of encouragement.[39]

B. Ἀγνωμοσύνη

There is only one reference to ἀγνωμοσύνη in this homily. However, the figure to whom the term is applied plays a major part, being set in contrast to Noah and is crucial to Chrysostom's appeal for the exercise of sincere forgiveness. In his handling of the parable, his picture of the wicked, unforgiving servant draws from Chrysostom the exclamation, Ὦ τῆς ἀγνωμοσύνης ὑπερβολή ("O what extremity of insolence!").[40] The limits of insolence or want of sensitivity have been reached in this individual. It is pertinent to note some of the descriptive terms that Chrysostom applies to this wicked servant. We are invited to look at his ἀπόνοια ("unreasonableness"),[41] and his ἀπανθρωπία ("inhumanity").[42] His actions are portrayed as ἀπάνθρωπος ("inhumane"),[43] and ὠμός ("savage"),[44] without any

---

[36] *In Gen. hom.* 27; PG 53,242 44; 243 22.
[37] *In Gen. hom.* 27; PG 53,242 4.
[38] *In Gen. hom.* 27; PG 53,239 60-61.
[39] *Cat. 1-8.* 7.1, 9-10; *Mart.*; PG 50,648 29-33.
[40] *In Gen. hom.* 27; PG 53,249 4.
[41] *In Gen. hom.* 27; PG 53,248 42.
[42] *In Gen. hom.* 27; PG 53,249 38.
[43] *In Gen. hom.* 27; PG 53,249 47.
[44] *In Gen. hom.* 27; PG 53,249 47.

thought of συμπαθής ("fellow-feeling"),[45] as ἀπηνής ("harsh"),[46] and as being applied ἀνελεής ("mercilessly").[47] Here indeed we are confronted with that egotistical arrogance that rides roughshod over the reasonable claims of fellow-humans, over reason and, as Jesus tells it, over the loving claims of a generous God of amazing mercy and forgiveness. In this regard it is instructive to see how much Chrysostom makes of the Lord's word, σύνδουλος (fellow-servant), in the text from the parable. He draws attention to the frequency of the evangelist's use of this term, stressing the absolute equality of the two servants.[48] Then he does the same thing, repeating it himself on nine occasions.[49] In addition, twice he makes the observation that they were ὁμογενής (of the same race) and that no superior-inferior relationship was involved.[50] In applying the text to his congregation he appeals on the basis of their own situation of mutual involvement in τοὺς ὁμοδούλους καὶ τοὺς ὁμογενεῖς, καὶ τοὺς τῆς αὐτῆς ἡμῖν φύσεως κοινωνοῦντας ("same-servanthood, same family, and sharing in our same nature").[51] All this intensifies the crime and draws out the harsh and arrogant content of ἀγνωμοσύνη.

Before leaving this term, it is needful to note that the cognate ἀγνωμόνων is used by Chrysostom in his comment on this homily about the offerings of Genesis 8:21 that states, "the Lord smelt an odour of fragrance". This, he says, did not apply to the ἀγνωμόνων Jews.[52] In their case, their offerings were an abomination (βδέλυγμα) because of τῆς προαιρέσεως τῶν προσαγόντων τὴν μοχθηρία ("the depravity of their choice of offerings").[53] The term ἀγνωμόνων has much the same content as ἀγνωμοσύνη, the context here indicating Chrysostom's perception of the brazen mindset that practised religious ritual without any acknowledgement of sin or reformation of conduct. "Insolent" would be a good translation, gathering up as it does that element of arrogance in the rejection of the reasonable claims of God upon them.

---

[45] *In Gen. hom.* 27; PG 53,249 6.

[46] *In Gen. hom.* 27; PG 53,249 20.

[47] *In Gen. hom.* 27; PG 53,242 32.

[48] *In Gen. hom.* 27; PG 53,242 56-60: Ὅρα πῶς συνεχῶς στρέφει τὸ ῥῆμα τοῦτο ὁ εὐαγγελιστής, Ὁ σύνδουλος αὐτοῦ, οὐχ ἁπλῶς, ἀλλ᾽ ἵνα μάθωμεν, ὅτι οὐδὲν μεταξὺ αὐτῶν τὸ μέσον ("See how the evangelist continuously turns to this word 'his fellowservant', and not merely once, that we might learn that there was absolutely nothing between them in status").

[49] *In Gen. hom.* 27; PG 53,248 51, 55; 249 14, 21, 26, 29, 33, 37, 47.

[50] *In Gen. hom.* 27; PG 53,248 45, 249.30.

[51] *In Gen. hom.* 27; PG 53,242 59-60.

[52] *In Gen. hom.* 27; PG 53,243 28.

[53] *In Gen. hom.* 27; PG 53,243 29-31.

C.   Γνώμη

As noted earlier, both εὐγνωμοσύνη and ἀγνωμοσύνη are built upon the γνώμη stem. There are fifteen occasions where Chrysostom uses γνώμη in this homily. The following features of Chrysostom's understanding of this faculty of the psyche are revealed in an examination of the passages where γνώμη occurs.[54] Inevitably, there is some overlap in this discussion with the previous material relating to the cognates, but as γνώμη itself is the main focus of this study, this direct examination of γνώμη reveals its features and role more clearly.

The γνώμη is the faculty of the psyche responsible for originating action. Chrysostom, in discussing the offerings of Noah, raises the question as to where he could have acquired this virtue of gratitude. He explains:

> But just as in the beginning the one who was born of the first formed human being, Abel I mean, when moved from his own inner resources, made his offering with great precision, so also in this time, with similar exactness, this righteous man [Noah] from his own mindset and his wholesome choice, as much as his human capacity allowed, brought his thanksgiving to the Lord through sacrificial offerings, as was his usual practice.[55]

Chrysostom makes the point that both Abel and Noah were motivated by their inner resources. The γνώμη and προαίρεσις of Noah are equated here with Abel's οἴκοθεν κινούμενος. This indicates that the effective impulse toward acting arises from the γνώμη along with the προαίρεσις, as seen in the references to Noah making his offerings from his οἰκείας γνώμης and προαιρέσεως. The parallel with Abel is comprehensive, the οἰκείας in Noah's case matching οἴκοθεν in Abel's. For Noah, the additional qualifying clause, κατὰ τὴν ἀνθρωπίνην δύναμιν ("according to human ability"),[56] makes clear the significance of the role of the γνώμη and the choice generated by it. The γνώμη is the principal motivating faculty

---

[54] By the term "faculty", I mean in Chrysostom's case, a power or ability of the psyche that is inherent, but which is subject to development. It is appreciated that Maximus the Confessor distinguished it from a faculty of the soul as being a mode of operation of the natural will, or, to cite Thunberg, *Microcosm and Mediator*, 226: "a disposition or *habitus* of will, such as man as individual and as fallen creature may establish for himself". I have no doubt that Chrysostom viewed it as a faculty, not making the distinction found in Maximus, but nevertheless holding to some positions about γνώμη common to them both.

[55] *In Gen. hom.* 27; PG 53,242 14-18: Ἀλλὰ καθάπερ ἐν ἀρχῇ ὁ ὑπὸ τοῦ πρωτοπλάστου τεχθείς, Ἄβελ λέγω, οἴκοθεν κινούμενος τὴν προσαγωγὴν ἐποιήσατο μετὰ πολλῆς τῆς ἀκριβείας· οὕτω δὴ καὶ νῦν ὁ δίκαιος οὗτος ἐξ οἰκείας γνώμης καὶ προαιρέσεως ὑγιοῦς κατὰ τὴν ἀνθρωπίνην δύναμιν, ὡς ἐνόμισε, διὰ τῶν θυσιῶν τὰς εὐχαριστίας ἀναφέρει τῷ Δεσπότῃ.

[56] *In Gen. hom.* 27; PG 53,242 17.

of the psyche. Thus, it is essential that the γνώμη be in a wholesome state if it is to effect a worthy result.[57] It remains to be seen how it relates to the passions and reason and other possible centres of motivation, but for the moment, it is sufficient to recognise this function.

Human ability and its application, he says, rest with the γνώμη and the προαίρεσις, the mindset and the choice. The immediate context, as noted above, refers to the knowledge of virtue that is embedded in human nature.[58] This section of the text suggests that this embedded knowledge must be a significant contributor to the γνώμη. The γνώμη must either contain a native element of intuitive moral knowledge, or have access to it through another faculty, perhaps the συνείδησις (conscience). The γνώμη portrait thus expands to include this natural moral element along with the intellectual and emotional elements, and the acquired elements already noted. This is significant for the essence of this study concerning the relation of the γνώμη to sin.

Flowing out of this passage is another issue of relevance to the role of the γνώμη, a feature that points to both the strength and the weakness of this faculty. On one hand, the embedded precise knowledge of virtue should make the γνώμη a tower of moral strength. It has not been left to journey without innate possession of the appropriate road map. On the other, Chrysostom, aware of both the volatility of humans and the vulnerability of the γνώμη to the effects of such forces as fear, adverse circumstances and various shaping factors, added the phrase κατὰ τὴν ἀνθρωπίνην δύναμιν ("according to human ability"), to allow for human weakness. In particular, he is conscious of the various possible conditions of the γνώμη and the resulting quality of the προαίρεσις. In this way, Chrysostom indicates that attitudes, choices and actions such as exhibited by Abel and Noah are within our reach, but they depend on us, upon the state of our γνώμη.

The γνώμη is the distinctive target of God's quest in the human soul. Chrysostom claims that Noah knew this fundamental reality of divine-human relationships: ἤδει σαφῶς, ὅτι γνώμην ἐπιζητεῖ μόνον ὁ Δεσπότης ("He knew quite clearly that the Lord seeks after only the γνώμη").[59] This may seem to be a piece of rhetorical hyperbole, but Chrysostom says this so often, and makes complementary similar claims for the place of the γνώμη in the economy of divine-human relationships, that it is reasonable to conclude that no hyperbole is intended. The γνώμη occupied a position of supreme importance in Chrysostom's theological anthropology.

---

[57] See fn. 62 below.
[58] *In Gen. hom.* 27; PG 53,242 8-11.
[59] *In Gen. hom.* 27; PG 53,242 22.

The γνώμη determines the choice (προαίρεσις) that is made. It is asserted that because Noah was aware that God looked only for the γνώμη he took great care in the choice of the offerings he made. As already noted in relation to εὐγνωμοσύνη, Chrysostom says that τῆς οἰκείας προαιρέσεως τὴν εὐγνωμοσύνην ἐπεδείξατο ("he demonstrated the rightmindedness of his own choice").[60] The προαίρεσις is governed by the γνώμη. The choice (προαίρεσις) is the expression of the mindset (γνώμη). The γνώμη is the faculty that is rewarded by God. Chrysostom says that God accepted Noah's right-minded choice and crowned his γνώμη. This shows how crucial a place the γνώμη had in Chrysostom's anthropology. Noah's mindset was crowned as the originating source of the choice made and the sacrifices offered. The feature is reiterated later in the homily when he makes the point that all our good works should originate from a healthy γνώμη.[61]

The well-disposed γνώμη affects the character of the offering. Chrysostom claims that Noah's mindset (γνώμη) "filled the smoke, the fatty stench, and all the nauseousness that is generated from that source, full of great fragrance".[62] The well-disposed γνώμη changed the character of the offering, giving it a beauty not inherent in it. Thus, any circumstance can be turned into an offering of great fragrance to the Lord by an appropriate γνώμη. Indeed, Chrysostom held that a healthy γνώμη is the cause of all our goodness. This is the reason he gives for the need in all circumstances to be eager to exhibit a healthy mindset.[63] The context of this assertion is a passage explaining why the Lord called the offerings of Jews an abomination. As noted above, Chrysostom charged this to the depravity of their προαίρεσις.[64] Hence, the need is at all times to be diligent in pursuing and expressing a sound γνώμη so that a healthy and appropriate choice will be made.

The γνώμη is closely related to the διάνοια, the faculty of thought. In explaining the critical importance of the γνώμη, Chrysostom relates it to, or perhaps even equates it with ἔνδοθεν διανοίᾳ, our innate faculty of thought. After asserting that a healthy γνώμη is the cause of our goodness he proceeds to fill out that concept by reference to the διάνοια, stating that God looks at our inner

---

[60] *In Gen. hom.* 27; PG 53,242 26-27.

[61] *In Gen. hom.* 27; PG 53,243 46-47: ...ἀπὸ γνώμης ὑγιοῦς ὁρμώμενοι τοῦτο διαπραττώμεθα, ἵνα καὶ τῶν καμάτων ἄξιον τὸν στέφανον κομισώμεθα ("...let us, being motivated by a healthy mindset, effect this [spiritual work] for ourselves, so that we might carry away a crown worthy of our toils"). See also *In 1Cor. hom.* 3; PG 61,30 14-16.

[62] *In Gen. hom.* 27; PG 53,242 30-33: Ὅρα πῶς ἡ γνώμη τοῦ προσάγοντος τὸν καπνὸν, καὶ τὴν κνίσσαν, καὶ πᾶσαν τὴν ἐντεῦθεν τικτομένην ἀηδίαν πολλῆς τῆς εὐωδίας ἐνέπλησε.

[63] *In Gen. hom.* 27; PG 53,243 35-37: Πανταχοῦ τοίνυν σπουδάζωμεν, παρακαλῶ, γνώμην ὑγιῆ ἐπιδείκνυσθαι ("Always, therefore, I exhort you, let us be eager to exhibit a wholesome mindset").

[64] *In Gen. hom.* 27; PG 53,243 30.

thinking as a basis for acceptance or rejection of our deeds.[65] This is parallel to the statement of line PG 53,242 22 that God seeks only the γνώμη. Also, here at lines PG 53,243 39-40 Chrysostom ascribes the starting-up of actions to the ἔνδοθεν διανοία, whereas only a few lines later at PG 53,243 45-46 he ascribes the same to the γνώμη.[66] In the history of the Greek language, διάνοια exhibits a semantic range which at least overlaps with γνώμη and which is similar in many respects to γνώμη. Thus, we find it used as "intention", "purpose", "thought", "spirit", "heart", and "opinion" as with γνώμη. The weight of its meaning appears to be upon the intellect with usages such as "process of thinking, intelligence, idea, notion, understanding and thinking faculty".[67] It is clear from this overlap that Chrysostom understood the γνώμη to involve an element of intellect, thought, or deliberation.

Further consideration of this significant passage is appropriate. It is asserted that a healthy γνώμη is of greater consequence and is more important to God than the size of the human resources that we may have at our disposal. Chrysostom suggests that God is in the habit of considering our inner mindset more than τοῖς παρ'ἡμῶν γινομένοις ("the things we do from our own resources").[68] The emphasis is upon the mindset rather than the deeds. It needs to be stressed that Chrysostom is insistent that all good works need to originate from a healthy γνώμη.[69] Chrysostom would have us believe that the state of the mindset determines the acceptance or rejection by God of our works. A remarkable assertion concerning the γνώμη in this regard is made in discussing an offering of Noah. Chrysostom argues that Noah's offering was accepted even though it was paltry to sight, as it was perfectly great when judged on the condition of his mindset.[70] Actions that appear trivial are counted as exceptionally great when they come from a healthy γνώμη. The cup of cold water is about the least a person can offer to another, but

---

[65] *In Gen. hom.* 27; PG 53,243 38-41: Ὁ γὰρ ἀγαθὸς Δεσπότης οὐ τοῖς παρ' ἡμῶν γινομένοις προσέχειν εἴωθεν ὡς τῇ ἔνδοθεν διανοίᾳ, ἀφ' ἧς ὁρμώμενοι ταῦτα διαπραττόμεθα, καὶ πρὸς ἐκείνην βλέπων ἢ προσίεται τὰ ὑφ' ἡμῶν γινόμενα, ἢ ἀποστρέφεται ("The good Lord is not in the habit of looking at the things we do from our own resources, as at our inner thinking, from which we are motivated to do these things. As he looks at that he gives his approval or disapproval of the things done by us.")

[66] *In Gen. hom.* 27; PG 53,243 45-46.

[67] LSJ, 405 *s.v.*

[68] *In Gen. hom.* 27; PG 53,243 38-39.

[69] *In Gen. hom.* 27; PG 53,243 45.

[70] *In Gen. hom.* 27; PG 53,244 18-21: Εἶδες τὰ παρὰ τοῦ δικαίου γεγενημένα, πῶς, ὅσον μὲν πρὸς τὴν ὄψιν τῶν γεγονότων, εὐτελῆ τυγχάνει, ἀπὸ δὲ τῆς ὑγιοῦς αὐτοῦ γνώμης καὶ πάνυ μεγάλα δείκνυται; ("Do you see the things that had been done by the righteous man, that according to sight they were just as any worthless thing, but by reason of being from a healthy mindset are shown to be superbly great?")

when issuing from a healthy mindset it is transformed into something wonderful in the eyes of God. This thought is developed further in a rather surprising way. He proposes that provided works are motivated by a healthy γνώμη, the crown is gained even if those works are unfinished.[71] Chrysostom, in developing his thought in this way, points to God's ineffable loving generosity for this marvel. He wanted to ensure that the main principle was not forgotten: it is on the strength of an inspection of the γνώμη alone that he awards the prize. Similarly, he asserts that God rewards a person because of the state of the γνώμη even when the intended good work is not implemented. Chrysostom gives the hypothetical example of someone in his congregation, who on seeing a beggar in the marketplace lifts heart and mind to heaven with compassion for the poor person. Even though, for some reason, it is not possible to assist and relieve the beggar's hunger, she/he receives the reward because of the right mindset (γνώμη).[72] The γνώμη with its thought and purpose is as good as the deed. Thus, the importance of γνώμη in the anthropology of Chrysostom and its place in his understanding of divine-human relationships is revealed yet again. From what follows in the homily, it is evident that this point is based upon the words of Jesus in the Sermon on the Mount about the adulterous gaze counting as if the deed itself had been implemented. Chrysostom observes that condemnation and punishment follow for a dishonest γνώμη as if the adultery

---

[71] *In Gen. hom.* 27; PG 53,243 50-52: Ἔστι γὰρ, ἔστι διὰ τὴν ἄφατον τοῦ Θεοῦ φιλανθρωπίαν καὶ τὸ ἔργον μὴ ἐπιτελέσαντας, ἀπὸ τῆς γνώμης μόνον τὸν στέφανον κομίσασθαι ("Doubtless, by reason of the ineffable love of God, even if we have not completed the work, it is possible to carry away the crown only on the basis of the mindset").

[72] *In Gen. hom.* 27; PG 53,243 57-59: κἂν μὴ δύναιο ἐπαρκέσαι καὶ λῦσαι τὸν λιμὸν, ἀπὸ τῆς γνώμης ἀπηρτισμένον ἔλαβες τὸν μισθόν ("Even if you were unable to supply anything to relieve his hunger, on the basis of having prepared your mindset you received your reward"). Chrysostom had great concern for the poor and never missed an opportunity to urge almsgiving upon his people. G.G. Christo (trans.), *St John Chrysostom: On Repentance and Almsgiving*, FOTC 96 (Washington, DC 1998) xvi, gives an apt summary of Chrysostom's attitude: "The homily *On Almsgiving* itself is especially rooted in St. Paul's epistles to the Corinthians, Thessalonians, and Romans. It bears the unmistakeable marks of Chrysostom's paternal *splanchna* (σπλάγχνα) that soothe human pain as a result of love, mercy, and forgiveness, all of which belong to the manifold aspects of the Mystery of Repentance."; see also, R. Brändle, "Jean Chrysostome: l'importance de Matth. 25.31-46 pour son éthique", *Vigiliae Christianae* 31 (1977) 47-52; B. Leyerle, "John Chrysostom on almsgiving and the use of money", *HTR* 87 (1994) 29-47; W. Mayer, "Poverty and society in the world of John Chrysostom", in L. Lavan, W. Bowden, A. Gutteridge and C. Kachado (eds), *Social and Political Archaeology in Late Antiquity*, Late Antique Archaeology 3 (Leiden 2006) 465-484.

had been put into effect.[73] Here the γνώμη with its thought and purpose is as bad as the deed.

The γνώμη is something we should secure or fortify for ourselves so that our deeds prove acceptable to God.[74] Chrysostom sees the γνώμη as a citadel that requires guarding against falling into a dishonest condition. It is clear that a faculty that requires such care must be significant in Chrysostom's anthropology. Here is a critical faculty of the psyche that must not be left open to attack.

This completes the possibilities that Chrysostom puts forth in this homily regarding the relation between mindset and action. A healthy γνώμη makes the insignificant deed great; it makes the unfinished one count as completed; it makes the intended but not implemented good work as though done. In each case, the γνώμη carries off the crown, the reward from a generous God. On the other hand, a depraved γνώμη ends in wrong choices, often in evil deeds and calls down condemnation and punishment.

The structure of the homily is particularly significant at the point where Chrysostom comments on the instructions given to Noah after the flood. It marks the transition from the discussion of the righteous Noah drawing grace from a generous God, and widens out to explain God's care for and generosity to humankind in the content and intention of those instructions. There he explains the text not only as evidence of the generous love of God, but also as warning of the danger that besets humankind in the tendency to harbour and express a φονική γνώμη (murderous mindset). From there he narrows the application to any individual in his congregation who bears a grudge against a neighbour, a point he then powerfully illustrates by use of the parable of the wicked servant. At the heart of this discussion looms the fearsome shadow of the φονική γνώμη, something which he suggests has been a permanent feature of humankind both before and after the flood. In following his argument, we see that Chrysostom, in considering the promise of God never again to curse the earth, takes up the statement of Genesis 8:21 in the Septuagint: "humankind's thinking (διάνοια) is fully wrapped

---

[73] *In Gen. hom.* 27; PG 53,244 8-11: Ὁρᾷς καὶ ἐνταῦθα πάλιν ἀπὸ τῆς μοχθηρᾶς γνώμης καὶ τὴν κατάκρισιν ἑπομένην, καὶ διὰ τὴν ἀπερίσκεπτον ὄψιν, ὡς εἰς ἔργον τῆς μοιχείας ἐξελθούσης αὐτῷ, τὴν κόλασιν ἐπηρτημένην; ("Do you see here in this instance the condemnation ensuing from the evil mindset, and on account of the careless imagination the correction inflicted as if the deed of adultery had already emerged?")

[74] *In Gen. hom.* 27; PG 53,243 11-13: Ταῦτα τοίνυν ἐννοοῦντες, πανταχοῦ τὴν γνώμην ἡμῶν ἀσφαλισώμεθα, ἵνα αὕτη τὰ παρ' ἡμῶν γινόμενα παρασκευάσῃ εὐπρόσδεκτα γίνεσθαι ("Therefore, considering these things, let us in all situations guard our mindset, so that it might render the things being done by us to be acceptable").

up securely in evil from youth".[75] So important does he think this text to be in emphasising God's ongoing love in the face of ongoing depravity that he repeats it twice more.[76] This focus continues with a reference to God's giving of these instructions as a restraint to the impulse (ὁρμή) to murder.[77] Then, in a dramatic monologue that lists a number of restraining factors that have to be resisted in the pursuit of homicide, he makes an appeal based upon the essential dignity of humankind as created in the image of God and as his vice-regent over creation. The appeal is made to any who may have hostile thoughts toward another: καὶ παῦσαι τῆς μοχθηρᾶς γνώμης ("bring your depraved mindset to an end").[78] Chrysostom then points to the fact that God gave these promises and instructions in order to restrain humankind's murderous γνώμη so that his purpose for humankind in populating the earth, controlling it, and enjoying it, might be fulfilled.[79] This murderous mindset is then reflected in Chrysostom's depiction of the parable of the wicked servant. The treatment of this parable takes up much of the latter part of the homily and culminates in his dramatic exclamation.

It is worth noting that Chrysostom bases his assumption of what appears to be the inherent depravity of the γνώμη upon the text from Genesis 8:21. This is evident when after the initial discussion stemming from the text he returns to make the following observation:

> See how he signified that because of their depravity he had brought the curse upon the earth. Then, lest we might think that they had changed for the better,

---

[75] LXX, Genesis 8:21 4-5: ὅτι ἔγκειται ἡ διάνοια τοῦ ἀνθρώπου ἐπιμελῶς ἐπὶ τὰ πονηρὰ ἐκ νεότητος, cited *In Gen. hom.* 27; PG 53,244 25-26.

[76] *In Gen. hom.* 27; PG 53,244 51-54.

[77] *In Gen. hom.* 27; PG 53,246 16-17: Ταῦτα δὲ ἐποιεῖ, ἄνωθεν προαναστέλλων αὐτῶν τὴν ὁρμὴν τὴν περὶ τὴν ἀνδροφονίαν ("He made these [regulations], checking beforehand from above their impulse for homicide").

[78] *In Gen. hom.* 27; PG 53,246 38-41: ἐννόει ὅτι κατ' εἰκόνα Θεοῦ δεδημιούργηται, καὶ ὅσης ἠξίωται παρὰ τοῦ Θεοῦ τῆς προεδρίας, καὶ ὅτι πάσης τῆς κτίσεως τὴν ἐξουσίαν ἀναδέδεκται, καὶ παῦσαι τῆς μοχθηρᾶς γνώμης ("Consider, that in the image of God he has been created, of what great privileged position he was thought worthy by God, and that he has received authority over all of creation; and bring your depraved mindset to an end").

[79] *In Gen. hom.* 27; PG 53,246 58-247 2: Εἶτα ἵνα μάθωμεν ἀκριβῶς τίνος ἕνεκεν τοσαύτην ταύτης τῆς ἐντολῆς τὴν ἀκρίβειαν ἐποιήσατο, καὶ ὅτι ἀναχαιτίζων τῶν ἀνθρώπων τὴν φονικὴν γνώμην φησὶν Ἡμεῖς δὲ αὐξάνεσθε καὶ πληθύνεσθε, καὶ πληρώσατε τὴν γῆν, καὶ κατα κυριεύσατε αὐτῆς· ("Then, in order that we might learn precisely why he made so much precision for this regulation, and that he was restraining the murderous mindset of human beings, he said, 'You, however, increase and multiply and fill the earth, and gain dominion over it;'").

and that it was because of this that he had made this promise, he said, "Humankind's thinking is fully wrapped up in evil securely from youth".[80]

Chrysostom is asserting here and in the following argument that humankind was the same, and would remain the same after the holocaust as before it: as possessing a tendency towards evil in its worst form. In order for this evil to be restrained, special grace was required so that humankind would neither be destroyed by divine judgment nor destroy itself in endemic homicide. God provided grace at that time in the promises and instructions that he gave to Noah and his family. This tendency is identified in Chrysostom's comments as the μοχθηρᾶς γνώμης (depraved mindset) and the φονική γνώμη (the murderous mindset). This is highly suggestive that Chrysostom's theological anthropology included the concept of a γνώμη that was depraved since the Fall.[81]

The γνώμη must be rightly tuned and tightly tensioned (τόνος). This feature emerges in the homily when Chrysostom emphasises the rapidity of God's response to any wholehearted approach to him, the Ninevites and the thief on the Cross being prime examples. God, Chrysostom asserts, Ἐπειδὰν γὰρ ἴδη τὸν τόνον τῆς ἡμετέρας γνώμης, καὶ πόθῳ ζέοντι προσιόντας ἡμᾶς, οὐ μέλλει, οὐδὲ ἀναβάλλεται ("When he sees the tension of our mindset and sees us coming near to a seething desire, he neither merely intends nor delays...").[82] In the discussion above, it has been established that Chrysostom saw the state or temper of the γνώμη as centrally significant in divine-human relationships. The γνώμη is referred to here as being in a condition of tension (τὸν τόνον) that God finds agreeable and to which he immediately responds. It is properly tuned or tensioned. The picture is of a cord being stretched or tightened. It could be said that it is at the right pitch or in tune or at its full strength, not slack or exhausted. Perhaps the image is of the stringing of a bow ready for shooting. The text under examination indicates that the γνώμη is at its appropriate tension when it is intensely concentrated on its goal, when its desire is seething or at boiling point. In itself τόνος is a somewhat neutral term. In a homily on Romans, Chrysostom suggests that Paul was trying to ἐκλύση τὸν τόνον ("unloose the tension") of his Judaising opponents.[83] As far as Paul was concerned, they were tense and overexcited in their opposition to the faith (something very familiar to Paul from his past as a rampaging Pharisee), and he

---

[80] *In Gen. hom.* 27; PG 53,244 47-52: Ὅρα πῶς ἐπεσημήνατο, ὅτι διὰ τὴν τούτων μοχθηρίαν τὴν κατάραν ἐπήγαγε τῇ γῇ. Εἶτα ἵνα μὴ νομίσωμεν, ὅτι ἐπειδὴ ἐπὶ τὸ βέλτιον μετεβάλοντο, διὰ τοῦτο αὐτὸς ταύτην ἐποιήσατο τὴν ὑπόσχεσιν, φησίν· Ὅτι ἔγκειται ἡ διάνοια τοῦ ἀνθρώπου ἐπιμελῶς ἐπὶ τὰ πονηρὰ ἐκ νεότητος.

[81] Further discussion of this issue is in Chapter 10 below.

[82] *In Gen. hom.* 27; PG 53,247.63-248 2.

[83] *In Rom. hom.* 12; PG 60,500 57-58.

was trying to slacken their nerve. Thus, τόνος could apply to a variety of attitudes with no moral judgement intrinsically involved, simply pointing to the intensity with which that attitude was held. The epithets occurring with τόνος determine its moral value in each instance. Elsewhere in Chrysostom's corpus, we find ἄτονος, "unstrung" or "slack",[84] and εὔτονος, "well-strung".[85] Given the discussion of this homily, in the context of divine-human relationships the γνώμη may be said to be εὔτονος when it is sound or healthy (ὑγιος). In contrast, it would be ἄτονος when it is ῥαθυμία (indifferent), μοχθηρά (depraved), or φονική (murderous).

Further to this tension or temper of the γνώμη, the two terms εὐγνωμοσύνη and ἀγνωμοσύνη are built upon the γνώμη stem and point to certain states of this faculty. Thus, εὐγνωμοσύνη points to a properly tensioned γνώμη and ἀγνωμοσύνη indicates a γνώμη that is slack or without proper tension. In other words, the proper temper (τόνος) of the γνώμη is expressed here in this homily as εὐγνωμοσύνη, rightmindedness, whereas the improper temper (ἄτονος) of the γνώμη is expressed here as ἀγνωμοσύνη, insolence. According to Chrysostom, the mindset is rightly tuned when the reasonable rights of God and fellow-humans are acknowledged. On the other hand the mindset is woefully unstrung and grossly out of tune when those rights are contemptuously disdained.

---

[84] *In laud. concept.*; PG 50,790 36, where ἄτονος is applied to nature (φύσις) when Zechariah argued the impossibility of producing children at his age due to his "unstrung nature". It was no longer tuned to the task. *In 1 Cor. hom.* 7; PG 61,60 58, it is applied to the soul (ψύχη) of fallen humankind that cannot defend itself against the Devil's craft.

[85] *Mart.*; PG 50,665 12, where the cognate εὐτονία is applied to the γνώμη. As τόνος was a critical concept in Stoic thought, this probably reflects Stoic influence upon Chrysostom. Amirav, *Rhetoric and Tradition*, 174, asserts that "Chrysostom reflects many features of a Stoic wise man: the "visible" things are neither good nor bad. They simply do not matter and have no moral bearing in themselves." This applies to a discussion of poverty and virtue, but Amirav suggests elsewhere (166, 186, 257) that Chrysostom often reflects Stoic thought. Among others to note some dependence by Chrysostom upon Stoic thought are: Kelly, *Golden Mouth*, 44: "his thinking …was steeped in the popular Stoicism which pervaded the culture", 92: "the sprawling Matthew commentary…shot through…with Stoic presuppositions"; R. Carter, "The future of Chrysostom studies: theology and Nachleben", in P. Christou (ed.), *ΣΥΜΠΟΣΙΟΝ: Studies on St John Chrysostom*, Analecta Vlatadon 18 (Thessaloniki 1973). [www.myriobiblos.gr/texts/ English/carter_future.html]; Brändle, "Johannes Chrysostomus I", 457; J.A. Brundage, *Law, Sex and Christian Society in Medieval Europe* (Chicago 1987) 84, gives an astute balance: "The Stoics presented special difficulties for the defenders of Christian orthodoxy for while the Fathers certainly adopted some of their most dearly held beliefs from the Stoics, and were conscious that they did so, they also felt compelled to reject other Stoic teachings, such as the contention that all sins are equally serious."; Schatkin, *John Chrysostom as Apologist*, 102, 104, 125, 138-9, 283-4.

III. Conclusion

It is evident from this examination of Homily 27 of Chrysostom's Genesis homilies that the γνώμη played a significant role in his theological anthropology. The frequency of usage in its various forms points to its significance in this regard. Even more significant is the part it plays in the contrast between Noah and the wicked servant who are presented by Chrysostom as belonging to opposite ends of what could be called the γνώμη tension spectrum, that has εὔτονος at one end and ἄτονος at the other. Other individuals and groups are made by Chrysostom to enter this spectrum at one end or the other. Abel joins Noah at one end along with the person wanting to help the beggar, and the person offering a cup of cold water, and those who through lack of resources or some other circumstance are unable to finish a commendable task. At the other end, the wicked servant of the parable is joined by Cain, unfaithful Jews, the person with the adulterous gaze, and humankind in general when its impulses and passions remain unchecked, even though Chrysostom acknowledges the essential dignity of humankind as the crown of creation. Each of these is marked by the state of their γνώμη, which is seen to be the target of God's quest in the human person, with the tension thereof determining both rewards and punishments. It affects the character of offerings, thoughts and works, making them acceptable or unacceptable. As a well-disposed γνώμη is the cause of all our goodness, God encourages it by providing means for its expression and wants it taught and practised. The γνώμη is a critical faculty of the psyche that originates action, is closely related to the faculty of thought (διάνοια), determines choice (προαίρεσις) and finds its expression in that faculty. It is a citadel that needs to be guarded. It appears to suffer from a critical flaw since the Fall, having propensity to depravity, murder and insolence, yet it appears to be the faculty to which the knowledge of virtue contributes. All this builds upon the foundation from the material previously considered, pointing to further issues to be investigated, namely: a more precise description of the relationship of the γνώμη to other faculties of the psyche; its autonomy in the grace-will tension in Chrysostom's theology; the shaping, settling and transformation of this faculty; and the issue of its association with sin.

CHAPTER 4

Authority of the Γνώμη

Chrysostom's homilies on Romans are a rich source for discerning his understanding of his anthropology in relation to the great themes of sin and grace. In all, there are seventy-one occurrences of γώμη in these homilies. The discussion of γνώμη as used in these homilies will be in three parts: in relation to its authority, accountability, and its significance for the issues of grace and sin. The focus of this chapter is upon authority, whereas the Romans' material on the two other issues will be incorporated into Chapter 10, "Sin and the γνώμη". In this chapter on authority, some discussion of the relation of γνώμη to προαίρεσις and other pertinent terms will be included. This will support and expand upon points that have been made above as well as introducing further features of the γνώμη as used by Chrysostom.[1]

Reference has been made to the fact that Chrysostom understood the γνώμη to be the ruling power in the psyche. Indeed, his anthropology appears to revolve around his view that the most critical function of the γνώμη was that of authority. Time and again he refers to the γνώμη as having mastery over the soul. Some facets of that mastery, control or authority have already been discussed above. Here, that authority will be more fully explored, especially in its relationships to other faculties and powers of the psyche. It will be seen: that the body and its members are controlled by it; that it has the power either to resist or to side with conscience; that it is lord over choice, and that desire or willing are directed by it; that it has final command of the passions; that it is the source of a person's attitudes; and that it lies as the responsible cause behind a person's actions. It will be demonstrated that Chrysostom understood the γνώμη to be endowed with such autonomy of authority that God himself respects it and does not put it under necessity; that every person has been endowed with an authoritative γνώμη and is responsible to God for its state and operation.

The body lies under the authority of the γνώμη. In a homily based on Romans 5:5-18, Chrysostom compares a person's body with a suit of armour. Like the armour, it is by nature neutral: no charge (ἔγκλημα) can be laid against it. The

---

[1] There is nothing written in recent times on the homilies in Romans in regard to γνώμη, but there are some works that bear upon this study: R.G. Tanner, "Chrysostom's exegesis of Romans", *SP* 17 (1982) 1185-1197; D. Trakatellis, "Being transformed", 211-229; D. Trakatellis, *Being Transformed: Chrysostom's Exegesis of the Epistle to the Romans* (Brookline, MA 1992); Aland, "Trustworthy preaching", 271-280.

controlling power over the body and its members is the "τὴν τῆς ψυχῆς γνώμην" ("the mindset of the soul").[2] The body becomes a weapon for good or evil as the γνώμη determines. Hence we find, as Chrysostom continues with the metaphor, a call for strong armour, a noble γνώμη, a good knowledge of warfare, and a commander.[3] He asserts that for the body to function as the divine commander intends, the controlling faculty, the γνώμη, must be appropriately conditioned. The required state is proposed as γενναῖας, high-born or noble, that is, one of superior values in bearing and thought, a necessity for the controlling faculty of the body which must always move within the accepted norms of the highest status in the culture, in this case of those who are called to reign with Christ.[4]

The γνώμη controls the effect of the conscience (συνειδός). Chrysostom, in an extended treatment of the law as discussed by the Apostle Paul in Romans 7:14, makes the point that in practice, conscience is subject to the whims and fancies of the γνώμη. It is when the γνώμη, the mindset, is in agreement with the law as applied by the conscience that its approval is given.[5] He points out that the knowledge of good and evil is a God-given foundational part of the nature of our

---

[2] *In Rom. hom.* 11; PG 60,487 7-9: Ὁ δὴ καὶ ἐπὶ τῆς σαρκὸς ἔστιν εἰπεῖν, τοῦτο κἀκεῖνο γινομένης παρὰ τὴν τῆς ψυχῆς γνώμην, οὐ παρὰ τὴν οἰκείαν φύσιν ("The exact thing may also be said about the flesh, which becomes this or that from the mindset of the soul, not from its own nature").

[3] *In Rom. hom.* 11; PG 60,487 39-42: Διὸ καὶ παντευχίας ἡμῖν δεῖ ἰσχυρᾶς, καὶ γνώμης γενναίας, καὶ τὰ τῶν πολέμων τούτων ἐπισταμένης καλῶς, καὶ πρό γε πάντων στρατηγοῦ ("For this reason we must have strong armour, a noble mindset, be well established in the arts of this war, and at least, foremost of all, a commander").

[4] *In Rom. hom.* 11; PG 60,487 40: This definition of γενναῖος I have composed from my understanding of the signification of the term from my reading in Greek literature over a long period. As an exemplary basis here, I point to Libanius' usage: *Or.* 14.24 9, where he combines it with θείας to speak of a noble and divine soul; *Or.* 15.28 8, with κάλος of a beautiful and noble mind; *Or.* 17.31 9, with κάλος in the funeral oration for Julian referring to his death as dashing the beautiful and noble hopes of the world; *Or.* 18.208 7, of Constantius ruining the noble soul of an army by bad training; *Or.* 22.20 13, linked with κάλος and φιλάνθρωπος to describe the noble, beautiful and humane treatment of Antiochene magistrates and councillors by the commissioner appointed to enquire into the riots of 387 over the statues; *Or.* 33.6 8, of a governor, who despite many faults had endured nobly some of the discomforts of office in very difficult circumstances. Each of these usages reflects the best ideals of the culture.

[5] *In Rom. hom.* 13; PG 60,510 32-36: Ἐπαινῶ τὸν νόμον, φησί, κατὰ τὸ συνειδός, καὶ αὐτὸν δὲ εὑρίσκω ἐμοὶ τῷ βουλομένῳ τὸ καλὸν ποιεῖν συνήγορον, καὶ ἐπιτείνοντά μοι τὸ βούλημα· ὥσπερ γὰρ ἐγὼ αὐτῷ συνήδομαι, οὕτω καὶ αὐτὸς ἐπαινεῖ τὴν γνώμην τὴν ἐμήν ("I approve the law, he means, in my conscience, and I find it in agreement with me when I am desiring to do good, intensifying my intention; even as I rejoice together with it, in this way also the law itself [through my conscience] approves my mindset").

inner beings.[6] This he equates with the law of my mind (νοῦς).[7] This innate law long preceded the Law of Moses, which in his thinking appears to be a more severe external expression of the innate phenomenon. He argues that the Law of Moses, in company with the conscience, pleads with and increases the intensity of the wish, desire or preference (βούλημα) to do good. Desire (βούλημα), however, is shaped by the γνώμη which, if it enthusiastically agrees with law-conscience, is praised by the law. Here the γνώμη is the faculty that is commended for placing desire on the side of the law and thus on the side of conscience (συνειδός). Γνώμη therefore, in his thought, has authority in the free human psyche not only over desire but also over conscience, in the sense that it is γνώμη and not conscience that has the last word. It is the final arbiter of the free soul.[8]

It is clear from the same passage in homily 13 that Chrysostom understood γνώμη to have authority over wish, desire or will as expressed there by βούλημα. In this homily, we see that Chrysostom distinguishes between God-given βούλησις ἔμφυτον, desire or natural willing, and the προαίρεσις, moral choice, which he defines as ...τὸ δὲ ἐξ ἡμῶν αὐτῶν γινομένη κίνησις, πρὸς ὅπερ ἂν αὐτὴν βουληθῶμεν ἀγαγεῖν ("...a motion from ourselves towards whatever we might wish to go after").[9] The προαίρεσις is also explained as our own willing (βούλησις ἐμέτερον) which originates with the γνώμη.[10] Thus, προαίρεσις, βούλησις, and βούλομαι are controlled by the γνώμη. The desire or wish βούλησις/βούλομαι is determined by the mindset (γνώμη) and then put into effect by the choice (προαίρεσις). This choice may or may not be in harmony with natural God-given

---

[6] *In Rom. hom.* 13; PG 60,510 36-39: Ὁρᾷς πῶς δείκνυσι τὴν μὲν τῶν καλῶν καὶ τῶν μὴ τοιούτων γνῶσιν ἐξ ἀρχῆς ἡμῖν καταβεβλημένην, τὸν δὲ νόμον Μωϋσέως ἐπαινοῦντα αὐτήν, καὶ ἐπαινούμενον παρ' αὐτῆς; ("Do you see how, from the beginning, the knowledge of what is good and what is not so has been laid down as a foundation in us, and that the law of Moses approves it and is itself approved by it?")

[7] *In Rom. hom.* 13; PG 60,511 13-14: Αὕτη οὖν, φησίν, ἀντίκειται τῷ νόμῳ τῷ φυσικῷ· τοῦτο γάρ ἐστι, Τῷ νόμῳ τοῦ νοός μου ("This [law of sin], he means, is opposed to the law of nature; this is what 'the law of my mind' means").

[8] As will be argued in Chapter 5, this authority is based upon the God-given autonomy of the γνώμη.

[9] *In Rom. hom.* 13; PG 60,510 26-28.

[10] *In Rom. hom.* 13; PG 60,510 28-29: Ἡ μὲν γὰρ βούλησις, ἔμφυτον καὶ παρὰ Θεοῦ· ἡ δὲ τοιάδε βούλησις, ἡμέτερον καὶ τῆς γνώμης ἡμῶν· The βούλησις in the latter clause refers back to the προαίρεσις. Although βούλησις is feminine, the adjective ἔμφυτον and the possessive pronoun ἡμέτερον follow the form as per W.W. Goodwin, *A Greek Grammar* (London–New York 1963 rep.) §925, "A masculine or feminine noun in the singular, denoting a class rather than an individual, may have a neuter predicate adjective, which is used as a noun." This translates then as: "For desire is a natural thing and from God, but such a desire [i.e. the προαίρεσις] is our own thing and from our mindset."

desire as that all depends upon the disposition of the γνώμη. This authority also covers another of the choosing verbs, the middle form of αίρέω, ἐλέσθαι meaning "to take for oneself, to choose".[11] In this same homily, it is argued that choosing (ἐλέσθαι) to yield to the better or the worse is a function of the authoritative mindset.[12] Modern commentators on patristic literature tend to make much of the function of προαίρεσις but to neglect that of the γνώμη. One example is that of D. Trakatellis, who has noted the critical role of the προαίρεσις in Chrysostom's exegesis of Romans. Relevant to our discussion is his perception that the term implies "a combination of volitional, intellectual, and emotional elements", and as being the "very core of ἄνθρωπος".[13] Trakatellis rightly demonstrates the importance of προαίρεσις in Chrysostom's thinking. However, he overlooks the even more critical role of the γνώμη, even though it figures in the most significant passage used by him to support his case, the one we have been considering. There Chrysostom describes and indeed defines the προαίρεσις, as noted above, in contrast to soul and body that are the works of God, as "a motion (κίνησις) from ourselves...our own and from our own γνώμη".[14] It is appreciated that Trakatellis is making a perceptive point about human freedom, but he stops short of showing how the προαίρεσις is determined by the γνώμη. Although he has argued persuasively for the place given to free choice by Chrysostom, this study has demonstrated that choice for Chrysostom is not in itself as free as we might be led to think. It may have been so at a point now long past, in the time of pre-Fall innocence. Now, Chrysostom would say, our considered choice is biased by the γνώμη. This does not destroy Trakatellis' argument, for the person is still free to choose, but may only do so within the constraints imposed by his/her own γνώμη. I think, however, that Trakatellis has collapsed into the προαίρεσις aspects that in Chrysostom's thinking belonged to the γνώμη. It is the γνώμη that, to use Trakatellis' image, is the very core of ἄνθρωπος in its fallen state, and which is the controlling faculty of the psyche.[15]

---

[11] LSJ, 41-42 *s.v.*

[12] *In Rom. hom.* 13; PG 60,518 24-27: Ἄν τοίνυν τῷ βελτίονι δῷς τὴν ψυχὴν καὶ τὸ σῶμα, ἐγένου τῆς ἐκείνου μερίδος· ἂν τῷ χείρονι πάλιν, τῆς ἐνταῦθα ἀπωλείας κατέστης κοινωνός, οὐ παρὰ τὴν φύσιν τῆς ψυχῆς καὶ τῆς σαρκὸς, ἀλλὰ παρὰ τὴν γνώμην τὴν κυρίαν ἀμφότερα ταῦτα ἐλέσθαι ("If therefore you give up your soul and body to the better, you will become part of that; but if, on the other hand to the worse, thereupon you have become a partner of destruction, not on account of the nature of your soul and flesh, but because of your mindset which has the authority to choose either of these things").

[13] Trakatellis, "Being transformed", 216.

[14] *In Rom. hom.* 13; PG 60,510 27-29; see fns 7 and 8 above in this chapter.

[15] In all there are seventy-one occurrences of γνώμη in these homilies on Romans. In comparison, προαίρεσοις, which is invested with much more importance by many patristic

Chrysostom was clear in his conviction that the γνώμη has final command over the passions. In homily 7, in an extended and lively discussion on the sin of jealousy (βασκανία) as it relates to attitudes to fellow-Christians who have attained or been awarded some honour, Chrysostom concludes that jealousy is worse than warfare for a number of reasons. Among these is that "warfare often is engaged upon for a reasonable cause"[16], whereas jealousy "is always nothing but madness and a satanic γνώμη".[17] These are strong words which put the onus squarely upon a distorted γνώμη as the cause of this mania. Chrysostom is intense in his language of condemnation of this state that so corrupts the soul. He asserts that the jealous γνώμη is unsurpassed by any venomous reptile or insect in its destructive poison. He blames it for crimes, from the slaying of Abel to the overthrow of churches and the engendering of heresies.[18] Also, there is no doubting as to where Chrysostom looked for the cause of this terrible scourge. Indeed, as he continued to discourse on the theme, he turned to speak directly of Satan and laid the ultimate guilt upon τὴν ἀκόρεστον τοῦ διαβόλου γνώμην ("the insatiable mindset of the devil").[19] The cause is traced to the controlling mindsets, the γνώμη of Satan and the γνώμη of the human agents who give rein to jealousy in their psyches.

In homily 8 a comparison is made between, on one hand, persons like Paul and the apostles of Jesus, and on the other, the present congregation including Chrysostom himself. Of the former he asserts that the shadows and the clothes of those men drove death away, but of the latter he remarks that our prayers fail to restrain our passions.[20] The cause of the immense difference between these groups

---

scholars, appears thirty-nine times, little more than half that of γνώμη. In addition, the εὐγνωμ- and ἀγνωμ- cognates provide another forty-six occurrences. Whilst word count is not the ultimate criterion in assessing the measure of a term's significance *vis-à-vis* other terms used by a particular author, it does give some guidance, and in this case the relative usage lends weight to the argument here presented.

[16] *In Rom. hom.* 7; PG 60,449 27-29: καὶ ὁ μὲν αἰτίαν πολλάκις ἔχει εἰπεῖν εὔλογον τοῦ πολέμου,...

[17] *In Rom. hom.* 7; PG 60,449 27-29:..δὲ οὐδὲν ἕτερον ἢ μανίαν καὶ γνώμην σατανικήν.

[18] *In Rom. hom.*7; PG 60,449 33-35: Τοῦτο γὰρ, τοῦτο τὰς Ἐκκλησίας ἀνέτρεψε, τοῦτο τὰς αἱρέσεις ἔτεκε, τοῦτο ἀδελφικὴν ὥπλισε χεῖρα, καὶ αἵματι δικαίου δεξιὰν βαπτισθῆναι ἐποίησε...("This very thing [jealousy] overturned churches, this gave birth to heresies, this made the brotherly hand to be baptised in the blood of the righteous...")

[19] *In Rom. hom.* 7; PG 60,450 10-13.

[20] *In Rom. hom.* 8; PG 60,463 59-464 1: Ποίας οὖν ἂν εἴημεν ἀπολογίας ἄξιοι, εἴ γε ἐκείνων μὲν καὶ αἱ σκιαὶ καὶ τὰ ἱμάτια θάνατον ἤλαυνον, ἡμῶν δὲ οὐδὲ αἱ εὐχαὶ τὰ πάθη καταστέλλουσι; Τί οὖν τὸ αἴτιον; Πολλὴ τῆς γνώμης ἡ διαφορά· ὡς τά γε τῆς φύσεως ἴσα καὶ κοινά ("Therefore, what worthy excuse might exist, if even the shadows and the clothes of those men drove death away?

he ascribes to a disparity in γνώμη. The point is explained by referring to the soul as a lyre prepared by Christ on which to make his music. Like all instruments, it needs the constant and watchful maintenance of the person in order to have it ever ready for Christ's use.[21] The problem is that it had become unstrung:

> Why then do you not prepare it in readiness for the hand of the artist, but slacken the strings and make it flat by luxurious living, thus rendering the whole lyre useless to him, when what is needed is to tighten the strings of the members, and to tension them with astringent spiritual salt? For if Christ sees it being tuned in this way, he will send out music through our souls.[22]

Here it is the soul and thus the whole being that is out of tune. Above it has been noted that the γνώμη is the faculty of the psyche which is required to be at the appropriate tension. If it is unstrung, then everything else follows. In this homily Chrysostom draws attention to the γνώμη as being the focal point of difference, indicating that it was the γνώμη, the mindset, which was responsible for this unstrung state and which had failed to apply the necessary discipline to keep the right tension in the soul. Chrysostom claims there was need for some strong spiritual discipline to tune the instrument to make it fit for Christ to play his music on it. As the controlling faculty in this process, the γνώμη must accept responsibility. Hence, Chrysostom points to it as the cause, on one hand, of the powerful deeds of the immediate followers of Jesus and, on the other, of the powerless prayers of the luxury-loving followers of his own day. It is pertinent to note that here Chrysostom makes a contrast between φύσις, nature, and γνώμη, mindset. As for our nature,…τά γε τῆς φύσεως ἴσα καὶ κοινά ("…the things of

---

What then is the reason for this? The huge difference is in the mindset, as the things of nature are equal and in common.")

[21] In Rom. hom. 8; PG 60,464 7-9: ἐπιθυμεῖ μᾶλλον τοῦτο ἡμῶν αὐτός, καὶ διὰ τοῦτο τὸ ὄργανον κατεσκεύασε τοῦτο, καὶ οὐ θέλει μένειν ἄχρηστον αὐτὸ καὶ ἀργόν, ἀλλ' ἀεὶ μετὰ χεῖρας ἔχειν αὐτὸ βούλεται ("He [Christ] eagerly desires this [to speak through us] more than us, and for this reason he prepared this instrument and does not wish it to remain useless and idle but desires to have it always in his hands").

[22] In Rom. hom. 8; PG 60,464 9-14: Τί τοίνυν οὐ παρασκευάζεις ἕτοιμον αὐτὸ τῇ τοῦ τεχνίτου χειρί, ἀλλὰ χαλᾷς τὰς νευράς, καὶ μαλακωτέρας ποιεῖς τῇ τρυφῇ, καὶ ἄχρηστον ὅλην κατασκευάζεις αὐτῷ τὴν κιθάραν, δέον ἐπισφίγγειν καὶ νευροῦν τὰ μέλη, καὶ ἐπιστύφειν τῷ ἅλατι τῷ πνευματικῷ; Ἂν γὰρ οὕτως ἡρμοσμένην αὐτὴν ἴδη, ἠχήσει καὶ διὰ τῆς ἡμετέρας ψυχῆς ὁ Χριστός. These strings were made from animal sinews and initially were shrunk appropriately in a chemical reaction. In use, the strings were tightened by pegs wrapped in cloth at their ends, precursors of the modern screws. The use of astringent salt in this text indicates that Chrysostom was perhaps suggesting a wholesale renovation, a restart of the process. This points to the depth of the problem. LSJ, τόνος, s.v. 1804, and ἄτονος, s.v. 272; M.C. Howatson (ed.), The Oxford Companion to Classical Literature (Oxford, 1989) 373.

nature are equal and common to all").[23] The γνώμη is where the difference exists. It is what is added to nature, whether it be zeal, faith and love on the one hand, or luxury on the other, that enriches or distorts the person, or, as is the point made by Chrysostom, the γνώμη of the person. It is the γνώμη, the mindset, that controls the quality of the tune which is played, or perhaps, whether or not a tune is played at all. Given that Chrysostom was addressing the issue of the power-debilitating passion for luxury that threatened his people, the γνώμη is held responsible as the controlling faculty of the passions.

Chrysostom's understanding of the authority of the γνώμη in the psyche was also expressed by attributing to it the locale and source of attitudes. Abraham is held up as a model of the righteous person who could step over all obstacles by the means of the lofty γνώμη gifted to him by God.[24] His confidence in the face of trials is attributed to the state of his mindset. In another passage relating to trials where Chrysostom comments on the "more than conquerors" of Romans 8:37, he asserts that even just the preparation of the γνώμη without having to suffer the actual trials enables the Christian to raise the trophies of victory.[25] It is evident that he saw the real battle to be one of the inner being rather than against external enemies. Above all it is a matter of the γνώμη, the mindset, and thus the great issues of life are decided in the γνώμη. The prodigal son is said to have become new from a change in his γνώμη alone.[26] This change in mindset is identified as the desire or will (βούλομαι) to go home. This desire is presented as having been generated in the γνώμη, the ἀπό with the genitive indicating the source from which the newness of attitude had its impetus. Chrysostom, with his vivid and persuasive oratory was calling for similar change in the attitude of the audience before him, signifying that, as seen in the prodigal, the γνώμη is the critical faculty in setting this orientation of the soul. An interesting insight into Chrysostom's social conscience is seen in a comment on Romans 13:6 in homily 23 on the virtue of paying taxes. Chrysostom traces social contract, from a human point of view, to the appointment and maintenance of governors to look after public affairs, to a

---

[23] *In Rom. hom.* 8; PG 60,464 1.

[24] *In Rom. hom.* 8; PG 60,461 17-18: Εἶδες πῶς τίθησι καὶ τὰ κωλύματα, καὶ τὴν ὑψηλὴν τοῦ δικαίου γνώμην πάντα ὑπερβαίνουσαν; ("Do you see how he [God] sets up both the obstacles and the lofty mindset of the righteous man [Abraham] who surmounted them all?")

[25] *In Rom. hom.* 15; PG 60,545 40-43: Οὐ γὰρ πράγματα ὑπομένοντες, ἀλλὰ τὴν γνώμην παρασκευάζοντες μόνον, οὕτω πανταχοῦ τὰ τρόπαια ἱστῶμεν κατὰ τῶν ἐχθρῶν ("For those not enduring action in battle, but by only preparing the mindset, so may we raise the trophies against our enemies").

[26] *In Rom. hom.* 10; PG 60,481.20-22: Ἀλλ' ἐπειδὴ ἐβουλήθη, γέγονεν ἄφνω νέος, ἀπὸ γνώμης μόνης καὶ μεταστάσεως ("But when he was desirous he became new from the change in his mindset alone).

κοινῇ γνώμη, a common mindset or shared conviction and consent.[27] This he applauds as being apropos to God's decree. It appears that here γνώμη is being used to express an aspect of the mind in its deliberative and consensual functions. In this sense γνώμη is the faculty of cause. Further to this, in homily 1, Chrysostom explains ὁρισθέντος, "being declared", in Romans 1:4 by heaping up, in his rhetorical genius, four terms of expression: δειχθέντος, ἀποφανθέντος, κριθέντος, ὁμολογηθέντος παρὰ τῆς ἁπάντων γνώμης καὶ ψήφου ("being exhibited, being displayed, being adjudged, and being acknowledged by the mindset and election of all").[28] The "all" refers to the various witnesses to the deity of the Son: the Old Testament prophets, his incarnation, his miracles, the Holy Spirit and his resurrection. These are listed both before and after the statement about the manner of their witness as coming from their combined γνώμη. The association of ψῆφος, meaning "vote" or, to tease out the image, "voting pebble",[29] indicates that this action flows from the γνώμη. The κοινῇ γνώμη of the previous text was expressed and observed in the appointment and maintenance of governors. In both cases a common attitude is envisaged, an attitude that is situated with the γνώμη.

There are a number of places in these homilies where the efficacy of the γνώμη to affect the quality of actions is made apparent. In a comment on Romans 12:1, the point is made that if we present ourselves as a sacrifice to God with an γνώμης ὀρθῆς ("upright mindset"), then in spite of any blemishes of slackness or worldliness that might exist, the fire of the Spirit will come down and make the sacrifice acceptable.[30] Chrysostom had pointed out that under the old system no blemishes were acceptable in a sacrificial offering and thus those who now offer themselves must exhibit more precision and purity than those of old. Yet, under the new, if the γνώμη is rightly disposed, then any few remaining spots will be taken care of by the perfecting power of the Spirit. This is the pastoral touch of Chrysostom that seeks the highest standard among his people, but that also appreciates the human weakness that requires encouragement to realise the capacity of the γνώμη to harness the power from above. In homily 21, the

---

[27] *In Rom. hom.* 23; PG 60,617 43-45: ἀλλὰ διὰ τοῦτο ἄνωθεν κοινῇ γνώμη πάντων ἔδοξε τοὺς ἄρχοντας τρέφεσθαι παρ' ἡμῶν ("but for this reason, [knowledge of the advantage gained from paying tribute to a king] from earlier times it seemed to the common mindset of all that rulers should be supported by us").

[28] *In Rom. hom.* 1; PG 60,397 58-60.

[29] LSJ, 2023 *s.v.*

[30] *In Rom. hom.* 20; PG 60,597 23-26: Κἂν ἔχῃς τι διαρρέον καὶ βιωτικὸν, προσαγάγῃς δὲ θυσίαν μετὰ γνώμης ὀρθῆς, κατελθὸν τοῦ Πνεύματος τὸ πῦρ, καὶ τὸ βιωτικὸν ἐκεῖνο δαπανήσει, καὶ τὴν προσφορὰν ἀνύσει πᾶσαν ("Even if you have some slipping away and worldliness, yet offer a sacrifice with an upright mindset, the fire of the Spirit coming down will consume that worldliness, and make the offering totally effective").

exhortation to giving with a generous spirit is illuminated by reference to the δαψιλής γνώμη (liberal mindset) that made the two mites of the widow much heavier than the many talents of others.[31] One might say of her: small offering, large heart, which would convey the sense of γνώμη very well. In homily 26, when explaining Paul's call for peace in dealing with those who have scruples about what they eat, Chrysostom points to the state of the γνώμη with which something is eaten as being the crucial issue. If the γνώμη of the eater is not changed, forcing a person to eat because of an external rule will only acerbate the problem. The state of the γνώμη determines the quality of the action: ...οὐ γὰρ τὸ φαγεῖν ποιεῖ ἀκάθαρτον, ἀλλ' ἡ γνώμη, μεθ' ἧς ἐσθίει ("...for it is not the eating that makes a person unclean but the mindset with which he/she eats").[32] The γνώμη holds the power either to fill actions with value or to empty them.

Chrysostom understood the γνώμη to be endowed with autonomy, which in his thought is a significant element of its authority. In commenting on the sovereignty of God, the divine potter of Romans 9:20-22, he stresses that the use and application of this metaphor does not imply the elimination of human freedom of choice (αὐτεξούσιος).[33] He follows on by giving a perceptive explanation of the proper approach to the biblical figures (ὑπόδειγμα) of which this metaphor is one.[34] He then places this αὐτεξούσιος with the γνώμη by asserting that God's authority (ἐξουσία) over the human clay does not entail any necessity or force (ἀνάγκη) over the γνώμη.[35] Indeed, if this were so, it would involve God in the moral creation of both good and evil persons, thus absolving them of all responsibility for their attitudes and actions.[36] Chrysostom is avowing God's

---

[31] *In Rom. hom.* 21; PG 60,603 48-50: Οὕτω καὶ ἡ χήρα πολλὰ τάλαντα ὑπερηκόντισε διὰ δύο λεπτῶν· δαψιλῆς γὰρ ἦν ἡ γνώμη ("In this way the widow went way beyond the scales through her two mites; for her mindset was so liberal").

[32] *In Rom. hom.* 26; PG 60,639 32-33.

[33] *In Rom. hom.* 16; PG 60,559 13-14: Ἐνταῦθα οὐ τὸ αὐτεξούσιον ἀναιρῶν τοῦτο λέγει, ἀλλὰ δεικνὺς μέχρι πόσου δεῖ πείθεσθαι τῷ Θεῷ ("Here this does not mean that he is destroying our autonomy, but showing us to what extent it is necessary to obey God"). See Aland, "Trustworthy Preaching", 280, who makes the comment on this passage: "One of Chrysostom's most important concerns is that the human *autexousion* is not nullified"; see also Trakatellis, "Being transformed", 217.

[34] *In Rom. hom.* 16; PG 60, 559-560.

[35] *In Rom. hom.* 16; PG 60,559 34-39: μὴ εἰς δημιουργίας λόγον νόμιζε ταῦτα εἰρῆσθαι τῷ Παύλῳ, μὴ εἰς γνώμης ἀνάγκην, ἀλλ' εἰς οἰκονομιῶν ἐξουσίαν καὶ διαφοράν ("...do not think that these things are said by Paul as an account of creation or about the constraint of the mindset, but about the authority and distinction of the divine arrangements").

[36] *In Rom. hom.* 16; PG 60,559 41-43: Καὶ γὰρ εἰ περὶ γνώμης ἐνταῦθα ὁ λόγος, καὶ τῶν ἀγαθῶν καὶ τῶν οὐ τοιούτων ἔσται αὐτὸς δημιουργὸς τούτων, καὶ ὁ ἄνθρωπος πάσης αἰτίας ἐκτός ("For if

respect for the autonomy of each person, an autonomy which lies in the authority of the mindset (γνώμη). An interesting sidelight is thrown on this in homily 14 where he explains that the subjection of creation to decay as being οὐχ ἑκοῦσα ("not willingly") meant that it was οὐχ ἵνα κυρίαν γνώμης οὖσαν δείξῃ ("not in order to show that its being (substance/essence) has independence of mindset").[37] Unlike human beings, creation is totally dependent in all facets of its being and existence. This explanation of the rhetorical personification of creation indicates that Chrysostom's position concerning humankind is that the distinctive feature of the essence of human beings is an authoritative independent γνώμη. In homily 19 we find him, when explaining the consequences of the unbelief that breaks a branch off the tree of divine election, acclaiming the greatness of the authority of both the προαίρεσις and the γνώμη. He says, Εἶδες ὅσον τῆς προαιρέσεως τὸ κῦρος; πόση τῆς γνώμης ἡ ἐξουσία; ("Do you see how great is the mastery of the moral choice? How great is the authority of the mindset?")[38] The text underlines the authoritative nature of the γνώμη in that good and evil are not immutable qualities of our beings but are dependent upon the mindset and the choice that flows from it. This authority of the γνώμη is again stated in a passage in homily 26 where Chrysostom encourages his people to give attention to the things of the Spirit rather than to be focused upon the things of the world. In so doing, he presents examples from both Old and New Testaments of those who walked that path. Then, in case the mention of such great models might have the opposite effect of discouragement, he tells them not to be troubled but to remember ...ὅτι πανταχοῦ τῆς γνώμης ἐστι τὸ κῦρος ("...that in all cases authority belongs to the mindset").[39] The ability to do what is required lies with them, in their own mindset.

Γνώμη, then, occupies a vital, authoritative role in the human psyche according to Chrysostom's usage of the term. It has authority over the body and its members. It has the power either to resist or to side with conscience. It has authority over desire, wish, and will, and determines choice. The passions find in it their high command. It is the locus of a person's attitudes. As the responsible cause of a person's actions, it determines their quality. It has been shown that Chrysostom understood that a significant element of the authority of the γνώμη is its endowment with autonomy by God, an autonomy that he holds inviolate, and

---

the speech here was about the mindset and the good and the bad, he himself will be the creator of these, and the human person be free of all blame").

[37] *In Rom. hom.* 14; PG 60,530 42.

[38] *In Rom. hom.* 19; PG 60,590 29-32: The use of κῦρος and ἐξουσία here is probably stylistic, there being no real difference of meaning in the terms in this context. At times Chrysostom refers to both προαίρεσις and γνώμη as authoritative in the soul. This does not affect their relative positions as made plain in numerous passages.

[39] *In Rom. hom.* 26; PG 60,642 32-35.

therefore entails the aspect of total responsibility. It is to the further examination of that autonomy that we now turn.

CHAPTER 5

The Autonomy of the Γνώμη

In one of the homilies to neophytes, Chrysostom comments that the inexpressible kindness of God is seen in the fact that he entrusted the care of our souls to ourselves. We are always free to choose or reject virtue, options that God has left ἐφ' ἡμῖν (up to us), particularly to our γνώμη. God has made us αὐτεξούσιοι (autonomous), and this self-determination is proof of his kindness and grace.[1] Reference has already been made above to this feature of autonomy in Chrysostom's anthropology, but his emphasis on the independence of the soul is such a significant characteristic of his theological thought that further treatment is required. It is not possible to come to an adequate grasp of his understanding of the human condition and the role of the γνώμη apart from an examination of the place of self-determination in his thinking. Allied to and implied in self-determination is the concept often found in Chrysostom's homilies of the need to make our contribution (τὰ παρ' ἑαυτῶν εἰσφέρειν). As these features are interwoven with other significant powers of the psyche that are raised by this text, and that bear upon the place and function of the γνώμη, it is necessary to address the following: (a) self-determination and γνώμη; (b) ἐφ' ἡμῖν (up to us) and γνώμη; (c) τὰ παρ' ἑαυτῶν εἰσφέρειν (bringing our contribution) and γνώμη; and (d) προαίρεσις (choice) and its relationship to γνώμη.

Before examining Chrysostom's homilies, it should be noted that the emphasis upon human autonomy was not unique to him among the Church Fathers. E. Gilson made the assertion in 1931 that "the emphatic way in which the Fathers of the Church insist on the concept of freedom"[2] has first claim upon our attention when reading them. This is typical of the opinion of most who have become familiar with the literature. Human autonomy was to Gilson and many scholars

---

[1] *Cat. 1-8 hom.* 8.22 1-6. This passage is treated more fully in section I below. In 1955 the French Benedictine scholar, A. Wenger, came upon eight of Chrysostom's hitherto unknown homilies to neophytes in a manuscript from the eleventh century at the Athonite monastery of Stavronikita. He published these together with a French translation and notes in 1957 as A. Wenger, *Jean Chrysostome, Huit catéchèses baptismales inédites*, SC 50 (Paris 1957). In 1963, P. Harkins produced an English translation of these, together with four other relevant homilies extant in other sources: Harkins, *Baptismal Instructions*. This publication contains a veritable mine of pertinent information and comment in the form of Harkins' endnotes, over 200 pages of them.
[2] E. Gilson, *The Spirit of Medieval Philosophy*, trans. A.H.C. Downes, Gifford Lectures 1931-1932 (London 1936) 304.

since, the outstanding feature of the theological thought of the patristic era. K. Ware is typical when he observes, "This God-given freedom of each human person is a master theme in patristic anthropology".[3] As the main concern of this study is the place of the γνώμη in Chrysostom's anthropology, it is not intended to cover ground that has already been well ploughed. The secondary literature has addressed issues such as synergism, the initiative of grace, the necessity of good works, predestination, freedom, providence, and the centrality of the προαίρεσις.[4] In comparison, very little has been devoted to discussing the γνώμη in Chrysostom's anthropology, a concept which I suggest has greater claims than others to central importance in his understanding of the human person and the associated web of relationships.[5] Nevertheless, some of these issues will be touched upon where they form the context of the particular occurrence of γνώμη under examination.

---

[3] K. Ware, "In the image and likeness: the uniqueness of the human person", in J. T. Chirban (ed.), *Personhood: Orthodox Christianity and the Connection between Body, Mind, and Soul* (Westport Conn.-London 1996) 1-13 at 10.

[4] W.R.W. Stephens, *Saint John Chrysostom: His Life and Times: A Sketch of the Church and the Empire in the Fourth Century* (London 1883³); Meyer, "Liberté et moralisme chrétien", 283-305; L. Meyer, *Saint Jean Chrysostome, maître de perfection chrétienne*, Études de théologie historique 19 (Paris 1933); E. Boularand, "La nécessité de la grâce pour arriver à la foi d'après Saint Jean Chrysostome", *Gregorianum* 19 (1938) 515-542; Baur, *John Chrysostom and His Time*, vol.1, 357-372; A. Kenny, "Was Chrysostom a semi-Pelagian?", *Irish Quarterly Review* 27 (1960) 16-29; Altaner, "Augustinus und Johannes Chrysostomus", 302-311; R. Brändle, "Synergismus als Phänomen der Frömmigkeitsgeschichte, dargestellt an den Predigten des Johannes Chrysostomus", in F. von Lilienfeld und E. Mühlenberg (eds), *Gnadenwahl und Entscheidungsfreiheit in der Theologie der Alten Kirche. Vorträge gehalten auf der Patristischen Arbeitsgemeinschaft, 3-5. Januar 1979 in Bethel* (Oikonomia 9), Erlangen: Theol. Fak., 1980, 69-89 and 113-121; H. Chadwick, "Freedom and necessity in early Christian thought about God", *Concilium* 166 (1983) 8-13; Collett, "A Benedictine scholar and Greek patristic thought", 66-81; Hill, "A Pelagian Commentator on the Psalms", 263-271; Phan, *Grace and the Human Condition*, 197-207; Hall, "John Chrysostom's 'On Providence'"; Brändle, "Johannes Chrysostomus I", 426-503; Aland, "Trustworthy Preaching", 271-280; Brändle, *Johannes Chrysostomus: Bischof*, 52-54; C.A. Hall, *Learning Theology with the Church Fathers* (Downers Grove, IL 2002) 161-176; C.A. Hall, "Nature Wild and Tame in St John Chrysostom's 'On the Providence of God'", in K. Tanner and C.A. Hall (eds), *Ancient and Postmodern Christianity* (Downers Grove, IL 2002) 23-37; R. Brändle, *John Chrysostom: Bishop-Reformer-Martyr*, trans. J. Cawte and S. Trzcionka, with revised notes by W. Mayer, ECS 8 (Strathfield, Australia 2004) 44-45; R.L. Wilken, "Biblical humanism: the patristic convictions", in R. Lints, M.S. Horton and M.R. Talbot (eds), *Personal Identity in Theological Perspective* (Grand Rapids, MI–Cambridge UK 2006) 13-28.

[5] It is only in the literature devoted to the seventh-century theologian, Maximus the Confessor, and the stream of thought that subsequently flowed from his works that γνώμη came into focus for attention and theological discussion.

In assessing Chrysostom's theological understanding on these issues, care needs to be taken not to overstate the case; there are moderating factors to be considered. For one thing, there is the general background of the social milieu in which Chrysostom worked and preached. He had to deal with Manichaeans with their denial of freewill and their doctrine of physically irresistible illicit sexual desire.[6] With this cloud hovering over his situation, it would have been necessary for him to emphasise both autonomy and responsibility. Then there is the ascetic training of Chrysostom to be taken into account. Though he had moved out from the monastic commune, the experience had left its mark upon him. With the habit of daily discipline firmly entrenched in his being, it is little wonder that the note of responsible freedom was one which he frequently sounded. Then, in addition, the role of grace in relation to the human will in Chrysostom's thinking should not be underestimated. It has been argued from his writings that faith is simultaneously the gift of God and a human response.[7] This view holds that it is neither all of one nor of the other, but a cooperative enterprise in which priority in time has no part. There is an insistence that the divine and the human blend in the production of faith. Faith belongs to both the consent of the will and the grace of God.[8] While human response was seen to be a definite necessity, it is clear that Chrysostom taught that it lies outside the ability of individuals to save themselves. His focus was on the cross of Christ and on reconciling grace as an act of God. Stephens summarises his understanding of Chrysostom's position, "faith and works are necessary conditions, but not efficient causes of salvation".[9] We find various writers maintaining that Chrysostom, although deeply concerned to press home the need for response, never abandoned his belief in the prevenience of grace.[10]

---

[6] O. Bardenhewer, *Patrology: The Lives and Works of the Fathers of the Church*, trans. T.J. Shahan (Freiburg–St Louis, MO 1908) 58-59, 96, 340.

[7] Collett, "A Benedictine scholar and Greek patristic thought", 74-75.

[8] Baur, *John Chrysostom and his Time*, vol. 1, 338; Brändle, *Johannes Chrysostomus: Bischof*, 53, states in reference to Chrysostom's *In Eph. hom.* 1; PG 62,12 49-51, "Wir werden gerettet weder durch die Gnade allein noch durch unsre Werke (allein), sondern durch beides." ("We become saved neither through grace alone nor through our work alone, but through both."); C. Stavropoulos, "Partakers of the divine nature", in D.B. Clendenin (ed.), *Eastern Orthodox Theology: A Contemporary Reader* (Grand Rapids, MI 1995) 190-191: "According to the tradition and teaching of the Eastern Orthodox Church, grace and human freedom are expressed concurrently and may not be understood the one without the other. There are not two separate moments. At the same time that a person freely makes the decision from within for the good of the Christian life, at that very same moment divine grace comes and strengthens him. Just as this grace is given to the individual, the individual makes a free choice."

[9] Stephens, *Saint John Chrysostom*, 407.

[10] Brändle, "Johannes Chrysostomus I", 472: "Ultimately John held fast to the prevenience of grace."; Aland, "Trustworthy preaching", 276: "This human cooperation does not compromise

Chrysostom, in a homily of instruction to baptismal candidates, encourages them to make their own contribution to the new life, but at the same time reminds them that everything they have as far as the faith is concerned is not ours but the Lord's, having received it all from him.[11] What we have to give is from the Lord in the first place. In view of this, it is to be concluded that Chrysostom appeared to place the initiative with grace. It is grace that does the seeking, "...for grace seeks out only the soul eager to receive it".[12] Again, "...for grace is ready and seeks out those who are eager to receive it".[13] It is true that the ground must be prepared, but nothing occurs apart from the God who seeks. Although these latter quotes are in reference to what we might call sanctifying grace, nevertheless it does indicate an understanding by Chrysostom of the vapidity of the human will apart from the grace of God. It should be noted that opinion on this matter does not flow only in one direction. R.C. Hill is one who voiced some doubts about Chrysosotom's commitment to the full gratuity of grace.[14] If the ambivalence that some have identified in him was more than an expression of his pastoral concern, then it strengthens the case for his commitment to the autonomy of the human individual.

I. Self-determination (αὐτεξούσιος)[15]

With those cautionary factors in mind, it is time to turn to Chrysostom's works. They reveal that he stressed self-determination at every turn. In particular,

---

the prevenience of grace...Christ gives human beings the dignity to be able to freely accept his offer. It is only the invitation which permits the freedom to respond."; Boularand, "La nécessité de la grace", 542, while he puts the dogmatic tension in Chrysostom's homilies down to an oratorical simplification or some other such problem, concludes positively: "Car, explicitement, Chrysostome attribue la première initiative à la vocation divine; nous n'obéissons qu'après avoir été appelés. ("For, clearly, Chrysostom ascribes the first initiative to the divine call; we do not obey until after we have been called.").

[11] *Cat. hom.*1; PG 49,225 20-24: Ἐπεὶ δὴ δὲ χρὴ καὶ τοῖς συνδούλοις τὰ παρ' ἑαυτῶν εἰσενεγκεῖν, καὶ τὰ παρ' ἡμῶν εἰσοίσομεν, μᾶλλον δὲ οὐδὲ ταῦτα ἡμέτερα, ἀλλὰ καὶ ταῦτα Δεσποτικά ("Since it is necessary for fellowservants to contribute their own things, then let us do that, but it is very much more the case that even these are not ours but the Master's").

[12] Harkins, *Baptismal Instructions*, 182,12.29, PG 49,256.

[13] *In Gen. hom.* 9; PG 53,76 61-77.1; Harkins, *Baptismal Instructions*, 333, n. 51.

[14] Hill, "A Pelagian commentator on the Psalms?", ITQ 63 (1988) 266, remarks: "So it is difficult for this pastor to concede the utter gratuity of grace. One looks almost in vain in the Commentary on the Psalms for an unqualified statement of it and of our complete dependence upon grace....His reading of the text is almost perverse in its being made to qualify a sense of God's impartial *philanthropia*".

[15] Chrysostom mostly uses the adjective as a substantive with the neuter article τό.

whenever providence, gifts of virtue, election, any hint of necessity or that God does everything appear in the texts from which he is preaching, Chrysostom is at pains to elucidate the relationship between God's work and human self-determination (αὐτεξούσιος). In his pastoral interest of not allowing any excuse for complacency or carelessness, he is quick to guard this autonomy by emphasising that whatever God does, he does not deprive us of self-determination or of the responsibility that it brings. In this regard we find him using a variety of verbs to make the point: God does not ἀνατρέπει (overturn), ἐξωθεῖ (banish, force out), ἀφίησι (send out, discharge), ἀφαιρεῖ (take away from); in med., ἀφελεῖται (deprive, bereave), λυμαίνοται (outrage, abuse), βλάπτει (disable, hinder, damage), or ἀναιρεῖ (lift up and carry away, abolish) the self-determination of the person.[16] It is both, a gift and an obligation, a privilege and a duty, a sovereignty and a stewardship.[17]

Of particular concern for this study is the faculty that Chrysostom saw to be endowed with this feature of autonomy. We find that it is applied in a variety of ways. Often, the reference is general and is identified simply with our person.[18] Similarly, he often speaks of our nature (φύσις) being created by God with this attribute.[19] On occasion, the προαίρεσις (choice) is mentioned as being self-determining.[20] It also appears to be applied to the βουλήσις (will or wish).[21] It is also applied to the γνώμη.[22] There is no need to discuss the general references to person and nature, but those where προαίρεσις, βουλήσις, and γνώμη come into focus are of concern. A discussion of the relationship between these faculties as Chrysostom saw them will be undertaken below. For the moment, a preliminary observation is made that all these terms share in this divinely endowed freedom

---

[16] *In Gen. hom.* 14; PG 53,117 20; *In Phil. hom.* 4; PG 62,209 17-20; *hom.* 8; PG 62,240 26-31, 50; *In Eph. hom.* 2; PG 62,17 38, *hom.* 4; PG 62,33 49; *In 1 Tim. hom.* 3; PG 62,515 40, 57-58; *In Matt. hom.* 6; PG 57,67 19, *hom.* 45; PG 58,471 34; *In Rom. hom.* 13; PG 60,509 4, *hom.* 16; PG 60,559 13, *hom.* 19; PG 60,583 37; *De mut. nom.*; PG 51,141 32.

[17] Whereas Chrysostom saw self-determination as a positive divine endowment, Platonism took the position that it was the essence of the beginning of evil. Sorabji, *Emotion and Peace of Mind*, 334, comments on Plotinus, *The Sixth Enneads* 5.1.1, paraphrasing as: "For souls that turn away, break loose, and become ignorant of the Father, the beginning of evil is pride (*tolma*) and willing (*boulēthēnai*) to belong to themselves alone. They are pleased with their own self-determination (*autexousion*) and create the greatest possible distance (*apostasis*) from the Father."

[18] *In Matt. hom.* 45; PG 58,471 34; *In Joan. hom.* 10; PG 59,6 27; *In 2 Tim. hom.* 8; PG 62,647 28.

[19] *In Gen. hom.* 19; PG 53,158 58, *hom.* 22; PG 53,187 6, *hom.* 23; PG 204,48.

[20] *In Gen. hom.* 14; PG 53,117 20; *In 1 Cor. hom.* 29; PG 61,247 36.

[21] *In Heb. hom.* 12; PG 63,99 41-42.

[22] *In Gen. hom.* 20; PG 53,169 57; *De perf. car.*; PG 56,283 42.

from necessity, and denote an accompanying moral responsibility. This is certainly the case in the contexts in which Chrysostom uses them. That they may be gathered up under αὐτεξούσιος by Chrysostom as seen above is sufficient to make the point. All have some bearing upon what is desired and how that may be gained within the bounds of the moral limitations already acceptable to the person or required by an acknowledged higher authority. In that sense they share the self-determination endowed upon the soul, but that is qualified by the relationships between them.

The text from *Cat.1-8*, 8.2, referred to at the beginning of this chapter, indicates more clearly the relationship between the self-determination of the soul and the γνώμη as Chrysostom understood it. The passage translates:

> For this is the greatest sure sign of his wisdom and his inexpressible lovingkindness, that he entrusted to us the care of the greater element in us. I mean the soul. He teaches us through his works that he made us to be autonomous (αὐτεξουσίους) and left it to be up to us (ἐφ᾿ ἡμῖν), that is to our mindset (γνώμη), both to choose virtue and to desert toward evil.[23]

Here the γνώμη is identified as the faculty in which the αὐτεξούσιος of the person is operational. It is the γνώμη that has been endowed with autonomy and upon which rests responsibility for the choices that are made. This is also seen in the homily on Genesis referred to above, where he states that "God has created our γνώμη self-determining".[24] It is clear from the remainder of that passage that the γνώμη is both free and responsible for one's choices. The contrast between ῥαθυμοῦντες (being careless), which we have seen is depicted by Chrysostom as a possible state of the γνώμη, and νῆψαι (to be sober-minded), indicates that the γνώμη is the autonomous faculty responsible for the choice of virtuous or evil paths. Again, in another place, Chrysostom, in discussing the human responsibility to respond to the things God has provided for the cure of our souls, refers to the self-determination of our nature. Using a medical metaphor, he makes the point that God "does not impose necessity upon us, but in applying the appropriate

---

[23] *Cat.1-8 hom* 8.22 1-6: Καὶ τοῦτο γὰρ τῆς αὐτοῦ σοφίας καὶ τῆς ἀφάτου φιλανθρωπίας τεκμήριον μέγιστον ὅτι τοῦ μείζονος ἐν ἡμῖν, τῆς ψυχῆς λέγω, τὴν ἐπιμέλειαν ἡμῖν ἐνεχείρισε διδάσκων ἡμᾶς δι᾿ αὐτῶν τῶν πραγμάτων ὅτι αὐτεξουσίους ἡμᾶς εἰργάσατο καὶ ἐφ᾿ ἡμῖν εἶναι κατέλιπε καὶ τῇ γνώμῃ τῇ ἡμετέρᾳ καὶ τὸ τὴν ἀρετὴν ἑλέσθαι καὶ τὸ πρὸς τὴν κακίαν αὐτομολῆσαι·

[24] *In Gen. hom.* 20; PG 53,169 57: Ὁρᾷς, ἀγαπητέ, πῶς αὐτεξούσιον ἡμῶν τὴν γνώμην ὁ Θεὸς ἐδημιούργησε, καὶ ὥσπερ ῥαθυμοῦντες ὑποσκελιζόμεθα, οὕτω καὶ νῆψαι βουληθέντες συνορῶμεν τὸ δέον; ("Do you see, beloved, how God created our mindset self-determining, and just as we are tripped up by being careless, similarly, by being prepared to be soberminded we will see the necessary thing to do as within our reach?")

drugs he allows everything to rest upon the γνώμη of the patient".[25] As γνώμη is singled out as the critical faculty that is involved, the direct link to the non-imposition of necessity indicates that αὐτεξούσιος must apply to it.

II. Up to us – ἐφ' ἡμῖν

The text from *Cat. 1-8* also contains the term ἐφ' ἡμῖν. This translates as "up to us", or "in our power".[26] The term has a long history in Greek philosophy, having been discussed by, among others, Aristotle (384-322 BCE),[27] the later Stoic Epictetus (c. 55-c. 135),[28] the Neo-Aristotelian Alexander of Aphrodisias (*fl.* c. 205 CE),[29] and the Neo-Platonist Plotinus (c. 205-260).[30] It is translated variously by those working in the relevant literature, but there is broad agreement that it implies personal causation or self-origination of something or other.[31] Definitions have been attempted such as "self-originating" and "the kinds of things that depend on us".[32] S. Hutton, in an editorial note to the work of R. Cudworth, a seventeenth-century author, asserts, "This term is used in Stoicism to denote moral responsibility".[33] This appears true, but the debate within Stoicism varied in relation to what this might apply. It appears that up until the second and third

---

[25] *In Gen. hom.* 19; PG 53,159 4: οὐ μὴν ἀνάγκην ἐπιτίθησιν, ἀλλὰ τὰ φάρμακα κατάλληλα ἐπιθείς, ἀφίησιν ἐν τῇ γνώμῃ τοῦ κάμνοντος κεῖσθαι τὸ πᾶν.

[26] Harkins, *Baptismal Instructions*, 128.22.

[27] Arist., *EN*, 3.5.1113b 3-1115a 3.

[28] Epict., *Enc.*, 2.2; 5; 19.2.31.2; *Discourses*, 1.1.

[29] Alex. Aphr., *De fato*, 33. 205 15-22.

[30] Plot., *Enneads*, 6.8.1-6.

[31] For this section and those that follow, there is a large corpus of secondary literature. In poring over the primary texts I have been guided by the following: B. Inwood, *Ethics and Human Action in Early Stoicism* (Oxford 1985); R. Dobbin, "Προαίρεσις in Epictetus", *Ancient Philosophy* 11 (1991) 111-135; S. Bobzien, *Determinism and Freedom in Stoic Philosophy* (Oxford 1998); A.A. Long, *Epictetus: A Stoic and Socratic Guide to Life* (Oxford 2002); Sorabji, *Emotion and Peace of Mind*; T. Brennan, "Stoic moral psychology", in B. Inwood (ed.), *The Cambridge Companion to the Stoics* (Cambridge 2003) 257-294; D. Frede, "Stoic determinism", in Inwood, *Cambridge Companion to the Stoics*, 179-205; C. Gill, "The school in the Roman imperial period", in Inwood, *Cambridge Companion to the Stoics*, 33-58; A.W. Price, "Aristotle, the Stoics and the will", in T. Pink and M. Stone (eds), *The Will and Human Action: From Antiquity to the Present Day* (New York 2003) 29-52; Sorabji, "The concept of will", 6-28.

[32] Bobzien, *Determinism and Freedom*, 332, 412.

[33] S. Hutton (ed.), Ralph Cudworth, *A Treatise Concerning Eternal and Immutable Morality; with a Treatise of Freewill*, S. Hutton (ed.), Cambridge Texts in the History of Philosophy (Cambridge–New York 1996) 155, n. 1.

centuries CE, the concept related to the purely mental procedures of assenting or not assenting to impressions, that is, to movements of the soul.[34] Bobzien suggests that this trend developed a focus upon choices, a trend that flowered under Middle Platonism.[35] Epictetus defines as follows:

> Of things, some are ἐφ' ἡμῖν, some are not. Ἐφ' ἡμῖν are conception (ὑπόληψις), impulse (ὁρμή), desire (ὄρεξις), exclusion (ἔκκλισις) and, in a word, as many as are our works. Not ἐφ' ἡμῖν are the body, acquisition, reputation, ruling, in a word, as many as are not our works. The things ἐφ' ἡμῖν are by nature free (ἐλεύθερα), unhindered (ἀκώλυτα), and free from embarrassment (ἀπαραπόδιστα), whereas the things not ἐφ' ἡμῖν are weak, servile, subject to hindrance, and belong to others.[36]

Bobzien asserts that Epictetus had an immense influence on thinkers of later antiquity including the Christians.[37] Thus, it is no great surprise to find Chrysostom echoing this principle within a Christian framework in a homily to neophytes. He compares and contrasts the approach of God in recruiting people for his kingdom with the generals who recruit soldiers for their armies:

> For this one [God] seeks only the things that are ἐφ' ἡμῖν, but those [generals] the things that are not ἐφ' ἡμῖν. For to be slave or free is not ours; further, to be tall or short, to be aged or physically perfect, or any such things are not ἐφ' ἡμῖν. But to be fair or good and draw near to these things [moral qualities] depends on our γνώμη. These things only God requires of us: those of which we are masters.[38]

The similarity to Epictetus is remarkable. Apart from Chrysostom's appreciation of the graciousness of God, the one critical difference is that whereas the later Stoic would place the ἐφ' ἡμῖν with the προαίρεσις, Chrysostom prefers the

---

[34] Bobzien, *Determinism and Freedom*, 403.

[35] Bobzien, *Determinism and Freedom*, 404.

[36] Epict., *Enc.*, 1.1-2.

[37] Bobzien, *Determinism and Freedom*, 403; so also Gill, "The school in the Roman imperial period", 33, states: "In the third and fourth centuries a.d. and later, Neoplatonic and Christian writers built on key Stoic ideas and absorbed them into their systems".

[38] *Cat. hom.* 2; PG 49,236 23-29: Οὗτος μὲν γὰρ τὰ ἐφ' ἡμῖν ζητεῖ μόνον, ἐκεῖνοι δὲ τὰ οὐκ ἐφ' ἡμῖν. Τὸ γὰρ δοῦλον εἶναι ἢ ἐλεύθερον, οὐχ ἡμέτερον· τὸ ὑψηλὸν πάλιν εἶναι καὶ βραχὺν, οὐκ ἐφ' ἡμῖν, τὸ γεγηρακότα καὶ ἄρτιον, καὶ ὅσα τοιαῦτα· τὸ δὲ ἐπιεικῆ ἢ χρηστὸν εἶναι καὶ τὰ παραπλήσια τούτοις, τῆς ἡμετέρας γνώμης. Καὶ ταῦτα ἡμᾶς ὁ Θεὸς ἀπαιτεῖ μόνα, ὧν ἡμεῖς ἐσμεν κύριοι·

γνώμη.[39] Pertinent to this is that Bobzien understands that προαίρεσις as used by Epictetus signifies the dispositions.[40] These are encompassed in the γνώμη by Chrysostom who sees it as controlling both the inner movements and the moral choices.

Indeed, Chrysostom understood a host of things as being ἐφ' ἡμῖν, up to us. Within our power is the ability to appreciate life as a march and a campsite, which entails the consequence of living in the light of eternity and not, therefore, laying up treasure on earth.[41] Virtue and vice are ἐφ' ἡμῖν.[42] Living a life worthy of our baptismal blessings is a moral quality that God has made ἐφ' ἡμῖν.[43] In this passage from Chrysostom's tenth homily on John's Gospel, in explaining "the power to become the children of God" of John 1:12, he links the ἐφ' ἡμῖν with τὸ αὐθάρετον (independence), αὐτεξούσιος (self-determination), and our ἐξουσία (power). In this way, he presses home both the possibility that is open to the baptised, together with the responsibility that devolves upon them. In a comment on John 6:44 that aimed to refute the Manichaean denial of anything being ἐφ' ἡμῖν (in our power) but that everything is totally fated, there is an insistence by Chrysostom upon this feature of autonomy as being definitely verified by this text in John that we are "masters of our γνώμη".[44] This I understand to mean that the mindset (γνώμη) is the locus of the mental impressions to which assent has been made or has been denied, since the τὸ ἐφ' ἡμῖν is identified with the γνώμη. Apposite to this is a section of a homily on Titus 1:3, where Chrysostom explains the command made about preaching. There he asserts that a divine command is ruled out as being ἐφ' ἡμῖν,[45] an assertion that appears to go against what he

---

[39] Sorabji, "The concept of will", 16: "Epictetus connects *proairesis* not only with freedom, but also with what is up to us (*eph' hēmin*). All that falls under *proairesis* is up to us. Moreover, unlike Aristotle, he holds that nothing is up to us except what falls under our *proairesis*".

[40] Bobzien, *Determinism and Freedom*, 403.

[41] *In Eph. hom.* 23; PG 62,168 10-11.

[42] *In Acta. hom.* 47; PG 60,331 34-38.

[43] *In Joan. hom.* 10; PG 59,76 26-41.

[44] *In Joan. hom.* 46; PG 59,257 58-62: 258.16: Τούτῳ ἐπιπηδῶσι Μανιχαῖοι λέγοντες, ὅτι οὐδὲν ἐφ' ἡμῖν κεῖται· ὅπερ μάλιστα βεβαιοῖ κυρίους ὄντας τῆς γνώμης. Εἰ γάρ τις ἔρχεται πρὸς αὐτὸν, φησὶ, τί δεῖ τῆς ἕλξεως; Ὁ καὶ αὐτὸ οὐ τὸ ἐφ' ἡμῖν ἀναιρεῖ, ἀλλὰ μᾶλλον ἐμφαίνει ἡμᾶς βοηθείας δεομένους ("The Manichees jump upon this [Scripture text] saying that it means that nothing lies in our power; the very text, the most significant one that confirms that we are masters of our mindset. Someone says, 'For if somebody comes to him, what necessity is there of drawing?' The text does not take away our self determination, but rather indicates that we stand in need of assistance.")

[45] *In Tit. hom.* 1; PG 62,666 36-41: Εἰ τοίνυν ἐπιταγή ἐστι, οὐκ εἰμὶ κύριος· ἐπίταγμα γὰρ πληρῶ. Τῶν γὰρ πρακτέων τὰ μὲν ἐφ' ἡμῖν κεῖται, τὰ δὲ οὐκ ἐφ' ἡμῖν· ἃ μὲν γὰρ ἐπιτάττων λέγει, ταῦτα οὐκ ἐφ' ἡμῖν· ἅπερ δὲ ἐπιτρέπων, ταῦτα ἐφ' ἡμῖν τυγχάνει. ("If therefore it is mandatory, I am not

otherwise teaches about human autonomy. One would think that true autonomy would permit a choice against the command. The terse "I fulfil a command" points to the actuality that a divine command is something one fulfils without deliberating much, if at all, about it, especially when the concept of future punishment for disobedience is made an essential element in the system.[46] This can only mean that the mindset (γνώμη) should be so conditioned that a positive response is the norm. One does not question the plain commands of God, but simply gets on doing them. This reflects the late-Stoic position of Epictetus in which ἐφ' ἡμῖν took on a role in ethics as a guide for life and actions, a guide based on "an already established theory of morals" and which had "become a perspective toward the future".[47] As far as Chrysostom was concerned, from the perspective of a Christian, those guidelines are well and truly established: the injunctions of God are sacrosanct and lay outside the things subject to us. He gives examples in what follows in the passage of the distinction between the things God does not allow and those he does, the latter being those where a condition is given that allows the hearer to become the "master of the things that were said".[48] The γνώμη needs to be trained to discern the difference and realise that its autonomy is a gift that needs to be exercised with godliness and care if we are rightly to use that which is ἐφ' ἡμῖν, that which depends on us.

III. Bringing our contribution – τὰ παρ' ἑαυτῶν εἰσφέρειν

Closely allied to ἐφ' ἡμῖν in Chrysostom's homilies is another expression that calls for attention as a facet of God-given human self-determination. From time to time in Chrysostom's *Baptismal Instructions* there occurs an expression that is characteristic of his approach to the relationship between humankind and God.[49]

---

in control; for I fulfil a command. Of the things to be done, some lie within our power but others do not. What God says as commands, these are not up to us; but those assigned on trust happen to be up to us.")

[46] *In Tit. hom.* 1; PG 62,666 54-57: Ταῦτα μὲν γὰρ καὶ ποιῆσαι, καὶ μὴ ποιῆσαι ἐφ' ἡμῖν· τὰ δὲ ἐπιτάγματα οὐκ ἐφ' ἡμῖν, ἀλλ' ἀνάγκη ἢ ποιῆσαι, ἢ μὴ ποιήσαντα κολασθῆναι ("For these things that are up to us we may or may not do; but the mandatory things are not up to us, but are a necessity, either for us to do or to incur punishment when not done").

[47] Bobzien, *Determinism and Freedom*, 338, 333. The Stoic "future" was concerned with happiness in the present life.

[48] *In Tit. hom.* 1; PG 62,666 52-54: οὐκέτι ἐπίταγμά ἐστι· τὸν γὰρ ἀκροατὴν ποιεῖ κύριον τῶν λεχθέντων, καὶ τὴν αἵρεσιν αὐτῷ δίδωσι τῶν πρακτέων ("This is not mandatory; he [God] makes the hearer master of what was said and gives that one the choice of the things to be done").

[49] The passages under discussion are *Cat. 1-8 hom.* 1.19, 2.1, 4.10, 4.11, 4.31, 5.19, 7.4, 7.24.

This expression, τὰ παρ' ἑαυτῶν εἰσφέρειν, is translated by P. Harkins as "to contribute one's fair share".[50] This translation is quite idiosyncratic and it raises the question as to the extent to which it matches the idiom current in Chrysostom's milieu. One hesitates to adopt Harkin's translation, but that may be due to an intrusion of one's own theological position into the situation. Putting that aside, the phrase is suggestive of what is up to us, having been noted as the "expression that marks the part man plays in co-operating with God in the work of salvation".[51] As such, an important aspect of the divinely gifted autonomy of the human person is being considered. The phrase is by no means unique to these homilies but is found throughout the corpus. As it directly involves the motions of the soul, this phrase has significance for the role and the autonomy of the γνώμη.

The expression translates: "to bring the things from ourselves", that is "to bring our own contribution". On the surface, at least, this indicates that Chrysostom understood that the human person must play an active part in the drama of divine-human relationships. The Stephens and Brandram translation of this phrase in one place in the two baptismal homilies that appear in the NPNF collection gives "to contribute of our own".[52] Turning to Wenger's French translation of the Stavronikita mss.,[53] we find some variety in the rendering of this phrase: 1:19, *maintenant d'y mettre du vôtre*; 2.1, *en apportant du vôtre*; 4.10, *il apporta...sa part*; 4:11, *à y répondre de votre côté* ; 4:31, *d'y mettre constamment du nôtre*; 5:19, *il a apporté tout sa part*; 7:4, *nous y mettons du nôtre*; 7:24, *nous y mettons du nôtre*. These amount to much the same thing: there is something of "yours" or "ours" which must be brought to or placed at the interests of salvation. The one variation is at 4.11, where Wenger uses the verb *répondre* and a fuller expression, *de vôtre côté*, in place of the possessive pronoun. This translation approaches Harkins' "your fair share". The context is of the abundance of the gifts that God had already bestowed upon the neophytes, gifts such as forgiveness, justification, and filial adoption. Thus though the verb used by Chrysostom does not in itself bear the sense of response, the context certainly does. This indicates that the original initiative comes from God. The contexts of each of the other occurrences indicate the same. In all but one instance Chrysostom refers to post-conversion life after having experienced God's grace in some way, such as revelation, mercy, forgiveness of past sins, and the shining

---

Abbreviated forms are found at 4.6 and 7.10. Various tenses and forms of the verb are used.

[50] Harkins, *Baptismal Instructions*, 30, 209 n. 27, 292 n. 22.

[51] Harkins, *Baptismal Instructions*, 209 n. 27.

[52] *John Chrysostom: Instructions to Catechumens*, hom. 1; trans W.R.W. Stephens and T.P. Brandram, in P. Schaff (ed.), NPNF Series 1, vol. 9, 160.

[53] Wenger, *Catéchèses baptismales*, 118, n. 1.

bridal robe of righteousness at baptism.[54] In 7.24 Cornelius appears to be an exception, suggesting the possibility that Chrysostom assumed a pre-conversion preparation that makes way for the reception of God's grace.[55] This raises a question, asked by many, 'Was it the case that Chrysostom taught that humans could take the initiative in seeking salvation?'[56] That apart, at least for the enlightened, justified and adopted person, there is an insistence upon an active part to play in receiving more grace. When it comes to the Christian walk, A. Kenny's conclusion in regard to Chrysostom's position is to the point: "Virtue is woven together out of God's grace and man's resolve."[57] A pertinent example of this is found in an important addition to the phrase at 4:11, where Chrysostom urges his people to incorporate the gifts received from God into their contribution:

> If God has anticipated you and presented you with such great gifts, and if in company with these great gifts you eagerly hasten to bring your own contribution, and together with the guardianship of those gifts already endowed you demonstrate precise administration, how shall he not again count you worthy of greater honour?[58]

This is "woven" indeed! Chrysostom sounds the note of responsibility clearly here, not the least in his choice of the term πολιτείας, which I have translated as "administration". The image is that of citizenship, in this case that of the heavenly, and stresses the responsible active part that the human participants in the privileges of that heavenly citizenship must play.

In regard to τὰ παρ' ἑαυτῶν εἰσφέρειν in these homilies to neophytes, there are direct links to γνώμη in the form of one of its cognates, the adjective εὐγνώμονων being found in two places, and γνώμη itself being present in another. In the second homily, it is made clear that what we bring from ourselves flows from a rightminded or properly disposed mindset (γνώμη) in its response to God's

---

[54] Occurrences at 7.4 and 7.10 referring to the blessings available at the tombs of the martyrs may appear more general but are clearly addressed to the neophytes.

[55] See 7.28 and 29 where Chrysostom pictures Cornelius as with "nothing whatever of the advantage of teaching" and who "showed so great zeal from his own resources".

[56] Harkins is certain that is the case; see *Baptismal Instructions*, 209 n. 27; see a perceptive discussion of this issue in A. Kenny, *Reason and Religion: Essays in Philosophical Theology* (Oxford 1987) at Chapter 7, "Grace and Freedom in St John Chrysostom", 103-120.

[57] Kenny, *Reason and Religion*, 110.

[58] *Cat. 1-8, hom.* 4.11 12-16: εἰ τοίνυν προλαβὼν τοσαῦτα ἐδωρήσατο, εἰ τὰ παρ' ἑαυτῶν μετὰ τοσαύτας δωρεὰς εἰσενεγκεῖν σπουδάσετε καὶ μετὰ τῆς φυλακῆς τῶν ἤδη παρασχεθέντων καὶ πολιτείας ἀκρίβειαν ἐπιδείξεσθε, πῶς οὐ μείζονος πάλιν ἀξιωθήσεσθε τῆς φιλοτιμίας;

largesse.[59] It is this mode of γνώμη that makes possible our willingness to bring our contribution and thus receive even more endowments. The fourth homily in this series is similar: the neophytes are exhorted to show enthusiasm (προθυμία) appropriate to the greatness of God's gifts already provided. This response from a well-disposed mindset (εὐγνώμονας) brings even more gifts. Chrysostom remarks here that God's reaction to such a mindset is to lavish his gifts upon us κἂν μικρόν τι εἰσενέγκωμεν ("even if what we contribute is small").[60] In another occurrence in this fourth homily, where Chrysostom lists the things that made up Paul's contribution, there is something similar. The Apostle Paul is held up as a model of response to the lavish expenditure of God in displaying τὴν γνώμην τὴν ἀκατάπληκτον ("an unruffled mindset"),[61] that is, one never astonished at the adverse circumstances of life. Other occurrences of γνώμη and its cognates in these homilies, though not directly associated with the τὰ παρ' ἑαυτῶν phrase, reinforce this pattern: God lavishes his bounty upon us; he expects the response of a well-disposed mindset so that he can pour out more gifts.[62] It appears that Chrysostom thought that a rightly disposed γνώμη is the essence of the τὰ παρ' ἑαυτῶν εἰσφέρειν, the things of our own with which we are to respond to our loving and generous God.

Turning to other parts of the corpus of Chrysostom's recorded homilies and writings, an illuminating use of the term is found in a homily on Genesis in a comment on Noah. There, according to Chrysostom, Noah gave direction to his thinking to focus on God and ignored those who mocked him. Chrysostom suggests that Noah "got the better of everyone because he had displayed his own contribution and attracted the grace that comes from above".[63] The participle ἐπισπασάμενος, which I have translated as "attracted", has the idea of dragging out or drawing forth. Hill translates it as "winning",[64] perhaps a little strong for the term, introducing an image that is not inherent in it. However, there is little doubt of Chrysostom's emphasis upon the need for the person to order his/her attitude in

---

[59] *Cat. 1-8, hom.* 2.1 10-13: εἰ μετὰ τὴν τοσαύτην φιλοτιμίαν εὐγνώμονες γενόμενοι τὰ παρ' ἑαυτῶν εἰσενεγκεῖν βουληθείητε, πόσης ὑμᾶς εἰκὸς ἀξιωθῆναι παρὰ τοῦ φιλανθρώπου Θεοῦ τῆς ἀμοιβῆς; ("after such great honour and you became rightminded, if you want to bring your own contribution, how great is the likelihood that you would be thought worthy of reward from our benevolent God?")

[60] *Cat. 1-8, hom.* 4.6 6-10.

[61] *Cat. 1-8, hom.* 4.10 10-17.

[62] *Cat. 1-8, hom.* 1.15 8-10, 1.18 9-12, 1.25 8-14, 2.14 12, 4.29 9-13, 5.18 5, 5.23 11-14, 5.24 1-4 and 8-11, 8.8 3-4.

[63] *In Gen. hom.* 23; PG 53,200 2: Τὰ γὰρ παρ' ἑαυτοῦ ἐπιδειξάμενος, καὶ τὴν ἄνωθεν χάριν ἐπισπασάμενος ἀνώτερος ἁπάντων ἐγίνετο·

[64] Hill, *Chrysostom, Homilies on Genesis 18-45*, 93.

a manner that would not only make it receptive to the overtures of grace, but that would also actually draw grace out from God. This passage on Noah also provides an important link between "our contribution" and the γνώμη. In this homily, Chrysostom continues to sing the praises of Noah as the one who "found grace in the eyes of the one who haunts the heart and who approved his γνώμη".[65] It is the γνώμη that provides our contribution. God visits the heart to ascertain the condition of the γνώμη to see if it is suitable to receive or attract his grace.

A significant variation of the formula appears in his homily thirty-two on Genesis. In summing up the lessons to be learned from the trials experienced by Abraham, Chrysostom points to the faithfulness of God, faithfulness available upon a certain condition. That condition is ἐὰν τὰ εἰς δύναμιν τὴν ἡμετέραν εἰσενέγκωμεν, which translates: "if we contribute the things within our power".[66] The clause is an expansion of the formula already noted and provides a further important window into Chrysostom's thinking. The emphatic "our power" verifies the claim that an application of our autonomy is required. There are certain things in our power that need to be applied if God's providence is to smile on us. Those things are listed in the text as ὑπομονὴν ("endurance"), καρτερίαν ("patience"), and εὐχάριστον γνώμην ("thankful mindset"). Again, the γνώμη is listed as being an important part of the contribution that is to be made from our own resources. In addition, it should be noted that endurance (ὑπομονή) and patient perseverance (καρτερία) are attitudinal states that are modal aspects of a person's mindset, the γνώμη.

In another homily on Genesis there is a passage discussing the Ethiopian eunuch in which the point is made that if we give evidence of applying all that is within our power, we will then receive grace from above.[67] Here the shortened formula, τὰ παρ' ἑαυτοῦ, and an element of the expanded form, τὰ εἰς δύναμιν, are brought together in an emphatic assertion of the required condition for receiving

---

[65] *In Gen. hom.* 23; PG 53,200 7-10: ἀλλὰ πρὸς ἐκεῖνον τὸν τὰς καρδίας ἐμβατεύοντα χάριν εὗρε, καὶ ἐκεῖνος αὐτοῦ τὴν γνώμην ἀπεδέξατο. See my discussion of this passage above in Chapter 2, "Discerning the γνώμη: Chrysostom, Theologian of the Mindset".

[66] *In Gen. hom.* 32; PG 53,305 12-14: Μὴ γὰρ, ἐὰν τὰ εἰς δύναμιν τὴν ἡμετέραν εἰσενέγκωμεν, τὴν ὑπομονὴν λέγω, καὶ τὴν καρτερίαν, καὶ τὴν εὐχάριστον γνώμην, συγχωρεῖ περιοφθῆναι ἡμᾶς ποτε; ("For if we contribute the things within our power, I mean endurance, patience and a thankful mindset, he never allows you to be disregarded, does he?")

[67] *In Gen. hom.* 35; PG 53,322 35-38: Οὐδὲν τούτων ἐλογίσατο ὁ βάρβαρος μὲν τὴν γλῶσσαν, φιλόσοφος δὲ τὴν διάνοιαν· ἀλλ' ἐννοήσας ὡς οὐ περιοφθήσεται, ἀλλὰ ταχέως ἀπολαύσει τῆς ἄνωθεν ῥοπῆς, εἰ τὰ παρ' ἑαυτοῦ καὶ τὰ εἰς δύναμιν ἐπιδείξαιτο, εἴχετο τῆς ἀναγνώσεως ("The foreigner, a lover of wisdom, counted these things nothing, both the language and the thought; but because he had reflected that if he demonstrated his own things, those within his power, he would not be disregarded, but swiftly would have the enjoyment of favour from above, he held fast to reading [the Scriptures]").

grace. This emphasis is strengthened by what follows in which we have a very clear statement of Chrysostom's thinking.[68] The assertion is made that God waits for the human contribution before giving his assistance. In the text πρότερον is significant. The person brings her/his share first and then divine assistance is displayed. In the eunuch's case, the cause of the appearance of the angel of the Lord to Philip with the message to go to the road on which the eunuch was travelling is identified by Chrysostom as the completion of all of what he had within his power to contribute. Three times in this passage the formula τὰ παρ' ἑαυτοῦ is used as Chrysostom strives to drive home this point. Chrysostom points to the motive of the eunuch for the journey he made to Jerusalem as evidence of the pious condition of his γνώμη.[69] In this case Chrysostom counsels his congregation that the particular contribution that constitutes sufficient evidence to God of a pious and well-disposed mindset is the giving of themselves to read the scriptures. This the eunuch had done. Chrysostom infers by this that the journey had been undertaken to gain understanding of the scriptures. This, then, must be one significant way he thought that the preparation of the γνώμη occurs.

The consistency of Chrysostom's thought on this issue is evident throughout the corpus of his writings. Chrysostom, commenting on Noah's claustrophobic experience in the ark in company with the animals, asserts that the abundance of divine assistance enjoyed by Noah was the result of his bringing τὰ παρ' αὐτοῦ πάντα εἰσήνεγκε ("all that he could contribute").[70] That contribution is described as "the steeliness of his mindset, the steadiness of his choice, and the faith which he displayed in God".[71] From Chrysostom's first homily on second Timothy, we find that though the spirit of power and of love for God is a gift of his grace, there is the prior requirement of our contribution.[72] In the following homily, in a

---

[68] *In Gen. hom.* 35; PG 53,322 41-46: Σὺ δέ μοι σκόπει τὴν τοῦ Θεοῦ σοφίαν, πῶς ἔμενεν ἐκεῖνον πρότερον τὰ παρ' ἑαυτοῦ εἰσενεγκεῖν, καὶ τότε τὴν οἰκείαν ἀντίληψιν ἐπιδείκνυται. Ἐπεὶ οὖν τὰ παρ' ἑαυτοῦ πάντα ἀπήρτιστο, λοιπὸν ὤφθη ὁ ἄγγελος Κυρίου λέγων τῷ Φιλίππῳ ("Consider with me the wisdom of God, how he was waiting first for that one [the eunuch] to bring his own contribution, and then he displayed his own giving in return. Therefore, after the eunuch had completed all of his contribution, finally, the angel of the Lord was seen speaking to Philip.")

[69] *In Gen. hom.* 35; PG 53,322 58-59: Ὅρα καὶ τὴν πρόφασιν αὐτοῦ τῆς ἀποδημίας, ἱκανὴν οὖσαν δεῖξαι τὸ φιλόθεον αὐτοῦ τῆς γνώμης ("See also the motive for his journey abroad, which is sufficient to show the piety of his mindset").

[70] *In Gen. hom.* 26; PG 53,237 31-32.

[71] *In Gen. hom.* 26; PG 53,237 28-30: αὐτοῦ τῆς γνώμης τὸ στερρὸν, καὶ τὸ ἀκλινὲς τῆς προαιρέσεως, καὶ τὴν πίστιν ἣν περὶ τὸν Θεὸν ἐπεδείκνυτο.

[72] *In 2 Tim. hom.* 1; PG 62,603 51-52: Ἀλλὰ σοὶ ἔδωκε τοὐναντίον πνεῦμα δυνάμεως καὶ ἀγάπης τῆς εἰς αὐτόν. Ἆρα καὶ τοῦτο ἀπὸ χάριτός ἐστιν, ἀλλ' οὐχ ἁπλῶς ἀπὸ χάριτος, ἀλλ' ὅταν καὶ ἡμεῖς πρότεροι ἐπιδειξώμεθα τὰ παρ' ἑαυτῶν ("But, inversely, to you he [God] gave a spirit of

passage emphasising that the endowment of the power of the Spirit is all God's work, he again refers to this principle in pointing to Cornelius who received the Spirit because he had made his own contribution of faith.[73] Cornelius is presented as a shining example in this sermon, the purpose of which Chrysostom states, is to "set right your mindset (γνώμη) and make you more steadfast for the future".[74] Here, our contribution is said to depend upon the rightly disposed γνώμη.

Further evidence of Chrysostom's position is found in Homily 42 on Genesis. In a passage commenting on Abraham's immediate and total obedience, the assertion is made that the daily help the patriarch received from God was the consequence of the effort he exerted. Again we find the phrase τὰ παρ' ἑαυτοῦ εἰσέφερε, "he brought his own contribution".[75] Chrysostom employs this example to exhort his hearers to practise every virtue so that they too might be rewarded. Three times in this paragraph, we find Chrysostom suggesting that we must supply something if we are to experience the help of God. Yet it is not merely effort itself that is rewarded; God, says Chrysostom, knows our thoughts and he supplies assistance to us when he sees the evidence of a healthy γνώμη.[76] Chrysostom

---

power and of love for him. Naturally, this is from grace, but not simply from grace, but at the time when we, first, shall display our own contribution").

[73] *In 2 Tim. hom.* 2; PG 62,612 52-55: Οὕτω τὸ πᾶν τῆς Πίστεώς ἐστιν. Ἐπεπήδησεν εὐθέως τὸ πνεῦμα ἐπὶ Κορνήλιον, ἐπειδὴ προλαβὼν τὰ παρ' ἑαυτοῦ ἐπεδείξατο, καὶ τὴν πίστιν εἰσήνεγκε ("Thus the whole work depends on faith. The Spirit immediately descended upon Cornelius, because having anticipated [God's favour] he displayed his own portion and brought his faith").

[74] *In 2 Tim. hom.* 2; PG 62,612 58-61: Ταῦτα τοίνυν εἰδότες οὐδὲ γὰρ ἁπλῶς εἴρηται ἡμῖν ταῦτα πάντα, ἀλλ' ἵνα διορθώσωμεν ὑμῶν τὴν γνώμην, καὶ ἀσφαλεστέρους εἰς τὸ ἑξῆς ἐργασώμεθα), πολλὴν τῶν εἰρημένων τὴν φυλακὴν ἐπιδείξασθε.

[75] *In Gen. hom.* 42; PG 54,385 47-49: Εἶδες πῶς ἐξ ἀρχῆς καὶ ἐκ προοιμίων τὰ παρ' ἑαυτοῦ εἰσέφερε, καὶ διὰ τοῦτο καὶ τὰ παρὰ τοῦ Θεοῦ καθ' ἑκάστην ἐκαρποῦτο μετὰ πολλῆς τῆς δαψιλείας; ("Do you see how from the beginning, even from the prelude, that he brought his own contribution, and because of this he bore fruit regularly in great abundance from God's contribution?")

[76] *In Gen. hom.* 42; PG 54,385 56-386 8: Ὁ γὰρ τὰ ἀπόρρητα τῆς διανοίας ἡμῶν ἐπιστάμενος, ἐπειδὰν ἴδῃ ὑγιῆ γνώμην ἐπιδεικνυμένους, καὶ πρὸς τοὺς τῆς ἀρετῆς ἀγῶνας ἀποδύεσθαι ἐσπουδακότας, παραχρῆμα καὶ τὴν παρ' ἑαυτοῦ παρέχει ῥοπήν, ὁμοῦ καὶ τοὺς πόνους ἡμῖν ἐπικουφίζων, καὶ τὸ ἀσθενὲς τῆς ἡμετέρας φύσεως ἐπιρρωννὺς, καὶ δαψιλεῖς τὰς ἀμοιβὰς χορηγῶν ("For when the one who understands our secret thoughts sees us demonstrating a healthy mindset in having made haste to strip for the contests of virtue, instantly, from his own contribution, he pours in the decisive propensity, as well as making our toils less burdensome, adding strength to the weakness of our nature, and bestowing an abundance of recompence"). A. Kenny, *Reason and Religion*, 108, makes a pertinent comment on ῥοπή: "ῥοπή meant a weight which tilted a balance to one side or the other. If this metaphor is to be taken seriously, we must say that, for Chrysostom, God's influence is decisive but by no means prevenient. He seems to picture the matter thus: our good will and the difficulty of doing good, are in different pans of a

adapts an image from the Olympic Games in order to suggest what makes a healthy γνώμη: it is one that hastens to strip for the contests of virtue. The condition of the γνώμη is critical in the reciprocal relationship that Chrysostom describes as being between God and humans: it is at the heart of the human contribution and therefore an expression of personal autonomy.

IV. Deliberated choice – προαίρεσις

Another facet of autonomy and freedom arises in the passage from the Titus homilies considered above. This is the element of deliberated choice that is a salient feature of Chrysostom's understanding of the divine-human relationship. Here the term αἵρεσις, choice, occurs. We encounter in αἵρεσις a term with a history in philosophical discussion that probably evolved from the common usage of the cognate verb, αἵρεω, to grasp, to become established in a technical sense as choice. This was preserved in the cognate term προαίρεσις, a term that had a significant place in Aristotle and a central place in Epictetus' ethics.[77] Bobzien argues that

> ...for Epictetus, προαίρεσις does not refer to a person's particular choice in a certain situation. First and foremost he uses the term to denote a disposition of the human mind which determines a person's individual choices.[78]

This implies that the intellectual deliberation expressed by Aristotle was incorporated by Epictetus in his use of the term. Long is definite on this when he asserts: "it [the προαίρεσις] is God's special gift of a rational, self-scrutinising, and motivating faculty".[79] Bobzien, however, suggests that Epictetus moved the focus from actions to choices, and asserted that choices are not subject to external compulsion but are dependent upon the προαίρεσις as defined as a disposition. In

---

balance. They are more or less in equilibrium; but God's ῥοπή comes and tilts the balance over to the right side." Hence my translation rendered here as "decisive propensity".

[77] Inwood, *Ethics and Human Action*, 240-242; Dobbin, "Προαίρεσις in Epictetus", 114, asserts: "Thus Aristotle assigns προαίρεσις a privileged position, one that it will continue to occupy in the philosophical tradition".

[78] Bobzien, *Determinism and Freedom*, 406; Brennan, "Stoic moral psychology", 292 n. 71, on Epictetus wrote: "*prohairesis*, I believe means one's own soul or *hêgemonikon* considered as the totality of one's disposition to assent"; Long, *Epictetus*, 207, claims: "But however *prohairesis* is translated, it is Epictetus' favourite name for the purposive and self-conscious centre of a person".

[79] Long, *Epictetus*, 211.

this, the emphasis is upon moral responsibility for our choices, not merely for our actions.[80] Then, Alexander of Aphrodisias combined the Aristotelian element of deliberate choice with the Epictetan/Platonic (Middle-Platonist) concept of responsible voluntary moral choice.[81]

In all of this, what is missing is a concept of will as now understood. R. Sorabji asserts that the concept of will evolved only gradually from Plato through to its full bloom in the Latin theologian, Augustine.[82] Others propose that there was no concept of an autonomous free will among the Greeks until after the third century CE, when Platonists and Christians were intent on resolving the presence of evil in a world created by and providentially directed by God.[83] J. O'Keefe goes even further in suggesting that the Cappadocian theologian, Gregory of Nyssa, could not enunciate a coherent explanation of sin because of a lack of such a concept.[84] Sorabji discerns in θυμός, as used by Plato, some suggestions of willpower but without any connection to freedom or moral responsibility.[85] Although the later Platonists such as Plotinus, and even Gregory of Nyssa made some connections that looked promising, Sorabji cannot find any substantial discussion that includes a full theory of the will before Augustine in the West and Maximus the Confessor in the East.[86]

This lacuna in the Greek philosophical tradition raises serious questions about the patristic theologians of the fourth century, of whom most, if not all, came through the Greek *paideia* before embarking upon their Christian ministries. Of first importance is the need to be assured that a true understanding of the will was in their possession. As indicated above, some have grave doubts. If the answer to that question is "no", then what is to be made of the many references in the Greek Fathers to will, self-determination and the insistence upon the authority that lies in the power of the human soul? Does, for example, the term προαίρεσις which

---

[80] Bobzien, *Determinism and Freedom*, 403.

[81] Bobzien, *Determinism and Freedom*, 402-403. Section 8.7, of this work, "The rise and fall of the problem to do otherwise and causal determination", 396-412, is a valuable discussion of this development.

[82] Sorabji, *Emotion and Peace of Mind*, 319. His discussion of the concept of the will, 319-340, is perceptive and balanced.

[83] Bobzien, *Determinism and Freedom*, 412; Price, "Aristotle, the Stoics and the will", 46: "Thus volitions appear to be absent from Greek philosophy, even where it looked most promising to find them."

[84] J.J. O'Keefe, "Sin, ἀπάθεια and freedom of the will in Gregory of Nyssa", *SP* 22 (1989) 52-59, at 52.

[85] Sorabji, *Emotion and Peace of Mind*, 323; Plato, *Republic*, 440.b. Sorabji also sees some possibilities in the *Republic* at 617.e. in reference to the use of choice (αἵρεσθαι), along with freedom and responsibility.

[86] Sorabji, *Emotion and Peace of Mind*, 324-325.

looked rather promising, unfold in the hands of the Fathers into a full bloom of free will? Or does it remain static in signification, or perhaps fade in comparison to another? J.N.D. Kelly asserted that all the Greek Fathers of the fourth century agreed that the human will remained free in spite of the Fall, and that we are responsible for our deeds, a position held in opposition to the Manichaeans.[87] Nevertheless, the questions remain, and an examination of Chrysostom's usage may be of assistance here.

Chrysostom made wide use of προαίρεσις. To take just three of his major works we find fifty-three references in his homilies on Genesis, thirty-eight in the Matthew homilies and thirty-nine in the Romans homilies. It is evident, especially given the history of the philosophical tradition of this term, that he saw it as important. In this regard, one may do no better than cite E. Nowak whose work on this term in Chrysostom is something of a benchmark:

> This is then a word of wide usage, loaded with philosophical resonances, which John uses for explaining his thought on the origin of evil. One should investigate some texts in order to grasp the nature and role of this προαίρεσις which is of essential importance to his work.[88]

For the purposes of this study, it will be sufficient to examine the usage in a small number of these occurrences. Chrysostom understood the προαίρεσις to belong to that class of internal powers or faculties that are autonomous. In a number of places it is presented as free, that is not bound by necessity. In a comment on Romans 2:8, Chrysostom is adamant that there is no defence before the final tribunal for those who without any force or tyrannising flee from the light to darkness, whose fall is of their own moral choice (προαίρεσις). No necessity is involved; the προαίρεσις is free to choose.[89] In the text, the term ἀπολογία, "defence", points to the presence of moral responsibility. In this instance, the προαίρεσις would be operating in flagrant opposition to the truth. In another homily where Chrysostom calls for a proper attitude toward afflictions and troubles, such as the unavoidable death of a son or the loss of property, he calls for

---

[87] J.N.D. Kelly, *Early Christian Doctrines* (London 1968[4]) 352.

[88] Nowak, *Le Chrétien devant la souffrance*, 61. Translation from the French is mine.

[89] *In Rom. hom.* 5; PG 60,425 51-55: Ἰδοὺ καὶ ἑτέρα κατηγορία πάλιν. Ποίαν γὰρ ἀπολογίαν ἂν ἔχοι ὁ τὸ φῶς φεύγων, καὶ τὸ σκότος αἱρούμενος; Καὶ οὐκ εἶπε, Βιαζομένους καὶ τυραννουμένους, ἀλλά, Πειθομένους τῇ ἀδικίᾳ· ἵνα μάθῃς, ὅτι προαιρέσεως τὸ πτῶμα, οὐκ ἀνάγκης τὸ ἔγκλημα ("See again another accusation. What sort of defence could a person have who is fleeing from the light and is choosing the darkness? He [Paul] does not say, being constrained and living under absolute rule, but 'being persuaded by injustice'; this is so that you may learn that the fall is a matter of moral choice, and that the crime is not one of necessity.")

his people to "let us make the thing of necessity to be one of our own choice".[90]
This is done in the situation by turning from the use of words of distress to those
of thanksgiving. Thus evil things which come to us undesirably (ἀβουλήτως) may
be transformed into freely chosen (προαιρέσεως) good deeds. Here προαίρεσις is
seen as autonomous by being set over against ἀνάγκη, necessity. In short,
Chrysostom would have us believe that an inner freedom overcomes any external
circumstances forced upon us. In an extended comment on Romans 8:7, there is a
passage that speaks of the gift of the grace of the Spirit. Chrysostom points out
that this "gift was not placed in us as a necessity of nature, but our freedom of
choice put it into our hands".[91] Here the freedom of the προαίρεσις is explicit with
ἐλευθερία (freedom) being given as its attribute. This is applied powerfully in the
text where, in a rhetorical parison, he presses home the peril of this responsible
freedom being used for self-imposed ruin: Εἰ δὲ σὺ τὸ φῶς σβεννύεις, τὸν ἡνίοχον
ἐκβάλλεις, καὶ τὸν κυβερνήτην ἐλαύνεις, σαυτῷ λογίζου λοιπὸν τὸ κλυδώνιον ("If
you quench the light, throw out the charioteer, and expel the pilot, then reckon the
wave [of passion] to your own responsibility").[92] Perhaps the most unambiguous
statement of the freedom of the προαίρεσις is made in a homily on 1 Timothy
where Chrysostom enumerates the things God does, and those his power enables
us to do for others in imitation of God in his service.

> I (God) formed the substance; you, beautify the faculty of choice. See how I love
> you and gave you power in the greater things. Beloved, look how much we have
> been honoured! Some who are unreasonable and arrogant say, "Why are we in
> control of our choice?" In all these things, as many as we have listed, in which
> we are able to imitate God, if there were no choice then it would not be possible
> for us to imitate him.[93]

From this, we see that Chrysostom held that the προαίρεσις is one of the greater
faculties: that it is a vital part of the autonomy given by God to human beings; that
its intended function is to operate in a way that its freedom is used to mould us
into God-likeness; that it is, like the late-Stoic προαίρεσις, teleologically oriented;

---

[90] In Rom. hom. 9; PG 60,473 25-27: Ταῦτα οὖν ἐννοοῦντες, ὃ τῆς ἀνάγκης ἐστί, ποιῶμεν τῆς
προαιρέσεως εἶναι τῆς ἡμετέρας·
[91] In Rom. hom. 13; PG 60,517 1-3: Ἐπειδὴ γὰρ οὐκ ἀνάγκη φύσεως τὸ δῶρον ἐνέθηκεν, ἀλλ'
ἐλευθερίᾳ προαιρέσεως ἐνεχείρισεν.
[92] In Rom. hom. 13; PG 60,517 8-10.
[93] In 1 Tim. hom. 15; PG 62,586 15-22: Ἐγὼ τὴν οὐσίαν εἰργασάμην· σὺ καλλώπισον τὴν
προαίρεσιν. Ὅρα πῶς σε φιλῶ, καὶ ἐν τοῖς μείζοσί σοι ἔδωκα τὴν ἰσχύν. Ὁρᾶτε, ἀγαπητοί, πῶς
τετιμήμεθα· καί τινες τῶν ἀλογίστων καὶ ἀγνωμόνων λέγουσι, Διὰ τί τῆς προαιρέσεώς ἐσμεν
κύριοι; Ταῦτα πάντα ὅσα διήλθομεν, ἐν οἷς δυνάμεθα μιμεῖσθαι τὸν Θεόν, εἰ μὴ προαίρεσις ἦν,
οὐκ ἂν ἦν ἡμῖν δυνατὸν μιμήσασθαι.

that it is our task to beautify it, that is to use it, and to persuade others to use it, as God intended, to make the right choices toward the destiny of our true beauty; and that it is invested with the power and autonomy to realise that destiny.[94] This is a complete picture of true free-will, containing the three elements looked for in such, i.e., freedom or control over internal motions (κύριος), responsibility (καλλωπίζω), and power (ἰσχύς and δυνατός). In a homily that covers Romans 8:12-27, in which he calls upon his people to address their lack of care for the poor, he brings his sermon to a conclusion by exhorting his people to draw the great physician, God, to their aid in seeking healing for this disorder. All God asks, he says, is that we bring to him the things that are ours, that is our προαίρεσις and our προθυμία.[95] What is interesting here is the coupling of προαίρεσις with προθυμία, eagerness, a term indicative of energy, suggesting therefore that not only is the προαίρεσις related to power in terms of self-determination, but also to power in terms of energy. This, as in the Timothy homily, supplies the will-power perspective noted as missing from the Greek philosophical hypotheses.

Much more could be said about Chrysostom's usage of προαίρεσις, but it is not the point of this study to give a full description. Rather the need is to discern the relationship of the προαίρεσις to the γνώμη in his anthropology or psychology and correlate that with the larger question of the locus of a principle of sin in the psyche. Before comparing προαίρεσις with γνώμη, it is well to note that the προαίρεσις, as one would expect of true free choice, is able to make evil choices as well as good ones.[96]

Both προαίρεσις and γνώμη are used independently in many places in the homilies. Much may be learned from these about their functions, but it is when they are used together that the distinction in their respective significations becomes apparent. Even where placed together they often look to be rhetorical synonyms so that it is difficult to discern between them. For example in an explanation of Romans 11:23 about the Jews, as natural branches, being cut off from the true olive tree of chosen Israel, Chrysostom, asserting that they cut

---

[94] Wilken, "Biblical humanism", 20-21: "More often, however, Gregory (of Nyssa) speaks of human freedom as moral freedom, the freedom to become what we were made to be. Freedom, as he puts it, is 'the royal exercise of the will', but will is much more than choice, more than deciding to do one thing in preference to another. It is an affair of ordering one's life in terms of its end, freedom oriented toward excellence (the original meaning of virtue) and human flourishing."

[95] *In Rom. hom.* 14; PG 60,540 27-32: Ἐπισπασώμεθα τοίνυν αὐτὸν, καὶ παρακαλέσωμεν συνεφάψασθαι, καὶ τὰ παρ' ἡμῶν συνεισενέγκωμεν, προαίρεσιν λέγω καὶ προθυμίαν ("Therefore, let us draw him in and call upon him to lay hold with us, and let us together bring our own contribution, I mean our choice and our eagerness").

[96] *In Rom. hom.* 16; PG 60,558 3-5; *hom.* 16; PG 60,561 21-25.

themselves off, points to the authority and autonomy of both the προαίρεσις and the γνώμη: "Do you see how great is the authority of the moral choice? How great is the authority of the mindset? For none of these things is immovable, neither your good nor his evil."[97] Although different terms are used, it appears impossible to distinguish any degrees of authority here. The point Chrysostom is making is that both Jews and Gentiles have the same autonomy attached to their choice and their mindset, and that both are fully responsible for the position in which they find themselves; hence the warning about their mutability. In another homily, Chrysostom argues that standing with someone in danger is different to standing with someone receiving honours; the former requires toil and labour, the latter much more, both προαίρεσις (choice) and γνώμη (mindset).[98] Elsewhere, both the choices and the mindsets of Patriarchs are commended in their offerings to God.[99]

There are passages in the homilies where these are terms used together in a way that makes the distinction between them clear. A definition of προαίρεσις is given by Chrysostom in an explanation of Romans 7:19-20 in the context of responsibility for sin. Leaving the sin issue aside for the moment, the definition shows plainly the relationship between these powers of the soul. There we find that the προαίρεσις is dependent upon the γνώμη for its operation:

> Do you see how, having discharged the substance (οὐσία) of the soul and the substance of the flesh of the accusation, he placed the whole of it instead upon the evil action. For if the soul does not will the evil, it has been acquitted, and if the person himself/herself does not effect it, the body also is set free, and the lot has its source in the evil moral choice (προαίρεσις) alone. The substance of the soul, the body and the moral choice are not the same, but the former two are the works of God, and the latter is a motion (κίνησις) happening from ourselves towards whatever we might desire it to go to. On one hand, desire (βούλησις) is natural and from God; but then, this kind of desire is ours and from our mindset (γνώμη).[100]

---

[97] *In Rom. hom.* 19; PG 60,590 29-32: Εἶδες ὅσον τῆς προαιρέσεως τὸ κῦρος; πόση τῆς γνώμης ἡ ἐξουσία; Οὐδὲν γὰρ τούτων ἀκίνητον, οὔτε τὸ σὸν καλὸν, οὔτε τὸ ἐκείνου κακόν.

[98] *In Rom. hom.* 7; PG 60,447 62-64.

[99] *In Gen. hom.* 27; PG 53,242 16; *hom.* 47; PG 54,431 41.

[100] *In Rom. hom.* 13; PG 60,510 19-29: Εἶδες πῶς καὶ τὴν οὐσίαν τῆς ψυχῆς, καὶ τὴν οὐσίαν τῆς σαρκὸς ἀπαλλάξας ἐγκλήματος, τὸ πᾶν ἐπὶ τὴν πονηρὰν πρᾶξιν μετέστησεν; Εἰ γὰρ οὐ θέλει τὸ κακὸν, ἀπήλλακται ἡ ψυχὴ, καὶ εἰ αὐτὸς αὐτὸ μὴ κατεργάζεται, ἠλευθέρωται καὶ τὸ σῶμα, καὶ μόνης τῆς πονηρᾶς προαιρέσεώς ἐστι τὸ πᾶν. Οὐ γὰρ ταυτὸν ψυχῆς οὐσία καὶ σώματος καὶ προαιρέσεως, ἀλλὰ τὰ μέν ἐστιν ἔργα Θεοῦ, τὸ δὲ ἐξ ἡμῶν αὐτῶν γινομένη κίνησις, πρὸς ὅπερ ἂν αὐτὴν βουληθῶμεν ἀγαγεῖν. Ἡ μὲν γὰρ βούλησις, ἔμφυτον καὶ παρὰ Θεοῦ· ἡ δὲ τοιάδε βούλησις, ἡμέτερον καὶ τῆς γνώμης ἡμῶν.

Here, in the context of sin, desire, βούλησις, is seen to issue from the γνώμη. Chrysostom is asserting that desire in itself is a neutral faculty as being a natural (ἔμφυτος) endowment from God. However, in practice it is controlled by the γνώμη, the mindset, and thus may be good or evil dependent upon the disposition of the γνώμη. The προαίρεσις is defined as a motion from ourselves towards an object of desire, which denotes that it is a preferred choice that has been made and is in motion. It is then referred to as "this kind of βούλησις" issuing from the γνώμη. Thus the προαίρεσις is a form of chosen desire that has its source in the γνώμη. If προαίρεσις retains anything from its tradition of deliberated choice, and I have no doubt that it did so for Chrysostom,[101] then either that deliberation has taken place in the γνώμη or at least is stored in the γνώμη.

In one of the Genesis homilies Chrysostom asserts that virtue and vice are to be found in the moral choice (προαίρεσις) of the mindset (γνώμη).[102] A contrast is made in the context of this passage between Abraham and Nachor in that they were brothers as far as nature was concerned, but in the choices they made they revealed vastly different mindsets. In an earlier homily, Chrysostom offers an explanation about the offerings of Cain and Abel by pointing to the difference in mindset (γνώμη) between the brothers.[103] That difference was seen in the choice (προαίρεσις) of offerings that were made. Cain's choice is described as indifferent, listless, apathetic (ῥάθυμος), thus revealing a mindset far removed from what God approves. In the passage in which this text is set the comment is made that "he [God] wants us to show our rightmindedness (εὐγνωμοσύνη) through these things

---

[101] W. Telfer (ed.), *Cyril of Jerusalem and Nemesius of Emesa* (Philadelphia 1955) 215, makes a comment about Nemesius of Emesa that is apposite to Chrysostom: "He no longer strives to maintain the consistency of the thought-world he left behind, for he sees it as a building, but as ruins. But that does not mean the abandonment of all his past studies. They become material, in as far as he finds them still sound and tenable, fit to contribute to a structure whose inspiration is new." Telfer claims that the essential outlines of Nemesius' treatise, *On Human Nature*, is a faithful representation "of the Christian outlook characteristic of the heyday of the Antiochene school"; F.G. McLeod, "Theodore of Mopsuestia revisited", *Theological Studies* 61(2000) 447-480 at 447, remarks that Nemesius was a contemporary of Theodore and that his work "is considered to be a reflection of the Antiochene tradition".

[102] *In Gen. hom.* 31; PG 53,290 65-67: Εἶδες πῶς οὐκ ἐν τῇ φύσει, ἀλλ' ἐν τῇ προαιρέσει τῆς γνώμης τῆς ἡμετέρας κεῖται καὶ τὰ τῆς ἀρετῆς, καὶ τὰ τῆς κακίας; ("Do you see how the things of virtue and evil lay not in nature, but in the moral choice of our mindset?")

[103] *In Gen. hom.* 18; PG 53,155 28-30: ἀλλ' ἡ διαφορὰ τῆς γνώμης λοιπὸν καὶ τῆς προαιρέσεως ἡ ῥαθυμία τοῦ μὲν εὐπρόσδεκτον ἐποίησε τὴν προσαγωγὴν, τοῦ δὲ ἀπόβλητον ("But, finally, the difference of the mindset and the indifference of the choice made the offering of one acceptable and of the other to be despised as worthless").

[offerings]".[104] The emphasis is upon the rightly disposed γνώμη that is expressed in the προαίρεσις. Earlier in this same homily, Chrysostom gives us something like God's *modus operandi*: "our Lord does not acknowledge difference of appearances, but on the basis of scrutinising the moral choice (προαίρεσις) crowns the mindset (γνώμη)".[105] This is then unpacked in his homily as noted above.[106] Elsewhere in the Genesis homilies Seth is said to have had the privilege of the firstborn, not his naturally, transferred to him διὰ τὴν τῆς προαιρέσεως εὐγνωμοσύνην ("on account of the rightmindedness of his choice"),[107] a feature Chrysostom then repeated to drive home his point, διὰ τὴν τῆς προαιρέσεως γνώμην ("the mindset of his choice").[108] It is evident that in Chrysostom's anthropology, the γνώμη stands behind the προαίρεσις as its ruling principle. The moral choice is an expression of the mindset.

Before leaving the προαίρεσις, it is necessary to ask why this term has been given prominence rather than γνώμη in commentators on the works of the Fathers prior to those of Maximus the Confessor. As mentioned above in Chapter 1, the Introduction, Demetrios Trakatellis and Christopher Hall do this very thing. Trakatellis in his survey of themes in Chrysostom's Romans' homilies has a section devoted to προαίρεσις, which he asserts "is for Chrysostom the very core of ἄνθρωπος".[109] Trakatellis makes some good points, but when noting the passage applying to Romans 7:19-20, he ignores the relationship to γνώμη, as discussed above in Chapter 4. The same applies to passages cited in regard to Romans 9:20, 22-23, where γνώμη figures frequently and significantly in Chrysostom's exegesis. It is appreciated that Trakatellos is not presenting a detailed coverage of Chrysostom's work, but it seems that the greater prominence given by Chrysostom to γνώμη, not only in the Romans' homilies but overall in his works, has escaped him. It is my opinion that γνώμη rather than προαίρεσις is the very core of ἄνθρωπος.

Christopher Hall, in his doctoral thesis on Chrysostom's *On Providence* (*Ad eos qui scandalizati sunt*), makes προαίρεσις the foundation of his approach even though the term appears only once in the document whereas γνώμη occurs eleven times, and its cognates, εὐγνωμοσύνη and ἀγνωμοσύνη twelve times between

---

[104] *In Gen. hom.* 18; PG 53,155 15-16: ἀλλὰ βούλεται καὶ διὰ τούτων δείκνυσθαι τὴν ἡμετέραν εὐγνωμοσύνην.

[105] *In Gen. hom.* 18; PG 53,154 38-40: ὅτι διαφορὰν προσώπων οὐκ οἶδεν ὁ Δεσπότης ὁ ἡμέτερος, ἀλλὰ ἐκ προαιρέσεως ἐξετάζων τὴν γνώμην στεφανοῖ.

[106] It should be noted that at *In Gen. hom.* 18; PG 53,155 39, Chrysostom varies this in that the προαίρεσις gets the crown. Nevertheless, there it is the γνώμη that is applauded.

[107] *In Gen. hom.* 20; PG 53,172 56-57.

[108] *In Gen. hom.* 20; PG 53,172 59.

[109] Trakatellis, "Being transformed", 216.

them.[110] It seems that Hall has given priority to the προαιρέσις due to his dependence upon the seminal work of Edward Nowak on Chrysostom's theology of suffering.[111] Hall certainly acknowledges the presence and importance of γνώμη and its cognates, which makes his presentation all the more intriguing. As Hall indicates, Nowak "explains Chrysostom's understanding of the mind's central role in the decision-making process of the προαίρεσις".[112] In this regard, Nowak notes the frequent coupling of γνώμη and προαίρεσις by Chrysostom:

> The second characteristic is the intellectual element which occurs with the decision of the προαίρεσις. Its choice is determined by the judgment which we bring upon things. This is the place at which the word γνώμη becomes visible as being used as an aspect of προαίρεσις. In this case, it seems that προαίρεσις stands as a sort of deconstruction [of nuances] analogous to those which come out when we translate it by *deliberated choice*, γνώμη being representative of the decision being supported upon grounds which clearly includes intellectual comprehension, and προαίρεσις the voluntary motion which makes the action to happen. Without doubt the προαίρεσις should not be confused with the knowledge of good and evil. God has entrusted this role to the conscience (συνειδός), but the προαίρεσις cannot occur apart from the cooperation of the intellect. Moral action with human beings belongs then to the προαίρεσις, which should nevertheless be founded upon the knowledge of the intellect for knowing what is good and what is evil.[113]

There is much in Nowak with which one must agree, dependence upon the γνώμη being the point in case. On the other hand there are some problems in this particular statement. In particular, Nowak makes the γνώμη an aspect (côté) of the προαίρεσις, thereby contradicting most of what he says in this paragraph about their relationship, that the προαίρεσις cannot operate without the intellectual element provided by the γνώμη.[114] The texts which he uses do not support his position, for all they say is that both the προαίρεσις and the γνώμη share the responsibility for evil.[115] He is reversing the order that Chrysostom appears to have held, that the προαίρεσις is an aspect of the γνώμη. Hall promotes προαίρεσις

---

[110] Hall, "John Chrysostom's 'On Providence'", 16.
[111] Nowak, *Le Chrétien devant la souffrance*, 62.
[112] Hall, "John Chrysostom's 'On Providence'", 21. By "mind's", Hall is referring to the frequent coupling of γνώμη with προαίρεσις by Chrysostom.
[113] Nowak, *Le Chrétien devant la souffrance*, 62. Translation from French is mine.
[114] Nowak, *Le Chrétien devant la souffrance*, 62: "C'est ici qu'apparaît le mot γνώμη, employé à côté de la προαίρεσις".
[115] *In Joan. hom.* 2; PG 59,37; *De diab. tent., hom.* 2; PG 49,261.

even though he too has much to say about γνώμη.[116] One excerpt is sufficient to illustrate:

> The essential point to grasp is that the indifferent things become good or bad according to the disposition (γνώμη) of the individual, which is in direct relation to how one will exercise the προαίρεσις or moral choice. Those who behave in a Christian manner or exercise Christian philosophy will make the right choice because their γνώμη and προαίρεσις have been molded by the Gospel.[117]

It is evident that Hall appreciates the importance of γνώμη in Chrysostom's anthropology. Yet, by giving προαίρεσις the dominant role in his presentation he has done two things: ignored the function of the γνώμη as principal; and he has collapsed into προαίρεσις functions, such as disposition, which Chrysostom viewed as belonging to the γνώμη. It is true that Chrysostom sometimes used the two terms synonymously, but in analysing his anthropological psychology, it is needful to maintain his distinction between them. In practice, it seems to me that Hall actually places γνώμη at the centre of his thesis on providence and suffering, thus contradicting his statement of methodological approach. This is evident in his comments on Chrysostom's treatment of Paul's attitude to his imprisonment as found in one of the homilies on Providence:

> Paul's perspective is shaped by the Gospel. Courage, boldness and perseverance are the result. The imprisonment itself is an indifferent thing. If Paul's perspective wasn't a mature one, he might well be suffering a great deal. But, Chrysostom insists, because he has a "φιλόσοφον γνώμην", an indifferent matter is turned to the good.[118]

Hall and Nowak make much of Chrysostom's statement in a homily on Colossians that appears to make the προαίρεσις the characteristic and therefore dominant faculty of human beings:

> For the choice (προαίρεσις) is more authoritative than the substance, and this rather than that is the person, for the choice (προαίρεσις) itself and not the substance casts one into hell or leads one into the kingdom; neither do we love nor hate anyone for being a person but for being such a kind of person.[119]

---

[116] Hall, "John Chrysostom's 'On Providence'", 22, 23, 34; 40-41, n. 85 includes a list of the γνώμη cognates used.

[117] Hall, "John Chrysostom's 'On Providence'", 34.

[118] Hall, "John Chrysostom's 'On Providence'", 37.

[119] *In Col. hom.* 8; PG 62,352 54-353 4: Τῆς γὰρ οὐσίας ἡ προαίρεσις κυριωτέρα, καὶ τοῦτο μᾶλλον ἄνθρωπος, ἢ ἐκεῖνο. Οὐ γὰρ ἡ οὐσία ἐμβάλλει εἰς γέενναν, οὐδὲ εἰς βασιλείαν εἰσάγει,

This statement needs to be understood in its immediate context where Chrysostom is explaining the meaning of ἄνθρωπος in relation to the language of the Apostle Paul who identifies sins with the person and their bodily parts. He points to the distinction Paul makes between the new humanity and the old humanity to show that no change has taken place in the substance of the person and their bodies, but in their preferred choices and actions. Thus, the real person is known by those features. Indeed, he argues that our judgement of others is made on that basis. Then, underlying this is the context of Chrysostom's theology that nature, including our God-created being, is not sinful but marked by nobility and essential dignity. This required him to deny the philosophies and ideologies that identified evil with the physical body and its appetites, such as Manichaeism and Neoplatonism with their dualism that saw the material world, especially the body, as inferior and subject to a pervasive corruption. Finally, this text should not be interpreted in isolation from the rest of his corpus in which the fuller picture of his anthropology comes to view. As indicated above, that picture, although it finds γνώμη and προαίρεσις working in concert, places γνώμη as a ruling principle to which the προαίρεσις is subject. I think that a text far more representative of Chrysostom's understanding of the distinctive feature of human beings is found in a comment on Romans 8:19-29:

> When he says that "it (creation) was not willingly made subject", it is not in order to show that it has independence of mindset (γνώμης), but that you may learn that the whole happened from the safekeeping of Christ, and was not an autonomous accomplishment.[120]

What is it that distinguishes humankind from the rest of creation? Chrysostom's answer is this: the independent, autonomous γνώμη. The προαίρεσις, though an important power in the soul in Chrysostom's anthropology, is dependent upon the γνώμη.

ἀλλ᾽ αὐτὴ ἡ προαίρεσις, καὶ οὐδένα οὔτε φιλοῦμεν, οὔτε μισοῦμεν ἢ ἄνθρωπος, ἀλλ᾽ ἢ τοιόσδε ἄνθρωπος.

[120] *In Rom. hom.* 14; PG 60,530 41-44: Ὅταν δὲ λέγῃ, *Οὐχ ἑκοῦσα ὑπετάγη*, οὐχ ἵνα κυρίαν γνώμης οὖσαν δείξῃ, τοῦτο λέγει, ἀλλ᾽ ἵνα μάθῃς, ὅτι τῆς τοῦ Χριστοῦ κηδεμονίας τὸ πᾶν ἐγένετο, οὐκ ἐκείνης κατόρθωμα τοῦτο.

V. Conclusion

This enquiry into human self-determination in Chrysostom's thought has demonstrated that all the capacities of the psyche to which he attached this autonomy are vitally related to the γνώμη. This applies to ἐφ' ἡμῖν, "up to us", which is identified with γνώμη in the homilies. The τὰ παρ' ἑαυτῶν εἰσφέρειν, our contribution, is seen to be dependent upon the state of the γνώμη and represented a crucial element of what is brought to God in the processes of salvation. The προαίρεσις, as deliberated moral choice, is somewhat of a partner in self-determination with the γνώμη. Nevertheless, important as it is in the paradigm of divine-human relationships, it is both derivative from and dependent upon the γνώμη. Direct and indirect application of the term αὐτεξούσιος, self-determining or autonomous, is made in a way that compels acknowledgement of the γνώμη as the master of those inner capacities that are the vehicles of expression of the feature that gives humankind its great dignity and unique position in the οἰκουμένη of God.

Before turning to the question of possible sources for Chrysostom's usage of γνώμη, there remains the need to discuss the critical feature of its capacity for development. In Chrysostom's homilies, the γνώμη is encountered in different modes: sometimes static and seemingly impossible to be moved; other times clearly readily subject to change. An examination of those states and the factors that enable that change is the task of the following chapter.

CHAPTER 6

Shaping the Γνώμη: The Decisive Responsibility

Τὸ πᾶν κειταῖ ἐν γνώμῃ

It has been demonstrated above that the γνώμη was a vital element in Chrysostom's anthropology. He understood it to be the ruling faculty of the psyche, the autonomous locus of determined policy, habits, and intentions. As it is the faculty that is continuously evaluated by God, its disposition is crucial in all the relationships of life. It is logical, with such an understanding of the operations of the soul, that Chrysostom would be committed to shaping, or rather re-shaping, the mindsets of his people. Indeed, he saw the church as a spiritual school, and his preaching as a significant vehicle of Christian education.[1] This points to the existence of an alternative *paideia* to that of the pagan Greek educational system, a Christian *paideia* that Frances Young calls: "a process of personal, social – indeed global – transformation effected by getting to know God and being reunited in the divine life".[2] A system of integrated intellectual, spiritual, moral and communal education was in place, particularly in the monastic movement, but also in the churches, in which the exegesis of Scripture was basic to the process.[3] The γνώμη was central to that process in Chrysostom's anthropology and in his

---

[1] *In Matt. hom.* 17; PG 57,264; Maxwell, *Christianization and Communication*, 88-117, discusses the importance of preaching as an educational tool in antiquity, and focuses upon Chrysostom's approach to it. See also Attrep, "The teacher and his teachings", 293-301; P. Allen, "The homilist and the congregation: a case-study of Chrysostom's homilies on Hebrews", *Augustinianum* (1996) 397-421 at 398; A. Hartney, "Men, women and money: John Chrysostom and the transformation of the city", *SP* 37 (1999) 527-534.

[2] F. Young, "Paideia and the myth of static dogma", in S. Coakley and D.A. Pailin (eds), *The Making and Remaking of Christian Doctrine: Essays in Honour of Maurice Wiles* (Oxford 1993) 265-282 at 281; see also Jaeger, *Early Christianity and Greek Paideia*, 86-102, who describes Gregory of Nyssa's ideas about a Christian *paideia*; Yazigi, "The eschatological pedagogy (παιδεία): the 'good'", 1-10, at 1-2 defines παιδεία as the instrument that forms the γνώμη and is the "bringing up" (ἀγωγή) and not merely the provision of knowledge. Available at http://www.aleppothodox.org/01-ar/90-news/90-news-2006/nov06-london_vst-lect2._Accessed 18 May 2007.

[3] Young, "Paideia and myth", 267, in a summary of Origen's approach states: "There is progressive transformation through the process and *paideia* takes place through the ministerial task of the church in the exegesis of scripture." A similar comment is made regarding Gregory of Nyssa at 273.

educational endeavours.[4] In order to grasp Chrysostom's usage of γνώμη in relation to sin and response, there is need to examine its capacity for development and the instruments that Chrysostom employed to condition it.

In a homily explaining the failure of the Jews to respond to the messianic claims of Jesus by his followers, Chrysostom claimed that the cause was due to the contention-loving condition of the Jews' γνώμη that was: "incurable and hard to alter".[5] This he derived from the metaphor of sleep, stupor or lethargy that is used in the text of Romans 11:8. He describes this lethargy as "the worst habit of the soul when it is in this incurable and unfeeling state".[6] Two things are of note here. First is the suggestion that the γνώμη is a habit (ἕξις) of the soul. It is the faculty in which habits are formed and solidified until they become salient features of a person's character.[7] The second thing is the development feature of the γνώμη as is implied in a habit. It is not a once for all fixed state but one that develops with time and experience. As this passage indicates, it may reach a state when it becomes fixed enough to be hard to alter, but that is down the track and not at the beginning. A third thing arises: if the γνώμη is subject to development or change, what are the factors that effect change? It is these three aspects of the γνώμη in Chrysostom's anthropology that is the concern of this chapter: (a) the γνώμη as a settled or fixed state, (b) the γνώμη as pliable and subject to development, and (c) the factors producing change and development in the γνώμη.

---

[4] S. Halliwell, "Philosophy and rhetoric", in I. Worthington (ed.), *Persuasion: Greek Rhetoric in Action* (New York 1994) 222-243, at 232, n. 11, commenting on a remark of Socrates on requisites for conducting public discourse wrote: "This means that the rhetorician, as someone who purports to deal with subjects as important yet disputable as justice and love, must, if his discourse is to have respectable claim to attention, possess an analytical and critical understanding of many major features of the world. Among these features is the psychology of the human mind itself, since it is upon this that every piece of rhetoric aims to work a persuasive effect. Because audiences are variable, the orator must have a grasp of the multifarious nature of human emotions, beliefs and mentalities. But it is not sufficient for this grasp to be coherent in abstract; it has to be capable of application in direct practice." Chrysostom had learnt his lessons well.

[5] *In Rom. hom.* 19; PG 60,584 19-21: Τὸ τοίνυν ἀνίατον τῆς γνώμης αὐτῶν καὶ δυσμετάθετον δηλῶν, *Πνεῦμα κατανύξεως*, εἶπεν ("Therefore he said, 'a Spirit of stupor', revealing the incurable and hard to alter state of their mindset").

[6] *In Rom. hom.* 19; PG 60,584 10-12: Κατάνυξιν, δὲ ἐνταῦθα τὴν περὶ τὸ χεῖρον ἕξιν τῆς ψυχῆς φησι, τὴν ἀνιάτως ἔχουσαν καὶ ἀμεταθέτως.

[7] See my discussion above of γνώμη as habit or τρόπος in Chapter 2 above. Sherwood, *Maximus the Confessor*, 61, in his introduction, discusses γνώμη as used by this later church Father who shows that the "γνώμη is related to election (προαίρεσις) as habit to act".

I. Γνώμη as settled convictions

Chrysostom often speaks of people's γνώμη in the sense that it is their authoritative opinion or understanding or teaching that is in view. There is, for example, the τὴν ἀποστόλων γνώμην ("apostles' γνώμη"),[8] τὴν Παύλου γνώμην ("Paul's γνώμη"),[9] and the γνώμη of teacher and disciples.[10] Here we have the settled ideas that have been established in one's being so that the whole mindset is in that direction. These are not passing opinions or ephemeral thoughts that flitter through the mind. These are those positions to which the totality of being is committed. This is particularly evident in the reference from the homily in Thessalonians. The context is Chrysostom's comment on 1 Thessalonians 3:8; namely, where Paul rejoices in the news that his disciples stood fast in the face of his sufferings. Chrysostom elaborates on Paul's anxiety for them and expresses the point thus, "For nothing else matters to a good teacher as long as the affairs of his disciples progress with him in harmony of mindset."[11]

Chrysostom asserts that Paul discounts his sufferings because of the comfort that true disciples bring to their teachers by faithfulness to their teachings. Good teachers are impervious to everything else that may happen as long as disciples progress in the γνώμη of the teacher. In fact, this is a shared γνώμη. This highlights the personal issue of inward conformity and the consequent expression in life as being the chief concern of the teacher. It is not merely information that is to be imparted, but mindset, attitude, spirit, the orientation of the psyche. Young's analysis of patristic *paideia* is pertinent here in that she reminds us of "the roots of Eastern theology where doctrine and spirituality are inseparable".[12] Chrysostom's comment is reminiscent of Paul's exhortation to the Philippians in 2:4: "Let the same mind be in you that was in Christ Jesus...". The γνώμη contains the same sense of commitment of the being. Thus to take up somebody's γνώμη is likewise to commit one's own γνώμη, and consequently one's own being, not only to their ideas but also to their praxis, the embodiment of those ideas into habits of life. In this context of teacher-student, to be κατὰ γνώμην with someone is to have settled one's life into the master's form of teaching.

In a comment on Paul's consternation over the fickleness of the Galatians, Chrysostom contends that disciples should hold to their teacher's γνώμη even

---

[8] *Comm. in Gal.*; PG 61,635 10, PG 61,635 47, PG 61,630 13.
[9] *Comm. in Gal.*; PG 61,635 5.
[10] *In 1 Thes. hom.* 4; PG 62,418 31.
[11] *In 1 Thes. hom.* 4; PG 62,418 31: Διδασκάλου γὰρ ἀγαθοῦ οὐδὲν ἂν ἅψαιτο λοιπὸν, ἕως ἂν τὰ τῶν μαθητῶν κατὰ γνώμην αὐτῷ προχωρῇ.
[12] Young, "Paideia and myth", 265.

when that teacher is absent as much as when present.[13] This underlines the commitment that is expected and that takes place in the γνώμη. The use of δέω (to bind, tie, fetter) here indicates the expectation of the normal obligation between disciple and teacher. It is not mere intellectual assent but something far less fragile. The strength of that obligation is evident from the illustration Chrysostom uses later in this commentary to show how a teacher's γνώμη is to be learned. He points out that Paul, in defending his integrity, is saying that "If any one desires to hear my defence, and to perceive in depth what is my mindset (γνώμη), let them look at my wounds...".[14] In a powerful image, he compares Paul to a soldier retiring from the front rank of battle, covered with blood and wounds that testify beyond all reproach as to his courage.[15] Such wounds are evidence of commitment. So with Paul: what greater evidence of commitment than this could there be? Indeed, wounds "send out a voice loftier than a trumpet",[16] better than words and arguments. It seems axiomatic to assert that whatever one is prepared to suffer for is what one truly believes, that to which one is truly committed. Hence, the γνώμη is the faculty of the psyche where settled convictions that determine action reside.

Along these same lines is a passage in a homily on 2 Thessalonians. There Chrysostom, having shown how the apostle Paul set aside the false teachers, uses γνώμη to announce Paul's teaching on the παρουσία (the expected end-time appearing of the Lord), and the anti-Christ: τὴν οἰκείαν γνώμην ἐκτίθεται ("he expounds his own γνώμη").[17] What is it that Paul expounds? What else but his own settled convictions, the things he believes in the depths of his being.

It appears, then, that the γνώμη was understood as including a deliberating or reasoning element. This element is identified as that in which thought has come to

---

[13] *Comm. in Gal.*; PG 61,660 20-24: Ἐνταῦθα γὰρ αἰνίττεται, ὅτι ἡ ἀπουσία αὐτοῦ ταῦτα εἰργάσατο, καὶ ὅτι τὸ μὲν μακάριον τοῦτό ἐστι, μὴ παρόντος τοῦ διδασκάλου μόνον, τοὺς μαθητὰς τὴν δέουσαν ἔχειν γνώμην, ἀλλὰ καὶ ἀπόντος ("He insinuates here that his absence had caused these things, and that blessedness is this: to have the mindset of the disciples bound not only when the teacher is present, but also when absent").

[14] *Comm. in Gal.*; PG 61,680 31-35: Καὶ εἴ τις ἀκοῦσαι βούλεται τῆς ἐμῆς ἀπολογίας, καὶ τὴν γνώμην μου καταμαθεῖν, βλεπέτω τὰ τραύματα,...

[15] *Comm. in Gal.*; PG 61,680 26-30: Οὐδὲ γὰρ εἴ τις στρατιώτην εἶδεν ἐκ παρατάξεως ἡμαγμένον ἐξελθόντα, καὶ μυρία τραύματα ἔχοντα, δειλίας τι κρίνειν αὐτὸν καὶ προδοσίας ἠνείχετο, ἐπὶ τοῦ σώματος τῆς ἀνδραγαθίας φέροντα τὴν ἀπόδειξιν ("For if anyone saw a soldier covered in blood and having countless wounds coming from his place in the line of battle, not even one person would accuse him of cowardice or hold him up for treason, because he carries the proof of his bravery upon his body").

[16] *Comm. in Gal.*; PG 61,680 24-25: Ταῦτα γὰρ φωνὴν σάλπιγγος ὑψηλοτέραν ἀφίησι πρὸς τοὺς ἀντιλέγοντας.

[17] *In 2 Thes. hom.* 3; PG 62,482 16.

a settled opinion which then shapes one's attitude to things. It is equivalent to saying, "My position on this issue is...", that is to say that the issue has been considered and thought through to a firm conclusion which becomes one's settled opinion on it. This is not a position from which the person will easily be moved. It is that to which the person is committed until more powerful evidence or argument or experience is encountered to cause a change. Such a change would be what we call a paradigm shift, that is, a change in the depths of one's being which becomes significant for all future actions. This concept of the γνώμη as referring to a settled opinion of the totality of being is illustrated well by Chrysostom's use of γνώμη in a homily in which he calls upon his people to pray for their leaders. He illustrates the point of the efficacy of such prayer with a common example from his society in which a king may pardon a condemned prisoner on the request of the people. The king has done so, says Chrysostom, "...because he was put to shame by the crowd, he changed his mindset (γνώμη)".[18] In order to translate into idiomatic English in the light of the surrounding text, this would usually translate: "the king repeals the (his) judgment". Γνώμη in this instance represents the settled opinion of the court, or probably of the king himself, both in relation to the guilt of the criminal and what ought to happen to him. Only a king could change the consequences of such a settled judgement. This reality, in itself, points clearly to the normal inflexibility of the γνώμη in its developed state. An examination of the two verbs used in the sentence together with the immediate context strengthens this understanding of γνώμη. The verb δυσωπέω, in its middle form as found here, has within it an element of unwillingness, shame being in view.[19] The rest of the text suggests some element of fear, it being the size of the crowd that influenced the decision. The other verb, ἀνατίθημι, which carries the meaning of "put back" or "retract",[20] "revoke",[21] being here in the middle voice, contains the element of doing something for oneself. The text then suggests that the constraint felt by the king is that of the safety of his own person or his desire for popularity. The king is shamed into it by the volume of popular opinion. As the king would have had at least a part in the original judgement, the γνώμη here includes the king's, thus strengthening the sense of rigidity that had to be overcome. The picture demonstrates the force of the γνώμη in its application to the individual: it is none other than the settled opinion of the totality of one's being, hence my preferred

---

[18] *In 2 Thes. hom.* 4; PG 62,490 25: Εἰ ἐπὶ ἀνθρώπων καταδίκους ἄνδρας καὶ ἀπαγομένους εἰς θάνατον δῆμος προσελθὼν ἐξητήσατο, καὶ τὸ πλῆθος δυσωπηθεὶς ὁ βασιλεὺς τὴν γνώμην ἀνέθετο...

[19] LSJ, 423 gives examples of this particular usage from Plutarch, *Coriolanus* 15, and Libanius, *Dec.* 39 17.

[20] LSJ, 123 *s.v.*

[21] LPGL, 125 *s.v.*

general translation as "mindset". In applying this to our relation to God, Chrysostom again uses δυσωπέω, but shifts the efficacy of such prayers from size or ambition to virtue.

The use of γνώμη as settled conviction is seen also in a comment on the Galatian letter. In discussing the attempt by "false brethren" (ψευδαδέλφους) to have Titus circumcised, Chrysostom asks why it was that these people were called false brethren when they were acting "κατὰ τὴν τῶν ἀποστόλων γνώμην" ("according to the apostolic mindset"),[22] the judgement made in Jerusalem which allowed circumcision for Jews among the followers of Jesus. Here again we are met with the expressed settled opinion of an authoritative body, the Jerusalem Council. Here is their judgement, their sentence, their settled deliberated conviction on an issue.

Further example of this use of the term is found in a comment on the opening address in Paul's letter to the Galatians. Chrysostom proposes that Paul's reference to "and all the brothers with me" (Gal. 1:2) is designed to get rid of any suspicion that he might be unorthodox. Chrysostom comments that Paul claimed that he had "many sharers of his mindset (γνώμη)...and what he wrote, he wrote even from their γνώμη".[23] The γνώμη here must refer to the settled understanding; the former to Paul's settled understanding of the Gospel and the latter to his companions' settled understanding of the Gospel. Alexander, in NPNF in translating these two occurrences of γνώμη, renders one as "doctrine" and the other as "accord".[24] These may give the sense, but something more precise is possible. In the first occurrence of γνώμη in this passage Alexander sounds in translation as if he was looking at the external aspect, and in "doctrine" gives an expression somewhat less forceful than the term implies. It has been argued in this study that γνώμη focuses upon the disposition of an internal source with all its intellectual and emotional content from which the external expression flows, and which is evident here in this context. Chrysostom is referring to the mindset of Paul, the settled position of his being about the issues on which he writes. If it is desired to use something akin to doctrine, then dogma would be far better; it carries much more the sense of tenacious personal conviction that is native to the concept. The second occurrence of γνώμη relates to Paul's Christian friends, the many who

---

[22] *Comm. in Gal.*; PG 61,635 10.

[23] *Comm. in Gal.*; PG 61,616 36-39: καὶ δεῖξαι ὅτι πολλοὺς ἔχει τῆς γνώμης κοινωνούς, συνέταξε τοὺς ἀδελφούς, δηλῶν ὅτι ἅπερ γράφει, καὶ ἀπὸ τῆς ἐκείνων γράφει γνώμης.

[24] *John Chrys., Galatians*; trans. G. Alexander, in P. Schaff (ed.), NPNF Series 1, vol. 13, 4: "Wishing therefore to remove their suspicion, and that he had many to support him in his doctrine, he has associated himself with the 'brethren', to show that what he wrote he wrote with their accord".

share his mindset, his settled deliberated opinions, to which they, too, are committed. When he writes, it is from the corpus of those settled opinions. He writes from a common γνώμη. Thus we could translate as "settled convictions" in both instances.

The distinction to which I have referred between the external expressions and the internal mindset is brought into focus in a comment on Paul's Galatian letter. In discussing the apparent arrogance of Paul's words and actions at the time, Chrysostom lets us into the secret of his own exegetical method. The key principle or rule (κανών) is … καὶ τὴν γνώμην ἐξετάζωμεν τοῦ λέγοντος ("…to scrutinise the γνώμη of the speaker closely").[25] Three times in this passage Chrysostom refers to the γνώμη. In looking at the actions of Abraham and Phineas, the bare facts mean nothing "…unless we add to them the γνώμη of those who do them".[26] Bare things are not enough; neither are "bare words…nor a single phrase".[27] These can easily lead us into turning the truth upside down. We need to take pains in order to see the products of Paul's γνώμη. We must therefore examine the intention or mind (διάνοια) of the apostle.[28] Chrysostom had already laid down the need to "turn towards the intention (διάνοια) of the writer".[29] The διάνοια is brought into view and placed in close association with the γνώμη to the extent that one is a gateway to the other. If we examine closely the διάνοια of the writer or speaker, Chrysostom claims that, in conjunction with other significant indicators, "we shall then know out of what kind of mindset (γνώμη) he was speaking these things".[30] Γνώμη thus includes intention or purpose. It is not surprising that the NPNF translators often translate γνώμη with one or other of these terms. In this homily, then, the distinction between the external expression and the inner source

---

[25] *Comm. in Gal.*; PG 61,629 6.

[26] *Comm. in Gal.*; PG 61,629 20-21: εἰ τὰ πράγματα μέλλοιμεν ἐξετάζειν γυμνὰ, μὴ προστιθέντες αὐτοῖς τὴν τῶν ποιούντων γνώμην.

[27] *Comm. in Gal.*; PG 61,629 1-3: Οὐδὲ γὰρ δεῖ τὰ ῥήματα γυμνὰ ἐξετάζειν,…οὐδὲ τὴν λέξιν καθ' ἑαυτὴν βασανίζειν.

[28] *Comm. in Gal.*; PG 61,629 22: Ἐξετάσωμεν τοίνυν καὶ τοῦ Παύλου τὴν διάνοιαν; Heath, "John Chrysostom, rhetoric and Galatians", 390, gives an informed discussion of the rhetorical principles of which Chrysostom made use in his commentary on Galatians. Heath points to intention, διάνοια, as a customary practice at: "The argument that one must attend to the intention behind the act is a key part of the standard division of the issue called counterstatement (ἀντίστασις), in which an action that would normally be criminal (for example, a general acting beyond his mandate) is defended on the basis of its beneficial consequences".

[29] *Comm. in Gal.*; PG 61,629 4: ἀλλὰ τῇ διανοίᾳ προσέχειν τοῦ γράφοντος. See LSJ, 405 *s.v.*

[30] *Comm. in Gal.*; PG 61,629 23-25: Ἐξετάσωμεν τοίνυν καὶ τοῦ Παύλου τὴν διάνοιαν, ἀφ' ἧς ταῦτα ἔγραφεν· ἴδωμεν αὐτοῦ τὸν σκοπὸν, καὶ τίς ἦν διόλου περὶ τοὺς ἀποστόλους, καὶ τότε εἰσόμεθα ταῦτα ἐκ ποίας ἐλέγετο γνώμης. Heath, "John Chrysostom, rhetoric and Galatians", 390, refers to the text of PG 61,629 and translates διάνοια as "intent", and γνώμη as "intention".

is made quite clear. It is, according to Chrysostom, impossible to know what the speaker means without discerning his γνώμη, without attending to the mindset from which the external expressions emanate. It is to be noted that words only have meaning within their context and they change meaning from one context to another. As far as Chrysostom was concerned, the primary context to take into consideration was the γνώμη, the mindset of the speaker. This was so for the simple reason that the γνώμη embodied the settled convictions of the person.

We can go a step further. There is an interesting combination of ideas brought together by Chrysostom in the passage under consideration. Not only was the διάνοια of a writer to be examined but also his σκοπός. This word may be translated as "aim" or "end" and therefore could be a stylistic substitute for διάνοια, but as it was another standard rhetorical principle, it is more likely that Chrysostom employed it as such.[31] It places the emphasis upon the end, at what the writer or speaker is aiming, thus it makes clear the sense in which διάνοια is to be understood: that is, the ultimate intention of the writer. When the writer has finished, what is the destination, or destinations if multiple aims are in view, at which we have arrived? Where, indeed, is he/she taking us? The γνώμη then contains the sense of embracing certain ideas so strongly that it desires to carry others with it. These are not tentatively held opinions; rather they are the strong convictions that have been riveted into the person's being to the extent that they would attempt to determine the destiny of other persons besides one's own.

Chrysostom adds another item for consideration when attempting to determine Paul's γνώμη. This is what he calls καὶ τίς ἦν διόλου περὶ τοὺς ἀποστόλους ("his total dealings with the Apostles").[32] His point appears to be that Paul always taught what he believed even when he was ahead of the apostles in discerning the implications of the Gospel in some issues, particularly the issue of circumcision. As Chrysostom notes in this passage, only after the Jerusalem council – Acts 15 – did the apostles preach that circumcision was not necessary, something that Paul had strongly held from the beginning of his ministry.[33] The point is they did not contradict him but after much discussion ruled according to his γνώμη. Chrysostom, in defence of Paul against the charge of arrogance, notes that Paul conducted himself with dignity and with due respect for the apostles at all times

---

[31] Heath, "John Chrysostom, rhetoric and Galatians", 373-375, and n. 20, discusses σκοπός in relation to multiple aims as being associated with rhetorical exegesis and a single aim with philosophical exegesis. This helps to understand some of the structural difficulties in Chrysostom's homilies.

[32] *Comm. in Gal.*; PG 61,629 23-24.

[33] *Comm. in Gal.*; PG 61,630 12-14: Αὐτὸς μὲν γὰρ ἐξ ἀρχῆς ταύτης εἴχετο τῆς γνώμης, ἣν καὶ οἱ ἀπόστολοι μετὰ ταῦτα ἐκύρωσαν τὸ μὴ δεῖν περιτέμνεσθαι.

during these encounters. How are we to determine Paul's γνώμη from all this? The γνώμη of a writer or speaker may be determined from the strength with which he/she holds and defends his convictions in the face of notable authorities. Here we are not encountering wavering and loosely held opinions. Here we meet consistent and strongly held convictions.

It is evident from the above that in the thought of Chrysostom the γνώμη could reach a settled state in which ideas and convictions are held with great tenacity. The totality of a person's being would be ruled by the mindset committed to these ideas, thus setting the agenda for life. These authoritative convictions would not only set the direction for one's own being but could be so strong that other persons could be carried along by the consistency and force with which they were defended and propagated. The γνώμη contains the notion of intention and purpose. Indeed, Chrysostom argued, examination of the intention (διάνοια) and aim (σκοπός) are sure gateways to discerning the γνώμη, the mindset of a person.

II. The Pliability of the Γνώμη.

Chrysostom had great confidence in the power of the Gospel to change those who heard it. In a comment on a prophecy of Isaiah about the salvation of God reaching out to the Gentiles, he asserted that:

> [the prophet] everywhere declaring that the power and the knowledge of these our Gospels will be poured out to the ends of the world converting the human race from a brutish manner and a hardened mindset (γνώμη) into a very gentle and tender people.[34]

This indicates that Chrysostom understood the γνώμη of the race to have been perverted and to some extent set in that distorted state, and that it requires the power and knowledge of the Gospel to be applied to it in order for it to change for the better. This does show that Chrysostom held that the γνώμη, though set, is able to be changed. Chrysostom's approach on this issue is significant, as it has been argued above that he understood that the γνώμη could reach a static state, a condition of settled conviction. This he applied particularly to heretics, about whom he counselled his people to avoid. Heretics, however, are not the normal category. The concept of the absolute inflexibility of the γνώμη in some people is

---

[34] *In Matt. hom.* 10; PG 57,188 5-10: πανταχοῦ δηλῶν ὅτι πρὸς τὰ πέρατα τῆς οἰκουμένης χυθήσεται τῶν Εὐαγγελίων τούτων ἡ δύναμις καὶ ἡ γνῶσις, ἀπὸ θηριώδους τρόπου καὶ σκληρότητος γνώμης εἰς ἡμερότητα πολλὴν καὶ ἁπαλότητα μεταβάλλουσα τῶν ἀνθρώπων τὸ γένος.

by no means the totality of Chrysostom's approach to the role of the γνώμη in the human psyche. In general, he treats the γνώμη as being able to develop and change, to move from an immature stage to one that is fully developed and set. In a comment on the ministry of John the Baptist he differentiates between the Pharisees and the crowds who were being baptised, by pointing to their respective mindsets (γνώμη). He describes the people as having an "unshaped" or "unmoulded" γνώμη.[35] The γνώμη had not yet reached its settled form. It was still flexible and open to change. It had not yet hardened so as to become impervious to the truth. This was distinctly different to that of the Pharisees whose desire was to seize him, and who were not open to the required change. Matthew makes this explicit: "The people came with one mindset and the Pharisees with another".[36]

In a comment on Galatians, Chrysostom interprets Paul's use of νήπιος "infant", as referring to the γνώμη and not as meaning physical age.[37] Γνώμη, then, may be used in reference to the degree of maturity attained by a person. Chrysostom uses it in this passage with νηπιωδέστερον, "more infantile".[38] In this particular instance, in Chrysostom's thought, childishness is expressed by submission to new moons and sabbaths, the elements of the cosmos, a pre-occupation with the shadows of the past rather than with the present substance of the faith. It is possible, he asserts, to have an infantile γνώμη or to have one that appreciates that we now live ἐν τῷ κρόνῳ, τῆς τελείας ἡλικίας ("in the time of the age of maturity").[39] The context indicates that he is comparing their pre-Christian existence with their Christian experience against the background of the dispensational change which occurred with the incarnation. At least those of the past age or dispensation had an excuse for their immaturity. Those who live post-incarnation do not, hence the epithet "more infantile". He goes on to say that all who are in Christ, by virtue of our adoption as sons, by the grace of God have already experienced a massive move in status and outlook:

---

[35] *In Matt. hom.* 11; PG 57,193 2-3: Ἀλλ᾽ οἱ μὲν ὄχλοι ἀπὸ γνώμης ἀπλάστου τοῦτο ὑπώπτευον· οἱ δὲ Φαρισαῖοι, ἐπιλαβέσθαι βουλόμενοι.

[36] *In Matt. hom.* 11; PG 57,193 11-12: Καὶ ἵνα μάθῃς ὅτι ἑτέρᾳ μὲν οἱ Φαρισαῖοι, ἑτέρᾳ δὲ ὁ δῆμος παρεγένοντο γνώμῃ.

[37] *Comm. in Gal.*; PG 61,657 10-12: Νήπιον ἐνταῦθα οὐ τὴν ἡλικίαν φησὶν, ἀλλὰ τὴν γνώμην.

[38] *Comm. in Gal.*; PG 61,657 12-15: ἐπειδὴ δὲ ἔτι νηπιωδέστερον διεκείμεθα, ἐκείμεθα, ἀφῆκεν ὑπὸ τὰ στοιχεῖα τοῦ κόσμου εἶναι, τουτέστι, νουμηνίας καὶ σάββατα· αὗται γὰρ ἡμῖν αἱ ἡμέραι ἀπὸ δρόμου σελήνης καὶ ἡλίου γίνονται.

[39] *Comm. in Gal.*; PG 61,657 17

> If, then, grace has made us freedmen instead of slaves, mature instead of infantile, heirs and sons instead of aliens, how is it not absurd, and indicative of extreme insolence to cut loose from this grace, and turn around back again?[40]

Although he makes much of the initial transformation which is experienced at conversion and baptism, he does not thereby rule out development, or, as the text here evidences, a backward movement away from whatever stage of maturity that already may have been attained. It is of note that Chrysostom here uses ἀγνωμοσύνη, the egotistical mindset that rides roughshod over the claims of reality and reason, as discussed in chapter three above. Its usage with ἄτροπος (foolish/absurd) in this passage is appropriate, as here God's grace is trodden under foot, a course that is as far from reason as it is from εὐγνωμοσύνη, that right-mindedness that recognises one's dependence on God and expresses its thanksgiving for all his benefits. With ἀγνωμοσύνη, the wrong end of the γνώμη scale has been reached. The utter absurdity of this infantile γνώμη is anticipated in the earlier passage where he employs a powerful metaphor, "Do you see how much the observance of days does for you? The lord and master of the house, the ruler of all, is reduced in rank to a lowly attendant."[41]

On the positive side, the capacity of the γνώμη to develop from immaturity to maturity is illustrated by Chrysostom in one of his homilies on Genesis. He compares Ham with Japeth, describing the former as younger than his brother in γνώμη even though he was older by age.[42] The passage is not dealing with development as such, but the use of the epithet νεώτερος (younger) is suggestive. There are degrees of maturity of the γνώμη, in this case possessed by different people but phrased in a context of growth. In Chrysostom's judgement, the development of Ham's γνώμη had not kept pace with his physical development or the development of his younger brother's γνώμη.

A different approach is taken by Chrysostom when he deplores the pliability of the γνώμη of the Galatians in falling into error. He proposes that, although Paul was prepared to submit to defending himself, he did not enjoy it. Indeed, he found it difficult to bear, especially the problem of …τὴν εὐκολίαν τῆς τῶν ἀπατωμένων γνώμης ("the pliability of the γνώμη of those who were deceived").[43] Here the

---

[40] *Comm. in Gal.*; PG 61,657 43-45: Εἰ τοίνυν ἀντὶ δούλων ἐλευθέρους, ἀντὶ νηπίων τελείους, ἀντὶ ἀλλοτρίων κληρονόμους ἐποίησε καὶ υἱοὺς ἡ χάρις, πῶς οὐκ ἄτοπον καὶ ἐσχάτης ἀγνωμοσύνης ἀφιέναι μὲν ταύτην, ὑποστρέψαι δὲ εἰς τοὐπίσω;

[41] *Comm. in Gal.*; PG 61,657 19-20: Ὁρᾷς ὅσον ἐστὶ παρατήρησις ἡμερῶν; τὸν κύριον, τὸν οἰκοδεσπότην, τὸν πάντων κρατοῦντα ἐν ὑπηρέτου καθίστησι τάξει.

[42] *In Gen. hom.* 29; PG 53,268 65-269 2: ἀλλ᾽ εἰ καὶ τὴν ἡλικίαν ἦν πρότερος ἐκείνου, ἀλλὰ τῇ γνώμῃ νεώτερος, καὶ ἡ προπέτεια αὐτὸν ἐξέβαλεν.

[43] *Comm. in Gal.*; PG 61,625 19-21.

mindset is described as εὐκολίαν, at ease, relaxed, lacking the tension required to render it fit for the service of God and thus an easy prey to deception. It is surprising to find Chrysostom so negative about this flexibility of the γνώμη when we often find him mourning its fixity. In this instance he finds its pliability a liability rather than an asset. The context indicates that he thought that the γνώμη ought to be stabilised as a barrier against false teachings. Instead of an open γνώμη there should be one that is closed to error. It should be open to truth and established in it and therefore closed to anything false. To use another metaphor from Chrysostom's repertoire that we have already encountered in this study, the strings of the instrument needed to be tightened so that it would be in tune with the divine truth.

There is no doubt that Chrysostom understood that change in a person's γνώμη was a possible reality. Indeed, there is, according to him, the need for change because the γνώμη may be in a distorted condition. At the end of a homily on 2 Timothy, Chrysostom urges his hearers to keep carefully in mind the things he had spoken to them. They were things, he says, which were not said without reason. He gives two reasons for his utterances: firstly, ἀλλ' ἵνα διορθώσωμεν ὑμῶν τὴν γνώμην ("so that we might set aright your mindset"), and then, καὶ ἀσφαλεστέρους εἰς τὸ ἑξῆς ἐργασώμεθα ("we might work for a more secure habit of mind").[44] This is of particular interest for this study. Chrysostom is attempting to help them διορθόω (to set straight, amend, restore to order)[45] their γνώμη. This aim may only reflect and apply to the particular situation, but in view of the initial change in the γνώμη that takes place at conversion and its pliability as already discussed, it is reasonable to conclude that this text has general application. Here he is addressing his congregation, so it seems clear that Chrysostom generally held that the γνώμη, even in believers, suffers some distortion and needs correction or restoring to order. This may refer to the basic distortion of a person's being which comes from the Fall, an issue taken up elsewhere in this study. More pertinent at this point is that he understood that the γνώμη could be set straight. It can be reconditioned by being educated out of its distortion. The γνώμη is not as rigid and set in its ways as one might be led to expect from some of the remarks that have been noted. Chrysostom worked on the basis of the possibility of change being a real option. The second clause indicates the goal of his teaching to be the production in his people of a habit of mind that is secure and not tossed around by the waves of heresy or circumstance. Paradoxically, he looks for a more settled mindset by using its pliability in a positive program of education. It is also apparent from this

---

[44] *In 2 Tim. hom.* 2; PG 62,612 59.
[45] LSJ 434 s.v.

that the goal will only be reached by the intense labour of the teachers. The verb, ἐργάζομαι, indicates something of the effort to be exerted.

Chrysostom was convinced of the dangers of careless living, especially by the baptised. He often warns against it. In one such passage where he thunders against post-baptismal carelessness, he questions the integrity of the faith of people who live that way. In a descriptive attack, he compares their behaviour to that of wild beasts and observes their capacity to be tamed.[46] He then poses a penetrating question: "What sort of defence will you have when you have led out your own natural meekness into an unnatural savagery?"[47] Both the question and its context are significant for our study. The difference between humankind and animals is perceived to be the possession of reason by the former. He says, Μηδεὶς τοίνυν ἐν τῇ τῶν ἀλόγων μενέτω μορφῇ ("Therefore let no one continue in the form of irrational beasts").[48] Also, in speaking of lions he remarks, καὶ τὸ λογισμοῦ ἐστερῆσθαι τὸ θηρίον ("the beast has been deprived of reason").[49] Another feature of humans is their free moral choice (προαίρεσις), a faculty to be treasured and not thrown away.[50] Throughout this passage Chrysostom asserts that human nature has a meek and not a wild temperament, that meekness or gentleness (πραότης) is a natural attribute in humankind. Again he asks the question:

> Therefore, what defence will you have, what pretty pretext will you be able to throw on the table, you who turns a lion into a human, but in your own case disregards a lion coming into being from a human? on one hand favouring the beast with that which is above nature, and on the other, for yourself, guarding nothing that is in accord with nature?[51]

By allowing oneself to become like an irrational wild animal, one fails to retain that which is consistent with one's nature. In this way one prostitutes free choice, perverts reason and horribly distorts nature. It is in the midst of this argument that Chrysostom refers to the possibility of taming another person. As an aside, he suggests the objection that the person to be tamed might validly raise:...τὸ μὴ

---

[46] *In Matt. hom.* 4; PG 57,49 56-50 5.

[47] *In Matt. hom.* 4; PG 57,49 47-48: ποίαν ἕξεις ἀπολογίαν, τὴν σεαυτοῦ πραότητα τὴν κατὰ φύσιν εἰς τὴν παρὰ φύσιν θηριωδίαν ἐξαγαγών;

[48] *In Matt. hom.* 4; PG 57,49 38-39.

[49] *In Matt. hom.* 4; PG 57,49 53.

[50] *In Matt. hom.* 4; PG 57,49 57-57,50 2: πῶς ἐπὶ σαυτοῦ μετὰ τῆς φύσεως καὶ τὸ τῆς προαιρέσεως προδίδως καλόν; ("...how, for youself, do you forsake the beauty of your moral choice along with that of your nature?")

[51] *In Matt. hom.* 4; PG 57,50 11-12: Τίνα οὖν ἔχεις ἀπολογίαν, ποίαν δὲ πρόφασιν εὐπρόσωπον προβαλέσθαι δυνήσῃ, λέοντα μὲν ποιῶν ἄνθρωπον, σαυτὸν δὲ περιορῶν ἐξ ἀνθρώπου γινόμενον λέοντα; κἀκείνῳ μὲν τὰ ὑπὲρ φύσιν χαριζόμενος, σαυτῷ δὲ οὐδὲ τὰ κατὰ φύσιν τηρῶν;

κύριον εἶναι τῆς ἑτέρου γνώμης ("...you are not the master of another's mindset").[52] It is the γνώμη that is understood as the wild beast in the person, or rather the faculty for allowing the irrational form of θύμος, anger, to roam free and wreak its manic damage on all and sundry. Thus, it is the γνώμη in which change has to occur, the beast that has to be tamed; not choice, reason or nature. It is none other than one's own γνώμη, the mastery of which is completely our own.[53] Of this, says Chrysostom, the taming or shaping of the γνώμη will restore the balance of nature. Reason will be restored, free choice will act responsibly and meekness shall again be the distinctive feature of human life. Thus the γνώμη is seen both as needing to be changed and, for the main part, as being open to the possibility of change.

It is to be emphasised that the γνώμη as seen by Chrysostom is autonomous. No other person is in a position to master it. Also, it is implied that if a person has given up their natural choice (προαίρεσις) they still retain their γνώμη by which the natural choice may be reached and activated. John Meyendorff refers to this distinction in his exposition of Orthodox theology. He points to the tradition in Orthodoxy of the distinction between the "natural will" and the "gnomic will".[54] For the moment, we rest with the position that the γνώμη is the key element by which human nature can be restored to its original harmony. In most cases the γνώμη can change and ought to be changed.

Imagery from the animal world is used by Chrysostom in another place to indicate the pliability of the γνώμη, its natural immaturity, and its need for assistance in stabilizing it in the right direction for development. Commenting on the introduction of the sign of circumcision, Chrysostom points to its function in relation to the imperfection of the γνώμη: to rein in its lack of purpose and restraint in future generations.[55] Circumcision would be akin to a bit in a horse's mouth, providing a stabilizing and directive force to the γνώμη to prevent those generations from giving in to their restless impulses. The implication here is that there is an inherent deficiency in the γνώμη that requires help to set it in the right direction. It is assumed by Chrysostom that such settling and stability is possible, the external sign of circumcision possessing for the Jews the potential to impact

---

[52] *In Matt. hom.* 4; PG 57,50 4-5.

[53] *In Matt. hom.* 4; PG 57,50 6-7: Νυνὶ δὲ τὸ σαυτοῦ θηρίον, καὶ οὐ πάντως κύριος εἶ ("Now, it [the γνώμη] is the wild beast itself, and you are totally master of it").

[54] Meyendorff, *Byzantine Theology*, 143.

[55] *In Gen. hom.* 39; PG 53,366 19-22: Ὅρα σοφίαν Δεσπότου, πῶς εἰδὼς τῶν μελλόντων ἔσεσθαι τὸ ἀτελὲς τῆς γνώμης, καθάπερ χαλινόν τινα ἐπιτιθείς, οὕτω τὸ σημεῖον τοῦτο τῆς περιτομῆς ἔδωκε, τὴν ὁρμὴν αὐτῶν τὴν ἀκάθεκτον ἐκκόπτων, ὥστε μὴ τοῖς ἔθνεσι συναναμίγνυσθαι ("See the Lord's wisdom, because he knew the purposelessness of future generations, how, just like someone placing a bit in a mouth, he gave them this sign of circumcision").

upon the internal faculty. Under the right circumstances the γνώμη is open to appropriate development.

In a homily on the creation account of Genesis, Chrysostom suggests that those who deny the existence of a personal divine Creator and who turn to various non-theistic explanations of the visible world have become dupes of the devil. This, Chrysostom avers, is a demonstration of the magnitude of his guile: "Consider how great is the guile of the devil, how he exploits the docility of the mindset (γνώμη) of those enslaved in error".[56] Here we clearly encounter the idea of the flexibility of the γνώμη. In this case Chrysostom would have us believe that it is as putty in the hands of the devil who no doubt attempts to configure it in accord with his own purposes. It is significant how those who are enslaved in error are described in Chrysostom's exhortation: ...μηκέτι τῇ πλάνῃ τῶν ἐξ οἰκείων λογισμῶν ἅπαντα φθεγγομένων προσέχωμεν ("...let us no longer be devoted to the error of those who loudly express everything from their own reasonings").[57] Chrysostom was strong on this issue of the autonomous use of reason that no longer confessed its dependence upon the Spirit of God. He perceived this as gross misuse of the faculty which, in its proper mode of dependence upon God, was intended by the Creator to be the ruling principle of the soul.[58] Reason, in its bid for an illicit autonomy became enslaved, and its place as ruling principle in the soul was taken by another faculty, the γνώμη, which was open to being shaped by numerous factors in the experience of life.

Chrysostom, then, held that the γνώμη normally operates with a certain degree of flexibility until a stage is reached where it becomes substantially fixed as in the case of heretics. For human beings in general it is developed over time according to the various influences that are applied in the course of life. For the Christian, in keeping with the New Testament notion of adoption, a substantial change in the mindset takes place at conversion. After baptism, change or development is still possible and, indeed, necessary. The γνώμη remains pliable as progress is made to the full restoration of nature in the image and likeness of God.

III. Instruments of Change

It has been established that though the γνώμη may become generally settled and fixed, it is, under certain circumstances, subject to positive change. What are those

---

[56] *In Gen. hom.* 7; PG 53,65 11-13: Σκόπει τοῦ διαβόλου πόση ἡ ἀπάτη, πῶς ἀπεχρήσατο τῇ εὐκολίᾳ τῆς γνώμης τῶν τῇ πλάνῃ δουλευόντων.
[57] *In Gen. hom.* 7; PG 53,65 27-29.
[58] This is clearly stated in *In 1 Cor. hom. 4*; PG 61,34; and *In 1 Cor. hom. 7*; PG 61,67-77; see Laird, "The theology of grace", 77-84.

circumstances? How is such change or development brought about? What may we learn about Chrysostom's understanding of the γνώμη from the way in which he prescribes change to take place?

It has been discussed above that Chrysostom, in his fourth homily on Matthew, always the pastor, addresses the need for change and transformation in his hearers. There we found his call for a change in their γνώμη.[59] Of particular concern to him is the destructive power of anger that he pictures first as a lion tearing its prey, then as a snake (not merely worms) eating away their innards. As there is a potion that is effective in killing worms, so also there is a powerful potion that will kill these snakes that engulf our vital inner life. This potion, which he asserts can extinguish every disease, and is basic to change in the γνώμη, is the blood or sacrifice of Christ.[60] In fact, Chrysostom points to a number of instruments by which the necessary change can be effected. The blood of Christ stands at the head of a list that is as follows: the precious blood of Christ, the divine scriptures, and almsgiving.[61] According to Chrysostom, they constitute a powerful triumvirate that "will enable us to put to death the passions that abuse our soul".[62] There are two more for consideration: preaching, primarily the exposition and application of scripture, and the remembrance of our sins, a form of ongoing repentance. These transforming agents will render the γνώμη right (ὀρθός), setting it at its correct tension (τονός), thus enabling it to function as divinely intended.

The blood of Christ is put at the head because it stands at the heart of the faith and as the basis of the believer's salvation. There are times when Chrysostom waxes lyrical when referring to the blood. In one place he piles up image upon image, declaring that: it washes from sins; by it heaven is made accessible; it brings us into the family of God; it produces the ongoing blooming of the image of our King within us; it generates extraordinary beauty in us; it does not allow the nobility of our souls to wither; it continuously waters and feeds our souls; it drives away demons and keeps them at bay; it leads into friendship with Christ; by it our

---

[59] *In Matt. hom.* 4; PG 57,50 4-6.

[60] *In Matt. hom.* 4; PG 57,50 34-37: Καὶ ποῖον ἂν εἴη τὸ ποτὸν, φησί, τὸ τὴν ἰσχὺν ταύτην ἔχον; Τὸ τίμιον αἷμα τοῦ Χριστοῦ, εἰ μετὰ παρρησίας ληφθείη· πᾶσαν γὰρ νόσον σβέσαι δυνήσεται τοῦτο,

[61] *In Matt. hom.* 4; PG 57,50 37-39: καὶ μετὰ τούτου τῶν θείων Γραφῶν ἡ μετ' ἀκριβείας ἀκρόασις, καὶ ἐλεημοσύνη τῇ ἀκροάσει προσγινομένη·

[62] *In Matt. hom.* 4; PG 57,50 39-41: διὰ γὰρ τούτων πάντων δυνήσεται νεκρωθῆναι τὰ λυμαινόμενα τὴν ψυχὴν ἡμῶν πάθη.

mind is made brighter than fire; by it our soul is made more lustrous than gold.[63] Much of this is spoken of the eucharist or the "mysteries" (μυστήρια) as the means by which the benefits of Christ's sacrifice are conveyed to the faithful participant. It was the direct link to the cross itself or, even more to the point, to Christ himself, as the one who died for us and imparts his life to us. Thus the initial application of the sacrifice of Christ to the soul was to be followed by regular application through the eucharist. This, in Chrysostom's judgement, provides the major shaping factor of the γνώμη.

The Scriptures are the second element of Chrysostom's triumvirate of transformation.[64] In the fourth homily on Matthew, in the lead into the wild beast passage, reference is made by Chrysostom to the scriptures as being the great instrument for effecting change in the γνώμη. Comparing them to the hairdresser's mirror, he asserts that one has only to look into them to discover one's own moral ugliness and the way to be set free from that deformity.[65] The scriptures, he insists, "not only point out our deformity but, if are willing, also transposes it into extraordinary beauty".[66]

Allied to the Scriptures in Chrysostom's methodology was preaching. He had no doubts that the γνώμη could be reached and grasped by compelling preaching. The persuasive presentation of ideas to the minds of the hearers would accomplish the desired result.[67] Near the end of the second homily on 2 Timothy, Chrysostom challenges the customary thinking (ὁ νομίζων) of his hearers in regard to the power of the priest in exercising a mediatorial role at the eucharist to sanctify them. He urges them to focus their minds upon God who works the grace, and not on the human agent who makes the offering. There is, he says, no superior-inferior

---

[63] *In Joan. hom.* 46; PG 59,261 11-41. The foregoing text is a précis of this huge section, some direct translation but mainly paraphrase, leaving out repetitions and other images. The following sections of the homily continue the theme.

[64] Hill, *Reading the Old Testament*, 183, writes that Chrysostom, along with the Antiochene theologians, appreciated the precision (ἀκρίβεια) of the Scriptures, and cites from a homily on Genesis, *In Gen. hom.* 15; PG 53,119 10-12.: "After all, they are not simply words, but words of the Holy Spirit, and hence the treasure to be found in even a single syllable is great".

[65] *In Matt. hom.* 4; PG 57,49 32-34: Κἂν βουληθῇς ἅπαξ μόνον ἰδεῖν εἰς τὰς τῶν ἁγίων ἐκείνων εἰκόνας, καὶ τὸ δυσειδὲς ὄψει τῆς διανοίας τῆς σῆς, καὶ ἰδὼν οὐδενὸς δεήσῃ λοιπὸν ἑτέρου εἰς τὸ ἀπαλλαγῆναι τῆς αἰσχρότητος ταύτης. "If you are willing once only to look at the icons of these saints, you will see the ugliness of your very own intellect, and when you have looked, then you will need as a necessity nothing other than to be delivered from this ugly deformity."

[66] *In Matt. hom.* 4; PG 57,49 27-29: οὐδὲ γὰρ δείκνυσι τὴν ἀμορφίαν μόνον, ἀλλὰ καὶ μετατίθησιν αὐτὴν πρὸς κάλλος ἀμήχανον, ἂν θέλωμεν.

[67] Hill, *Reading the Old Testament*, 192, conveys well the attitude of Chrysostom in this matter: "It was his explicit conviction that what was written in the sacred text bore on the lives of the readers, and there were various ways in which the intended beneficiaries could access it".

offering dependent upon the status of the human offerer because it is God, not the human agent, who does the sanctifying. All humans are on the same level before God; the one essential is the presence of faith.[68] With this understanding of the direct relationship between the individual and God and the consequent critical nature of personal human response, Chrysostom urges his hearers to attend to his words. They need to change their basic thinking, something they may do by heeding what he has to say. In applying this, he points to their γνώμη. He is convinced that his teaching is the instrument by which change in their γνώμη can be brought about. It is through the application of his words that the γνώμη can be set right and be rid of its distortion.[69] The indication is that the γνώμη contains, among other elements, a cognitive and rational element or is closely related to such. It is noteworthy that in the NPNF the translation of γνώμη in this instance is "minds".[70] A few lines later we hear Chrysostom saying "...let us register them [the things spoken] upon our intellect (διάνοια)".[71] The thinking faculty, διάνοια, is thus linked closely with the γνώμη.[72]

In this same place, Chrysostom expresses his concern that his congregation should have his teachings not only registered in writing on their minds, but also ἔχωμεν ἀεὶ κεκολαμένα τῷ συνειδότι ("cemented ever in our consciences").[73] There is a link between mind, conscience and γνώμη. It may be that Chrysostom recognised the γνώμη as the arbiter between the thinking faculty and the conscience, reflecting the conflict between our faculties as suggested by the apostle Paul in Romans 2:14-15, or perhaps even contained in them both. Whatever the relationship, for Chrysostom the significance of the γνώμη and the means by which change in it can occur were of prime importance. He held that the γνώμη could be set aright by instruction that is aimed at it through the thinking faculty, and by appropriate impact upon the conscience. This explains why

---

[68] This does not mean that Chrysostom denigrated the rulers of the church, for he defends them and calls for respect to be given to them elsewhere in his works, e.g., *Comm. In Gal.* ; PG 61,623 57-624 7. See *In Tit. hom.* 1; PG 62,668-670, for an extensive insight into the responsibilities and trials of a bishop in the context of a call for prayer for such leaders.

[69] *In 2 Tim. hom.* 2; PG 62,612 58-61: Ταῦτα τοίνυν εἰδότες (οὐδὲ γὰρ ἁπλῶς εἴρηται ἡμῖν ταῦτα πάντα, ἀλλ᾽ ἵνα διορθώσωμεν ὑμῶν τὴν γνώμην...) ("Therefore, knowing these things, for we have not said these things just for the sake of it, but so that we might make straight your mindset...").

[70] *John Chrys., 2 Tim.;* trans. J. Tweed, in P. Schaff (ed.), NPNF Series 1, vol.13, 483.

[71] *In 2 Tim. hom.* 2; PG 62,613 3-614 3: Προσέχωμεν τοίνυν ἀκριβῶς, προσέχωμεν τοῖς λεχθεῖσι μετ᾽ ἐπιμελείας, ἀπογράψωμεν αὐτὰ ἐπὶ τῆς διανοίας τῆς ἡμετέρας,

[72] See also *In Gen. hom.* 18; PG 53,155 56, 59, *In Gen. hom.* 42; PG 54,386 3, *De sanc. mar.*; PG 50,646 25-29.

[73] *In 2 Tim. hom.* 2; PG 62,614 1.

Chrysostom understood the blood or sacrifice of Christ as basic to change in the γνώμη. The key issue is the control and shaping of the γνώμη. Not only is freedom from destructive passion to be found in taming the γνώμη, but also freedom from the tyranny of an evil conscience. It was shown above that in Chrysostom's anthropology the γνώμη exercises control over the conscience, but that did not prevent the conscience from impacting upon and adding to the shaping of the γνώμη under suitable circumstances.

A related matter in a comment on the apostle Paul is found in a homily on Genesis. There Chrysostom observes that a particular γνώμη was produced by the discernment of an underlying purpose (ὑπόθεσις) to an event in Paul's experience.[74] His subsequent γνώμη or mindset is determined not so much by the event itself, but by his understanding of this underlying cause. It is the assumption he made, his thinking on the possible cause or purpose of the event, that shaped his γνώμη to face what lay ahead. Here again the thinking faculty is closely associated with the γνώμη. What one thinks about an event becomes determinate for one's thinking and approach to life in the future. The point here is, that in Chrysostom's understanding, whatever impacts upon our thinking is instrumental in changing our mindset, our γνώμη. This is why Chrysostom was a dedicated preacher: people needed to be taught well in the scriptures so that their reflections on their experiences would be guided to make an appropriate impact on their γνώμη. Both the teaching received and one's reflections on events in the light of the scriptures are shining examples of formative factors of the γνώμη.

Almsgiving was mentioned as another instrument by which change in the γνώμη could be effected. Chrysostom spoke frequently and at length on almsgiving. Here again is a topic about which, in the context of repentance, he becomes somewhat lyrical, "I specifically mean almsgiving, the queen of virtues, the very best advocate, which quickly raises people to the triumphal arches of heaven."[75] Almsgiving is presented as one of the roads to repentance. Here is where words become deeds, where the state of γνώμη is observed in a very practical and obvious way. Overall, Chrysostom gives it a very positive role in the Christian life, seeing it as a vital part of training (γυμνάζω) for repentance.[76] As

---

[74] *In Gen. hom.* 27; PG 53,225 52: ἀλλ' ἐπειδὴ ἡ ὑπόθεσις τῶν γινομένων τοσαύτην αὐτῷ τὴν γνώμην κατεσκεύαζεν, ὡς μηδὲ ἐπιστρέφεσθαι πρὸς τὰ ἐπιόντα δεινά.

[75] *De paen. hom.* 3; PG 49,293 9-12: Λέγω δὴ τὴν ἐλεημοσύνην τὴν βασιλίδα τῶν ἀρετῶν, τὴν ταχέως ἀνάγουσαν εἰς τὰς ἁψῖδας τῶν οὐρανῶν τοὺς ἀνθρώπους, τὴν συνήγορον τὴν ἀρίστην. Μέγα πρᾶγμα ἐλεημοσύνη·

[76] *De paen. hom.* 3; PG 49,292 34-35: Περὶ μετανοίας τὸν λόγον ἐγυμνάζομεν πρώην καὶ ἐλέγομεν, ὅτι πολλαὶ καὶ ποικίλαι ὁδοὶ τῆς μετανοίας, ἵνα εὔκολος ἡμῖν γένηται ἡ σωτηρία.

repentance, μετάνοια, refers to a change of mind, the claim that almsgiving is a factor in changing the γνώμη is well warranted.[77]

In a number of places, Chrysostom advocates the value of the continuous remembrance of our sins as a means of developing a proper γνώμη for approaching God in prayer. In a homily where Chrysostom discusses the parable of the Pharisee and the publican, he analyses the different mindsets of these men in their prayers. He declares:

> For just as it is good to remind oneself of one's sins, so it is also good to forget one's virtuous deeds. What does this mean? That the remembrance of virtuous deeds sets one up for boastfulness, whereas the remembrance of sins represses that kind of thinking (διάνοια) and makes one humble; the former creates more negligence, the latter produces more zeal.[78]

Chrysostom, in describing the two men at prayer, paints the Pharisee who was consumed with grand thoughts of his own piety as a ship so overloaded with cargo that it suffered great losses and became a piece of wreckage that never left the harbour. On the other hand, the person who was conscious of his sins approached God in prayer with "much rightmindedness" (εὐγνωμόσυνη), that is with a rightly disposed γνώμη, attained his goal and was duly justified.[79] Here then is another factor in the shaping of the mindset. The truly repentant must keep their past sins before their eyes, not as an exercise in morbidity, but in order to fashion the γνώμη to become steadfast in the pursuit of holiness. As Chrysostom clearly stated in another homily:

> Do you see how great a good it is to call our sins to mind? For if this man had constantly remembered these sins of his, he would not have become a savage

---

[77] Christo, *On Repentance and Almsgiving*, xiv, observes: "Repentance is ordained by God as a perpetual conversion for the human being to exercise his free choice correctly in order to recapture his image in its pristine state and heal it. Repentance enables the human being to strive for and eventually achieve the likeness of God which Christ's redemptive work restored once and for all."

[78] *Non desp.*; PG 51,366 31-37: Ὥσπερ γὰρ ἁμαρτημάτων μεμνῆσθαι, καλόν, οὕτω κατορθωμάτων ἐπιλελῆσθαι, καλόν. Τίνος ἕνεκεν; Ὅτι ἡ μὲν τῶν κατορθωμάτων μνήμη πρὸς ἀλαζονείαν ἡμᾶς ἐπαίρει, ἡ δὲ τῶν ἁμαρτημάτων μνήμη καταστέλλει τὴν διάνοιαν καὶ ταπεινοῖ· καὶ ἐκείνη μὲν ῥαθυμοτέρους ποιεῖ, αὕτη δὲ σπουδαιοτέρους ἐργάζεται.

[79] *Non desp.*; PG 51,365 44-54. See also *Non grat.*; PG 50,658-659, and *Utinam*; PG 51,306 57ff. See also *De paen. hom.*7; PG 49,328 19-22, from a homily of which the authenticity as a work of Chrysostom has been questioned by senior scholars in the field, but has been included by Christo in the group on which he has based his monograph. There is compelling evidence to ascribe this homily to Severian of Gabala, which may suggest a common source of theological formation for both men in their Syrian background.

person, something far less than human. This is why I constantly say, and will not rest from saying, that it is altogether exceedingly useful for us and a necessity that we continuously remember that we had been transgressors. For nothing is thus able to produce a wise, reasonable and gentle soul as the continuous remembrance of sins. [80]

It is seen, then, that whatever has significant impact upon the mind, conscience, or affections, is effective in producing change in the γνώμη, the mindset or basic orientation of a person's being. In particular, Chrysostom pointed to the blood of Christ for its impact upon the conscience and for its consequent effect of focusing vision upon the things of God. The Scriptures, especially the teaching of them and the expositional approach to them given by Chrysostom and other trusted preachers, were another vital instrument of conditioning the γνώμη towards godly health. Almsgiving, as representative of altruistic action that protects us from the hardening of self-centredness in our beings, was seen as another crucial element in training the γνώμη. In Chrysostom's system, almsgiving was included as a road to maturity under repentance. Ongoing repentance, including the remembrance of past sins, also was claimed as a factor in properly shaping the γνώμη.

IV. Conclusion

In Chrysostom's anthropology, the γνώμη was understood as the faculty of the soul that would develop into the agenda-setting ability for life and destiny. Eventually it would become settled into a habitual state which would determine responses to ideas and circumstances in the encounters of daily life. For some it would become fixed in opposition to the truth, and would reject the overtures of grace; for others it would remain pliable and respond positively. The Christian, at conversion and baptism, receives an initial transformation of the γνώμη that forms the basis for further development in God-likeness. The Christian is expected to make use of the instruments of change provided by God to mould the γνώμη in accord with his desires. These instruments of ongoing change are discerned as the

---

[80] *De decem.* ; PG 51,27 35-43: Ὁρᾷς ὅσον ἐστὶν ἀγαθὸν ἁμαρτημάτων μεμνῆσθαι; Καὶ γὰρ οὗτος, εἰ διηνεκῶς τούτων ἐμέμνητο, οὐκ ἂν οὕτως ἄγριος ἐγένετο καὶ ἀπάνθρωπος. Διὰ τοῦτο συνεχῶς λέγω, καὶ λέγων οὐ παύσομαι, ὅτι χρήσιμον σφόδρα καὶ ἀναγκαῖον τὸ διηνεκῶς μνημονεύειν ἡμᾶς τῶν πεπλημμελημένων ἡμῖν ἁπάντων· οὐδὲν γὰρ ἐργάσασθαι δύναται, ὡς ἡ διηνεκὴς τῶν ἁμαρτημάτων μνήμη.

blood or sacrifice of Christ, especially as experienced in the eucharist, the sacred scriptures and the preaching of them, almsgiving, which he called the queen of virtues, and which together with the remembrance of sins he considered as essential elements of continuous repentance.

This concludes the first part of this study. The γνώμη has been identified as the ruling faculty of the soul and its features and functions described. Chrysostom taught that every person is master of their own γνώμη and therefore responsible for its state, their responses, their spiritual formation and their sins. Chrysostom believed the shaping of the γνώμη to be the decisive responsibility of every person. Everything depends on it.

It is to the issue of sin and its locus in the γνώμη that attention must be given. Before that is done, the sources of Chrysostom's understanding of the γνώμη will be discussed in order to confirm the above picture from the significant formative factors of his theological anthropology in which the γνώμη had such a critical place.

CHAPTER 7

In the Rhetorical School of Libanius

In attempting to understand the usage of γνώμη by Chrysostom, the question arises as to what sources were influential in the development of his vocabulary and the meaning of critical terms in his writings. Some obvious sources come quickly to mind: his home environment, especially the influence of his mother, his education in the Greek παιδεία,[1] his early interest in the law, his six years in the ἀσκητήριον of Diodore, and the six or seven years of ascetic life and study when he committed the whole of the New Testament to memory. For the purpose of the focus on γνώμη in this study, the ascetic years may be dismissed as a major source as there are only nine occurrences of the word in the New Testament. Also, because this period stands at the end of what we might call his period of formal education, it seems clear that he came to that time with a large working vocabulary and conceptual system already on hand.[2] There is not much that can be said about the home except the normal generalities in regard to class and Christian background.[3] With regard to his interest in law, that soon waned, and though that episode may

---

[1] Παιδεία is used in the sense of an educational system including its goals, literature, guiding principles and methodology. By the end of the fourth century CE, two great παιδεία were vying for ascendancy in the Roman empire: one, the Greek παιδεία based upon the literature of the Classic period of Greek history, and promoted by the pagan rhetors and philosophers of the old order; the other, the Christian παιδεία based upon the life and ministry of Jesus Christ and which looked to the Hebrew Scriptures and the writings of the apostles of Jesus and those who were associated with them in following the Christian faith, and that was promoted by its preachers and teachers; See Chapter 6 above, "Shaping the Γνώμη", esp. note 2, for the discussion of the Christian παιδεία; the standard work on the Greek παιδεία is W. Jaeger, *The Greek Παιδεία*, 3 vols, trans. G. Highet (New York 1943-1945); see also A.-J. Festugière, *Antioche païenne et chrétienne: Libanius, Chrysostome et les moines de Syrie* (Paris 1959) 211-244, who discusses the Greek παιδεία including its advantages and disadvantages from a Christian perspective. Cf. Mitchell, *The Heavenly Trumpet*, 401-402, for the rival *politeias*, the opposing civilizations, and the goal of Chrysostom's epideictic rhetoric aimed at creating a new social order.

[2] It is obvious from his explanation of 1 Cor. 1:10 in the distinction he makes between νοῦς and γνώμη that he brought his educational background to bear on the text, for there is nothing explicit in the New Testament which he could have used. See *In 1 Cor. hom.* 3; PG 61,23 7-28 and my discussion above in Chapter 2.

[3] See John Chrys., *De sac. 1-6*; SC 272,1.5; A.H.M. Jones, "St John Chrysostom's parentage and education", HTR 46 (1953) 171-173; Baur, *John Chrysostom and His Time*, vol. 1, 1-7; Kelly, *Golden Mouth*, 4-6.

have had some role in developing his rhetorical expertise, it is most unlikely that it was a major source for the particular vocabulary under investigation here. At best, it would have been affirmative.[4] In regard to his experience in the ἀσκητήριον, that may have had its part, but I suspect that, at best, it only confirmed much of what had been already put in place as far as the vocabulary and ideas relating to the faculties of the psyche were concerned. No doubt adjustments and perhaps additions were made in the light of the specific Christian knowledge gained with Diodore, but much of the basic schema would have remained as Diodore came to Antioch as a highly educated lay-person.[5] It has been noted by Campenhausen that Diodore was a dialectician trained in the Aristotelian school, a philologist, theologian and biblical scholar.[6] This would have been significant not only for Chrysostom's approach to exegesis and use of Scripture, but also for the value he placed on what he had gained from the Greek παιδεία. It appears that he had taken his own advice when he counselled Christian parents to attend to the schooling of their children. He did not advocate desertion of the pagan school system, but was happy enough for the plasterers, his characterisation of the philosophers and rhetor-sophists of the Greek παιδεία, to do their work on the walls provided the building was solid and firm in Christian virtue.[7] In his own case, although his concern was for building in each life an enduring edifice of true virtue through the Christian παιδεία, he would not cast away the literary heritage of his previous

---

[4] John Chrys., *De sac. 1-6*; SC 272,1.4; Heath, "John Chrysostom, rhetoric and galatians", 372, thinks that as many of Libanius' pupils became advocates and that judicial rhetoric was taught in the rhetorical schools of late antiquity, Chrysostom absorbed the techniques of that branch of rhetoric. This seems probable, but the extent to which γνώμη figured in the specialised vocabulary of judicial rhetoric is conjectural. He was already familiar with γνώμη from his literary studies, and if it figured among the specialised judicial vocabulary it would have strengthened its significance for him; Thurén, "John Chrysostom as rhetorical critic", 195, takes a contrary position to Heath on Chrysostom's use of judicial rhetoric; J. Fairweather, "The Epistle to Galatians and Classical rhetoric: parts 1 and 2", *Tyndale Bulletin* 45 (1994) 1-38 at 3, asserts that Chrysostom analysed Paul's letter as both apologetic (judicial) and deliberative.

[5] Baur, *John Chrysostom and His Time*, 89-103; Kelly, *Golden Mouth*, 11 and 18-19.

[6] H. von Campenhausen, *The Fathers of the Greek Church* (London 1963) 143; Baur, *John Chrysostom and His Time*, 93, asserts of Diodore: "He also wrote against Paganism, Plato and Aristotle, the Jews, the Manichaeans, Melchisidekites, and Arians, astronomers and astrologers and their fatalism, and so forth." This indicates knowledge of their teachings, and as Diodore was educated in Athens it is assumed that much of this was gained there. See also C. Schäublin, "Diodor von Tarsus", TRE, 763-767.

[7] John Chrys., *Oppugn.*; PG 47,367 9-12: Τί οὖν; κατασκάψομεν τὰ διδασκαλεῖα, φησίν; Οὐ τοῦτο λέγω, ἀλλ' ὅπως μὴ τὴν τῆς ἀρετῆς καθέλωμεν οἰκοδομήν, καὶ ζῶσαν κατορύξωμεν τὴν ψυχήν ("What then? Does it mean that we shall raze the schools to the ground? This I do not mean, but to act in such a manner that we should not destroy the edifice of virtue, or bury the soul that is alive.")

education but make good use of it in the ministry of preaching in which he excelled. The years under the instruction of the Greek παιδεία, especially the final years in Antioch's famous rhetorical school, stand out as the time in which Chrysostom's vocabulary was not only formed, but also consolidated to become a permanent feature of his psyche. Though much was added in the following years of Christian instruction and meditation, Libanius, in particular, had left the imprint of the teacher upon him.[8]

Significant consequences accrued from Chrysostom's formal education in the Greek παιδεία that was completed with four years in the rhetorical school of the famous sophist-orator, Libanius. There he developed an exceptional talent for rhetoric, advanced his outstanding command of Classical Attic, and became steeped in the literary heritage of the Greek παιδεία. The tutelage of Libanius, a master *par excellence* in these arts, provided Chrysostom with the best possible opportunity to shape his being with those elements that in time would make him a select exponent of persuasive oratory in the service of the Christian church. In those years, it is evident that an indelible mark was made upon the intellect and mindset of Libanius' talented pupil. Many scholars have testified to the influence of those years, especially in regard to his rhetorical skill and his proficiency in language of the lassical elite.[9] Under Libanius, not only the skill, but also the

---

[8] For discussions of Libanius' life, school, works and influence, including translations of many of his works see Festugière, *Antioche païenne et chrétienne;* P. Petit, *Les Étudiants de Libanius* (Paris 1956) esp. 40-42 and n. 129, which points to the problems of confirming a relationship between Chrysostom and Libanius with any certainty; B. Schouler, *La Tradition hellenique chez Libanios* (Lille–Paris 1984); D.A. Russell (trans.), *Libanius, Imaginary Speeches: A Selection of Declamations* (London 1996); S. Bradbury, *Selected Letters of Libanius: from the Age of Constantius and Julian,* TTH 41 (Liverpool 2004); R. Cribiore, *Gymnasts of the Mind: Greek Education in Hellenistic and Roman Egypt* (Princeton–Oxford 2005), in which Libanius figures significantly; R. Cribiore, *The School of Libanius in Late Antique Antioch* (Princeton–Oxford 2007); A.F. Norman (trans.), *Libanius: Selected Orations,* 2 vols, LCL 451-452 (Cambridge, MA–London 1969-1977).; A.F. Norman (trans.) *Autobiography and Selected Letters,* 2 vols, LCL 478-479 (Cambridge, MA–London 1992).

[9] A. Naegele, "Johannes Chrysostomus und sein Verhältnis zum Hellenismus", *Byzantinische Zeitschrift* 13 (1904) 73-113; Ameringer, *A Study in Greek Rhetoric,* though Ameringer does not discuss any particular link to Libanius; Baur, *John Chrysostom and His Time,* vol. 1, 304-314, and at 22-28, where discussing Chrysostom's rhetorical training he remarks that he found it very improbable that Chrysostom would not at least have heard Libanius, and that it is highly probable that Libanius was his teacher. At 22-23, he lists the proponents in the early debate over this issue; D.G. Hunter, "Borrowings from Libanius in the *Comparatio regis et monachi* of St John Chrysostom", *Journal of Theological Studies* n.s. 39 (1988) 525-531; D.G. Hunter, *A Comparison Between a King and a Monk; Against the Opponents of the Monastic Life: Two Treatises by John Chrysostom,* SBEC 13 (New York 1988); D.G. Hunter, "Libanius and John Chrysostom: new thoughts on an old problem", *SP* 22 (1989) 129-135; D.G. Hunter, "Preaching

vocabulary of the teacher became that of the student.[10] The correspondence between Libanius and Basil of Caesarea indicates how wide of the mark are those who disparage the influence of the Greek παιδεία upon Christian leaders in late antiquity. There is little doubt that the influence of Libanius on his students was profound and lasting. This is evident from a letter Libanius wrote in answering a letter from Basil calling him a sophist in the derogatory sense that he used his rhetorical skill ...καὶ τὰ μεγάλα μικρὰ ποιεῖν, ὁπότε βούλεται, καὶ τοῖς μικροῖς περιτιθέναι μέγεθος ("...capriciously to make great things small and to bestow greatness on small things").[11] He comments on Basil's reading of the Old Testament:

> Therefore, cling closely to the books that you say are inferior in style but better in thought, and may nothing hinder you. As for the things that are always ours, and were at first yours, the roots remain and will remain while you exist; and no period of time will ever cut them off, not even if you water them the very least.[12]

Libanius was right, and this is obvious in Chrysostom who eventually came to oppose Libanius who was a leading spokesman for the Graeco-Roman pagan worldview. There is little doubt that what Chrysostom learnt from Libanius during the years under his tutelage left a huge legacy of thought, understanding and opinion in his psyche. It is in his opposition to his former teacher that the extent of this influence of the Greek παιδεία upon Chrysostom becomes evident. He had

---

and propaganda in fourth-century Antioch: John Chrysostom's *Homilies on the Statues*", in D.G. Hunter (ed.), *Preaching in the Patristic Age: Studies in Honor of Walter J. Burghardt* (New York–Mahwah, NJ 1989) 119-138; A. Hartney, *John Chrysostom and the Transformation of the City* (London 2004) 33-52, discusses both the Classical roots and the ambivalence of Chrysostom toward the Classical tradition.

[10] The claim of M. Edwards, "Pagan and Christian monotheism in the age of Constantine", in S. Swain and M. Edwards (eds), *Approaching Late Antiquity: The Transformation from Early to Late Empire* (New York 2004) 211-234, that the Hellenic tradition had little effect on the writers of Greek Christianity, has been answered in a review article by A.P. Johnson, "Approaching late antiquity: the transformation from early to late empire", *Theological Studies* 66 (2005) 891-892: "Yet, while the Church in the West accepted Romanness, the Hellenic tradition is claimed to have had little effect on Greek theologians (Edwards's (sic) second essay). The emphasis on the particularity of Christianity (vis-à-vis Neoplatonism) is a salutary move; but explaining away the common vocabulary shared (even if for different purposes and within different theological frameworks) by pagan and Christian thinkers only obfuscates the discourse(s) on the divine in Late Antiquity".

[11] Basil, *Epist.* 339.1 2-4.

[12] Basil, *Epist.* 340 21-26: Βιβλίων μὲν οὖν ὧν φῂς εἶναι χείρω μὲν τὴν λέξιν, ἀμείνω δὲ τὴν διάνοιαν, ἔχου καὶ οὐδείς κωλύοι. Τῶν δὲ ἡμετέρων μὲν ἀεί, σῶν δὲ πρότερον, αἱ ῥίζαι μένουσί τε καὶ μενοῦσιν ἕως ἂν ᾖς καὶ οὐδεὶς μήποτε αὐτὰς ἐκτέμοι χρόνος, οὐδ' ἂν ἥκιστα ἄρδοις.

learned from an earlier stage of the παιδεία that its chief aim was moral formation, the creation of a person of virtue.[13] From Libanius' works it is clear that this principle was reinforced.[14] The issue of the ethical power of the Greek παιδεία over against that of the Christian gospel became the battleground of these orators of contrasting world-views. As Hunter has noted:

> It was axiomatic in antiquity that a virtuous life could sustain an apologetic argument, and to Libanius the life of Julian or of Socrates was a sign of the superiority of Hellenic παιδεία and λόγοι.[15]

Chrysostom was no less aware of this principle. Hunter observes that Chrysostom, in possibly what was his first published work, the *Comparatio regis et monachi*, had plagiarised speeches and other works of Libanius for the purpose of demonstrating the superiority of the Christian teachings in producing virtue.[16] The Christian monk, he argued, was the true philosopher, the true paragon of virtue. The Christian faith had produced living icons of the ideal that the Greek παιδεία had set but could not reach. One of the conclusions drawn by Hunter from this exchange is the suggestion that "the ethical interests which dominated Chrysostom's preaching throughout the rest of his life may have been definitively shaped by this pagan-Christian conflict".[17] The impact of Libanius, the leading defender of paganism in Antioch and perhaps in the empire, is manifest.

---

[13] Jaeger, *Early Christianity and the Greek Παιδεία*, 86-100; Downey, *Antioch in the Age of Theodosius the Great*, 63-64, observes: "Thus the student learned to analyse and explain a text in its literary, moral, and technical aspects. Of these, the moral content was the chief end of study, for the goal of all education was the formation of character and preparation for life".

[14] Libanius' works are replete with the theme of virtue; a very few examples of the many references are to be found at *Or.* 12.20, 12.96, 13.43, 14.31, 15.45; *Ep.* 19.6, 19.16, 35.3, 37.5; see the comment by Liebescheutz, *Barbarians and Bishops*, 172: "The declamation of secular rhetors included a considerable element of moralizing. Libanius, and no doubt many other sophists, insisted that rhetorical education had a moral objective".

[15] Hunter, "Libanius and John Chrysostom", 131; R.E. Carter, "St John Chrysostom's rhetorical use of the Socratic distinction between kingship and tyranny", *Traditio* 14 (1958) 367-371 at 371, notes: "It has often been remarked that the Fathers of the fourth century defended Christianity against paganism by means of the literary education they had acquired in the pagan schools. Chrysostom's use of the king-tyrant distinction is a striking example of this practice". Carter applies it to more issues than addressed here, notably to Church-State relations.

[16] Hunter, "Borrowings", 525. This is expanded in his "Libanius and Chrysostom", 129-135, at 135 where he concludes: "Ethics and apologetics are intimately linked for Chrysostom, and this represents a lasting legacy from Libanius."

[17] Hunter, "Preaching and propaganda", 133. This article gives a fuller account of the struggle by focusing upon the material relating to the riots in Antioch in 387 CE that culminated in the

There is reason to think that this influence extended to vocabulary and ideas except where terms were derived predominantly from the Christian context. Otherwise, it appears that Chrysostom used terms common to the culture of the Hellenic παιδεία. This applies particularly to those terms that were used to refer to the operations of the human psyche. Thus, the concern of this part of the study is twofold: first, to judge the affinity or otherwise of Chrysostom's usage of γνώμη to that of Libanius, and consequently, to appreciate its harmony with the literature of the παιδεία; second, to discern the range of its signification from that grand context in order to understand the application made by Chrysostom.

A survey of Libanius' works reveals that γνώμη was used extensively by him in the same ways as discerned in the works of Chrysostom. This includes many of the terms used in various English translations to cover the diverse nuances of γνώμη in its semantic range. It is evident that both rhetor-sophist and Christian preacher drank at the same well, the Greek παιδεία, and absorbed its vocabulary into their own psyches. As the student was directed by the teacher in what to read as well as how to read, this dependence guaranteed the sharing of a common stock of words, stories, images and concepts. It is no surprise to find that there are significant affinities between the two scholars in their use of γνώμη. Some of these are discussed below.

One area of similarity is found in the use of γνώμη as signifying the normally fixed habit of a person's being, what we call one's mindset. This is encountered in the funeral oration for Julian where Libanius drew attention to the emperor's capacity to focus his mind on philosophical speculations in the midst of various diversions such as the hippodrome, the circus, and even the revelry of banquets. He could move among the promiscuous mob he had to entertain, having a drink and allowing others to indulge, but ἐπιτρέπων αὐτὸς λόγους ("...he, himself, would be turning towards rhetorical argument").[18] The verb, ἐπιτρέπω, which Libanius uses here, signifies in the context the orientation of Julian's inner being towards the promotion of speculative enquiry. This was the fixed habit of his psyche. Nothing could change (μεθίστημι) his γνώμη, his mindset, in this regard. His mind was set in that direction and he would turn instinctively toward it.[19]

Closely related to this preceding usage of γνώμη is its use to signify the locus for persistence in the face of adverse circumstances or, antithetically, the locus of weakness and wavering under the weight of unfavourable conditions. Both men

---

destruction of the imperial statues; see Cribiore, *The School of Libanius*, 142-143, on student imitation of a teacher and its application to Chrysostom.

[18] Libanius, *Or.* 18.170-171.

[19] See Chapter 6 above for discussion of this feature in Chrysostom.

used γνώμη in these ways.[20] Libanius tells how Socrates did not allow his imposed poverty to alter his way of life, ἀλλ' ἐτήρησεν ἀκίνητον τὴν γνώμην διὰ τέλους... ("but he guarded unmovable his γνώμη through to the end..."). [21] His mindset did not flinch under the circumstances. Julian is described as being steadfast under injustice when an intimate advisor of his was expelled from the palace by a corrupt prefect. Libanius wrote, καὶ οὐκ ἐγένετο χείρων τὴν γνώμην τοσαῦτα ἀδικούμενος ("...and as much as he suffered injustice, it did not come to pass that it mastered his mindset").[22] On the other hand, we find the inhabitants of the fortress isle of Thilutha having their γνώμη agitated (ταράξας) by Julian's threat to return and deal with them in his campaign.[23] They certainly did flinch.

Allied to this is the variety of epithets that are attached to γνώμη, signifying the various states in which this faculty could be found. These epithets of the γνώμη are nothing less than portraits of the persons to whom the specified γνώμη is ascribed.[24] Libanius recounts the deeds of Julian when fighting the barbarians on the Rhine frontier. In so doing, he pauses to use a favourite technique of the rhetor, the comparison, in observing the worth of two of the strategies that Julian discarded in favour of a third. One, he suggests, was of no great consequence, the other of great danger, the one indicative of a small mindset (μικροῦ τὴν γνώμην) and the other of an irrational one (ἀλογίστου).[25] Neither was worthy of a great general. The portraits are clear, luminously setting off Julian's mindset. Chrysostom, too, used a wide variety of epithets with γνώμη. A feature of his preaching was that he marshalled an abundance of descriptive words to press home to his hearers the burden of his heart, the epithets used in conjunction with γνώμη being a particular instance of this. They range from ἀγαθή, good, on the positive side, to σατανική, satanic, on the negative. They encompass the whole gamut of moral and spiritual states and emotions. In every case, the state described appears to refer to the basic orientation of the person's being: this is the kind of person this one is. Take, for example, two epithets, πονηρᾶς (evil), and ἀσθενεστέρας (more feeble), which are found together in a homily addressing the

---

[20] This flexibility of the γνώμη in Chrysostom is discussed in Chapter 6 above.
[21] Libanius, *Dec.* 1.18.
[22] Libanius, *Or.* 18.86.
[23] Libanius, *Or.* 18.219.
[24] My inspiration for the use of the term "portraits" here comes from Mitchell, *The Heavenly Trumpet*, 70-75, in her treatment of the epithets applied by Chrysostom to the Apostle Paul that she classes as "miniature portraits". Her introductory remarks and footnotes on the function of epithets in the literature and oratory of antiquity are very helpful. Their significance for my understanding of the role of γνώμη had been recognised before her book became available, but the image I thankfully borrow.
[25] Libanius, *Or.* 18.55.

incident of the rich young ruler. Here he employs the comparison figure, contrasting the rich young ruler with the Pharisees. At the reply of Jesus to their questions, the Pharisees grew fierce, whereas the young ruler was cast down. To Chrysostom, these responses indicated that whereas the former had come to Jesus with an evil γνώμη, the latter had come with one that was very feeble.[26] The epithets are descriptive of the kind of persons these people were in their inner beings. Their mindsets, the basic orientations of their beings, are in view. In Chrysostom's view, the Pharisees were fundamentally evil because they did not want the truth and reacted violently when they heard it. The rich young man was essentially weak, because he desired the truth but was enslaved by a governing passion. In both cases, their reactions were no mere passing emotions but were expressions of their γνώμη, the basic mindsets of their beings.

In the funeral oration for Julian we find that Libanius viewed the γνώμη as having a central role in the soul as an arbiter of good and evil. In mentioning how Julian repudiated the use of force in procuring conversions from one faith to another, Libanius pictures a person under duress offering a sacrifice with the hand, but being censured and accused by their own γνώμη for their weakness.[27] No real conversion takes place, only what Libanius calls a σκιαγραφία, a painting with shadows, a mirage or an illusion. The action with the hand is against the normal fixed mindset of the person who is functioning out of character in doing this. The γνώμη is seen as equivalent to conscience, a faculty shaped by παιδεία and experience. This matches Chrysostom's perspective on the γνώμη in which he regarded this faculty as the control centre of a person's moral convictions, although his Christian conviction did not allow him to equate it with the conscience.[28]

Another area of comparison to Chrysostom relates to the technique of understanding a writer, a speaker or a teacher. Chrysostom insisted that one must discern the γνώμη, the mindset, of the communicator in order to grasp the essence of their teaching. It is no surprise to find that Libanius shared that principle. Indeed, it is probable that Chrysostom learnt it from the sophist himself in the first place. Enumerating the content and extent of Julian's education and subsequent understanding, Libanius speaks of Julian's teacher and guide:

---

[26] John Chrys., *In Matt. hom.* 63; PG 58,604 36-41: ἀλλ' ἄπεισι κατηφής· ὅπερ οὐ μικρὸν σημεῖον ἦν τοῦ μὴ μετὰ πονηρᾶς γνώμης αὐτὸν προσελθεῖν, ἀλλ' ἀσθενεστέρας, καὶ ἐπιθυμεῖν μὲν τῆς ζωῆς, κατέχεσθαι δὲ ἑτέρῳ πάθει χαλεπωτάτῳ ("But he goes away downcast, which was no small sign that he did not come to him with an evil mindset, but with one quite weak. Though his heart was set on life he was bound by another most dangerous passion").

[27] Libanius, *Or.* 18.122.

[28] See Chapter 4 for the discussion of Chrysostom's view of the γνώμη as the controlling faculty of the conscience.

...a Spartan (Λακεδαιμόνιος), a priest of virtue, a leader of the παιδεία, one who knew, if indeed anyone has done, the secrets of Homer's mindset, at least, of all those who sang and danced to Homer's tune.[29]

More was required than merely reading Homer's words. The inner convictions of his mindset needed to be detected if one was to appreciate what he intended to impart. Hence the reference to his chorus (χορός), his following, those who had drawn near to him in their thinking, and metaphorically sang the same song and danced the same dance. The task, though daunting, might be accomplished by listening to the chorus as well as to the maestro himself. Libanius' Christian student was to apply this principle to his congregation when he advised them not to look merely to the words of the speaker but also to his mindset (γνώμη) in order to acquire an accurate knowledge of what was taught.[30]

Another use of γνώμη that was common to both men was that of the plans or aspirations of the heart. Libanius tells us that Julian on his Persian campaign had the γνώμη, the mindset, the aspiration, to set foot on all the territories of the Persian empire.[31] Here we see the determined mindset that dreams great plans for the future. With this usage, we encounter the aspirations of the heart, the core hopes and desires of the person. Here γνώμη gathers up the deepest expressions of the thinking mind. These are not fleeting passions, the impulses of the moment, but determined, deliberated policies and cherished ambitions that are to be pursued, often with disastrous consequences as they were in Julian's case. Chrysostom also often used γνώμη in this way to express the purposes of the heart. A pertinent example is the comment in a homily on Matthew where he refers to the text from Luke where Jesus told his disciples that he passionately desired to

---

[29] Libanius, *Or.* 15.27: ἀλλ' ἀνὴρ Λακεδαιμόνιος, ἱερεὺς δικαιοσύνης, ἡγεμὼν παιδείας, εἰδώς, εἴπερ τις, τῆς Ὁμήρου γνώμης τὰ ἀπόρρητα καὶ σύμπαντός γε τοῦ περὶ τὸν Ὅμηρον χοροῦ... I have translated δικαιοσύνη in its semantic sense of righteousness rather than justice as the context is contrasting Hellenic humanity with barbarian savagery, and calls for humane, merciful treatment of penitent rebels and not the strict justice of deserved punishment. The argument is that the emperor, a fine product of the παιδεία, could do no other; for a discussion of χορός in relation to a school or followers of a teacher, see M. Griffith, "'Public' and 'private' in early Greek institutions of education", in Yun Lee Too (ed.), *Education in Greek and Roman Antiquity* (Boston 2001) 23-84, esp. 43-47 (Section 3a Chorus); P. Wilson, *The Athenian Institution of the Khoregia* (Cambridge 2000). In this translation, I have chosen to tease out the imagery of the term.
[30] John Chrys., *In Rom. hom.* 15; PG 60,518 14-20.
[31] Libanius, *Or.* 18.260. καὶ γνώμην δὲ εἶχεν ἐπιβῆναι πάσης ὅση Πέρσαις...

eat the Passover meal with them.[32] Chrysostom explains this desire as being an expression of the harmony of Jesus' mindset with his impending vicarious suffering on the Cross; it was, he said, "κατὰ γνώμην".[33] Here is that determined and daring pursuit of policies and plans that have been formed in the depths of the soul. As with Libanius, so with Chrysostom, γνώμη in these contexts points to a mindset moulded to represent the settled hopes and deliberated desires of the being.

Another point of comparison relates to the shaping and development of the γνώμη. Both Libanius and Chrysostom saw the need for education as a crucial factor in this process. For Libanius, the Greek παιδεία, the education system, which at its higher levels by the fourth century of our era had been in the hands of the sophists and philosophers for the best part of a millennium, was the one thing that could effect this process successfully. It is no surprise to find him frequently extolling the value of the Greek παιδεία. In his speech on his return to Antioch after a number of years in Athens, Nicomedia and Constantinople, it was the eloquence of the παιδεία that took centre stage in his encomium of the city and its citizens. Glanville Downey comments:

> Thus, Libanius said, "just as in former times the fortunes of Greece were divided between two cities, Athens and Sparta, today the fair possessions of the Greeks are divided between two cities, Antioch and Athens" – and here Libanius made the revealing comment that Antioch was to be considered Greek, on a par with Athens, for men were to be called Greeks because of their eloquence rather than their birth. Here Libanius was echoing the famous passage in the *Panegyric* of Isocrates. The great orator of classical Athens and the rhetorician of Roman Antioch both looked to Greek παιδεία, Greek culture, as the norm of civilization.[34]

In the course of this speech, Libanius referred to eloquence as ὁ νοῦν πόλεως, "the mind of a city".[35] He devotes fourteen sections to the praise of eloquence as it existed in Athens and Antioch as evidence of the value given to the ἡ τῆς σοφίας ἐπιθυμία ("passion for wisdom")[36] by the citizenry of these two cities. It is evident that the way in which the citizens thought about themselves in relation to the world in which they lived was to be found in the eloquence of their public orators,

---

[32] K. Aland et al. (eds), *The Greek New Testament* (Stuttgart 1996⁴) Luke 22:15: Ἐπιθυμίᾳ ἐπεθύμησα τοῦτο τὸ πάσχα φαγεῖν μεθ' ὑμῶν πρὸ τοῦ με παθεῖν.
[33] John Chrys., *In Matt. hom.* 81; PG 58,734 8.
[34] Downey, *Antioch in the Age of Theodosius the Great*, 93-4. See Libanius, *Or.* 11.184-185.
[35] Libanius, *Or.* 11.181. This paragraph is based on sections 181-194 of this oration, following parts of it rather closely.
[36] Libanius, *Or.* 11.182.

senators, officials, lawyers and judges, all of whom were the product of the παιδεία. Nothing surpassed this passion for wisdom in Athens, not the greatness of its war-ships, or the tactical brilliance of its battles, or the expanse of its rule. Its wisdom was the greatest asset. Indeed, as it was in Athens, so also is it in Antioch, πάντα δὲ ἐλάττω τοῦ τῆς σοφίας ἔρωτος ("...everything else is less than the love of wisdom").[37] Wisdom, Libanius argued, had not lain passive in Antioch. It had come to life and taken wings in eloquence. In turn eloquence had proved to be the most beneficial of all things. Eloquence was the expression of a knowledgeable, confident, and virtuous mindset. As far as Libanius was concerned, that mindset had been shaped by the παιδεία. This was the case with the orators and the officials who had οἱ τὰς πόλεις ταῖς γνώμαις ὀρθοῦντες ("guided accurately the cities with their mindsets").[38] Then, "the earnestness of the mindset of a judge who held the most courts", not only brought eminence to the city, but also "laid up for himself an everlasting remembrance of glory".[39]

In one of his *Declamations*, the imaginary speeches composed for public consumption and the training of students in rhetorical invention, he had a son arguing rather ironically that his father, at whom the law the son was proposing was directed, had prepared his γνώμη through the education, the παιδεία, provided for by this parent.[40] In another speech, we find Libanius reminding the emperor Julian of how the old gods had led his intellect (διάνοια) to greatness through the study of Plato, thus preparing his γνώμη for his imperial responsibilities, including oratory.[41] Another example is found in a section of the oration "Against the Refugees". There Libanius extols the splendour of eloquence or artistic speech (λόγους). In so doing he compares those who are eloquent to the oracles or prophets, saying, ὃ γὰρ ἐκείνοις τὰ πνεύματα, τοῦτο τούτοις ἡ γνώμη ("...for what the spirits are to those [the prophets], the mindset is to these [the eloquent]").[42] This interesting comparison indicates that the γνώμη is the faculty that provides the wisdom of foresight to the orator, but Libanius insists that this is only so if the γνώμη has been adequately shaped by education, that is by the Greek παιδεία. The

---

[37] Libanius, *Or.* 11.182.

[38] Libanius, *Or.* 11.188.

[39] Libanius, *Or.* 11.194: ὁ γὰρ οὐ πλεῖσται σύνοδοι, τῆς αὐτοῦ γνώμης σπουδὴν ἐνδείξας εἰς ἀείμνηστον κατέθετο τὴν δόξαν.

[40] Libanius, *Dec.* 39.6.

[41] Libanius, *Or.* 13.13 1-6. See also *Or.* 15.28 and *Or.* 12.30 for the education of Julian's διανοία by the παιδεία. In *Or.* 17.31 Libanius uses an athletic metaphor in describing how he prepared his own διάνοια to be able to laud Julian's achievements adequately. See *Or.* 11.192 for a similar comparison.

[42] Libanius, *Or.* 23.21 11-12: ὃ γὰρ ἐκείνοις τὰ πνεύματα, τοῦτο τούτοις ἡ γνώμη. See also *Or.* 11.192 for a similar comparison.

content, character and competence of the γνώμη depend upon education. It is something that is acquired or formed over time. The next sentence makes this very clear. "One may assert to be immortal only those who carry through with education, for even though they come to the end of their natural life they yet live on in fame."[43] Rhetoric was an essential element of the Greek παιδεία, but much more was included. Rhetoric, as the chief instrument of the παιδεία by the fourth century, inculcated a weighty knowledge of the past through the literature of bygone golden ages. Indeed, it transmitted the wisdom, values and experience of the past, thereby expanding the experience of the γνώμη, both of individuals and communities, thus enabling those so educated to make a significant mark in the world and leave a legacy of fame behind them. Those who fled their studies in a time of trouble also fled their immortality.

The importance of proper education to the development of the γνώμη is seen in an oration that Libanius addressed to Theodosius after the riots of 387 CE. In this speech, he refers to the breakdown of normal life that occurred. Among other things, he mourned the collapse of the rhetorical school. He described the scene as follows:

> Nobody teaches and no one learns. The skin is diseased, the voice loses its strength, the mindset has been forced to wander around in confusion, and someone, having started on one subject is carried off course to another.[44]

Denied its proper instruction, the γνώμη falls into chaos and ceases to develop as required. As far as Libanius was concerned, progress in shaping the γνώμη could only be made through the disciplined study provided by the παιδεία. As such, Libanius was representative of the παιδεία itself. It was the revered institution for the training of a cultured elite with suitably moulded mindsets, who then could give appropriate service in and leadership to the various institutions of the state.

Chrysostom shared this appreciation of education. It was natural that Chrysostom would largely replace the priority of the literature of the Greek παιδεία with that of the Christian faith that he subsequently whole-heartedly embraced. Thus, the Christian scriptures became the dominant force in shaping, or rather re-shaping his γνώμη. This was not accomplished by erasing the vast emporium of knowledge and experience he had gained in the Greek παιδεία, but rather by capturing, purifying and subjugating it to the new master who ruled his

---

[43] Libanius, *Or.* 23.21 12-14: μόνους δὲ τοὺς διενεγκόντας φαίη τις ἂν καὶ ἀθανάτους εἶναι φύσει μην ἐλευτῶντας, δόξῃ δε ζῶντας.
[44] Libanius, *Or.* 19.61: διδάσκει δὲ οὐδεὶς οὐδὲ μανθάνει. νοσούντων μὲν ἡ χρόα, οὐκ ἐρρωμένων δὲ ἡ φωνή, πεπλανημένων δὲ ἡ γνώμη, καί τις ἐπ' ἄλλον ὁρμήσας λόγον ἐπ' ἄλλον ἀπηνέχθη.

soul. After Chrysostom became a priest, he then carried concern for the condition of the γνώμη to his congregation. As a preacher, he set about the task of re-shaping their mindsets. As J. Maxwell has commented:

> One of Libanius' students, John Chrysostom, saw himself as teacher and the church as his classroom where he educated large groups of people in Christian theology, ethics, and history. Standing in church, he told his audience, "This is a spiritual school." Sermons have not been included in traditional studies of education in the ancient world, but they are extremely important sources in this field when education is considered in a variety of contexts as the transmission of knowledge.[45]

Hence, we find Chrysostom in his sermons calling for change in the γνώμη, and pointing to the Scriptures as a vital instrument for effecting that change.[46] He was confident that his preaching, which was based on exegesis of the biblical texts, would straighten out their γνώμη of any doctrinal and ethical distortions.[47] Whatever differences separated the pagan Sophist and his one-time student, the Christian preacher, they were united in seeing the formation of the γνώμη as the critical task of their chosen vocations. Both also approached this mission by using the literature of their respective world-views as vital instruments of mindset transformation.[48]

Another similarity of the usage of γνώμη is in its relation to διάνοια, the intellect, understanding, or process of thought.[49] In Chrysostom, the two terms are found often side by side in what appears almost as equivalents, or at least in the form of a hendiadys. However, as discussed elsewhere in this study, a distinction between their significations is at times clearly seen.[50] Libanius also uses γνώμη in these ways of relationship to the διάνοια. In an oration to Julian in which he pleaded for his friend, Aristophanes of Corinth, Libanius attempts to predispose Julian toward generosity by pointing to the emperor's greatest attribute, his universal care of his subjects: "to have extended your thinking (διάνοια) even as

---

[45] Maxwell, *Christianization and Communication*, 88-89. Chrysostom is cited from *In Matt. hom.* 17; PG 57,264.

[46] John Chrys., *In Matt. hom.* 4; PG 57,50 37-39 points to three effective instruments: the blood of Christ, the Scriptures and almsgiving.

[47] See the discussion in Chapter 6, Section 2 above, on *In 2 Tim. hom*; 2, PG 62,612 58-61: ἀλλ' ἵνα διορθώσωμεν ὑμῶν τὴν γνώμην, καὶ ἀσφαλεστέρους εἰς τὸ ἑξῆς ἐργασώμεθα ("in order that we might straighten out your mindset, and labour for a more secure habit of mind").

[48] See John Chrys., *Mart.*; PG 50,646 25-29, where the διάνοια of the Syrian monks had been instructed in Christian thought and discipline, φιλοσοφία.

[49] LSJ 405 *s.v.*, for semantic range.

[50] See Chapter 3 above for discussion.

far as every family and person".[51] There immediately follows a reference to those who do not understand this outlook. They are τοῖς μὲν γὰρ βραχυτέροις τὰς γνώμας ("to those who are lesser in mindsets...").[52] At first sight, it is difficult to distinguish between διάνοια and γνώμη in this instance as the contrast appears to be between a superior intellect and a smaller one. Julian had stretched his thinking, his intellect; theirs were fixed at a lower point. So the distinction should be made in that Julian's thinking was allowed to develop further whereas the others had terminated the development of their intellects at an earlier stage. The end results were two distinctive and, in this instance at least, somewhat contrasting mindsets. However, Libanius did not desire to make such a simple comparison. He wished to emphasise the intellectual effort Julian had exercised in reaching such a summit of virtue compared with the objector who was content to live short of such excellence and who failed to perceive Julian's greatest asset.[53] Thus, when considered in relation to the context and purpose of the oration, the restoration of Aristophanes was well within the reach of Julian's γνώμη already shaped through the stretching of his διάνοια, something not understood by those of lesser application. The same distinction is encountered toward the end of the long funeral oration for Julian. There Libanius, in a rhetorical apostrophe, turned to address the gods with a number of questions, one of which was, τί μεμψάμενοι τῆς γνώμης ("Why did you complain of his γνώμη?").[54] Then, having spelt out Julian's deeds together with the attributes of his character, he climaxed in a fervour of triumphant exclamations culminating in a rhetorical paraprosdokian: ὦ τέλους τῆς διανοίας ἀναξίου ("O, what an unworthy outcome of his intellect")![55] Julian's deeds spoke of the excellence of his intellect, yet the unexpected τέλος suggested that the gods had found something in his mindset that offended them. Libanius was at a loss to see what that might have been. It could not have been his intellect, his deeds, his devotion to the gods, his chastity, his justice, his intelligence, his valour or virtue – all of which were as great as, if not greater than, the lassic models.[56] From Libanius' dilemma it is evident that, as with Chrysostom, the γνώμη was

---

[51] Libanius, *Or.* 14.25 5-6: τοῦτο δ' ἐστὶ τὸ καὶ μέχρι γένους ἑκάστου καὶ ἀνδρὸς τὴν σὴν τετάσθαι διάνοιαν.

[52] Libanius, *Or.* 14.25 6-7: τοῖς μὲν γὰρ βραχυτέροις τὰς γνώμας. "for to those smaller in mindsets", τὰς γνώμας being an accusative of specification.

[53] Libanius, *Or.* 14.25 4-5: ἴστω τὸ μέγιστον τῶν σῶν ἀγνοῶν ("...let him [the faultfinder] know that he fails to recognise his [Julian's] greatest quality").

[54] Libanius, *Or.* 18.281.

[55] Libanius, *Or.* 18.282 3.

[56] Libanius, *Or.* 24.36, notes the constant focus of Julian's διάνοια on the gods. The classical models mentioned are Hippolytus for σωφροσύνη, Rhadamanthys for δικαιοσύνη, Themistocles for σύνεσις, and Brasidas for ἀνδρεία.

understood as something more than mere intellect, but as a faculty that combined with intelligence elements of attitudes, character, virtues and vices. One could view it as the battleground of reason and passion, not in the sense of a swift short encounter, but rather as a long drawn out campaign. Libanius was certain that with Julian that inner struggle had long been won by reason, religion and virtue. The god-fearing pagan teacher could not fathom why the gods should judge Julian's γνώμη as being otherwise. Considering again the references to Julian's education and the performance of his imperial duties in the speech as given by Libanius in Antioch in 362 CE, Julian's superior or stately mindset (ὑψηλὴ γνώμη) was seen by him to be the result of a thought process (διάνοια) that had been brought to greatness through study. The relationship between γνώμη and διάνοια as used by Libanius equates with what is found in Chrysostom: it was predictable in its outcomes. The properly nurtured διάνοια would result in a proper γνώμη, which in turn would issue in appropriate attitudes and actions, all of which would attract the favour of the gods. This is why Julian's death so disturbed Libanius' own γνώμη, although in the end it was insufficient to effect radical change in him.

Another way in which Libanius used γνώμη the same as Chrysostom was when he referred to a person having performed a deed in his/her γνώμη but was prevented by circumstances of doing it in real action. In a speech to the people of Antioch about the emperor's anger, he explained how a person may be incapable of performing a particular service but will do so in their mindset (γνώμη). This would be evident, he asserted, by observable behaviour such as "eager agreement, joy at the prospect and the depression over the regrettable result".[57] Nothing of this had been seen in the Antiochenes. Another instance is found in a letter to Datianus. Libanius tells how it was his intention to assist his friend but was prevented so doing by the fact that his horse had bolted. His friend thought he had been negligent of him, so we find Libanius pleading that he be judged on the basis of his γνώμη in which he had determined to act, and not on his apparent negligence in the failure to perform.[58] Libanius argued in like manner before the emperor Theodosius when appealing for leniency toward Antioch after the riots of 387. Libanius, by then a fading symbol of the old order of paganism, came before a Christian emperor who was intent on eliminating the power of the pagan past. He had come to Constantinople to plead with all his rhetorical skill for the city he so loved, but was self-elected and without the authority of an official embassy. Thus, he suggests that the substance of his efforts should be assessed on his γνώμη, his mindset, the inner stance of his being, rather than any external criteria: "I shall be

---

[57] Libanius, *Or.* 16.22.6-8: γνώμη δὲ καὶ τῷ σφόδρα συμβουληθῆναι καὶ τῷ φαινομένης ἐλπίδος ἡσθῆναι καὶ τῷ τῆς τοῦ πράγματος φύσεως ἐναντιουμένης ἀθυμῆσαι.
[58] Libanius, *Ep.* 1446.6.1-3.

judged, I hold in principle, by my γνώμη rather than by want of legal authority to take the initiative to give this answer.".[59] It is evident that the γνώμη was understood by Libanius to be the critical faculty of the psyche where the decisive attitudes and intentions of the person are determined. This is confirmed by the accusation made by Libanius in the oration on the emperor's anger, that the Antiochenes had failed to make their γνώμη rise above their circumstances, thus, neither in deed nor in mindset had they performed in an acceptable manner.[60] This emphasis on the γνώμη being as acceptable as the act itself, even if the intention is never accomplished, or even if adverse consequences occur as the result of an act, is a feature that has been noted in this study of the usage of γνώμη by Chrysostom.[61]

Allied to this aspect is Libanius' claim that the gods take note of the γνώμη in their assessment of humans. In a letter of consolation after Julian's death to Seleucus, the chief priest of a province under Julian, Libanius belittles his own works as being trifling in comparison to those of his friend, but proposes that his γνώμη is the thing with which the gods are pleased. He pleads, τὴν γνώμην δὲ οἶμαι καὶ παρὰ τοῖς θεοῖς εὐδοκιμεῖν ("...but I think that my mindset (γνώμη) is held in esteem even among the gods").[62] Here, as with Chrysostom, when a person stands before the all-seeing deities the focus of attention is turned upon the inner workings of the psyche, in particular the γνώμη.[63] This thinking is found in Libanius who asserts that an act, which appears evil and brutal, may be quite virtuous when the γνώμη behind it is discerned. This comes up in several of the *Declamations*, pointing probably to customary defences when supposed criminal acts are being examined. In one declamation, a father who is a war hero is on trial for killing his son. He defends himself by claiming he did this act for the sake of the city. Such a motive, he claims, should discharge him from any criminal guilt. He supports his case by referring to the laws of damage, the laws of homicide, and to well-known instances of history when generals burned their own ships or crops in the cause of defeating the enemy. From these he draws the conclusion: τῆς τοίνυν γνώμης εὐδοκιμούσης ἀπήλλακται καὶ τὸ πραχθὲν αἰτίας ("Accordingly, when the mindset (γνώμη) is held in esteem, the action is exonerated from guilt").[64] In another declamation, a similar defence is offered by Orestes for the

---

[59] Libanius, *Or*. 19.2.5-6: κριθήσεσθαι γὰρ ἡγοῦμαι τῇ γνώμῃ μᾶλλον ἢ τοῖς οὐχ ὑπάρξασι τοῦ δοῦναι κυρίοις.
[60] Libanius, *Or*. 16.22.
[61] See Chapter 2, Section 3 above.
[62] Libanius, *Ep*. 1473.1.
[63] John Chrys., *In Gen. hom*. 20; PG 53,166 43; *hom*. 29; PG 53,200 7-9.
[64] Libanius, *Dec*. 42.17 13-14.

murder of his mother. He brings forth several arguments, the deeds of his mother, the command of Apollo, and the hypothetical cases of killing robbers who attack a person, an enemy in self-defence, and an adulterer who has taken one's wife. All these are the defence of motive, the reasons of the heart. Thus, we find him saying that no charge would be brought against such, ἀλλὰ τὴν τούτου γνώμην εἰδὼς ὡς ἀριστέα μᾶλλον θαυμάσει ("but knowing the mindset (γνώμη) of this person, one will admire him rather as a monument of honour").[65] It is being insisted that it is the motive which is the critical factor in judging the virtue or vice of an action. What was intended in the γνώμη is the thing to be considered, not the action in itself, divorced from this inner cause. The disposition of this faculty, the γνώμη, is the decisive factor in attributing praise or blame. That this was Libanius' own position and not just that of one of his imaginary creations appears clear from the discussion above. Here again we are face to face with Chrysostom in his usage. The apparent brutal action of Phineas, or the deceit of Jacob or the intended infanticide of Abraham, are all to be judged and applauded on the basis of the disposition of the γνώμη.[66]

An interesting similarity to Chrysostom in regard to γνώμη lies in a particular element of Libanius' belief system. This relates to his understanding of the relation between providence and one's own γνώμη. In an oration given at the request of the Emperor Julian when he came to Antioch in July 362, Libanius praised Julian for his self-effort in concert with his dependence upon τοῖς κρείττοσι ("the higher powers").[67] Julian, who had turned from his Christian upbringing to the traditional paganism, does not appear to have embraced some of its extreme practices of complete abandonment to forces outside his own abilities. Libanius appreciated that Julian did not depend blindly upon the normal range of oracles available to the generals of armies and made use of by many of them. Julian, it is claimed, equated such an attitude with ῥᾳθυμία, sloth or indifference. Rather than depending upon the γνώμη of others, he chose to depend on his own. Julian would not trust the interpretations of omens and oracles to anything but his own mindset. So much was this the case, that Libanius says that in effect Julian had set himself up in place of the Pythia, the famous oracle of Apollo at Delphi.[68]

---

[65] Libanius, *Dec.* 6.15 15.

[66] John Chrys., *In Gen. hom.* 53; PG 54,466 58-60: εἰπειδὴ κατὰ θεοῦ γνώμην ἐγένετο, καὶ οὐ τοῖς γεγονόσι προσέχομεν, ἀλλὰ τῷ σηοπῷ τῶν γινομένων, καὶ τῇ τῶν πεποιηκότων γνωμῇ.

[67] Libanius, *Or.* 13.48.

[68] Libanius, *Or.* 13.48. This is probably a piece of rhetorical hyperbole, Libanius wishing to fit Julian into his own ideal of an emperor-sage. There is testimony to the extensive practice of divination by Julian in Ammianus Marcellinus, *Rerum Gestarum*, 21.1 7-13, 22.12 7-8. Nevertheless, this soldier, who accompanied Julian on the Persian campaign, testified that it was

There is here with Libanius a synergism of γνώμη and κρείττων very similar to the relationship between γνώμη and πρόνοια (Christian Providence) in Chrysostom. In both the sophist and his pupil, there is an emphasis upon a mindset that acknowledges an over-ruling higher power, yet recognises that the course of events also depends upon one's own decisive action.

As further evidence of this aspect is the reflection in another oration to Julian six months later, where Libanius again extols the emperor, this time for his γνώμη (mindset), τύχη (luck), labours and skills.[69] It was the combination of these elements, he asserts, that had ensured victory against the barbarians on Julian's front on the Rhine. This bringing together of γνώμη and τύχη is significant, because τύχη points to something beyond human control, the act of a god (Fortune), providence, or fate. This is the same dualism as we find in Chrysostom. The individual person must strive with all their power, with everything that is at their disposal, their mindset, skill and toil. However, there is an element that is out of their hands, and which needs to be acknowledged. In the same breath, dependence on that other must never give place to sloth. As suggested by Libanius' presentation where the grammar connects τύχη directly to Julian as his fortune, τύχη favours those who set their whole beings, particularly the γνώμη, to the task. This is reminiscent of Chrysostom as discussed elsewhere in this study. In the beginning of homily 27 on Genesis, he focuses upon εὐγνωμόσυνη, a rightly disposed mindset (γνώμη) as the means by which Noah called forth more and greater goodwill to himself from God.[70] It is also significant that Libanius reflected on Julian's apparent setbacks as having been "by the mindset of the gods, an integral part of your more honourable destiny".[71] This amounts to a doctrine of providence in which all circumstances are woven into a fabric of ultimate benefit for the human actor on the stage of history. This is both near to and far from Chrysostom. The concept was much the same for the Christian bishop, but the

---

only the wise, the *sapiens*, who could acquire the knowledge to divine the signs. He describes Julian as "so learned and so zealous to acquire all knowledge".

[69] Libanius, *Or.* 12.52: καὶ διὰ την σὴν καὶ γνώμην καὶ τύχην καὶ μόχθους καὶ τέχνας οὐ καθ' ἑκάτερον τοῦ πολέμου τὸ στόμα τοῖς βαρβάροις ὑπῆρχε κρατεῖν. Norman, Libanus: *Selected Orations*, 1.69, translates γνώμην here as "resolution", but a mindset developed in wisdom is probably in view. In 12.54 Libanius referred to Julian's return from battle to his books that had provided the inspiration (ὁρμηθεὶς) and wisdom for his victory.

[70] See Chapter 3 above. See John Chrys., *In Acta. hom.* 47; PG 60,332, where he mourns the small number of those who live rightly, thus leaving the mind of many open to a denial of Providence on one hand, and the denial of personal autonomy on the other; see D. Amand, *Fatalisme et liberté dans l'Antiquité grecque* (Louvain 1945) esp. 502 and n. 5.

[71] Libanius, *Or.* 13.18: Πάλιν τοίνυν ἐνεθυμήθην, ὅτι καὶ ὅσα σοι τῆς τιμῆς ἀφαιρεῖν ἐδόκει, καὶ ταῦτα τῆς καλλίονος μοίρας ἦν γνώμη θεῶν.

divine mindset that controls the guiding hand was understood as very different. Nevertheless, both Libanius and Chrysostom recognised a divine γνώμη that ordered the lives of humans.[72] On the other hand, both of them placed emphasis upon the human response, the disposition of the human γνώμη.[73]

Just as in Chrysostom, Libanius viewed γνώμη as the faculty where conversion is effected. He speaks of the conversion of Julian from Christianity to "the true (τὴν ἀλήθειαν) gods".[74] In his account, he referred to Julian as having left his family estates to lie fallow, focusing rather on the preparation of his soul. There was a greater fruitfulness for which to prepare. He cultivated or healed (θεραπεύω) it, Libanius claims, by devoting himself to philosophy. As might be expected, the rhetor was adroit in his choice of words. The verb θεραπεύω has a semantic range, dependent upon context, that includes: to cultivate, to treat medically, and to serve or to worship.[75] Each of those contexts is used here by Libanius: the family estates lying fallow as cultivation was required elsewhere, the turn from acknowledgement of the "false" Christian God to the "real gods", and the reference to the "doctor" (ἰατρός), the philosopher under which Julian's γνώμη was healed, made fruitful and oriented to serve the right deities. Thus, Libanius not only indicated what was wrong but also where the ailment lay and how it could be, indeed from his viewpoint how it was, remedied. The γνώμη was the problem; it was wrongly oriented; it required the curing properties of philosophy from the Greek παιδεία. Chrysostom said much the same when calling for conversion from paganism to the Christian faith. From his point of view, the problem was also located in the γνώμη, but was rather more complex than the sophist would allow.

---

[72] The event of Julian's premature death in 363 in retreat in his abortive Persian campaign caused Libanius some serious doubts about his beliefs as he says that his first reaction was to commit suicide, *Or.* 1.135. His monody over Julian, composed some two years after the emperor's death, reveals that the event was "the stroke that both smote and shattered our souls, so that for the best man and for anyone who has a desire to live morally good, life is no longer worth living", *Or.,* 17.1. Even allowing for rhetorical hyperbole, it is evident from the tone of the monody that Libanius had been shaken. However, in the same work Libanius provides a justification for the opposition of heaven to Julian for the invasion of Persia; *Or.* 17.20, Norman, *Selected Orations,* 1.263: "you tried to exact a punishment disproportionate to the crime". This indicates that Libanius' mindset (γνώμη) remained firm in spite of the blows it had received.

[73] Reuling, *After Eden,* 157, makes the comment, "John Chrysostom was a utopian defender of the possibilities of the human will and for him this would seem a fatalistic way of thinking. Fate and free will would seem to be paradoxically intertwined in an unresolved tension: they were only to be unravelled by the champions of the Pelagian controversy, both camps appealing to the writings of the golden-mouth preacher of Antioch."

[74] Libanius, *Or.* 12.32-34. The following discussion is based on this passage, which I will use without further references.

[75] LSJ 792 *s.v.*

The cure in this case was to be found in the Christian Scriptures and the sacraments of the Church. In homily 19 on Genesis, he proposed that the faculty requiring attention for the cure of the soul affected by sin, was the γνώμη.[76]

In 380 CE, Theodosius, the Christian emperor, issued an edict that all peoples in the empire should practice the Christian trinitarian faith as defined by the Nicene Creed. Although the edict promised retribution for offenders, this was not actively pursued.[77] Others were not so tolerant: bands of Christian monks took up the cause and began to ravage pagan temples. In an address to the emperor in 386, Libanius reminded the emperor that a show of force would not be instrumental in converting the people to Christianity. The emperor's decrees did not do it; neither would the destruction of temples. The mindset (γνώμη) of the people was the thing that needed to be changed.[78] This would be a matter of intellectual persuasion, not that of an imperial edict or the might of the sword. As with Chrysostom, Libanius was aware that the citadel that needed to be taken was not the temples that marked the landscape, but rather the mindset of the people that determined their religious allegiance.[79]

Besides the features described above, a number of other parallels are evident in the works of Libanius. It is not intended to discuss these in detail as many simply fall within the semantic range of γνώμη as generally used by most writers of the Hellenistic cultures of antiquity. We have discerned in Libanius a number of parallels in his usage of γνώμη to that of Chrysostom. Both saw it as a fixed habit of the mind, a locus of various set attitudes such as persistence and weakness. They understood it to be the arbiter of good and evil. In order to comprehend a writer or speaker, both perceived the need to grasp the γνώμη of the person communicating. The γνώμη was, for both, the location in the soul of plans and aspirations. Both were strong in their belief that it is shaped by education.

---

[76] John Chrys., *In Gen. hom.* 19; PG 53,159 4; *In 1 Cor. hom.* 3; PG 61,26 20-21.

[77] J. Stevenson (ed.), *Creeds, Councils, and Controversies: Documents Illustrative of the History of the Church A.D.337-4* (London 1966) 160-161. Apart from a couple of glaring exceptions, Theodosius pursued a policy of leniency in his dealings with the great variety of ethnic and religious diversities under his rule. The wording of the edict suggests that it was aimed at non-trinitarian adherents within Christianity, and not particularly at pagans. A decade would pass before his position became such that he proscribed pagan worship; see I. Sandwell, "Outlawing magic or outlawing religion?: Libanius and the Theodosian Code as evidence for legislation against pagan practices in the fourth century AD", in W.V. Harris (ed.), *Understanding the Spread of Christianity in the First Four Centuries: Essays in Explanation,* Columbia Studies in the Classical Tradition 27 (Leiden–Boston 2005) 87-124.

[78] Libanius, *Or.* 30.27: εἰ δὲ ταῖς κατασκαφαῖς ἐγίγνοντο τῆς γνώμης αἱ περὶ ταῦτα μεταβολαί, πάλαι ἂν σῇ ψήφῳ τὰ ἱερὰ κατέσκαπτο· πάλαι γὰρ ἂν ἡδέως.

[79] See Chapter 2 above.

Libanius had a similar understanding of the relation of γνώμη to διάνοια. Also, both thought that γνώμη was the critical motivating faculty of actions, and that the disposition of the γνώμη was acceptable even if the deed could not be performed. Both believed that the γνώμη was the object of divine scrutiny and evaluation, and that it was the faculty that determined relationships with the divine, especially in matters beyond human control. Indeed, they acknowledged a divine γνώμη that ordered human life. Libanius, as did Chrysostom, understood the γνώμη as being crucial in the process of conversion from one faith to the other.

It is clear from these parallels that Chrysostom had absorbed the vocabulary and concepts of the Greek παιδεία applying to the faculties of the psyche. Certainly, this was the case with γνώμη, which figures so centrally in Chrysostom's writings. As Libanius, along with the rhetor-sophists of the Second Sophistic looked to the literature of the Classical past for their education, it is no surprise that much of the vocabulary and many of the concepts of that formative era of Greek culture should have been in current use in the late antiquity of Chrysostom's time. Whilst diversity was to be found in all places, a strong common base held the upper echelons of society together in a thought-world that had permeated and dominated the civilizations of the Mediterranean and their conquests for a major part of a millennium. It is to the formative period of that thought-world that we now turn.

CHAPTER 8

Γνώμη in the Formative Greek Παιδεία

It has been established in the first part of this study that γνώμη is a significant concept in Chrysostom's anthropology. Turning to the New Testament, which he knew by heart, and the Septuagint with which he was also exceptionally familiar, one is struck by the paucity of the incidence of γνώμη in this biblical literature. There are a bare nine occurrences in the New Testament and twenty-four only in the Septuagint that covers the whole of the Old Testament including the Apocrypha.[1] This strengthens the case for Chrysostom's education in the Greek παιδεία being the foundational source of his intellectual framework, and that his time in the rhetorical school of Libanius was a critical factor in his development. The affinity in usage of γνώμη by Libanius and Chrysostom has been demonstrated above. Their debt to the Greek παιδεία is clear. This part of this study, therefore, examines the usage of γνώμη in the Greek language in its formative era. This is done with the purpose of discerning the effect of the main literature of the Greek παιδεία upon Chrysostom's vocabulary and his anthropology, literature that he not only knew intimately, but a substantial portion of it by heart. Some points need to be made in relation to this search.

First, it is undertaken because of the relative homogeneity of Greek culture over a long period, eleven centuries for the purpose of this study. It is appreciated that there were significant political, economic, and social changes and developments during this time that contributed to the evolution of the language of the Greeks. However, the persistence of the Classical Greek παιδεία through most of this era provides an important linguistic connection between Chrysostom's age and the past.[2] Antioch in the fourth century, though in transit through the changes from a purely pagan Graeco-Roman city to one where Christianity was asserting its presence, was yet a shining jewel of the culture of the Greek παιδεία. It was one of the foremost cities of the empire, and every leap year its Olympic Games

---

[1] New Testament: Acts 20:3, 1 Cor 1:10, 7:25, 7:40, 2 Cor 8:10, Phlm 14, Rev 17:13, 17:17 (2); Old Testament (LXX): 1 Esd 6:21, 7:5; 2 Esd 4:18, 4:19, 4:21 (2), 5:3, 5:5, 5:9, 5:13, 6:1, 6:3, 6:12, 6:16, 7:21; 2 Macc 4:39, 11:37, 9:20, 14:20; 4 Macc 9:27; Dan 2:14, Ps 82:4, Prov 2:16, 12:26. Most, if not all, of these OT references are from literature of the Exilic and Post-Exilic periods. There is a startling absence of the term in the Pentateuch and the literature of the Pre-Exilic eras of the Judges and the kingdom(s), suggesting that the compilers of the LXX may have been faced with the absence of an equivalent term in the early Hebrew literature.

[2] Jaeger, *Early Christianity and the Greek Παιδεία*, 140 n. 1.

heralded its commitment to that element of Hellenism and the παιδεία that emphasised physical beauty and strength. Even more so, Antioch's reputation for its schools, especially the rhetorical school under its leading citizen, Libanius, enshrined it as a famous centre of Greek culture, arts and literature in the East.[3]

Secondly, Chrysostom, as a native of Antioch, was a product of the Greek παιδεία of his day. As such, not only was he familiar with the Greek classics as taught in the rhetorical schools but he had them embedded in his being.[4] Libanius, the rhetor under whom Chrysostom studied, mentions in a letter to Postumianus, a member of a noble Roman family, some of the authors studied by this former pupil, a list no doubt typical of the curriculum of his school,

> ...you have filled your soul with Homer, Hesiod, and the rest of the poets, and Demosthenes, Lysias, and the rest of the orators. Herodotus, Thucydides, and all their company could claim that there is room for them too in your intellect, and as witness of this they could cite the many fine orations you have composed.[5]

From Chrysostom's own writings it may be added to this list, Zeno, Plato, Diagoras, Pythagoras, Euripides, Menander, Aristotle, and the Stoics.[6] Even though at times he disparaged the pagan philosophers and rhetors, and contested even his own master, Libanius, he "never disowned", as von Campenhausen noted, "his careful philological training".[7]

Then, care must be taken, as J. Barr makes clear, to recognise that "etymological fact is historical and relative",[8] and not to err by looking for the essence of a word that persists unchanged through time. The purpose of this

---

[3] Downey, *Antioch in the Age of Theodosius the Great*, 1-15, 58, 85.

[4] Baur, *John Chrysostom and His Time*, 306; Naegele, "Johannes Chrysostomos", 73-113, esp. 92-93.; E. Martin, "Golden mouths and speaking bodies: John Chrysostom's depiction of Christian martyrs", *eSharp* 8 (Autumn 2006) 1-20, at 4-5; D. Constantelos, "Hellenic paedeia and church fathers: educational principles and cultural heritage", Greek Orthodox Archdiocese of America art. 8 (New York 2003) http://www.goarch.org/print/en/ourfaith/article8143.asp. Accessed 1 January 2007; D. Constantelos, "John Chrysostom's Greek Classical education and its importance to us today", *Greek Orthodox Review* 36 (1991) 109-129.

[5] Libanius, *Epist.* 1036, Norman, *Auto.*, 181, vol. 2, 403.

[6] John Chrys., *Adv. Jud. hom.* 3; PG 48,886 30-3; *In Rom. hom.* 3; PG 60,414 6-7.

[7] Campenhausen, *The Fathers of the Greek Church*, 143; Mayer and Allen, *John Chrysostom*, 26-27, include the advanced rhetorical training under Libanius as one of the factors that "contributed strongly to the content of his preaching and to the characteristics of his style", and also observe that "The traces of John's rhetorical education can be seen in every aspect of his sermons' structure, content and delivery."; Brändle, *John Chrysostom: Bishop – Reformer – Martyr*, 32, notes that he "inserts many quotations from the works of Greek poets and philosophers into his orations".

[8] J. Barr, *The Semantics of Biblical Language* (London 1961), 159.

present section of study is to investigate the early history of the usage of γνώμη to see what it signified at that time, and what affinity of meaning may have existed between Chrysostom's usage and the literature of his education. The principle that will guide this investigation is that provided by L. Wittgenstein, "the meaning (signification) of a word is its use in the language".[9] The issue here is not that of essence but of dependence: what source or sources shaped Chrysostom's use of this term γνώμη, and what does this convey of the signification of the term as he used it. The point is that the persistence of the Greek παιδεία over a millennium preserved the basic meanings of this term. Though it accrued various nuances in its usage over time, the fact that it was defined by Aristotle as a faculty or power of the soul or psyche, and was treated as such by the Hellenic philosophic and sophist tradition, it retained much of its Classical significance by the fourth century CE.

One reservation that must be made is that this survey cannot be exhaustive. It takes note of the early period up until the fourth century BCE. Particular attention is given to Thucydides, as there appears to be quite an affinity between the usage of γνώμη in the *History* and the usage of Chrysostom. Aristotle's discussion of γνώμη in his *Ethica Nicomachea* is examined, as concepts in that work were foundational to discussions of the operation of the psyche through much of the Greek παιδεία. Attention is also paid to Aristotle's *Rhetorica* which also contains basic material relating to γνώμη. In addition, while Chrysostom disparaged the Greek philosophers, particularly for their dependence upon the "Egyptians" and the false deities of the pagan world, Aristotle would appear to have been free of those failings and to have been more in tune with Chrysostom's mindset.[10] As the speeches of Demosthenes, the great political orator of fourth century Classical Athens, were mandatory study texts in the rhetorical schools a millennium later, an examination of these is deemed necessary. This list, although selective, will be sufficient to provide a firm base for understanding Chrysostom's use of the term.

I. Early period

Homer and Hesiod have been identified as being familiar to Chrysostom, thus providing the starting point for this study, but there are no occurrences in Homer, and only one in an extant fragment from Hesiod that provides nothing pertinent to this study. An excellent survey of the use of γνώμη up until the end of the fifth

---

[9] L. Wittgenstein, *Philosophische Untersuchungen: Bi-lingual Edition*, trans. G.E.M. Anscombe (London² 1958) 20.
[10] John Chrys., *In Rom. hom.* 3; PG 60,413 46-415 51.

century BC has been made by Peter Karavites.[11] In tracing the origins of the term, he begins with the sixth century with Theognis, and ends with a sampling among the Presocratics such as Democritus, Critias and Gorgias. The survey, within the limitations of a journal article, is reasonably thorough with good coverage of Sophocles, Euripides and Aristophanes, and with special attention to the historians, Herodotus and Thucydides.[12]

The survey by Karavites reveals the wide range of connotations for which this term was utilised. He gives fifty-three different English translations of γνώμη. This suggests that nailing down a single meaning of γνώμη during this period with any attempt at precision is a difficult if not an impossible task. Many would say that it is undesirable to do so. The development of language over time, especially in periods of great change in society, which was the case in the fifth-century Greek world, makes it difficult to grasp hold of the signification of a word that makes it appropriate for application in a particular context. There must be good reasons why this happens but these are not always apparent.

For Theognis in the sixth century, γνώμη signified mainly "reasoned opinion", "prudence" or "judgment".[13] The fifth century witnesses what Karavites calls an "increase in the elasticity"[14] of the term with a subsequent "evolution in the usage of the term in the latter part of the fifth century and beginning of the fourth".[15] All this seems rather overwhelming, especially as the list appears to be a mixture of diverse concepts confirming Karavites' comment regarding the elasticity of the term in its development. However, an analysis of these results indicates that certain patterns emerge. The list, for all its seeming diversity, breaks down to a few categories that have a common base. This analysis, using his translations, is set out in the table below.

---

[11] Karavites, "*Gnome's* nuances", 9-34. With the exception of Thucydides, I have relied heavily upon his article for this section. I have checked most of his translations and though I would make changes in some instances, I accept most of them as satisfactory. The analysis of this material is mine.

[12] This latter feature is in harmony with the phenomenon that I have observed that Greek historians in general made more use of γνώμη than most other categories of ancient Greek authors apart from rhetoricians and Christian writers. This may be due to the crucial importance of mindset, γνώμη, for soldiers and political figures in times of warfare. Nothing has changed in this regard.

[13] Karavites, "*Gnome's* nuances", 9.

[14] Karavites, "*Gnome's* nuances", 10.

[15] Karavites, "*Gnome's* nuances", 17.

Cognition	Wisdom	Character	Judgement	Purpose	Political
mind (as the seat of thought)	Under-standing	nature	idea	purpose	proposal
Faculty of un-derstanding	insight	temper	opinion	intent (reason for human activity)	motion
intelligence	acumen	mark	view	plan	political acumen
intellectual ability	good sense	feelings	expectation	strategy	political persuasion
thinking process	prudence	attitude	reasoned conclusion/ opinion	policy	resolution
deliberation	respect	disposition	persuasion	will	judgement
reason	counsel	mettle	conviction	decision	judicial decisions
thought		spirit	judgement	consent	verdict
knowledge		resolution	verdict	accord	sentences
		will-power	advice		accord
		determination	counsel		

Six categories have emerged with each having a nuance common to that group. In the first category, Cognition, I have grouped the terms that have their primary reference to the faculty of thought or intellect. I have listed these in order of their increasing intensity from the mind as something substantive, through the cognitive processes to the outcome of knowledge. The second category, Wisdom, gathers those terms in which wisdom in judgement comes to the fore. The order here follows the process through from its conception to its expression.

The third category, Character, focuses on the usage in which the disposition of a person is the dominant nuance. Once again, I have given them an order, this time working from a general term, nature, to those stressing a specific characteristic such as determination. Under Judgement, I have grouped the terms that reflect the concept of an opinion held or expressed, from the mere idea through to verdict, in which a conviction has become an expressed judgement, to counsel in which an element of wisdom is suggested in the opinion being given or sought. The fifth category, Consent, groups those terms in which the element of autonomous free will is present. The order here moves from intent to formulated policy, and on to the exercise of will. Finally, under Political, the grouping collects those uses of γνώμη where it appears in a political context such as an assembly or a court. Again, the list works from the beginning of the process with a proposal, through to its end in the sentence consequent upon the verdict.

Whilst I have separated these terms into separate categories, it should be noted that there is interlinking between them. For example, opinion and judgement must be present in formulating strategies or plans as under Purpose. The point of separating out words for this category of Purpose is that will is deemed as the critical element, since the exercise of judgement toward a goal is in view. Likewise, the Wisdom category is obviously a nuanced extension of the Judgement category with the sense of wise judgement being seen by the translator as the demand of the context. Other categories are also linked: all judgements have some cognitive element involved; cognition also plays a part in Purpose, especially where plans, strategy and policy are concerned; the same obviously applies to the Political category, but as many of these come from speech or persuasion contexts, the rhetorical nature of the speeches involved demands the recognition of the presence of emotive elements that brings the Character category into the picture. Both the content and the context of these speeches also bring wisdom into the political picture. Character does not stand isolated; it combines at least elements of intellect, emotions and convictions. Thus, although a particular nuance is appropriate for a particular context, γνώμη brings together some or even all of these elements with the context designating the dominant aspect. There is a common thread between the meanings and categories that have been noted. Although γνώμη in one context leans toward signifying judgement, in another purpose, and in another temper, and so on, all these point to some state or activity of the human psyche where intellect, will, conviction and emotions combine in a perceptible attitude or stance. Thus, the variety of usage encountered in the earliest known period of the Greek language may not be as haphazardly diverse as Karavites suggests. It is this combination of elements in γνώμη that has surfaced in this study of Chrysostom's usage. The cognitive and the emotive, character traits, conviction, purpose, judgement, and even the corporate policy elements have been encountered in his homilies. All these, it has been argued, are integral to the mindset that, in his anthropology, stands at the very centre of functional and practical human existence.

In particular, Karavites makes some interesting observations that are pertinent to this study and the usage of γνώμη in Chrysostom. In commenting on Sophocles, he notes that there is a discernible basic meaning to the term. He writes:

> Basically, however, the use of *gnome* in Sophocles continued to denote that part of man that is associated with his natural ability to learn through life's experiences, to understand events, and on the basis of this understanding to draw intelligent conclusions or judgments . . . By *gnome* Sophocles refers to the intelligent side of man, his ability to arrive at logical conclusions. No matter what the individual case might be, the thinking process, *gnome*, is the common characteristic of human judgment.[16]

Two things are of note here. First, with the ascription to γνώμη of intelligence, the thinking process, an element of deliberation is discerned as being basic to the term. This element was to remain fundamental throughout the history of its usage. Karavites observes the same thing in Thucydides:

> A quick glance at the text of Thucydides and it becomes evident that *gnome* appears in multiple forms, practically all of them associated with some sort of tortuous thinking process.[17]

This can be taken further, for a glance at the table indicates that γνώμη was employed to designate the mind, the faculty of understanding, the thinking faculty itself. The second point to note from Karavites' comment on Sophocles concerns the reference to an educational aspect of life's experiences. The γνώμη is seen as being formed by deliberation upon past events or experiences. This formational feature of γνώμη persists throughout its history, and is found as such in Chrysostom's usage. Further to this, Karavites notes from Euripides the role of education in the formation of a γνώμη σοφή, a prudent mindset, which generates the quality of mercy.[18] He attributes to education the "loftiness of purpose (γνώμη)"[19] of both Pericles of Athens, and Brasidas the Spartan, in their speech-making. The γνώμη is viewed in much the same manner by Chrysostom as being shaped over time, in Chrysostom's Christian view pre-eminently by Scripture, Sacraments and Christian discipline (φιλοσοφία). A third thing arises from Karavites comment on Thucydides in that the tortuous thinking process suggests

---

[16] Karavites, *"Gnome's nuances"*, 11-12.
[17] Karavites, *"Gnome's nuances"*, 24.
[18] Karavites, *"Gnome's nuances"*, 14.
[19] Karavites, *"Gnome's nuances"*, 25.

that there is more than the intelligent side of the human psyche involved in γνώμη. The presence of emotional factors is thereby indicated. Karavites seems to have overlooked this element, thus making the γνώμη much less complex than the usages in the texts allow. This complexity, as evidenced in the Classical texts, such as Thucydides, is discussed in what follows.

II. Thucydides

There are good reasons to think that Thucydides is especially significant for this study. Thucydides appears to have been a favourite of Libanius and one that students of the rhetoric schools universally studied. In his autobiography, Libanius relates an incident about the theft of his favourite copy of Thucydides' *History* which he carried around on his travels.[20] This loss he calls μεγάλῳ ("a great thing"). He was δηχθεῖς ("deeply irritated") by its loss, was ἀνιαρόν ("in pain"), for with it, he says, εὐφραινόμενος μᾶλλον ἢ Πολυκράτης τῷ δακτυλίῳ ("he had enjoyed himself more than Polycrates with his ring").[21] When it was recovered, he "was set free [from his pain] and was exceedingly glad, just like someone over a child who turned up quite unexpectedly after having been missing for quite a while".[22] He also mentions how he had been ἐπεπόνθειν ("emotionally moved") by reading it, just as previous readers had so been.[23] Libanius liked his Thucydides, and there is little doubt that he drilled his students in it. It is worth noting that Libanius' lost book turned up when a student of another rhetor in Antioch, having purchased it from someone, brought it to read in class, further evidence of the place of Thucydides in the curriculum of the rhetorical schools. Chrysostom would have been made familiar with the *History* during his years under the tutelage of Libanius, keeping in mind that the training of memory was a vital component of rhetor-sophist education and that Thucydides was one of the

---

[20] Libanius, *Or.* 1, 148-150, Norman, *Libanius: Autobiography,* 478, vol. 1, 216-219, translations are mine. Further short citations in this paragraph are from this text.

[21] This ring was Polycrates' most valuable possession which he threw away in the sea on the advice of Amasis, king of Egypt, and which was returned to him in the belly of a fish presented to him by a fisherman. See Herodotus, 3.40; A.F. Norman, "The book trade in fourth-century Antioch", *JHS* 80 (1960) 122-126 at 124, suggests that this copy was about 150 years old at the time.

[22] Libanius, *Or.* 1, 150: οἷα ἄν τις ἐπὶ παιδὶ τὸν ἴσον μὲν ἀφανισθέντι χρόνον, φανέντι δὲ οὐ προσδοκηθέντι περιχαρὴς ἀπηλλαττόμην.

[23] See also Festugière, *Antioche païenne et chrétienne,* 216 n. 2, which refers to this incident.

ancients that was committed to memory in that system.[24] Chrysostom probably would have encountered Thucydides in his schooling in the earlier grammarian stage of the Greek παιδεία.[25]

Unlike γνώμη in the works of the patristic era, this term has received special treatment by a number of classical scholars for Thucydides' usage of it in the *History*.[26] It is not the aim of this study to add anything to the results of that scholarship, but rather, for the purpose of comparison, to garner from them a considered understanding of the usage of this term in the *History*. Thucydides' *History* is significant for the development of the usage and meaning of γνώμη in the history of the Greek language.[27] The *History* contains 174 occurrences of γνώμη with a frequency ratio of 11.59 per 10K, which is very high in comparison with other Greek writers.[28] This suggests that the term had an importance in Thucydides common to only a handful of his contemporaries and those who followed soon after. P. Huart, whilst recognising the variety of meanings in Thucydides' usage, pointed to a feature which he saw as unique, saying:

> Further, he attributes an exceptional importance to the word [γνώμη]: γνώμη becomes the symbol of all that which man is able to realise by the power of his reflection, and which constitutes his dignity; Thucydides had faith in γνώμη,

---

[24] J.W.H. Walden, *The Universities of Ancient Greece* (New York 1909) 211, 214; Norman, "The book trade", 123, comments on the practice of the pagan teachers disdaining the use of stenographers, "in keeping with their tradition of memorisation..".

[25] Walden, *The Universities of Ancient Greece*, 201-202; Libanius, *Or.* 1.8, relates how he, as a young man, becoming frustrated with his low quality rhetors, turned from them and gave himself solely to the memorising of the Classical writers, a task to which he devoted himself for five years. He did this, he claims, under a teacher with a phenomenal memory who gave him a great appreciation of the classics. Norman, *Libanius: Autobiography*, vol. 1, 61, n. b, suggests this man was a *grammatistes* (elementary schoolmaster). Cribiore, *The School of Libanius*, 147-169, and esp. 164 and n. 24, makes some pertinent comment about the curriculum of these various levels of the παιδεία.

[26] From the vast scholarly output on Thucydides I have chosen the specialist studies on γνώμη as follows: Huart, *Le Vocabulaire;* Huart, *Γνώμη chez Thucydide*; L. Edmunds, *Chance and Intelligence in Thucydides*, Loeb Classical Monographs (Cambridge, MA 1975); J.J. Price, *Thucydides and Internal War* (Cambridge 2001); R.D. Luginbill, *Thucydides on War and National Character* (Boulder, CO 1999); G. Perusek, "Strategy and changing moods in Thucydides", *Poroi* 3.2, (2004) 1-20, http://inpress.lib.uiowa.edu/poroi/papers/perusek041001. html. Accessed 10 August, 2007; Price, *Thucydides and Internal War*, 3, says it well: "The scholarship on Thucydides may cause despair and fatigue by its sheer mass".

[27] Huart, *Le Vocabulaire*, 505.

[28] G.R. Crane (ed.), Perseus Digital Library Project, Tufts University. http://w.w.w.perseus.tufts. edu. Accessed 22 August 2007. The comparative figures are: for all Greek texts, 3.70 per 10K; prose, 3.82; rhetoric 6.28; drama, 5.32, tragedy, 5.17; Herodotus, 9.19.

because he saw in it a sure guide to conduct, the intellectual principle which should – or must – allow him to resist blind impulses; it is by it that man, to recapitulate a famous formula, is truly "the measure of all things".[29]

This certainly endows γνώμη with special significance for human life, both for the inner being and external conduct. This aspect of γνώμη as constituting the dignity of the person is echoed in Chrysostom, especially in his insistence upon its αὐτεξούσιος, autonomy, and its ἐξουσία, authority.[30] Chrysostom qualifies this from his Christian perspective by making a distinction between φύσις (nature) and γνώμη, investing nature with original dignity, and teaching that inappropriate operation of both γνώμη and προαίρεσις (choice) betrays that dignity. On the other hand, not only do these faculties of the soul retain the dignity gifted to them, but they also undergo a purifying transformation at conversion and baptism.

Not only does Thucydides, according to Huart, invest γνώμη with the essence of humankind's dignity, but also with the burden of its destiny. Γνώμη, as the intellectual principle which is set over against τύχη, fortune or fate, on one hand, and against ὀργή, impulse, mood, passion or anger, on the other, sums up the role that γνώμη plays in some of the main figures, primarily Pericles, in Thucydides' account of the Peloponnesian war.[31] L. Edmunds' has been similarly impressed in his study of the τέχνη-τύχη and γνώμη-τύχη antitheses in the *History*. He discerns γνώμη in what he calls its normative sense, that is ξύνετος ("intelligent"), as the guiding principle of Athens' first citizen, Pericles, and, in their better moments, of the Athenians as a whole. Edmunds claims that Thucydides himself saw γνώμη as one of the great historical forces of human life and endeavour.[32] We find Edmunds saying, in his discussion of Pericles' first oration,

In fact, the thematic first noun of the prooemium, gnome, proves to be the leitmotiv of Pericles in the *History*, and the concept of gnome proves to be the basis of Pericles' policy. Along with *chremata*, gnome is the basis of Pericles' military strategy (2.13), and although this word appears twice only in the Funeral Oration, it is clear that Pericles regards gnome as the guiding principle of Athenian life, since he speaks of the Athenian holidays as "rest for the gnome" (2.38.1). Gnome is the standard to which he recalls the Athenians in the third speech, at the time of the plague.[33]

---

[29] Huart, *Γνώμη chez Thucydide*, 173. Translation from the French is mine.

[30] John Chrys., *In Gen. hom.* 20; PG 53,169 57; *De perf. car.*, PG 56,283 42; *Cat. 1-8*, 8:22.1-6.

[31] Τύχη, Thucydides, 1.144 4, 2.64 6; Edmunds, *Chance*, 66, 75; Luginbill, *Thucydides on War*, 66; ὀργή, Thucydides, 2.21; Edmunds, *Chance*, 4, 11-15; Price, *Thucydides and Internal War*, 24, 309; Perusek, "Strategy and Changing Moods", 8.33; Huart, *Γνώμη chez Thucydide*, 33.

[32] Edmunds, *Chance*, 4-5.

[33] Edmunds, *Chance, 8*.

This usage of γνώμη is reflected in Chrysostom, who held that the disposition of the γνώμη determines human destiny.[34] Also in Chrysostom is found a similarity to the struggle with τύχη, except that τύχη is replaced by πρόνοια, providence, where the relationship is not intended to be one of conflict, but one of dependence and acceptance. Nevertheless, Chrysostom, with his compassionate understanding of humanity, was quite aware of the reality of the struggle of his people with the adverse circumstances of life. Therefore, with the perception of the Christian, the γνώμη remains the critical factor, but is given a basis for hope that fortifies the γνώμη and does not desert it in contrary circumstances, as so often was the case in the *History*. Luginbill has discerned γνώμη in Thucydides as being the arbiter between ὀργή and τύχη, with τύχη representing the human psychological reaction to the uncertainties of the future.[35] As an arbiter, it is not very successful, mainly because it is a weak force under the control of the emotional impulses of hope or fear.[36] Chrysostom also sees it as an arbiter, but one that, for the Christian, has been delivered from its intrinsic weakness by the transformation that takes place at conversion and baptism, an initial transformation of the γνώμη that forms the basis for further development in its intended role.[37]

Huart's and Edmund's analyses of γνώμη in the *History* have much to commend them. However, there is a problem concerning their understanding of γνώμη as being normative in usage when encountered as intelligent, that is as ξύνετος γνώμη.[38] In this sense it would be considered as being primarily and essentially a rational faculty, somewhat of a function of reason. This may be acceptable if normative is being used in the sense of an ideal standard that in practice is beyond reach. However, as Edmunds continues his discussion, he refers to γνώμη as retaining its "normal connotation of 'intelligence' or 'reason' as opposed to unreasoning passion".[39] This appears contrary to the story Thucydides relates, where, for the most part, his presentation of γνώμη runs counter to its use as intelligent γνώμη, being seen overwhelmingly as under the control of irrational passions. Predominantly, with few exceptions, the participants are swayed by adverse circumstances, false hopes and unfounded fears. As Luginbill has observed,

---

[34] John Chrys., *In Matt. hom.* 1; PG 57,22 56; *hom.* 6; PG 57,67 45-49.

[35] Luginbill, *Thucydides on War*, 56-60.

[36] Luginbill, *Thucydides on War*, 60, 65.

[37] John Chrys., *Comm. in Gal.*; PG 61,657 43-45.

[38] Edmunds, *Chance*, 9-10; Huart, *Γνώμη chez Thucydide*, 173.

[39] Edmunds, *Chance*, 10.

In general, Thucydides thought of "intelligent" *gnome* as being confined to exceptional individuals (such as Pericles) and manifested only under extraordinary circumstances (such as the siege of Plataea).[40]

Luginbill has made a balanced study of the role of γνώμη in human nature in Thucydides' *History* in relation to the tension between ὀργή and τύχη. He recognises that γνώμη is presented in the *History* primarily as fickle and changeable, often subject to passions with its rational element being crushed out of the picture by the course of events.[41] In this he agrees with Edmund's position that bad luck is regarded by Thucydides and Pericles as a subjective phenomenon, a psychological reaction to adverse circumstances, and not, as regarded by many of the ancients, as a purely external determining factor in human history. Edmunds sums up: "Pericles regards the individual soul as the locus of chance; and he seems to deny implicitly that the city as a whole can be affected seriously by chance (2.60-64)".[42] Luginbill, in contrast to the popular view, locates the rise of fear and anger because of these circumstances to the responses of the γνώμη and the διάνοια and the φρόνημα, these terms probably being used somewhat as rhetorical synonyms, all pointing to faculties of consideration or deliberation in the psyche.[43] Thus, as Luginbill argues, Thucydides presents γνώμη as:

essentially emotional in nature...the line between thinking and feeling is hard to draw...in Thucydides' schema the cognitive functions of *gnome* also have severe limitations.[44]

Luginbill attempts to apply the ὀργή – τύχη – γνώμη paradigm to the national characters of the protagonists of the Peloponnesian war, an enterprise fraught with some hazards, but it is with the function of γνώμη in the human psyche that his work is of value to this study.[45] Luginbill, surprisingly in view of his comments

---

[40] Luginbill, *Thucydides on War*, 59.

[41] Luginbill, *Thucydides on War*, 57.

[42] Edmunds, *Chance*, 71.

[43] Luginbill, *Thucydides on War*, 72-73.

[44] Luginbill, *Thucydides on War*, 58.

[45] T. Rood, "Review article of Robert D. Luginbill, *Thucydides on War and National Character*", *Bryn Mawr Classical Review* (1999) 2000.02.20, http://ccat.sas.upenn.edu/bmcr/ 200/2000.02.20.html, suggests that, whilst there are serious problems with his discussion of national character, his section on "Risk and Reason", *tyche* and *gnome*, is "one of the best sections of the book". In Luginbill's defence, it should be noted that it is not merely significant individuals but also the various city-states, the πόλεις, that are a focus of the action and the attitudes which are displayed and to which the term is applied. As G. Murray, *A History of Ancient Greek Literature* (New York 1897) no page nos, Chapter Eight, "Thucydides", asserted:

about the ambiguous nature of γνώμη as found in the *History*, appears to accept that an objective rational approach will always result in the right outcome. Thus, the failure of γνώμη must be due to the uncertainty of human knowledge and not in its lack of rationality.[46] He still accepts that γνώμη, if rarely reaching a rational ideal, represents in some way the deliberative component of the psyche. Though he does qualify this, and comes down with weight upon a more emotional portrayal of this faculty:

> .....it (γνώμη) is a highly subjective and emotional sort of reason, fallible in the extreme, and susceptible to being influenced by rhetoric and events....While it may represent the reflective and deliberative part of Man's nature, it is not without an emotional side, and the conclusions it draws are liable to be erroneous.[47]

This is true, as γνώμη in Thucydides' usage combines elements of reason and emotion in varying degrees according to the individuals in view. Luginbill points to the expression of a lack of rationality in actions as stemming from the γνώμη and usually ascribes that lack, not to the uncertainty of human knowledge but to the emotional element. This, indeed, is the basis of his analysis and conclusions, for he summarises as follows, "In the preceding chapter, we found that while reason (*gnome*) is the master of the psyche in Thucydides' system, it is in most cases an irresolute and highly emotional master."[48] Nonetheless, that uncertainty has a part in the operations of the psyche is undeniable. The ancient recourse to τύχη is evidence sufficient to make the point. It could and did affect the participants in the *History* to varying degrees, depending upon the state of their γνώμη. The uncertainty may have contributed to failure, but the emotional element of the γνώμη was a determinant factor as to the strength of the impact of such forces upon the individuals and peoples involved.

An interesting example of the triumph of the γνώμη over τύχη and irrational ὀργή is related about the battle of Mantinea 418-417 BCE. On one occasion, the Spartans had incurred some losses due to an error of tactics and were being

---

"There is perhaps nothing in literature like his [Thucydides'] power of half personifying a nation and lighting up the big lines of its character". Accessed from Peitho's Web, 31 August 2007. Whether or not it was appropriate for Thucydides to do this is a question outside the scope of this chapter.

[46] Luginbill, *Thucydides on War*, 57.

[47] Luginbill, *Thucydides on War*, 57. See also his comment on page 56, "overlooking the non-rational features of *gnome* necessarily causes confusion in understanding the *History's* psychological mechanics...And it is just such a subjective aspect of *gnome* that has generally been overlooked in the critique of Thucydides' work".

[48] Luginbill, *Thucydides on War*, 65.

accused of cowardice and ineptitude, idleness and sluggishness. Yet, after the initial setbacks, they were ultimately victorious in the battle. So, after returning home with their shame erased, it was considered that the mishaps were due to τύχη being against them, but that their γνώμη had remained constant, hence the victory.[49] The γνώμη had not been changed by temporary adversity.

However, that the γνώμη is seen to have an emotional element or is swayed by emotions is clear; the text of Thucydides testifies to this. One example is the exhortation of Gylippus to the Syracusans prior to a naval battle with Athens. In his attempt to stir them to up to their best efforts, he argues that it is legitimate, ἀποπλῆσαι τῆς γνώμης τὸ θυμούμενον ("...to sate the raging passion of your mindset...")[50] in retribution on the aggressor. The most intense passion is ascribed here to the γνώμη, an intensity that would normally squash the rational component of this faculty. This may not be so, as seen in another incident. When the Syracusans became aware that the Athenian expeditionary force to Sicily in 415 BCE had reached Rhegium, they set aside their former scepticism and made preparations πάσῃ τῇ γνώμῃ ("with all their mindset") (6.45.1). Of interest is the translation of R. Warner, "with all their energies",[51] which suggests the totality of their beings. The Crawley/Feetham translation gives "threw themselves heart and soul into the work".[52] We might translate in our idiom "with all their heart". Here is seen both the critical function of the γνώμη and something of its nature. A person or an entity is only giving of their all when their mindset (γνώμη) is totally focused on the task in hand. As to its nature, the indications from this context are of both rational and emotional elements working in concord. Passion is certainly present. This appears to mean that the emotional elements of the γνώμη are controlled, or perhaps focused, by the rational elements therein. As seen above, Chrysostom follows this usage when referring to the basic orientation of the being, as in his explanation of the γνώμη of the Syrophonecian woman, when she approached Jesus for the healing of her child, as having made "a violent attack".[53]

G. Perusek is another who has noted this in the *History* in reference to the mood of the Athenians when rushing into war (2.9.1). He writes, comparing it to the German word, *Geist*:

---

[49] Thucydides, *History*, 5.75.3.

[50] Thucydides, *History*, 7.68.1.

[51] R. Warner (trans.), *Thucydides: The Peloponnesian War*, Penguin Classics (Harmondworth 1972²) 438.

[52] R. Crawley (trans.), R. Feetham (rev.), *Thucydides: The Peloponnesian War*, GBWW 6 (Chicago–London–Toronto–Geneva 1952 repr.) 521.

[53] John Chrys., *In Matt. hom.* 22; PG 57,305 58, 306, 9,12,16.

First the use of *gnome* makes it difficult to differentiate feelings from mentalities...Just as *Geist* is hard to translate from German to English, because it means both *mind* and *spirit*, *gnome* encompasses feelings and judgments.[54]

This is similar to Chrysostom who, in his usage, also points to an emotional element in the γνώμη. Furthermore, pertinent to this issue, the presence of an emotional element does not necessarily negate the rationality or the strength of the γνώμη but, indeed, may enrich it. Chrysostom, for example, indicates that the lack of pity in the wicked servant of Matthew18 severely distorted his γνώμη and resulted in behaviour that was entirely irrational (ἀπόνοια).[55] It may be observed that the wicked servant was not pictured as devoid of emotion in his γνώμη. As seen earlier in this study, it was distorted by harshness and savagery. Much depends upon the emotional state of the γνώμη. The presence of an element of compassion in the γνώμη of the servant would have changed the outcome. Agreement with Luginbill on the point of the γνώμη being a highly subjective and emotional sort of reason is clearly seen here. Although both Thucydides and Chrysostom view the γνώμη as having a rational element, rarely do they present it as entirely such. It is interesting to note that one of the exceptional examples of intelligent γνώμη that Luginbill uses from the *History* actually demonstrates the presence, not absence, of emotional elements. In the *History* at 1.75, the Athenians indicate in their defence that the principal motive for this display of ξύνεσις (intelligent) γνώμη in their actions was δέος (fear), although one might allow in its context that this is proper fear.[56] Coupled with γνώμη in its positive or ξύνεσις (intelligent) state, one might call this fear intelligent or rational. Nevertheless, whether this fear is proper or otherwise, it is an emotional element, an element that does not render the γνώμη irrational in this instance, but rather enhances its rationality. Thucydides, according to Luginbill, in the drama of politics and war saw the γνώμη of the protagonists governed by either hope or fear, "two basic emotions of the γνώμη".[57] Γνώμη may well be seen as the orientation, stance or

---

[54] Perusek, "Strategy and changing moods", 5.18.
[55] John Chrys., *In Gen. hom.* 27; PG 53,248-249; Those familiar with Charles Dickens' *Hard Times* will remember that the Gradgrind children who, having been brought up to suppress the emotional element of their psyches, turned out to be unmitigated disasters, totally unable to cope with life and who, we would say, acted quite irrationally. For other similar examples in real life and literature, see Wood, *Epistemology*, 175-176.
[56] See Edmunds, *Chance*, 58-61, for this "proper fear".
[57] Luginbill, *Thucydides on War*, 65.

attitude of the mind, what I would call the mindset, but never as a totally rational faculty of the psyche if rationality is to be defined as being without emotion.[58]

Thucydides presents the γνώμη as the master of the psyche, with the role of evaluating the experiences and circumstances of life together with the urges and passions of one's own psyche, in order to determine the best way forward.[59] Though failure often occurs due to weakness in the γνώμη, the strength of the γνώμη in the face of adverse circumstances is sometimes seen in the *History*. This triumph of the rational over the irrational is applied by Thucydides not only to individuals, but also to the collective γνώμη. The collective mood is seen as critical to the state of the γνώμη and thus to conduct in the war.[60] Γνώμη in Thucydides is not concerned with abstract thinking but always has action in view. It is focused upon the formulation of policy: what to aim at and what means to employ to achieve that end.[61] Here again is a feature reflected in Chrysostom's usage.[62] The fact that γνώμη and προαίρεσις, moral choice, are frequently linked together in Chrysostom's works also indicates the practical nature of γνώμη.

This comparison could be extended, but sufficient has been presented to demonstrate the affinity between Thucydides and Chrysostom in the usage of γνώμη. Just as γνώμη is a term of crucial importance in Thucydides, so it is in Chrysostom. Both see it as endowed with dignity and of carrying the burden of destiny. It is understood by both as possessing rational and emotional elements, and as being the master of the psyche, responsible to control the passions and to adopt appropriate attitudes to external forces beyond its control. In both, though rational, it is not concerned with abstract thinking but is directed toward action, towards an end and the means to attain it. A little has been said of its weaknesses, but both the *History* and Chrysostom's homilies abound with incidences of its vagaries, its failings, and its distortions and its defeats. On the other hand, both hail its potential and its victories, though it would appear that Thucydides laid down his pen in distress, whereas Chrysostom left his work assured of the ultimate attainment of the goal set for the γνώμη.

---

[58] Recent studies in cognitive linguistics have indicated that emotion is an essential element to true cognition. See "Introduction", 13, including n. 34, above.

[59] Thucydides, *History*, 1.140.1, 2.59.5, 2.61.2, 3.38.1; Luginbill, *Thucydides on War*, 54-66, esp. 57; Price, *Thucydides and Internal War*, 51-53, 309; For Chrysostom, see Chapter 4 above, "Authority and the Γνώμη".

[60] Thucydides, *History*, 2.9.1; Perusek, "Strategy and changing moods", 18, 77; Price, *Thucydides and Internal War*, 302.

[61] Thucydides, *History*, 1.32.5, 1.53.2, 1.62.3, 4.32.4; Huart, *Γνώμη chez Thucydide*, 12-13, 77-79; Huart, *Le Vocabulaire*, 316.

[62] John Chrys., *Comm. in Gal.*; PG 61,641 9; *In Gen. hom.* 27; PG 53,243 50-59; *In 2 Cor. hom.* 3; PG 61,414 46-52.

III. Aristotle

Whereas the link from Chrysostom to Thucydides seems to be clear enough, the same cannot be said for a link with Aristotle. Nevertheless, the influence of Aristotle, although not always overt, was deep and wide in the ancient world. Other philosophers crowded the scene to leave their evident marks in various schools. Some, like Plato, also had wide currency and influenced thought universally. However, in times and places where Aristotle himself tended to be lost to sight, his concepts continued to permeate even where they did not dominate. Ammonius Saccas and his disciple, Plotinus, incorporated much of Aristotle's terminology into their Neoplatonism.[63] Thus, although Chrysostom's education in philosophy may have been dominated by Plato[64] and the current Neoplatonism, Aristotle at least lurked in the background. Examination of Aristotle's thought reveals significant affinity between his approach to γνώμη and the usage of Chrysostom.

P. Huart mourned that after Thucydides a degenerated usage of γνώμη replaced the focus upon the intellectual principle that is found in the *History*. Plato was blamed for this, but as he rarely uses the term, that may be an overstatement.[65] Aristotle certainly did not lose the sense of the rational and intellectual in his treatment of γνώμη. Indeed, three aspects are clearly presented: as a faculty of the

---

[63] R. Sorabji, *The Philosophy of the Commentators 200-600 AD: A Sourcebook*, vol. 2: *Physics* (Ithaca, NY 2005) 1: "The Philosophy of the Commentators of 200-600AD constitutes the transition from Ancient to Medieval Philosophy. This period started with the Aristotelian (Peripatetic) School battling against Stoics and Platonists. But soon Neoplatonism became dominant, swallowing up the other schools, while still displaying their influence, especially that of the Aristotelian, Alexander of Aphrodisias. He like most of the others, did much of his own Philosophy through the medium of commentary on the earlier Philosophy, and that is why the Greek philosophers of this period can be called commentators. Alexander's commentaries, and most but not all of the surviving ones are on Aristotle."; M.L.W. Laistner, *Christianity and Pagan Culture in the Later Roman Empire together with an English translation of John Chrysostom's "Address on Vainglory and the Right Way for Parents to Bring Up Their Children"* (Ithaca, NY–London 1951) 22-23, summarises the situation well: "Neoplatonism, however, was an impressive attempt, by combining with the teaching of Plato, elements derived from Aristotle and the Stoics and also from the Pythagoreans who, after a long period of obscurity had again emerged into greater prominence shortly before the beginning of the Christian era, to create a systematic body of ideas which would still conform to the Greek philosophical tradition and at the same time would more effectively combat the enemy without."

[64] Kelly, *Golden Mouth*, 8; E. Osborn, *Ethical Patterns in Early Christian Thought* (London–New York–Melbourne 1976) 120-121, who comments on the combination of Platonic and Stoic themes in one of Chrysostom's later works, *To Olympias*.

[65] Huart, Γνώμη *chez Thucydide*, 175.

soul it is rational, natural, and practical. These three aspects are woven together in his discussion.

Aristotle's *Nicomachean Ethics* contains a brief discussion of the γνώμη in Book 6.11.1143a. There are eight occurrences of the term here in a passage that merits detailed study. Along with νοῦς, intuitive reason or intelligence, σύνεσις, understanding, and φρόνησις, practical wisdom or prudence, γνώμη is categorised as a δύναμις, a power or a faculty of the human soul.[66] It is also described as an ἕξις, a state, quality or habit of mind.[67] With these other terms it is also called a τὸ φυσικόν, a natural endowment, which people possess by nature, φύσις.[68] According to Aristotle the γνώμη has the function of judging, discriminating or distinguishing. The field of judgement allotted to it is that of discernment of the reasonable or the fair or the equitable. As we saw above, it is concerned with conduct. In that it discerns the reasonable or equitable, the γνώμη is a step beyond σύνεσις, i.e. it is not merely a matter of judging things rightly according to strict law so that a correct legal understanding is achieved, but judging with a sense of equity or kindness so that a true judgement is achieved. This indicates that the γνώμη was understood to contain some moral and emotive elements.

The γνώμη is said by Aristotle to extend to the same things as νοῦς (intuitive reason), φρόνησις (practical wisdom or prudence), and σύνεσις (understanding).[69] This appears to mean that they merge or converge in a person, and are applied to the same issues. The various faculties mentioned have a common interest and a common task. Each provides its own individual perspective, but are brought together to make the necessary judgement of matters of practice or conduct, which are termed the ἔσχατα (ultimates). In this process the γνώμη is considered along with the other faculties τὸ φυσικόν (a natural endowment). Aristotle here means by natural endowment something that comes from experience rather than by logical demonstration.[70] Intuitive reason (νοῦς) and judgement (γνώμη) come with a particular age. It is expected of those who "have reached years of discretion" (Rackham), or "years of reason" (Ross).[71] This indicates that the γνώμη develops

---

[66] Arist., *EN*, 1143a.28. In order to make use of accepted traditional understandings of the various terms used here, and without extended discussion of each, I have followed the translations of W D. Ross (trans.), *Nicomachean Ethics*, GBWW 9 (Chicago 1952) 392-393, and H. Rackham (trans.), *Aristotle: Nicomachean Ethics*, LCL 19 (Cambridge Mass. 1934) 358-363.

[67] Arist., *EN*, 1143a. 25.

[68] Arist., *EN*, 1143b.6-7.

[69] Arist., *EN*, 1143a.25.

[70] Arist., *EN*, 1143b.13-14: διὰ γὰρ τὸ ἔχειν ἐκ τῆς ἐμπειρίας ὄμμα ὁπῶσιν ὀρθῶς ("...because they have from experience eyes that see truly").

[71] Rackham, *NE* 1143a; Ross, *NE* 339; Arist., *EN*,1143a 25-27: ἐπὶ τοὺς αὐτοὺς ἐπιφέροντες γνώμην ἔχειν καὶ νοῦν ἤδη καὶ φρονίμους καὶ συνετούς; ("...upon the same we attribute

over time, perhaps reaching a fixed state in later years. This is characteristic of Chrysostom's usage of the term.

A further observation is to be made from Aristotle. As the ultimates are grasped by intuitive reason and not by argument or deductive reasoning, the γνώμη shares in this characteristic. Because it has developed over time, its judgements are often immediate. It is already determined by the experiences that have been encountered and by the psychic processes that have turned those experiences into attitudes that become instinctive to the individual. Hence, the γνώμη is described as an ἕξις, a state, quality or habit of mind. Indeed, Chrysostom laboured in teaching to that end.

Finally, considering this passage in the *Ethica*, it should not be disregarded that γνώμη is discussed by Aristotle as a faculty of the rational part of the psyche. It may include an emotive element, but essentially, as far as Aristotle is concerned, it is that natural faculty of the rational part of the mature psyche that intuitively makes correct and equitable judgements about matters of conduct. In this dissertation, it has been argued that in the hands of Chrysostom this is only partly true. Whilst he appears to have adopted the basic anthropology of Aristotle, he parted company with the pagan philosopher by ascribing the fundamental flaw in humankind as applying to the γνώμη. According to him, both the rational and the emotive are also flawed, but they meet in the γνώμη, which if it were untouched, would produce the ideal of which Aristotle wrote. It does not because it cannot. As far as Chrysostom was concerned, true moral judgement and moral conduct are only possible within the Christian faith. Chrysostom points up the lack in his own early education when he asserts that the traditional Greek παιδεία, which he had received, could not produce the virtue that it claimed as its glory.[72] The necessary transformation and moral formation that would truly inform the γνώμη are found only in Christianity, the one and only true φιλοσοφία.

There is no guarantee, or perhaps even likelihood, that Chrysostom was directly familiar with Aristotle's *Rhetorica*. G. Kennedy points out that the work was never published by the author, disappeared to Asia Minor, and only came to the surface in Athens and Rome some time in the first century. By then, it appeared outdated as a rhetorical handbook, but was later to serve as providing additional insights into Aristotle's ideas on politics and psychology. Kennedy observes that the work is fundamental to the subject, and that some of its ideas, and a considerable amount of its terminology were absorbed by his followers and

---

deliberated judgment [mindset] for they already have reason, and practical wisdom and understanding?"; See also the discussion on φρόνησις at 1142a 7-19.

[72] Hunter, "Libanius and Chrysostom", 132.

subsequently disseminated.[73] Its influence was indirect but effectual in some respects. For understanding γνώμη it is helpful. There are three types of usages of γνώμη in Aristotle's *Rhetorica*. It is used in referring to a juror's oath, to maxims and to a person's inner conviction. Firstly, we find it being used as the dicast's (juror's) oath.[74] R. Roberts, taking note of the context of forensic oratory, translates the passage, "I will give my verdict according to my honest opinion.".[75] This is acceptable, but it falls short of Aristotle's argument here that written law must never be allowed to be the final criterion but must be used subject to universal law or the law of nature. Thus, the appeal is to something more elevated than "honest opinion". It suggests, rather, the highest understanding one may have of a matter. Liddell and Scott propose "to the best of one's judgement" in reference to this passage.[76] This is much more to the point. In view of the discussion in this study, perhaps "noblest mindset" for "γνώμη τῇ ἀρίστη" would sit better here. This would recognise both the solemnity of the oath and its call to consideration at a higher level than mutable written law operates. "Honest opinion" seems more casual in our idiom than the situation demanded. The oath indicates that deep consideration of the matter will be given at the highest level of moral principles possible to the juror's mindset. Aristotle describes this τὸ γνώμη τῇ ἀρίστη κρινεῖν as ἐκ τῶν εἰκότων ("what is likely to be true").[77] That is to say, it is a matter of considered opinion at the highest level, the very best estimation, but not necessarily of fact. It is what the dicast believes after careful deliberation.

Aristotle also uses γνώμη in his *Rhetorica* as a maxim, a brief sentence that expresses a piece of wisdom concerning conduct.[78] Aristotle explains a maxim as a general statement "about questions of practical conduct, courses of conduct to be chosen or avoided".[79] It indicates something that is thought to be universally true. It need not be true, only commonly agreed upon and therefore taken as truth. Maxims, he asserts, invest speech with a moral character. They make the moral purpose apparent and prominent. Indeed, they are a general declaration of moral principles. It is interesting to note that this is the meaning with which the term has come across into the English vocabulary. *Gnome*, in English, apart from that piece of statuary in the garden or the dwarfs of folklore, bears the idea of the opinion of

---

[73] G. Kennedy, *A New History of Classical Rhetoric* (Princeton, NJ 1994) 62-63.

[74] Arist., *Rhetorica*, 1375a.29-30: καὶ ὅτι τὸ γνώμη τῇ ἀρίστη τοῦτ' ἐστίν, τὸ παντελῶς χρῆσθαι τοῖς γεγραμμένοις.

[75] W.R. Roberts (trans.), Aristotle, *Rhetorica*, GBWW 9 (Chicago 1952) 619.

[76] LSJ, 854 s.v.

[77] Roberts, *Rhetoric*, 652; Arist., *Rhetorica*, 1402b.33.

[78] Roberts, *Rhetoric*, 641-643. The term is used a number of times in this sense in an extended passage from 1394a.19-1395b.19.

[79] Roberts, *Rhetoric*, 642.

the wise or proverbial wisdom. It contains the idea of established thinking or inherited attitudes on a given topic, often involving a moral judgment.[80] In early Greek literature, it often needs a μῦθος or fable to explain it.[81] It should be noted that myths convey not mere meaning but also feeling at an instinctive and foundational level. This combination of wisdom, established thought, instinctive feeling and moral stance is indicative of the use of γνώμη during the Patristic period. Chrysostom, in common with many of the Fathers, uses it in such a way with the recasting of the moral element as containing values that may be valid or distorted according to the tenets of the Christian scriptures that were applied to the person or people being discussed.

Aristotle's third use of γνώμη in his *Rhetorica* is similar to Chrysostom's use of the term when referring to a person's settled conviction. Aristotle uses it in this sense to refer to a person's sense of inner conviction. In describing an exchange between Peisander and Sophocles, he points out that Sophocles is reported as saying that whereas the other ephors were bribed to do the condemned action, he, Sophocles, had done it from his mindset (γνώμη).[82] Therefore, he should not be put to death. Here we encounter the settled mindset of the inner being. External circumstances are not the issue. It is what the person has decided in the heart.

From these it is evident that in the fourth century BCE the ideas of careful deliberation and settled conviction were contained in γνώμη. It is to be noted that a moral decision was involved, that moral principles were expressed. The issue is always one of moral conduct. Furthermore, the opinions held are firmly held. They have had to endure the law court on one hand, and the vagaries of public attitudes on the other. They are held even under pressure to the contrary, and are therefore a true reflection of the inner workings of the psyche. These features were echoed in Chrysostom in the fourth century CE.

---

[80] Murray, *A History of Ancient Greek Literature*, 56; R.P. Martin, "Gnomes in poems: wisdom performance on the Athenian stage", Princeton–Stanford Working Papers in Classics, 2005, 11-12.

[81] P.E. Easterling and E.J. Kenny (eds), *The Cambridge History of Classical Literature*, vol. 1 (Cambridge 1985) 700-701.

[82] Arist., *Rhetorica*, 1419a.35: οἱ μὲν γὰρ χρήματα λαβόντες ταῦτα ἔπραξαν, ἐγὼ δὲ οὔ, ἀλλὰ γνώμῃ.

IV. Demosthenes (384-322 BCE)[83]

A significant corpus of the Greek παιδεία in use for rhetorical training in late antiquity was that of the speeches of Demosthenes, the politician-orator of Classical Athens. R. Cribiore, in discussing Lucian of Samosata's (c.125-c.190 CE) satirical essay on the differences between the short and long paths to rhetorical excellence and its application to the time of Libanius and Chrysostom, portrays the long road as presented by Lucian as follows:

> The guide for the hard road is the traditional teacher of rhetoric who in leading a young man up forces him to follow most carefully the footprints of ancient writers such as Demosthenes and Plato. With him, the young man will have to endure the sweat and fatigue of a long climb that will last many years.[84]

It has been shown that under Libanius the young man who was to become known as Chrysostom had climbed that road, suffered the sweat and experienced the fatigue of the intensive study of the old masters of the Greek παιδεία. Libanius belonged to the traditional school as far as his best students were concerned.[85] Although he may have been forced to change to a shorter curriculum for many of his students, he still treasured the long hard road as the true path to the accomplished sophist.[86] Thus, the speeches of Demosthenes would have become almost second nature to Chrysostom. The widely agreed "affinity between Demosthenes and Thucydides"[87] is further reason to assume that this political orator of Classical Athens served Chrysostom as a well-used model that left its

---

[83] Again, as with Thucydides, one faces a vast ocean of secondary literature, on Demosthenes in particular, and the institutions of fourth-century Athens in general. Although reading has been more extensive, the following have been chosen as especially pertinent to this study: J. Ober, *Mass and Elite in Democratic Athens: Rhetoric, Ideology, and the Power of the People* (Princeton, NJ 1989), D. Stockton, *The Classical Athenian Democracy* (New York 1990); H. Yunis, *Taming Democracy: Models of Political Rhetoric in Classical Athens* (Ithaca, NY 1996); L. Foxhalk and A.D.E. Lewis (eds), *Greek Law in its Political Setting: Justifications not Justice* (Oxford 1996); S.A. Usher, *Greek Oratory:Tradition and Originality* (New York 1999). This does not include those works cited below that are substantially translations of various speeches, and contain valuable insights in their introductory chapters.

[84] R. Cribiore, "Lucian, Libanius, and the short road to rhetoric", *GRBS* 47 (2007) 71-86 at 73; See also R. Cribore, *The School of Libanius*, 174-196, for an extended discussion of the two paths.

[85] H. Yunis, *Taming Democracy*, 18, asserts: "The post-Aristotelian rhetorical tradition never cut the tie to democratic Athens; Demosthenes and other fourth-century orators whose work had been preserved in writing remained vibrant sources and models of style".

[86] Cribiore, "Lucian, Libanius", 85-86.

[87] Yunis, *Taming Democracy*, 240 and n. 7.

imprint upon him in various ways. The fact that Libanius wrote his *Hypotheses to the Speeches of Demosthenes*, mainly brief explanatory abstracts to each of the speeches, indicates the importance of Demosthenes, not only for the currency of his written speeches in fourth century CE for rhetorical education, but also for the particular place they had in the formation of Libanius' students.[88] It is fitting, then, to turn to those speeches to examine the usage of γνώμη by this rhetor-politician of fourth century classical Athens. I have taken all the speeches that have been preserved under the name of Demosthenes into account for this study even though some have been identified as being authored by other writers. As most of those thought to be spurious have been acknowledged as genuine fourth-century compositions, I have worked on the assumption, supported by the testimony of Libanius' *Hypotheses*, that the corpus was passed on throughout antiquity in almost identical composition (but not with the same numbering) as it has survived down to our present era.[89] Regarding those that are thought to be spurious, there are good reasons to include them in this analysis. Considering the nature of the legislative and legal processes of democratic Athens, especially the large number of persons directly involved in decision-making, it can be safely assumed that whoever wrote them, despite any differences in style that occur, they describe those processes and the terminology in use at the time with reasonable accuracy.[90]

An analysis of the one hundred and six occurrences of γνώμη in the corpus reveals three features of Demosthenes' usage: the critical place of γνώμη in the legislative processes of the Athenian democracy; the decisive role of γνώμη in the judicial processes; and the similarity of general usage to that of Chrysostom.[91]

---

[88] D.A. Russell, *Libanius: Imaginary Speeches*, 5, comments that the *Hypotheses* "reminds us that Demosthenic scholarship was the core of Libanius' rhetorical skills".

[89] See C. Gibson (trans.), "Libanius' *Hypotheses* to the orations of Demosthenes", in C. Blackwell (ed.), *Dēmos: Classical Athenian Democracy*, at A. M Mahoney and R. Scaife (eds), *The Stoa: A Consortium for Electronic Publication in the Humanities*, [www.stoa.org], 2003 © 2003, for a translation of the *Hypotheses*, in which there are assertions by Libanius that he was aware that some of the speeches were probably written by some other person.

[90] D.M. MacDowell (trans.), *Demosthenes Speeches 27-38*, The Oratory of Classic Greece 8 (Austin. TX 2004) 14-16; I have included the collection of Preambles (*Exordia*) that have come down under Demosthenes' name although the authenticity of these has been questioned in the past. Yunis, *Taming Democracy*, 287-289, esp. n. 3, has presented a summary of the arguments for the authenticity of the whole collection based on the work of F. Blass, *Die attische Beredsamkeit*, 3 vols (Leipzig 1887-1898²) 3.1, 322-328, and A. Rupprecht, "Die demosthenische Prooemiensammlung" *Philologos* 82 (1927) 365-432, and R. Clavaud, *Démosthène: Prologues* (Paris 1974) 5-55; see S.A. Usher, *Greek Oratory*, 244 including n. 1 and n. 2 re authenticity.

[91] Given the political or judicial nature of these speeches, it is to be noted that much of the usage of γνώμη by Demosthenes naturally comes under that aspect of γνώμη that I have termed

In regard to the proceedings of the assembly, γνώμη (mindset) was used by Demosthenes to denote a motion, or proposal sent to it for debate and resolution.[92] The practice in Athens at the time was for issues to be brought to the council (βούλη) who possessed the authority to set the business agenda of the Assembly and to present to it legislation through the president for the day. The Council either formulated recommendations on these issues that were then passed on as proposals, or it simply left the issues open for the assembly to form proposals from the ensuing debate.[93] The recommendations of the council represented the deliberated mindset of that body. In *De Corona (On the Crown)*, a speech made by Demosthenes in a people's court, a number of times he refers to the decision, sanction or approval of the Council as their γνώμη (mindset). In one place in his speech, to prove a point he was making, he asked that the decree of Callisthenes be read. This decree in proposal form had been approved by the council for presentation to a special assembly. It was their γνώμη, their deliberated mindset, that this proposal should be presented.[94] The same phraseology is used in this speech in reference to another decree being introduced to the assembly by the generals; again it was the council's γνώμη that this be allowed.[95] In the same way, two decrees proposed by Callas had also gained the γνώμη of the council for their presentation to the assembly.[96] In the same speech, reference is made to another proposed decree presented by the president of the assembly. In this instance, the combined γνώμη of the council and generals is in view.[97] It is clear from these instances that γνώμη means more than mere opinion; the council was passing the proposals on to the assembly as the result of measured deliberations. Not all proposals that came to them were given the same attention, though one might suggest that as some items were of a non-critical character, the lack of a formulated proposal from the council could be interpreted as an expression of their indifferent mindset on the issue. It is the nature of γνώμη as deliberated mindset as

---

political in the analytical chart in section 1 of this chapter, although the overlaps will be apparent. Thus, in normal translation, it would be preferable to use something less inflexible and more suitable to the nuance appropriate for the context than "mindset" on every occasion. For the sake of analysis, I have been consistent in order to exhibit the frequency and nature of this term, and to ensure its global signification is not lost in translation.

[92] Demos., *1 Philipp.* 11, 30; *Halon.* 19; *Cor.* 164.

[93] See Stockton, *The Classical Athenian Democracy*, 57-116, for the political and legal institutions and processes of fourth century Classical Athens, esp. 77 and 87-89; See also Ober, *Mass and Elite*, 132-141.

[94] Demos., *Cor.* 37.

[95] Demos., *Cor.* 75.

[96] Demos., *Cor.* 115, 116.

[97] Demos., *Cor.* 164.

seen here that is significant in Chrysostom's anthropology as discussed in this study. It has been noted repeatedly that he used the term with this meaning in mind.

In the collection of the model introductions attributed to Demosthenes, we find γνώμη used to describe the views or opinions of the speakers in the assembly debates.[98] In order to appreciate the force of γνώμη in these contexts it is necessary to remember that the Athenian assembly was by no means an easy place to display one's oratory, a lesson that Demosthenes had learned by hard experience. In his early attempts, he had been howled down by a rowdy and unruly element among the members in attendance.[99] R. Wallace sums up the situation well: "In assemblies, Courts, and theater, Athenians were free to say almost anything, including blatant vituperation".[100] He gives pertinent examples and refers to the noise and shouting. Although Wallace notes the complaint of the old oligarch, "that 'crazy people' and any base fellow who wants to, stands up and speaks and obtains what is good for him and those like him, any citizen who wants can speak on equal terms",[101] he presents three factors as to why in practice few could take advantage of this provision. They are: *thorobus*, the hubbub of noise directed at the speaker; the constraint to indulge the Athenian demos; and the fear of assassination at the hands of one of the powerful generals and his gang.[102] Thus for the most part, only the competent and practised rhetors dared to rise to address the crowd, persons whom Demosthenes in one Introduction designated as ...τῶν εἰωθότων γνώμην ἀπεφήναντο ("...those who had been accustomed to proclaim their convictions").[103] Ober describes these as, "a recognizable 'set' of men who played a special role in the political life of the πόλις".[104] Apparently, it was not the

---

[98] Demos., *Exord.* 1.1; 2.2; 7.2; 18.1; 25.1; 25.3; 56.3; See also *Syntax.* 11; *Symm.* 2; *1 Philipp.* 5; *2 Philipp.* 14.

[99] Plutarch, *Dem.* 6-7, relates something of the struggle of Demosthenes' early attempts to enter the lists; see also Demos., *Exordia* 4.1; 56.3; *2 Olynth.* 29, *Syntax.* 20. Ober, *Mass and Elite*, 132, asserts that numbers attending have been estimated as up to 6,000, but economic and other social factors probably limited the number free to attend.

[100] R.W. Wallace, "The power to speak – and not to listen – in ancient Athens", in I. Sluiter and R.M. Rosen (eds), *Free Speech in Classical Antiquity*, Mnemosyne Suppl. 254 (Leiden 2004) 221-232 at 222; Yunis, *Taming Democracy*, 11, asserts: "Politics in Athens was intensely competitive; to volunteer to speak in Assembly was to enter the fray, and it would have discouraged the faint-hearted".

[101] Wallace, "The power to speak", 221.

[102] Wallace, "The power to speak", 222-223.

[103] Demos., *Exord.* 1.1; see also *1 Philipp.* 1.

[104] Ober, *Mass and Elite*, 107-108; M.H. Hansen, *The Athenian Ecclesia II: A Collection of Articles 1983-1989* (Copenhagen 1989), has written a persuasive study (originally published as "The numbers of rhetores in the Athenian ecclesia, 355-322 BC", *GRBS* 24 (1984) 123-155),

place for expressing passing whims or impulsive fantasies. Some orators might speak *ex tempore*, but in order to be heard and given credence they needed to address the assembly only with opinions that had been thought through and firmly embedded in their beings.[105] This indicates the character and content of γνώμη, its signification, in this context. Essentially, as argued throughout this study, it refers to the deliberated mindset. This is evident in another of these introductions where Demosthenes describes the scene where a speaker might say something contrary to some other member's γνώμη. In such cases, the person being contradicted should be called upon to adopt the principle, σκοπείτω πάνθ' ὑπομείνας ἀκοῦσαι, "waiting patiently to listen, let him consider all aspects".[106] Only such focused concentration, which had to be won by the power of the oratory, was able to bring about a change in the γνώμη, again demonstrating the nature of this faculty. Just as Chrysostom pointed to the condition of the γνώμη of the Pharisees as being the cause of their rejection of the preaching of John the Baptist, so Demosthenes points to the γνώμη of some members of the assembly as being the stumbling-block to their capacity to listen to good advice.[107] These people, like the Pharisees, were disposed in their mindsets only to receive what they liked to hear and to block out what, in Demosthenes' judgment, they most needed to heed.

In relation to the usage of γνώμη in the juror's oath of the people's courts, it was seen above that Aristotle's definition allowed for some flexibility and diversion from strict law. The suggestion was that this was in recognition of emotive elements being involved, indeed as being deliberately courted in order to effect a fair judgement. Demosthenes is in concert with Aristotle in this, but in providing the context of the realities of the trial as a fuller background of explanation, he brings a critical insight into the working of the γνώμη. In his speech against Aristocrates, he makes the point that the jurors may give a verdict that is incorrect without losing their integrity to their oath. He explains that in practice the verdict of the γνώμη is somewhat subject to the speakers to whom they

---

that asserts at page 121 that active rhetors in the assembly over a period of thirty-four years (355-322 BCE) numbered no fewer than 700 to 1400, much greater than traditionally thought. However, at 122 he acknowledges that among them there was a small group who were prominent: "On the other hand, there can be no doubt that a few 'professional' or 'semi-professional' politicians did exist in Athens and did in fact move a considerable number of decrees in the *ecclesia*; the lexicographers report that Timarchos moved more than 100 decrees".

[105] C. Wooten, *A Commentary on Demosthenes' Philippica I: with Rhetorical Analyses of Philippica II and Philippica III* (New York 2008) 43, notes that "uninformed and unskilled speakers were hooted off the speaker's platform".

[106] *Exord.* 18.1.

[107] John Chrys., *In Matt. hom.* 11; PG 57,193 10-13; Demos., *Exord.* 25.1.

listen.[108] The rhetorical ability of the speakers to sway reason and stir passion becomes a vital factor in moulding and changing their γνώμη. Both rational and emotional elements are involved that, together with the uncertainty that embraces life, are able to shape the γνώμη to give what may be an erroneous finding. Without doubt, the γνώμη was the faculty that had to be focused or tuned as the juror's chief instrument of judgement. In one court case, Demosthenes addresses the jurors thus: καὶ τηρήσατε τὴν γνώμην ταύτην ἐφ' ἧς νῦν ἐστέ ("guard this mindset that you now rely on").[109] Whereas Aristotle suggested that the emotional element was required to produce a fair verdict, Demosthenes implies that the emotional element could be used to distort the verdict. We find him giving the following advice: περὶ πάντων ὧν ἂν ἀκούητε, τοῦθ' ὑποθέντες ἀκούετε τῇ γνώμῃ ("concerning everything that you may hear [in this court], listen to it after establishing this [scenario] in your mindset").[110] This injunction is immediately followed with an emotionally charged descriptive question, designed to bias the jurors' mindsets against his adversary. Demosthenes well knew why it was possible for a juror to retain his integrity, ἀλλὰ γνώμῃ διαμαρτὼν ἀποτυχεῖν, "but miss the [correct judgement] by going astray in the mindset".[111] The persuasive skill of the orator could produce such a result, demonstrating that the γνώμη was the controlling faculty in decision-making, a facet of γνώμη about which Chrysostom was emphatic. Also indicated here is the presence of significant emotional elements in the γνώμη as recognised by Chrysostom.

This phenomenon of retaining integrity whilst being in error, lays bare the inherent weakness of the γνώμη that hinders it from being a font of absolute truth and perfect trustworthiness. The speech referred to concerns the prosecution of Timocrates for the attempted introduction of a law whereby he could make substantial profits. At one place in the speech, Demosthenes accuses him of premeditated malice and not simply of going astray in his γνώμη.[112] This was not a matter of an honest error of judgement. Earlier, Demosthenes had pointed out how Timocrates had evaded the normal legal processes of introducing legislation; had he taken the proper path he might only have been accused of the lesser and perhaps non-indictable fault, that of failure through having gone astray in his γνώμη, the honest mistake to which the γνώμη is open. Apparently, the γνώμη

---

[108] Demos., *Aristocr.* 96. γνώμῃ τῇ δικαιοτάτῃ δικάσειν ὀμωμόκασιν, ἡ δὲ τῆς γνώμης δόξα ἀφ' ὧν ἂν ἀκούσωσι παρίσταται· ἡ δὲ τῆς γνώμης δόξα ἀφ' ὧν ἂν ἀκούσωσι παρίσταται ("They had taken oath to pronounce judgement by their most civilised mindset, but the opinion of the mindset that is supported will be from those they may hear").

[109] Demos., *Mid.* 213.

[110] Demos., *Mid.* 108.

[111] Demos., *Tim.* 48.

[112] Demos., *Tim.* 110.

came into play in all participants in the lawsuit: that of the defendant in framing and presenting his defence, of the prosecutor in the persuasive oratory of his attack, and of the jurors in their decision-making. Thus, apart from the doubt thrown on Timocrates' integrity in this suit, it is apparent that, even if integrity is retained, what seems a fundamental weakness of the γνώμη could distort the outcome. As noted above in Thucydides, it is as open to the passions as it is to reason. In addition, the γνώμη, even when not driven by unbridled passion, is latently open to the vagaries of environment and experience that are significant in determining levels of knowledge, wisdom and ignorance. Uncertainty thus casts its shadow over both past and future. For the jurors, the Athenian juror's oath covered such exigencies: it allowed for the normal distortions of the γνώμη. For the rest, it depended upon their integrity.[113] As discussed in chapter 3 above, Chrysostom was well aware of the inherent weakness of the γνώμη, but he saw answers to it in the generous love and grace of God.

Both the critical composition and significance of the γνώμη are suggested by Demosthenes in his speech on the false embassy where he calls upon the Court, acting with μιᾳ γνώμη, a united mindset, to punish the collaborators.[114] From what we know of the composition of the Athenian people's courts, it would have been a remarkable phenomenon to gain unanimity on such an issue. Yunis notes that panels of judges ranged from 201 for some minor private suits to over 2,000 for major public cases.[115] In an arena where human passions as well as human intellect were not only powerfully present, but recognised as being so by the orators who addressed them, it was necessary that persuasive rhetoric harness both reason and passion for such an outcome. This would have been especially so because Athens had a reputation for pride in their πραότης (mildness).[116] Not mere

---

[113] See Demos., *Cor. Trier.* 18-19 where he argues before the council that the task of the lawyers engaged by his opponents to present their case is simply to declare their γνώμη (mindset), and not to put monetary interests before those of justice by zealously striving to distort the facts in order to ensure their pay. This seems somewhat ironic, as Demosthenes was as zealous and wily an orator as any in putting or defending a case. Nevertheless, he was pointing to the exemplary main function of a speaker in all the venues of Athenian democratic debate, that of stating their considered opinion, their deliberated noblest mindset, their γνώμη. No more and no less was required.

[114] Demos., *Fals. Leg.* 299.

[115] Yunis, *Taming Democracy*, 5 n. 11. Ober, *Mass and Elite*, 141, limits the range from 200 to 500.

[116] For Demosthenes' usage of πραότης, see M.D. Hall, "Even dogs have Erinyes: sanctions in Athenian practice and thinking", in L. Foxhalk and A.D.E. Lewis (eds), *Greek Law in its Political Setting: Justifications not Justice* (Oxford 1996) 73-89 at 74 n. 3. Her perceptive contribution on punishment in Athens demonstrates that this reputation was more real in the claim than in the practice. She concludes at 88-89 that Athens was no better or no worse than

assent but merciless assent was required, thus demonstrating the nature of the γνώμη as something beyond plain understanding and inclination, but as incorporating elements of passion. C. Carey argues that pathos was seen as fundamental to effective rhetoric:

> *Pathos* is defined broadly by Aristotle (*Rhetoric 1356a, 1377b*) as 'creating a certain disposition in the audience'. Aristotle was not the first rhetorician to stress the importance of *pathos*. Emotional appeal formed a major component of the rhetorical handbooks that were circulating in his day (*Rhetoric 1354a*). He mentions Gorgias, Quintilian, Thrasymachus and points to usage by Homer, Thucydides, Hesiod and Aeschylus.[117]

Demosthenes did not hesitate to generate pathos in one or more of its forms as the situation required. As the γνώμη is the faculty that combines both reason and passion, it was the target of such persuasion oratory. This is observable in a speech against Callippus where the appeal made is to the jurors to refrain from changing their γνώμη from working with three established principles: the merits of the case, without partisanship, and based on justice. His call, a choice between established principles and persuasive speakers, is μηδὲ μεθ' ἑτέρων τὴν γνώμην γενόμενοι ("they should not be going after the mindset of other speakers").[118] The element of devotion or commitment to a principle or a person evident here involves the presence of passion in the γνώμη. It is noteworthy that the appeal regarding allegiance or devotion was not merely a matter of principles versus persons, but was focused on the γνώμη of those persons. This applied to less significant relationships. In a letter to Heracleodorus, Demosthenes warns this orator against supporting the unjust prosecution of a friend of his. He says that he has a high opinion of Heracleodorus and would be greatly upset, "if, after motivating myself to feel well disposed towards you, I should be forced instead to take the opposite mindset".[119] The devotion to his friend was far greater than that to the eminent

---

other πόλεις at the time. This does not negate my point, as the orator had to address the self-image, their mindset regarding themselves.

[117] C. Carey, "Rhetorical means of persuasion", in I. Worthington (ed.), *Persuasion: Greek Rhetoric in Action* (New York 1994) 26-45 at 26-27.

[118] Demos., *Callip.* 2; See V. Bers (trans.), *Demosthenes Speeches, 50-59*, The Orators of Classical Greece 6 (Austin, TX 2003) 12-15, who on philological and stylistic grounds ascribes this speech to Appolodorus, both in the writing and the delivery. Others suggest that it was written by Demosthenes for Apollodorus, a client, and who probably delivered this speech to the court. As these details are not relevant to the issue of this study, I have taken the simpler path in analysis by leaving the third party out of the discussion.

[119] Demos., *Epis.* 5.4: εἰ παρωρμηκὼς ἐμαυτὸν εὐνοϊκῶς ἔχειν σοι τὴν ἐναντίαν γνώμην μεταλαβεῖν ἀναγκασθείην.

orator. A strong emotional element was directing a change in his γνώμη towards Heracleodorus. Thus radical change in attitude or disposition takes place in the in the γνώμη, and such change in that faculty is rarely achieved by appeal to reason alone. Here, too, we find parallels with Chrysostom: his awareness of the γνώμη as the citadel of the psyche to be targeted with persuasive oratory in the service of God; and the very nature of his calling as a minister of the Gospel in impressing his mindset, inasmuch as it follows Christ, upon his people.

As seen above, Chrysostom held that true unity in actions and collaboration in ventures are the province of the γνώμη. Demosthenes had worked with that principle a millennium previously. He was well aware that something more than mere intellectual assent was required, and that bare appeal to the intellect alone would fail to produce the desired solidarity of purpose and perseverance. It is not surprising that, when persuading the assembly to join forces in resisting Philip of Macedon, we find him calling them to do so ὁμοθυμαδὸν ἐκ μιᾶς γνώμης ("with one passionate accord from one mindset").[120] The source of total accord, of effective passionate united resistance is to be found in the γνώμη, the faculty of the psyche that has the capacity to combine both reason and passion in appropriate balance. In another speech, he cautions the Athenians not to hold past grudges against the Thebans and thereby have them join with Philip in his invasion. If they go down that path, he asserts, they will καὶ μιᾷ γνώμῃ πάντων φιλιππισάντων ("with one mindset all be Philippised").[121] In another call for unity of purpose and action he asks for two things, first, ὁμόνοιαν ("oneness of mind or reason"), and second, δὲ πάντας ἐκ μιᾶς γνώμης τοῖς δόξασι προθύμως συναγωνίζεσθαι ("for all, from one mindset in the formation of opinions, to struggle together zealously in the contest").[122] This reveals another dimension to the application of γνώμη, that of the disposition of the mindset. Not only is its distinction from a decision made with the mind or reason made evident, but also the need for an element of zeal in the mindset in order to carry out the intention in the face of a powerful enemy. An appropriate emotional element must augment the rational element in the mix of the mindset. Athenians failures in the past had highlighted the disparity between νοῦς (mind or reason) and γνώμη (mindset). This is similar to the distinction Chrysostom makes between these faculties in his homily on 1 Corinthians 1:10 that has been discussed above in Chapter 2. Chrysostom explained that the

---

[120] Demos., *4 Philipp.* 59: ὁμοθυμαδὸν, from θυμός, of which LSJ, 810, s.v., emphasises the emotional passionate aspect of the soul. We may tease out ὁμοθυμαδὸν, as follows: one and the same passionate spirit. This is a vital element of effective one accord. See also LPGL, 657, s.v., which notes θυμός usage in the patristic era as "the active non-intellectual principle in the soul".

[121] Demos., *Cor.* 176.

[122] Demos., *Epis.*, 1.5.

emotional element required for real unity, and that was lacking in mere intellect, was to be found in a γνώμη that was brimming with love.[123]

As did Chrysostom, it is apparent that Demosthenes understood the γνώμη as being subject to development and change. The role of the political orator was nothing other than to shape the γνώμη of others to think and feel similarly to himself.[124] In an essay praising the young Epicrates, we find Demosthenes speaking of the need to train the γνώμη so that it might be made suitable for the responsibility of office in the administration of the Athenian πόλις.[125] This could be done, he suggests, by the study of philosophy. Demosthenes noted that Epicrates was already showing promise by his choice of sports. In choosing chariot racing, he exhibited "the sign of a good soul and a prudent mindset (γνώμη)".[126] Here, as in Chrysostom, it is to be noted that the προαίρεσις (choice) was determined by the state of the γνώμη. Demosthenes, although he did not truly belong to the aristocratic class, shared their outlook in his preference for chariot racing.[127] He advised Epicrates that training for foot races helped neither courage nor morale, and that practising boxing destroyed the γνώμη as well as the body. Thus, what were thought to be both helpful and hindering activities in the shaping of the γνώμη are made known. The appropriately shaped and disposed mindset was critical for the role that it played in the life of the Athenian πόλις. Chrysostom followed suit in his vocation, in recognition of the role of the γνώμη for life and godliness. He spent his life shaping the γνώμη of his congregations and colleagues with the appropriate instruments, especially the Christian Scriptures and the sacraments.

Like Chrysostom, the emphasis in Demosthenes is upon contributing our part and at the same time remaining dependent upon the divine: ἂν θεὸς θέλη ("if god will"),[128] that is, upon the higher powers beyond human control. In this text, Demosthenes was insistent that the Athenians could not be passive, weak and negligent and then expect to see things come out in their favour. There is need for toil and exertion, for them to become independent, their own men and not dependent upon others. As seen above, this is Libanius; it is also Chrysostom; but in Chrysostom's understanding it was neither the capricious pantheon of the Greeks, nor the haphazard ways of indecipherable Fortune, but the consistently

---

[123] John Chrys., *In 1 Cor. hom.* 3; PG 61,23 7-28.
[124] Usher, *Greek Oratory*, 277-278.
[125] Demos., *Erot.* 55: καλὸν οὖν παρεσκευάσθαι τὴν γνώμην, ἵνα μὴ τότε πλημμελῆς ("Therefore it is good to have prepared your mindset so that at that time you may not err").
[126] Demos., *Erot.* 24: ...καὶ ψυχῆς ἀγαθῆς καὶ γνώμης φρονίμου κοινόν ἐστιν σημεῖον·
[127] See Ober, *Mass and Elite*, 252-253, for a discussion of the highborn and sports.
[128] Demos., *1 Philipp.* 7; see also *In Exordia* 2.3.

faithful trinitarian God of Christianity who was empowering and watching in providential care and determined the outcome. Demosthenes was insistent that only a γνώμη that was disposed willingly to contribute their wealth and their bodies to the service of the πόλις could entertain any expectation of future freedom.[129] Philip was the prime example of such a γνώμη. He had achieved his past victories and extended his empire because, said Demosthenes, "he, being equipped with the necessary mindset trampled upon them and possessed them all".[130] As this study has shown, Chrysostom would have heartily agreed.

Agenda-setting has been noted above as a function of the γνώμη in Chrysostom's usage of this term. Demosthenes so uses γνώμη to describe what he thinks Philip of Macedon is doing: he "is drunk with the greatness of his achievements and he dreams of many more like them in his mindset".[131] In Chrysostom it was noted that the γνώμη was the locus of the imagination. The γνώμη is the faculty in which dreams for the future occur and plans are formulated. LSJ, under the entry for ὀνειροπολέω, suggest the translation for πολλὰ τοιαῦτ' ὀνειροπολεῖν ἐν τῇ γνώμῃ in this text: "builds many such castles in the air".[132] However, sufficient value has not been given to the force of γνώμη in this construction. The γνώμη is not a faculty of empty dreams but one of deliberated judgement, of policy, of direction. The context indicates that Philip's dreams for the future were built on the solid achievements of the past and were far from being castles in the air. Milns translates this as "has many similar aspirations revolving in his mind".[133] This is more to the point, as Demosthenes is referring to rational aspirations and not to drunken fancies. Perhaps this is a rhetorical figure of embracement where Demosthenes is paradoxically combining Philip's euphoria derived from past victories with his sober aspirations for the future. Subsequent history would confirm this. Perhaps, to acknowledge that Demosthenes' language was something more than rhetorical strategy, a measure of intoxication or euphoria may have been involved, but it was not the drunkenness of vain fantasies. Philip, more than any other leader at the time, was in the position to indulge his

---

[129] Demos., *1 Philipp.* 7

[130] Demos., *1 Philipp.* 6: καὶ γάρ τοι ταύτῃ χρησάμενος τῇ γνώμῃ πάντα κατέστραπται καὶ ἔχει, τὰ μὲν ὡς ἂν ἑλών τις ἔχοι πολέμῳ, τὰ δὲ σύμμαχα καὶ φίλα ποιησάμενος· καὶ γὰρ συμμαχεῖν καὶ προσέχειν τὸν νοῦν τούτοις ἐθέλουσιν ἅπαντες, οὓς ἂν ὁρῶσι παρεσκευασμένους καὶ πράττειν ἐθέλοντας ἃ χρή.

[131] Demos., *1Philipp.* 49: ἐγὼ δ' οἶμαι μέν, ὦ ἄνδρες Ἀθηναῖοι, νὴ τοὺς θεοὺς ἐκεῖνον μεθύειν τῷ μεγέθει τῶν πεπραγμένων καὶ πολλὰ τοιαῦτ' ὀνειροπολεῖν ἐν τῇ γνώμῃ.

[132] LSJ 1231, s.v.

[133] J.R Ellis, and R.D. Milns (trans and eds), *The Spectre of Philip: Demosthenes' First Philippic, Olynthiacs, and Speech On the Peace; A Study in Historical Evidence*, Sources in Ancient History 1 (Sydney 1970) 32.

dreams without much fear of disappointment or disaster. Demosthenes, unlike many of his fellow Athenians, was not labouring under the illusion that Philip was doing something other than setting his agenda of future conquests. In the debate concerning the dispute about the ownership of the island of Hallonesus, Demosthenes reminded the assembly of the cunning of Philip in the way in which he changed course in his dealings with them. The distrust of the Athenians led him to change his agenda in his approach to them, from one of acting as an eager benefactor to that of being an upholder of universally agreed justice. This justice, he asserted, was being denied to him, when in reality, claimed Demosthenes, he was denying the Athenians their previously acknowledged rights. Demosthenes noted that Philip, by their actions, was caused …μεταβάλλειν αὐτοῦ τὴν γνώμην ("…to change his mindset").[134] It is in the γνώμη that ideas are consolidated, and thus orient the being towards particular actions. This is also seen in Demosthenes' speech on his writ against Meidias. He claimed that his opponent had distorted the reality of the situation by choosing to put himself forward as the victim rather than the aggressor. That he should choose such a path, Demosthenes argued, was due to…τὴν ἀναιδῆ γνώμην ("his shameless mindset").[135] It was the disposition of his γνώμη that had set the agenda for his defence.

Before concluding this survey of Demosthenes' usage of γνώμη, a general comment should be made. To do this it is needful to return to an issue raised in my Introduction, Chapter 1, regarding insistence upon applying Chrysostom's pastoral concern as a necessary interpretive tool for understanding his theology. In the single-mindedness displayed in that, it seems that he had learnt well from this ancient master. Demosthenes had used his rhetorical skill not as an end in itself, but as a means to an end, the recovery and preservation of the Athenian spirit of democracy and independence. In relation to this feature, Kennedy makes the pertinent observation: "He [Demosthenes] alone of Greek orators shared, perhaps without much realizing it, Plato's belief in absolute values and rejection of rhetorical relativism".[136] With Chrysostom there is indeed affinity, but with two vital distinctions: he was most certainly aware of the source of the absolute values that he believed and preached, and he was consciously deliberate in his rejection of rhetorical relativism.

Closely related to this is another lesson that he probably learned from the speeches of the master he was required so diligently to study. Yunis observes that of the three models of rhetoric under consideration in his essay, those of Plato,

---

[134] Demos., *Hallon.* 21.
[135] Demos., *Mid.* 91.
[136] Kennedy, *A New History of Classical Rhetoric*, 80.

Thucydides and Demosthenes, only Demosthenes' were "pure praxis".[137] This is similar to Chrysostom in that he was involved in the pastoral life of his people, face to face with the realities, distractions and temptations of life in the city. He was neither writing nor conversing from the theoretical distance of the philosopher as Plato, nor was he reporting from the remove of the historian as Thucydides, but like Demosthenes, he was speaking in the midst of the fray with the urgency of the decisive moment of his congregations' destiny pressing upon him. This feature of pure praxis may account for his departure from the rhetoric models when he thought it necessary so to do in the interests of his people rather than being a slave to protocols that might enhance his own reputation. In the event, he did not need to worry about reputation; the appellation he gained says it all.

It is no great exaggeration to suggest that a study of the speeches of Demosthenes creates the impression that the destiny of the fourth–century Athenian democracy was determined by γνώμη. The whole process of the political life of Athens was ultimately dependent upon both the individual and collective γνώμη of the members of the assembly and the council. From a proposal introduced by the πρυτάνεις (president), the opinions of individual members, through to the final application of the confirmed judgement, Demosthenes applies this term to every step in the process. A similar feature marks the trials, both public and private, of the people's courts. The term is also used for the approval or the sanction of the council of 500. The prime feature of γνώμη as deliberated mindset found in Demosthenes is echoed in Chrysostom. This strongly suggests that he derived his understanding of the significance of this term from those speeches and the other Classical authors he studied in the Greek παιδεία. Other features found in the speeches also find their echo in Chrysostom: the presence of intellectual and emotional elements; the locus for becoming set in views and opinions; its inherent weakness; agenda setting; its need for development and education; as the target of persuasive oratory; the paradoxical confidence in self effort and humility in recognition of the need for dependence on the divine; and the focus of human destiny. The parallels speak volumes as to the influence Demosthenes had upon the thought and vocabulary of the young student a thousand years in the future.

---

[137] Yunis, *Taming Democracy*, 18-21.

V. Conclusion

It has been shown that all of this material from the Classical Greek παιδεία is reflected in Chrysostom's use of γνώμη. There is the emphasis upon moral exhortation aimed at internal transformation issuing in virtuous conduct, an emphasis that dominates in his homilies.[138] The settled conviction of the mindset encountered in Chrysostom is here. As suggested, Chrysostom also taught that the rationality of the γνώμη is ever modified by emotional elements, for better or for worse as the case may be. As master of the psyche and in control of the passions, the γνώμη carried the burden of destiny. Attitudes to external forces beyond human control were determined by the disposition of γνώμη. It could be the harbourer of weaknesses that led to failure, or of strengths that led to victories.

With the understanding of the γνώμη that Chrysostom harvested from the formative literature of the Greek παιδεία, he was enabled to teach a relevant doctrine of sin that allowed for the full dignity of the person, and the full freedom of the human will, and that laid upon a faculty of the soul a responsibility that the individual or the group could not escape. Before discussing that doctrine of sin, the question arises as to whether or not he was alone in his particular usage of γνώμη. To what extent was he a member of a theological community that thought similarly about the place and function of the γνώμη in the human psyche? To that question we now turn.

---

[138] Young, "The rhetorical schools", 192-193; Mühlenberg, "From early Christian morality", 212, makes the pithy comment that "Chrysostom did philosophise about the inward struggle of virtue against the temptations of the Evil One but rather surprises his flock when he kind of x-rays their customary habits with the light of a Christian morality".

CHAPTER 9

The Antiochene Camaraderie

It has been established above that the Greek παιδεία contributed significantly to the vocabulary of Chrysostom's theological anthropology. This has been discussed in relation to Libanius (Chapter 7), and to the formative Greek παιδεία (Chapter 8). Before discussing his usage of γνώμη in relation to the issue of sin, it is beneficial to investigate another significant source of his language and thought, the theological tradition of the early church, especially that in which he first lived and worked at Antioch. It is not intended to cover the distinctive features or the broad issues of that tradition but to focus on one thing: the usage of γνώμη by a small number of writers who have been deemed to constitute the core of the Antiochene school.[1] Concentration here will be upon Diodore of Tarsus (died c. 390), and Chrysostom's companion student in Diodore's ἀσκητήριον, Theodore of Mopsuestia (350-428), and Theodoret of Cyrus (c. 393-c. 458), the later representative of Antiochene thought and methodology. This study cannot be exhaustive, for, in spite of the ravages of controversy that led to the destruction of much of Diodore's output, and that of Theodore, the amount of material that has been recovered of the output of those two worthies, together with the extant works of Theodoret, comprises a substantial corpus.[2] Without moving the concentration

---

[1] There is a growing literature as to the nature and characteristics of this phenomenon. The question of definition on the basis of a distinctive exegetical approach has been addressed briefly in Chapter 1 above; A. Schor, "Theodoret on the 'school of Antioch': a network approach", *JECS* 15 (2007) 517-562, in taking a different direction, has contributed a perceptive study based on social network theory to the possible nature of the school, suggesting that it was a "socio-doctrinal network, a group of clerics bound by a call and response of doctrinal language". Whilst I think that Schor's approach is somewhat limiting in its perception of the scope of the Antiochenes, it does add a valuable aspect to that which is already agreed upon as to the nature of the school. Hence the title I have given to this chapter: "The Antiochene Camaraderie"; see also R.B. ter Haar Romeny, "Eusebius of Emesa's Commentary on Genesis and the origins of the Antiochene school", in J. Frishman and L. Van Rompay (eds), *The Book of Genesis in Jewish and Oriental Christian Interpretation: A Collection of Essays*, TEG 5 (Leuven 1997) 127, who suggests in this commendable essay that "The Antiochene School is best described as a school of thought (*Richtung*), rather than an institution (*Lehranstalt*) such as the School of the Catechists in Alexandria".

[2] Whilst I have perused the writings that have survived only in Syriac and/or Latin, I have used only those extant in Greek. For a study such as this that depends on the occurrence of a particular word, in the interests of precision it is not valid to second-guess what exact Greek word may lay behind the possible equivalents in extant non-Greek texts.

of this study away from Chrysostom, a sizable amount of sufficient material is presented from these writers, more than ample to support the main thrust of this work. The chapter will conclude with a brief reference to the wider patristic context, including a special mention of Maximus the Confessor, who in his theological writing systemised the essence of some of what Chrysostom presented piecemeal in homiletic form.

I. Diodore of Tarsus

There are twenty-eight occurrences of γνώμη in the extant fragments of Diodore's Commentary on the Psalms.[3] Analysis of these texts reveals close similarity to Chrysostom's usage. A significant feature of Chrysostom's usage of γνώμη was summed up in the clause: God inspects the γνώμη (mindset). One application of this principle concerned the approach to God in prayer, an issue Diodore takes up in expounding the fourth Psalm as a hymn on providence. Diodore asserts that it is not the righteous life of the person praying but the γνώμη he/she brings to prayer that determines the validity of the petition before God. On this premise, Diodore asserts that there is a ἡ δικαία αἴτησις ("righteous petition"),[4] one that is in harmony with God's character and his providential law.[5] Such alone is acceptable to him and brings a speedy answer. Conversely, there can be no assurance of being heard by God if the request falls outside those parameters. Diodore is emphatic that a request in prayer definitely will be heard when it is conditioned by a righteous γνώμη. This, he says, is a principle of universal application because the Psalmist "proposes his own personal experience as generally embracing all those who have such a mindset, that is, one which is righteous and divinely sanctioned…"[6]

---

[3] Citations are from J.M. Olivier (ed.), *Diodore of Tarsus: Commentarii in Psalmos.* vol. 1: *Commentarii in Psalmos I-L*, CCSG 6 (Turnhout 1980). The only other occurrence of Diodore's usage outside this *Comm. Pss*, is one in *Fragmenta in epistulam ad Romanos* (in catenis), in K. Staab (ed.), *Pauluskommentar aus der griechischen Kirche aus Katenenhandschriften gesammelt* (Münster 1933) 83-112. For literature directly pertinent to this section, see R.C. Hill (trans.), *Diodore of Tarsus: Commentary on Psalms 1-51*, WGRW 9 (Atlanta, GA 2005).

[4] Diod., *Comm. Pss* 4.2a 13.

[5] Diod., *Comm. Pss* 4.2a-2b. "Asking righteously" or "righteous petition" occurs five times in section 2a within the space of eleven lines, twice in section 2b, plus another one each in sections 3 and 4.

[6] Diod., *Comm. Pss* 4.2a. 10-13: Τὸ δὲ ἑαυτοῦ πρόσωπον ὑποτίθεται ἐνταῦθα περιλαμβάνων πάντας τοὺς τοιαύτην ἔχοντας γνώμην, δικαίαν τέ φημι καὶ ὁσίαν·

This distinction between life and mindset is significant for our perception of the nature, role, and the importance of γνώμη as used by Diodore. As Providence applies to the circumstances of life, Diodore explains that adverse circumstances brought on by our own fault and sin are to be endured with patience and cannot be proper matter for effectual prayer. Conversely, those troubles that come only from external causes can and should be the substance of righteous petitions with the expectation of a prompt hearing. The issue here is of a self-seeking, self-absorbed γνώμη over against a God-discerning, God-dependent γνώμη. The righteous petition is one that takes account of God's character and his providential purpose. The suggestion in Diodore's treatment is that our petitions, just as much as all other parts of our lives, need to be ordered by a righteous γνώμη. The orientation of the γνώμη determines not only the choices made, the responses given, the direction pursued, but also the petitions uttered. Prayer must be included for, in Antiochene thought, the γνώμη determines what petitions will be answered.

In comments on the following Psalm, Diodore again points to the need of the right γνώμη in prayer. He understood the psalmist, speaking for the nation at the time of their Babylonian captivity, as claiming the blessings of divine providence because of their conversion from the worship of idols and its associated evils, to the acknowledgement of the true God, together with the concomitant desire to bring about justice in the land. This change is explained by Diodore as release from the former γνώμη and restoration to a sound mind.[7] With this healing of the γνώμη comes the assurance that God hears and answers the prayers of his people. Hence, the concerns of prayer obviously change with the change of mindset to sanctioned requests, in this instance the restoration of the Temple and the establishment of justice.

Another area of accord between Chrysostom and Diodore on the role of γνώμη relates to the judgement of God. Diodore comments on the psalmist's distinction between voluntary and involuntary sins: those that come from within ourselves and those that are forced upon us by chance external factors such as torture. Diodore understands that the latter transgressions, which are designated ἀλλότρια ("alien")[8] by the psalmist and ἔξωθεν ("from outside") or οὐκ ἀφ'ὧν ("not from us"),[9] by Diodore, merit God's pardon, whereas the former, those that are ἐκ τῶν ἐφ' ἡμῖν ("from those up to us"),[10] are subject to condemnation. Diodore asserts that the basis of condemnation for these voluntary sins, however small they may

---

[7] Diod., *Comm. Pss* 5.8. 1-2: Ἐγω οὖν, φησίν, ἐπειδὴ λοιπὸν ἀπήλλαγμαι τῆς τοιαύτης γνώμης – ἐσωφρονίσθην γὰρ ἀφ' ὧν ἔπαθον.
[8] Diod., *Comm. Pss* 18.13b-14a.
[9] Diod., *Comm. Pss* 18.14c.
[10] Diod., *Comm. Pss* 18.4c.

appear to be, is the γνώμη of the transgressor.[11] This indicates just how much value Diodore, and those taught by him, placed on the γνώμη in their theological anthropology.

Another critical area of life experience where Diodore, like Chrysostom, maintains that God looks at the γνώμη is that of repentance and conversion. Diodore, in keeping with his historical hermeneutic, relates Psalms 27-30, though viewing them as prophetically composed by David, to the experience of Hezekiah with the Assyrians. Diodore, in his explanation of the text of the twenty-ninth Psalm, has Hezekiah ἐφυσιώθην τὴν γνώμην ("puffed up in his mindset")[12] about the victory over the Assyrians, a victory he ascribed to his own virtue. He notes that the consequences of this self-opiniated γνώμη were the aversion of God's face from him and the onset in his life of various afflictions and troubles. These disasters brought him to his senses so that he confessed and repented of his destructive γνώμη.[13] It is evident from this that Diodore understood the γνώμη as the critical human faculty in God's dealings with us. It is seen to be the cause of the problem, the target of God's chastening actions, and the subjective centre of confession and repentance. It is pertinent to note Diodore's comment on this process in the second Psalm in this group: "after his mindset was improved he confessed the truth".[14]

As with Chrysostom, Diodore understood the γνώμη to be the disposing faculty of the psyche, thereby determining a person's dominant stance or attitude, and ultimately one's destiny. This is evident in his comments on the forty-eighth Psalm in an extended passage on the folly of trusting in wealth and making it the governing pursuit of life. In his explanation of the text, he calls this passion for possessions a "feverish delusion" (τύφος),[15] the expression of a γνώμη that denies the dignity of the Creator's gift of reason to them. As a result, such persons fail to comprehend what God requires of them, and so live and die like the beasts, the irrational creation. The γνώμη is presented by Diodore as a controlling, distorting, and darkening faculty and, in the end, as being responsible for one's destiny. We have noted that Diodore described Hezekiah's reaction to victory in battle as one of unseemly pride, a puffed up mindset which had similar consequences to those

---

[11] Diod., *Comm. Pss* 18.14c, esp. 7-8: Ὁ γὰρ ἡμεῖς ἑκόντες πράττομεν φαῦλον, κἂν ᾖ τὸ μικρότατον, τοῦτο ἐκ τῆς γνώμης τοῦ ἑλομένου μειζόνως καταδικάζεται ("A bad thing that we willingly perform, even if it is the smallest, is greatly condemned on the basis of the mindset of the one who makes the choice").

[12] Diod., *Comm. Pss* 29.6c-d 7-8.

[13] Diod., *Comm. Pss* 29.6c-6d; 29.8b; 29.13a; see also *Comm. Pss* 27.pr. 4; 27.1b-c.

[14] Diod., *Comm. Pss* 27.1b-c: βελτιωθεὶς τὴν γνώμην, ὁμολογεῖ τὸ ἀληθές; See Hill, *Diodore Comm. on Psalms*, 85, who translates as "change of heart" here.

[15] Diod., *Comm. Pss* 48.13a-1s4b, esp. 14a 1.

as related in Psalm 48, except that there recovery occurred for Hezekiah after his repentance.[16]

Diodore's comments on Psalm 9 also demonstrate the authority of the γνώμη in the psyche. The psalmist cries out to God for his intervention against those who exploit the poor. Diodore describes this call as a request for God's retribution to be superior to their γνώμη.[17] It is a prayer for justice for the victims of the oppressing nations whose γνώμη, later in this Psalm, is identified as πλεονεκτική ("grasping").[18] In the event, the retribution was retribution indeed, for the one act brought justice to the victims and swept the oppressors right out of the land. Diodore focuses in on the grasping γνώμη in his comment by asserting that the purpose of the thoroughness of God's intervention was that this γνώμη should disappear from the land. It needed to go, for it had driven the oppressors to their evil deeds. It dominated the oppressors internally as much as it subjugated their victims externally.

This affinity with Chrysostom is linked to another feature of γνώμη common to both that is found in this passage: its association with διάνοια (thought/thinking). Diodore explains that the grasping person "did everything because he had this overriding thought (διάνοια) that there was nothing of interest to God in the things that happen".[19] The usage of διάνοια here appears almost synonymous with γνώμη which occurs a few lines later. The over-riding διάνοια is part of the settled mindset that is the driving force behind the exploitation of the poor. Diodore's usage of γνώμη parallels that of Chrysostom in associating it with volition, especially προαίρεσις (moral choice). This relationship is seen in the commentary on Psalm 9 where προαίρεσις is associated with the grasping γνώμη in its condemnation.[20] The choices taken were the result of grasping or greed being the dominant state of the γνώμη. Diodore explains a section of Psalm 17 that deals with God's protection of the psalmist, as God repaying him by acting for him κατὰ ταύτην μου, θησί, τὴν γνώμην καὶ ἐπ' ἐμοῦ πεποίηκας ("according to this mindset of mine").[21] Diodore refers this γνώμη to the psalmist's treatment of his adversaries. The context makes it clear that the γνώμη in view here is that which is expressed by the consistency of his moral choices in relation to his enemies:

---

[16] Diod., *Comm. Pss* 27.pr. 4; 27.1b-c; 29.6c; 29.6d; 29.8b; 29.13a.

[17] Diod., *Comm. Pss* 9.33a.

[18] Diod., *Comm. Pss* 9.39 4.

[19] Diod., *Comm. Pss* 9.32a: Ἐπειδὴ τοῦτο μάλιστα κατὰ διάνοιαν ἔχων ὅτι οὐ μέλει τῷ θεῷ πραττομένων, πάντα ἐποίει.

[20] Diod., *Comm. Pss* 9.36b.

[21] Diod., *Comm. Pss* 17.29 1.

> Therefore, for this reason that I eagerly sought not to wrong those who were conspiring against me, the Lord took vengeance for me compatible with this choice (προαίρεσιν) of mine...For it is his custom...to guard from injustice those who choose (προαιρουμένους) not to act unjustly.[22]

Besides using προαίρεσις, Diodore also has recourse to αἱρέω, using it in the middle voice, meaning to take for oneself/to choose: "For he saw me keeping his laws and choosing not to wrong anyone".[23] He also employed ἐκλέγω, also in the middle voice, meaning to pick out for oneself/select: "Those who on the whole select for themselves the better way, you also select with the aim of guarding them from every evil thing."[24] Diodore sums up by gathering all this together under γνώμη as already cited. The choice flows from the γνώμη. Similarly, αἱρέω in its aorist middle participial form, ἑλουμένου, appears with γνώμη in the comment previously referred to on the eighteenth Psalm, where the basis for judgement of even what seems a trivial bad action is said to be τοῦτο ἐκ τῆς γνώμης τοῦ ἑλομένου ("the mindset of the one who chose").[25] As held by Chrysostom, it is not so much the deed but the γνώμη motivating the deed and the προαίρεσις flowing from the γνώμη that are accountable. Elsewhere, Diodore applies the details of Psalm 44 to the Messianic reign of the Lord Jesus. Among these are the joyful virgins who enter their vocation without being under any pressure, but: ὡς ἑκουσίᾳ τῇ γνώμῃ ἑλόμεναι τὸ σεμνὸν σχῆμα ("with a voluntary mindset choose this august role").[26] Not only does the choice flow from the γνώμη but its quality is also determined by the state of the γνώμη. Saul is presented as a prime example of this in Psalm 35 where Diodore comments that he ἐπιβουλεύων μὲν τῇ γνώμῃ, τοῖς δὲ ῥήμασι κολακεύων ("he was conspiring with his mindset, but flattering with his words").[27]

Diodore, as did Chrysostom, understood the γνώμη as a faculty requiring development. In Diodore's writings, we encounter it in various stages from instability, in the process of development, and in settled states. The hardened or settled mindset was noted above in the greedy, grasping oppressor. Hezekiah's mindset was witnessed in a vital moment of development. It can be no surprise,

---

[22] Diod., *Comm. Pss* 17.25a-26: Διὰ ταύτην οὖν, θησί, τὴν αἰτίαν, ἐπειδὴ ἔσπευδον μὴ ἀδικεῖν τοὺς ἐπιβουλεύοντας, ἀνταπεδίδου μοι ὁ κύριος κατὰ ταύτην μου τὴν προαίρεσιν...καὶ γὰρ ἔθος αὐτῷ...θυλάττειν δὲ ἀπὸ ἀδικίας τοὺς ἀδικεῖν μὴ προαιρουμένους.

[23] Diod., *Comm. Pss* 17.22a: Ἑώρα γάρ <με>...θυλάττοντα τοὺς αὐτοῦ νόμους καὶ οὐχ αἱρούμενον ἀδικεῖν οὐδένα.

[24] Diod., *Comm. Pss* 17.27a: Καὶ τοὺς καθόλου, φησίν, ἐκλεγομένους τὸ βέλτιον, τούτους καὶ αὐτὸς ἐκλέγει εἰς τὸ θυλάττειν αὐτοὺς ἀπὸ παντὸς κακοῦ.

[25] Diod., *Comm. Pss* 18.14c.

[26] Diod., *Comm. Pss* 44.16a.

[27] Diod., *Comm. Pss* 35.2a.

then, that formative factors in the development of the γνώμη are found in what we have of Diodore's works. One of these formative instruments is experience. The commentary on Psalm 27 relates how the notable victory over the Assyrians dramatically affected Hezekiah's mindset, unfortunately for the worse, a case of negative development in this instance.[28] God did not leave it at that but intervened with his chastening visitations, which eventually brought about the needed change in Hezekiah's γνώμη. This experience was critical as a shaping factor of this faculty. In another place, the biblical text about seeking for guidance by God's law evokes the comment that this is a prayer for instruction so that a basis would be provided "that I might improve and set right my γνώμη".[29] Holy Scripture is recognised as a factor in the development of the γνώμη. Along with that goes the responsibility to act on the instruction so given by improving and setting right (διορθόω) one's γνώμη. This requirement of a right or upright (ὀρθός) mindset was encountered in Chrysostom, as discussed in Chapter 4 above.

In the fiftieth Psalm, Diodore gives something of a definition of γνώμη. In commenting on the text of Psalm 50:19, "…a contrite spirit is a sacrifice to God, a contrite and humble heart the Lord will not despise", he explains the meaning of πνεῦμα (spirit) as γνώμη (mindset): "Instead of sacrifices we offer to you our mindset – this is what spirit means – one that has been humbled and a heart that has suffered."[30] This is remarkable, as it indicates that Diodore understood γνώμη to be the very core of the human soul. It is to be noted that he also appears to use γνώμη synonymously with καρδία (heart). The humbling (ταπεινόω) attached to καρδία in the Scripture text is applied to γνώμη in the commentary, and a different word, ταλαιπωρέω (suffered), replaces the τρίβω (crushed/contrite) of the Scripture in the relation to καρδία, at first sight a rather strange phenomenon for a scholar who, along with the other Antiochenes, strived for precision (ἀκρίβεια) in his work. There is a mixing of terms here as though there is little or no difference between the two faculties, καρδία and γνώμη, both referring to the same core of the being, each, perhaps, from a different perspective, the former relating more to the spiritual, and the latter more to the intellectual. It has been seen in Chapter 1 above that Chrysostom sometimes used γνώμη very much as we would use heart in English. It has already been observed here that the same applies to Diodore as

---

[28] Diod., *Comm. Pss* 27.pr.4.

[29] Diod., *Comm. Pss* 26.11: παίδευέ με, θησίν, ἔνθα χρὴ ἵνα βελτιωθῶ καὶ διορθωθῶ τὴν γνώμην.

[30] Diod., *Comm. Pss* 50.19 1: Προσέρομεν σοι, θησίν, ἀντὶ τῶν θυσιῶν γνώμην – τοῦτο γὰρ λέγει πνεῦμα -- ταπεινωθεῖσαν καὶ καρδίαν ταλαιπωρηθεῖσαν...

shown in the translation by Hill of his comments on Psalm 27.[31] Finally, we should not rush past the importance of the γνώμη in Diodore's theological anthropology as revealed in this passage, "instead of sacrifices our γνώμη – this is what πνεῦμα means". It startles like a huge clap of thunder without any pre-warning rumbles. The offering up of a mindset that has been appropriately humbled is the worthiest sacrifice of all. It is nothing less than the offering up of our spirit, the very core of our beings. Indeed, this, in the opinion of the Antiochenes, is why God haunted the καρδία: to inspect the γνώμη.

It is evident that Diodore and Chrysostom were in harmony in their usage of γνώμη. Are there any differences between them? The answer is a resounding "No!" There are occasions in Diodore as with Chrysostom where a different English translation would be less stilted than "mindset" without seriously affecting the meaning. The writer has encountered numerous examples in this research of translators resorting to "will", a common practice by patristic scholars, and given that γνώμη governs choice, this is not in the category of something to be wondered at. The frequent use of γνώμη by the Antiochenes in relation to God's determined purposes has probably abetted this practice, for in those instances it is invariably translated as "will". Nevertheless, it should be kept in mind that when a translation other than mindset or mentality is used, one is looking at a function or aspect of this faculty and not at some other power of the soul.

II. Theodore of Mopsuestia

Chrysostom's life-long friend, Theodore,[32] who became bishop of Mopsuestia, was a prolific writer whose works suffered much the same fate as those of Diodore, especially when he was posthumously anathematised at the Council of

---

[31] Note 8 above; I have already suggested that the paucity of the usage of γνώμη in the *Koine* Greek of the New Testament may have been due to its replacement at the common level by καρδία.

[32] A. Mingana (ed.), *Commentary of Theodore of Mopsuestia on the Nicene Creed*, Woodbrooke Studies 5 (Cambridge 1932) 3, refers to a letter from Chrysostom that was written near the end of his life when in exile in the Cucusus. See John Chrys., *Ep.18-242;* PG 52,668-669 for this letter, 112; For literature relevant to this section, see R.A. Greer, *Theodore of Mopsuestia: Exegete and Theologian* (Westminster 1961); J.McW. Dewart, *The Theology of Grace of Theodore of Mopsuestia*, Studies in Christian Antiquity 16 (Washington, DC 1971); F.G. McLeod, *The Image of God in the Antiochene Tradition* (Washington, DC 1999); G. Kalantzis (trans.), *Theodore of Mopsuestia: Commentary on the Gospel of John*, ECS 7 (Strathfield 2004); R.C. Hill (trans.), *Theodore of Mopsuestia: Commentary on the Twelve Prophets*, FOTC 108 (Washington, DC 2004).

The Three Chapters (Second Council of Constantinople) in 553. Fortunately, a significant number of his writings have survived in various forms and languages, preserved by followers who looked to him for wisdom in the midst of the great controversies that engulfed the church in the late fourth and early fifth centuries, and by later generations who valued and repeated his insights as the epitome of orthodoxy.[33] Theodore, deemed to have been much more the desk theologian-expositor than Chrysostom who excelled in the homiletic art, is a valuable source of Antiochene thought.[34] As the extant Greek corpus is quite considerable, this study will focus on two of his works, the *Commentarius in xii prophetas minores* and the *Commentarii in Joannem*.[35]

Once again, the God inspects the mindset (γνώμη) feature, characteristic of Chrysostom, is present in Theodore. Although there is nothing akin to the vivid image of his colleague's "...nevertheless he [Noah] found favour in the eyes of the one [God] who haunts the heart, and to him his attitude (γνώμη) was acceptable",[36] the articulation of this principle is plain for all readers to see. He interprets a reference to the selfishness of the people concerning Temple oblations as the fruit of an ἀσεβὴς γνώμης ("ungodly mindset"),[37] which makes any and every oblation unacceptable to God. The condition of the γνώμη determines the quality of the offerings. He employs the same usage in a comment on Malachi's denunciation of the offering up of crippled animals. God, he says, dismissed these paltry offerings because they were offered from a φαύλη γνώμη ("paltry mindset").[38] Similarly, fasting was unacceptable unless exercised with an ἀγαθή γνώμη ("good mindset").[39] Not only did Theodore understand that the γνώμη determined acceptability in the Temple, but also that it was critical to God's spending time with his people. In a comment on an oracle of Hosea about this, he states that the

---

[33] See Mingana, *Commentary*, 6-7, re the loss of much of Theodore's output.

[34] H.B. Swete (ed.), *Theodori Episcopi Mopsuesteni. In Epistolas B. Pauli:Commentarii, The Latin Version with the Greek Fragments with an Introduction, Notes and Indices*, vol. 1 (Cambridge 1880, 1882) lxxvii-lxxviii, gives a valuable observation on the differences between Chrysostom, Theodore, and Theodoret.

[35] The detailed analysis of γνώμη in these two works covers twenty-seven percent of the total usage in his extant works.

[36] John Chrys., *In Gen. hom.* 23; PG 53,200 7-9: ἀλλὰ πρὸς ἐκεῖνον τὸν τὰς καρδίας ἐμβατεύοντα χάριν εὗρε, καὶ ἐκεῖνος αὐτοῦ τὴν γνώμην ἀπεδέξατο. See Hill, *Homilies on Genesis 18-45*, 93, who so translates.

[37] Thdr. Mops., *Ho.* 9.4c. References to Theodore's commentary on the Minor Prophets in this section are given in the form, and refer to the sections, and where appropriate the line numbers, in the critical text of H.N. Sprenger, *Theodori Mopsuesteni Commentarius in XII Prophetas*, Biblica et Patristica 1 (Wiesbaden 1977).

[38] Thdr. Mops., *Mal.* 1.13b 2.

[39] Thdr. Mops., *Zach.* 7.7. 6.

reason that God was shunning such intimacy with them was that οὐδὲ κοινωνῶ τῆς γνώμης ὑμῖν ("...I have nothing in common with your mindset").[40] This was because it was a γνώμη that was eager to embrace an evil lifestyle. Theodore suggests that this aversion was mutual, for in spite of the grace and love shown to them by God, "they did not change the γνώμη they held so as to incline towards me [God]".[41] On a positive note, Theodore gives us a glimpse of the γνώμη that seizes God's attention in a pleasing way. In one of the extant fragments of Theodore's commentary on John's Gospel there is a noteworthy observation about John's comment on Jesus loving Lazarus and his sisters, Mary and Martha, at the time of his friend's sickness. Theodore says that John had introduced this note into the narrative to show how much God appreciated "the virtue of those who had a harmonious mindset about this",[42] that is, the desire for every circumstance to work for the glory of God. There is much to indicate that Theodore understood the γνώμη to be of special interest to God.

Also found in Theodore is that aspect of γνώμη that presents it as the causal faculty of various rebellious actions. The murmuring of the people in John 6:41-42 is ascribed to their δυκόλια γνώμη ("peevish or discontented mindset").[43] Judas Iscariot's outburst against Mary at Bethany in John 12:3-8 is described as the consequence of his κακίτην γνώμην ("pernicious mindset").[44] In Hosea, where Israel's unfaithfulness to God in idolatry is likened to a woman who drifted from her husband to other men, Theodore asserts this was the consequence, in both cases, of a πορνικῇ γνώμῃ ("unchaste or adulterous mindset").[45] In the same vein, Israel's complete apostasy and embracement of error was the product of this adulterous γνώμη.[46] It is clear from this that not just some passing fancy was involved, but rather the adoption of a lifestyle stance. When Hosea takes up another image for their apostasy, that of a stubborn heifer, Theodore explains this metaphor in the context of their fall away from God as an instance of a natural appetite finding inappropriate expression through an intemperate γνώμη: "As with a heifer, by the motion of natural desire towards indiscipline, they [Israelites] stood off from his [God's] service, and with an undisciplined mindset they leaned

---

[40] Thdr. Mops., *Ho.* 11.9c.

[41] Thdr. Mops., *Ho.* 5.4 1: οὐδὴ γὰρ μεταβαλλόμενοι γνώμην ἔσχον τοῦ νεῦσαι πρὸς ἐμέ.

[42] Thdr. Mops., *Joan.* 86,1-6: εἰς τὸ δεῖξαι τῶν τὴν ἀρετὴν σύμφωρον ἐχόντων περὶ τοῦτο τὴν γνώμην.

[43] Thdr. Mops., *Joan.* 37 2.

[44] Thdr. Mops., *Joan.* 103.col.2 22.

[45] Thdr. Mops., *Ho.* 3.4 2.

[46] Thdr. Mops., *Ho.* 4.12b 1.

towards the service of idols."[47] This accords with Chrysostom's assertion that the passions, as a constituent of φύσις (nature), are not intrinsically evil, but are subject to the γνώμη, and that the character of their expression will reflect the state of the γνώμη.[48] In another place, Theodore stresses the point that crimes of destruction and sacrilege performed by Tyre and Sidon against Israel and denounced through Joel were the outcome of their μνησικακοῦντες γνώμη ("grudge-bearing mindset").[49] A raging assault by Edom is "evidence of an enduring mindset of hatred toward them [Israel]".[50] He observes that an ἀσεβεῖ τῆ γνώμη ("irreverent mindset")[51] lies behind the oppression of the poor by the powerful. A comment on Zechariah points out that neglect of the work entrusted to the returned exiles was the effect of a μοχθηρία γνώμης ("depraved mindset").[52] Theodore's preamble to Nahum includes some of the lessons to be learned about God from the examples of his dealings with Nineveh and Babylon. One of these is the fear of the retribution that he visits upon "those who have an irremediable mindset for falling".[53] This is a γνώμη that is set indeed. Also in Theodore's comments on Nahum, references occur to Israel's enemies as acting against them ὑπὲρ ὧν μοχθηρία γνώμης ("under the influence of a depraved mindset"), and ὑπὲρ ὧν ἀπονοία καὶ μοχθηρία γνώμης ("under the influence of a foolish and depraved mindset").[54] It is of note that at line 82 of this passage this depravity of the γνώμη is termed by Theodore οἰκείας μοχθηρία ("innate depravity"). Although not analysed in depth for this study, there is pertinent material in his commentary on the Psalms about the nature of sin. Theodore presents a clear definition of sin in a comment on Psalm 54. R.A. Norris gives the essence of the text as, "sin is rooted in an inimical disposition of the will (γνώμη) which expresses itself in outward action (πρᾶξις) and deliberate intent (πρόθεσις)".[55] Sin flows from a hostile mindset, a statement in complete accord with Chrysostom.

The motivating function of the γνώμη is even more evident in Theodore's comments on texts that refer to divine judgement or retribution. An instance of

---

[47] Thdr. Mops., *Ho.* 4.16a 2-3: δίκην γὰρ δαμάλεως κινήσει τῆς θυσικῆς ἐπιθυμίας νευσάσης, ἀπέστητε μὲν τῆς δουλείας τῆς ἐμῆς. ἀκολάστῳ δὲ γνώμῃ πρὸς τὴν εἰδώλων ἐνεύσατε θεραπείαν.
[48] See Chapter 4 above for discussion re Chrysostom and the passions.
[49] Thdr. Mops., *Joel* 3.4-8.
[50] Thdr. Mops., *Am.*1.11 14-15: ἄρχι τέλους τὴν αὐτὴν τοῦ μίσους περὶ αὐτους ἐπιδειξάμενοι γνώμην.
[51] Thdr. Mops., *Hab.* 1.3a.
[52] Thdr. Mops., *Zach.* pr.1 16.
[53] Thdr. Mops., *Nah.* pr.1 68: τοὺς ἀδιόρθωτον ἐπὶ τῷ πταίειν ἔχοντας τὴν γνώμην.
[54] Thdr. Mops., *Nah.* pr.1 79-84.
[55] R.A. Norris, *Manhood and Christ: A Study in the Christology of Theodore of Mopsuestia* (Oxford 1963) 157-159. See Thdr. Mops., *Exp.* Ps. 54.4a.

this is Hosea's oracle against the leaders who made alliances with Egypt and Assyria. These leaders would suffer by the sword of those very powers for undisciplined (ἀπαιδεύτως) use of their tongues. Theodore looks behind the tongue to their γνώμη as being the responsible faculty. It is the same scornful, petulant γνώμη, he says, that marked their ancestors in Egypt at the time of the Exodus when "they poured contempt on God's gifts to them".[56] This brought divine judgement on them then; this would bring judgement upon them in the present.[57] This is consistent with Joel's call to arms to visit judgement on the nation as being aimed, says Theodore, at ταύτην ἔχετε τὴν γνώμην κατὰ τῶν ἐμοὶ ("their mindset that is biased against those belonging to me").[58] It was for the grudge-bearing γνώμη that motivated the rapacious crimes of Tyre and Sidon that retribution would break upon them.[59] Theodore assigns the cause of the threatened enemy invasion of Israel, as announced in Amos' oracle, to Israel's γνώμη.[60] Likewise, on Obadiah, Theodore blames the γνώμη of the Idumeans, the Babylonians, and any Israelites complicit in those nations' crimes for the promised judgement upon them.[61] Theodore makes a like comment on Micah's oracles about the penalty to be inflicted on various towns of Philistia: it was due to the culpability of their depraved γνώμη.[62] Similarly, Lachish, a fortified town of Judah, is addressed as deserving of punishment for their irreverent γνώμη.[63] Theodore asserts that an attempt to overthrow the priesthood was also due to an irreverent γνώμη, a situation that brought painful irritation to God and moved him to a display of his wrath.[64] Without doubt, this list tells us that Theodore thought that God had his eye on the γνώμη.

It is evident from the foregoing list of occurrences that Theodore understood that the γνώμη was the faculty that bore the chief responsibility for sin and for the consequent divine judgement.[65] He makes a pertinent comment on John 15:7,

---

[56] Thdr. Mops., *Ho.* 7-8.16d 2-3: ἐξεφαύλιζον τὰς εἰς αὐτοὺς γεγενημένας παρὰ τοῦ θεοῦ δωρεάς.
[57] Thdr. Mops., *Ho.* 7.16c; 7-8.16d.
[58] Thdr. Mops., *Joel* 3.9-11 3.
[59] Thdr. Mops., *Joel* 3.4-8 8.
[60] Thdr. Mops., *Am.* 6.14 1.
[61] Thdr. Mops., *Abd.* Pr.1 17; Pr.1 44; 1.16 3; 1.16 13.
[62] Thdr. Mops., *Mi.* 1.11c 2.
[63] Thdr. Mops., *Mi.* 1.13b 3.
[64] Thdr. Mops., *Zach.* 14.1-2 25-30.
[65] This paragraph anticipates the issue to be addressed in Part 3, Chapter 10 below. It is presented here as part of Theodore's overall usage of γνώμη, rather than being omitted here and included in the discussion of Chrysostom's perception of the issue.

Jesus' application of the image of the vine and the branches, which demonstrates the extent of the role of the γνώμη in our responsibility before God:

> He means, it is necessary, for those who are spiritually joined together with the Lord to have their mindset suitably comparable to the grace that has been given to them, for they are pruned when they are indifferent, but they bear much fruit when they carefully manage their divine citizenship.[66]

God expects that the state of the γνώμη will be comparable (ἀνάλογος) to the divinely given grace. The indifferent γνώμη, one that is idle or wants to take a holiday from the cultivation of that grace, thereby despising and neglecting it, results in the chastening hand of the divine gardener. On the other hand, a γνώμη that inclines to nurturing or cultivating the heavenly citizenship by godly living ensures much fruitfulness. Theodore thus indicates that the γνώμη is critical in this relational response. In another place, Theodore illuminates the significance of the γνώμη for this aspect in his depiction of the division of the Commandments in two parts: εἴςτε τὴν περὶ θεὸν γνώμην καὶ εἰς τὴν περὶ τον πλησίον ἀγάπην ("the mindset in regard to God and the love in regard to our neighbour").[67] Theodore leaves us in no doubt that God inspects the γνώμη.

Responsibility is exercised in choices made. In this matter, another similarity to Chrysostom is seen in the interaction of the γνώμη and the will, especially προαίρεσις (moral choice). Theodore brings these together in his preamble to Nahum:

> When God allowed them to display their own moral choice, they used this with so much more depravity of mindset and with so much more savagery and wickedness of manner as to attack all the people of the ten tribes and take them captive. Because they had considered everything with a rapacious attitude, they laid waste their cities and, along with them, whatever they came across.[68]

---

[66] Thdr. Mops., *Joan.* 129 41-44: Δεῖ, θησι, τοὺς πνευματικῶς τῷ Κυρίῳ συναπτομένους ἀνάλογον ἔχειν τὴν γνώμην τῇ χάριτι τῇ δοθείσῃ αὐτοῖς ἐπεὶ ῥαθυμοῦντες κολάζονται τῆς δὲ κατὰ θεὸν πολιτείας ἐπιμελόμενοι πολὺν οἴσουσι καρπόν. References to Theodore's *Commentary on John* are given in the form and refer to the fragment number and line numbers from the critical edition of R. Devreese (ed.), *Commentarii in Joannem (e catenis)*, in R. Devreese, *Essai sur Théodore de Mopsueste;* Studi e Testi 141 (Rome 1948) 301-409.

[67] Thdr. Mops., *Zach.* 5.1-4 10.

[68] Thdr. Mops., *Nah.* pr.1 11: ἐπειδὴ δὲ ἐνδέδωκεν αὐτοῖς ὁ θεὸς τὴν προαίρεσιν ἐπιδεῖξαι τὴν οἰκείαν, ὥστε τοσαύτῃ μὲν ἐχρήσαντο μοχθηρίᾳ γνώμης τοσαύτῃ δὲ ὠμότητι καὶ τρόπου κακίᾳ, πάντας μὲν τοὺς τῶν δέκα φυλῶν ἐπιστρατεύσαντες αἰχμαλώτους λαβεῖν, πορθήσαντές τε αὐτῶν τὰς πόλεις καὶ τὰ προσόντα αὐτοῖς δι᾽ ἁρπαγῆς ποιησάμενοι παντά.

It appears that God had lifted his restraint on the Assyrians and allowed their faculty of choice to follow their γνώμη that was brimming with depravity and waiting to burst forth in extreme violence as described. As with Chrysostom, so too Theodore understood that the γνώμη expressed itself through the choices that were made. This dependence of choice upon the γνώμη is clearly stated in a passage on Hosea dealing with offerings of oblations where the people's choices brought divine reproach upon the γνώμη from which those choices flowed,

> They chose never to offer any of those oblations that had been gratifying to him [God]. Then, to show that he was reproaching them for their mindset, he says: the Deity was not pleased with them.[69]

Theodore describes the process of conviction and conversion as occurring in the γνώμη. He takes Hosea's prophecy of the eventual conversion of Israel and its return to God as applying to the return from exile under Zerubbabel at the time of Cyrus. He portrays this conversion as a μεταβαλοῦνται τὴν γνώμην ("change of mindset").[70] Theodore also comments that the unfaithfulness of Israel was the result of a γνώμη that had been shaped by a yearning, a craving for an adulterous mindset. Such a γνώμη allowed them to stand utterly aloof from God.[71] Theodore understood that the γνώμη was critical in setting the direction of life. Radical change for better or worse in individual or community necessitated the conversion of the γνώμη. It should be noted that this comment by Theodore includes the notion that the γνώμη could be influenced by a powerful passion which, when entertained, would shape the γνώμη to allow sinful actions such as pushing God out of one's thoughts and life. A fuller explanation of the process of conversion is given in his explanation of Joel's call for repentance by turning back to God with all their heart. Theodore treats this with a five-fold elaboration:

(a) μεταβαλώμεθα τὸν λογισμόν (to change their reasoning);

(b) νεύσωμεν ὁλοκλήρῳ τῇ διανοίᾳ (to incline with their whole intellect toward God);

(c) an accusation of practising penitential rites οὐκ ἐκ διαθέσεως ("without engagement of their disposition");

(d) τὰς καρδίας δὲ ἑαυτῶν διανοίγοντές τε καὶ γυμνὰς προσάγοντες τῷ θεῷ (to lay open their hearts and present them naked before God); and

---

[69] Thdr. Mops., *Ho.* 9.4a 8-10: οὐδὲν τοῦ τῶν αὐτῷ κεχαρισμένων εἵλοντο πώποτε ποιῆσαι. εἶτα δεικνὺς ὅτι ὀνειδίζων αὐτοῖς τὴν γνώμην λέγει οὐ μὴν τοῦ θείου τούτοις τερπομένου.

[70] Thdr. Mops., *Ho.* 3.5a 2.

[71] Thdr. Mops., *Ho.* 4.12b 1.

(e) δῆλοι γένησθε τῆς περὶ αὐτὸν ἀντεχόμενοι γνώμης (to make visible that they were clinging to their changed mindset regarding him) by putting off their former wickedness.[72]

The last element appears to sum up the process: their γνώμη had changed. Reasoning, intellect, disposition, heart and deed are involved. Some of the terms referring to faculties of the soul may well be synonymous, or partly so, with γνώμη here. As with Chrysostom's usage, these terms are closely linked together, suggesting that the γνώμη contains a substantial intellectual component. It is pertinent that Theodore does this with a biblical text in which the prophet Joel mentions only one faculty, the καρδία (heart). It is evident that Theodore thought that because the γνώμη is often swayed by passions, there was need to expand on the prophet's words in order to convey the full conscious rational responsibility involved in a true radical change from the worse to the better. The Antiochenes, though fully aware of the emotional element of the γνώμη, always insisted upon free and full responsibility for repentance as much as they did for apostasy. Theodore's comment on Joel's call for a solemn assembly explains that this gathering was intended to be for self-examination: ἐπὶ τῇ μεταμέλεια τῆς γνώμης ("for the purpose of repenting of their mindset").[73] It is no surprise, then, in another context, to find Theodore explaining the conversion of the Ninevites in response to the preaching of Jonah as μεταθεμένους τῆς πρόσθεν γνώμης ("a change of their former mindset").[74] This change enabled them to see the better thing, the veneration of God.

Thoughts of nurture, indifference, and shaping lead to a consideration of γνώμη development. Theodore was in accord with Chrysostom in this matter, for he describes the γνώμη, not only in various settled states as already noted above, but also in contexts where it exhibits the capacity to change for better or for worse. An instance of the latter is found where Theodore explains that the Israelites, in spite of God's intimate treatment of them, had daily intensified (ἐπιτεινόντων) their adulterous γνώμη to the point where punishment and exile would be visited upon them.[75] Continual change for the worse was taking place. The preamble to Zechariah depicts the returned exiles as ἀμφίβολον ἔτι τὴν γνώμην ἔχειν ("possessing a wavering mindset"),[76] one that was ambiguous and not at all set. In contrast, the response of the Ninevites to the preaching of Jonah is described as

[72] Thdr. Mops., *Joel* 2.12-13.
[73] Thdr. Mops., *Joel*, 2.15-16 5-6.
[74] Thdr. Mops., *Jonah*, pr.1 173.
[75] Thdr. Mops., *Ho.* 1.2b 27.
[76] Thdr.Mops., *Zach.*, pr.1 31.

ἀναμφίβολον τὴν γνώμην ("unambiguous"),[77] an unqualified belief brought about by great fear. This incident points to two factors instrumental in γνώμη development that we have met in Chrysostom, instruction and fear. On this occasion, objective data and subjective emotion, or appeal to rational intellect and appeal to sentiment, both component elements of the γνώμη, combined to produce God's desired outcome. Elsewhere, Theodore ascribes the lack of belief in Jesus by his brothers as being the fruit of οὐ τελείαν περὶ αὐτοῦ γνώμην ἔχοντες ("an immature mindset").[78] This indicates that further growth was both needed and possible. Instruction, teaching, and preaching claim a prime place in Theodore's perception of causative factors in γνώμη change. In discussing the returned exiles as narrated by Zechariah, Theodore attributes the change in their fortunes to μεταβαλόντες τὴν γνώμην ("a change in their mindset").[79] The challenging ministry of Zechariah and Haggai had motivated this change in the γνώμη, from neglect towards the construction of the Temple, to zeal and effort for it.

Theodore's perception of the dominant power of the γνώμη in the psyche comes to the fore in his comments on an interesting aspect of the judgement theme in Micah. The passage is as follows:

> From the beginning, you deliberately preferred an antagonistic and bellicose mindset towards me, unwilling to listen to my oracles, but warring with your own peace more than with any other entity. At least, you have received the present war as the benefit of your disobedience.[80]

Apart from declaring the ironic benefit of foreign invasion that issued from adopting a hostile γνώμη towards God, Theodore suggests that this chosen γνώμη became all-consuming and self-destructive. People given over to this mindset shut out the voice of God and, incongruously, go into battle with the wrong enemy, essentially themselves. In so doing they destroy their own well-being and any possibility of a comprehensive peace. In this viewpoint, the γνώμη plays a determining role in the soul. Like Chrysostom, it is apparent that Theodore held that the γνώμη was responsible for human destiny. This is clear where Theodore uses the image of the leaven in the flour in an oracle of Hosea to expand on the pervasive power of the γνώμη. The evil γνώμη of some who rebelled against Jeroboam and set up the northern kingdom of Israel is likened to handful of

---

[77] Thdr. Mops., *Jonah*, 3.5 3.
[78] Thdr. Mops., *Joan.* 41 4.
[79] Thdr. Mops., *Zach.* 8.10 17.
[80] Thdr. Mops., *Mi.* 2.8a 1-3: ὑμεῖς δὲ ἄνωθεν ἔχθραν τινὰ καὶ πολεμι᾽αν γνώμην εἵλεσθε πρὸς ἐμέ πείθεσθαι μὲν τοῖς λεγομένοις οὐκ ἐθέλοντες πολεμοῦντες δὲ τῇ οἰκείᾳ εἰρήνῃ μᾶλλον ἤπερ ἐτέρῳ.

leftover already leavened dough. Just as when that dough is mixed into a new lot of flour and the leaven works its way through the whole, so τὴν γνώμην τῆς κακίας ("the evil mindset")[81] had affected the entire nation. Thus, when Hosea's condemnation of the northern kingdom strikes a universal personal note of finding no one to call upon God, Theodore directs attention to the σύμφωρνον γνώμην ("harmonious mindset")[82] of the people that motivated this lack of recognition of God. This communal γνώμη, a theme stressed by both Theodore and Chrysostom, also by Thucydides long before them in another context, is presented as the paramount factor in the shaping of national destiny.[83]

This examination of Theodore's usage of γνώμη parallels that of Diodore and Chrysostom in every respect where comparisons are possible. In the case of these three exegetes, this phenomenon could be attributed to the influence of a mentor upon his students. Another consideration suggests that it could be ascribed to the Greek παιδεία as a lasting element of the heritage of their common general educational experience, including their rhetorical training. No doubt, the latter was a critical factor, but it is quite plausible to allow that Diodore showed the way to his young colleagues for the usage of that common intellectual legacy to good effect in the explanation of the faith and the Scriptures that had transformed their lives. It will be of particular interest to see to what extent Theodoret of Cyrus trod the same path, to see if the γνώμη was as critical to his anthropology as it was to the older members of the Antiochene camaraderie. It is to him that we now turn.

III. Theodoret of Cyrus

The available material in Theodoret's writings for the analysis of his usage and perception of γνώμη is so vast that a separate tome should be devoted to it. As this study focuses on Chrysostom, only one document has been chosen as representative of the place γνώμη held in Theodoret's anthropology. This is his commentary on Paul's letters, *Interpretatio in xiv epistulas sancti Pauli*. As will be seen, it is more than adequate for the task, containing a rich insight into the critical role of γνώμη as used by the Antiochene camaraderie.[84]

---

[81] Thdr. Mops., *Ho.* 7.4c-5a.

[82] Thdr. Mops., *Ho.* 7.7c.

[83] See Chapter 8, section II above.

[84] In the process of this research, besides the analysis of the commentary on Paul's letters, in J.-P. Migne (ed.), *Interpretatio in xiv epistulas sancti Pauli*; PG 82 36-877, I have made a detailed analysis of his usage of γνώμη in *Interpretatio in Psalmos*, and *De providentia orationes decem*, and consulted the occurrences of γνώμη in *Graecarum affectionum curatio, Eranistes, Haereticarum fabularum compendium*, and *Quaestiones et responsiones ad orthodoxos*. From

Theodoret joins the Antiochene chorus in asserting that God inspects the γνώμη. In a comment on Romans 9:14 where Paul rejects any thought of injustice with God, the argument Theodoret proffers is ὡς οὐ τῇ φύσει προσέχειν ἔθος τῷ τῶν ὅλων Θεῷ, ἀλλ᾽ ὅτι γνώμην ἀρίστην ἐπιζητεῖ ("it is not the habit with the God of all to turn towards nature; rather he seeks after a noble mindset").[85] In the case in point, God did not find it. They deserved what they suffered. Individually and corporately, the state of the γνώμη is the object of his search. The implication is that one cannot help one's nature, but responsibility is ours for the condition of γνώμη. God's dealings with Israel are tendered in support of this assertion. In a different context, the discussion on the appeal to the Corinthians to support the offering for the Jerusalem poor, Theodoret points to a principle by which God works in the matter of giving: τὰ δὲ προσφερόμενα τῇ δυνάμει εἴωθεν ὁ τῶν ὅλων Θεός· οὐ γὰρ τὴν ποσότητα, ἀλλὰ τῆς γνώμης ὁρᾷ τὴν ποιότητα ("The God of all is accustomed to measure offerings on the basis of ability, for it is not a matter of quantity, but the quality of the mindset that he keeps in sight").[86] Again, the γνώμη is the focus of God's attention. An almost identical statement is made on a comment on 1 Timothy 5:10, where God is said to seek the quality of the γνώμη and not the quantity of service.[87] Theodoret explains the division of wooden and clay vessels into either τίμια (honourable) or ἄτιμα (dishonourable) on the basis of the respective γνώμη involved.[88] It is interesting to note that Paul is said to use the same criterion as God when he speaks of Timothy as his beloved son. Theodoret does not want his readers to make a comparison with children who can be irritable at times, but to focus on the γνώμη. Paul's assessment, he says, was not based upon Timothy's nature; it was his γνώμη that Paul appreciated so much.[89]

Another usage of γνώμη of Theodoret's in common with Chrysostom is his insistence upon its autonomy. In an extended discussion of predestination, he fiercely defends the independence of the γνώμη. The heart of the argument is that the only reason one can argue against divine election is the very possession of the

---

these, which are only seven out of the twenty-five extant works in Greek on the TLG, it was evident that so much was available that it was beyond the scope of this chapter to cover the total corpus. In choosing the work for presentation, I decided it would be advantageous to choose something other than the texts covered by Diodore and Theodore. The *Int. Pauli* is ideal in this regard. For literature directly relevant to this section see R. Hill, "Theodoret's Commentary on Paul", *EB* 58 (2000) 1-21; R.C Hill (trans.), *Theodoret of Cyrus: Commentary on the Letters of St Paul*, 2 vols (Brookline, MA 2001).

[85] Thdt., *Int. Pauli*; PG 82,153 52-54.
[86] Thdt., *Int. Pauli*; PG 82,425 18-21.
[87] Thdt., *Int. Pauli*; PG 82,820 6-7.
[88] Thdt., *Int. Pauli*; PG 82,844.
[89] Thdt., *Int. Pauli*; PG 82,832 20-31.

gift of an αὐθαίρετον (independent) γνώμη, otherwise there would be complete silence. He defends the justice of God on this ground. If there is no independent γνώμη, there can be no blame.[90] He outlines the charge as being that they were quite unlike the clay under the potter's hand:

> But you resist and argue. Thus, you neither are bound by natural necessities nor do you transgress unlawfully against your mindset, but you willingly welcome evil with warmth and it is in a spirit of independence that you receive the troubles that would lead to virtue. So then, the sentence of the God of all is right and just, for he punishes sinners who have the effrontery to do this with their mindset.[91]

The autonomy of the γνώμη is starkly clear here. Theodoret has graphically underlined not only its independence but also its capacity for insolence. In its worse state it disregards the innate goodness of nature, embraces evil with enthusiasm, and rejects the overtures of grace inherent in the hardships with which God would turn them to virtue. It throws all God's gifts and care in his face with brazen effrontery. Theodoret indicates that under these circumstances there is no argument for injustice in God. The autonomy of the γνώμη is its own answer. This discussion on God's justice ends with a statement regarding the metaphor, vessels of wrath prepared for destruction: καλεῖ τοὺς αὐθαιρέτῳ γνώμῃ τοῦτο γεγενημένους ("...[vessels of wrath] he calls those who had become this by their independent mindset").[92] Theodoret makes various assertions concerning the extent of this autonomy in his commentary. A person's autonomy and independent γνώμη are not undermined by law, though it is not always beneficial to use the mindset's freedom from them as loss may occur.[93] Paul's pedigree and his list of accomplishments in Philippians 3 brings the comment that the pedigree apart, Εἶτα τὸ λοιπὸν τῆς γνώμης ("the rest are of the γνώμη").[94] Everything within our control, which birth is not, is attributed to the γνώμη, a clear assertion of its critical role in the psyche. Things forced upon us by circumstances, including unwilling sins, do not impair the autonomy of the γνώμη. Indeed, τὰ παρὰ γνώμην γιγνόμενα συγγνώμης ἀπολαύει τινός ("the things that happen contrary to our mindset enjoy

---

[90] Thdt., *Int. Pauli*; PG 82,157 1-10.

[91] Thdt., *Int. Pauli*; PG 82,157 19-25: Σὺ δὲ ἀντιτείνεις καὶ ἀντιλέγεις. Οὐ τοίνυν φυσικαῖς ἀνάγκαις προσδέδεσαι, οὐδὲ παρανομεῖς παρὰ γνώμην, ἀλλ᾽ ἑκὼν ἀσπάζῃ τὴν πονηρίαν, καὶ αὐθαιρέτως καταδέχῃ τοὺς πόνους τῆς ἀρετῆς. Ὀρθὴ οὖν ἄρα καὶ δικαία τοῦ Θεοῦ τῶν ὅλων ἡ ψῆφος. Ἐνδίκως γὰρ κολάζει τοὺς ἁμαρτάνοντας, ὡς γνώμῃ τοῦτο ποιεῖν τολμῶντας·

[92] Thdt., *Int. Pauli*; PG 82,160 13-14.

[93] Thdt., *Int. Pauli*; PG 82,268 11-18.

[94] Thdt., *Int. Pauli*; PG 82,580 21-22.

some forgiveness").[95] A special case of this principle occurs in Theodoret's comments on the one wife rule for a leader in 1 Timothy 3:2. A second marriage after the death of the first wife is permissible and does not breach ἐγκράτεια (self control), for it is not a matter of ἐκ γνώμης but of ἐκ περιστάσεως ("from circumstances").[96] It is something that lies with the (φύσις) nature of the particular person and thus not something for which one is accountable. A widower may feel constrained to seek a second wife, and this constraint is outside the realm of γνώμη. Another aspect is that the grace of God does not nullify the autonomy of the γνώμη. This is made explicit in Theodoret's explanation of Paul's example of giving by the Macedonians in 2 Corinthians 8. The grace of God was: οὐ τὸ τῆς γνώμης ἐκβαλὼν αὐθαίρετον ("not to exclude the independence of their mindset").[97] Indeed, grace and the autonomous γνώμη were designed to work together and complement each other. In comments on Philippians 1:29-30, Theodoret asserts that grace does not destroy the autonomy of γνώμη but is given to instruct it. The lesson to be learned is that the mindset deprived of grace is rendered helpless, unable to do good works. Both the enthusiasm (προθυμία) of γνώμη and the grace of God are required, as grace cannot help where there is no enthusiasm, and enthusiasm without grace cannot reap the wealth of virtue.[98] The suggestion here is that the γνώμη supplies the enthusiasm and grace provides the enabling power. This principle is applied to the twin gifts of believing and struggling, each of which requires responsible cooperation to deliver their rich harvest. For Theodoret, the field of operation of the autonomy of the γνώμη is established as extending to all matters where freedom and responsibility may be exercised, but precludes any circumstance where constraint, pressure, or anything beyond one's control makes them impractical and thus free from accountability. This autonomy allows the greatest of benefits to be acquired, and the worst of errors to be committed. Independence dependent upon grace is the order of the day. Theodoret is emphatic that the γνώμη enables persons and communities to attain their destiny when it is exercised in harmonious unity with the grace of God.

Closely related to autonomy of the γνώμη is the issue of authority. For what is it responsible? As with the other Antiochenes discussed in this study, Theodoret understood the γνώμη to be responsible for and in control of the power of choice. Theodoret's interpretation of the text of 1 Corinthians 3:13-15 concerning the responsibilities of teachers throws the accountability for implementation on to the listeners: "The teacher instructs in the divine things, but the hearers choose what is

---

[95] Thdt., *Int. Pauli*; PG 82,753 24-25.
[96] Thdt., *Int. Pauli*; PG 82,805 20-29.
[97] Thdt., *Int. Pauli*; PG 82,421 46.
[98] Thdt., *Int. Pauli*; PG 82,568 44-53.

to be done according to the independence of their mindset".[99] Clearly here, the γνώμη dictates the exercise of choice. Similarly, in the issues of taking people to court in 1 Corinthians 6:5-6, Theodoret asserts that of the two options for disputes between believers, the choice either to suffer wrong or be examined before fellow-believers is placed back upon their own γνώμη.[100] In reference to 1 Corinthians 16:2, the choice (προαιρουμέναις) of the amount of giving is left to their γνώμη.[101] Part of Paul's defence of his delay in visiting the Corinthians is described as: "nor do I have sudden changes of mindset, so as to choose (αἱρεῖσθαι) now this thing, now that one".[102] Here again the choice is dependent upon the state of the γνώμη. Also, in the pursuit of perfection now brought within reach by the evangelical instruction, Theodoret declares that the γνώμη is the critical faculty: ἐν τῇ αἱρέσει τῆς γνώμης κεῖται τῆς τελειότητος ἡ κατόρθωσις ("the successful accomplishment of perfection lies in the choice of the mindset").[103] This is elaborated by emphasising that the more rigorous features such as fasting and selling all one's possession are Ταῦτα γὰρ οὐ νομοθεσία ἀλλ' αὐθαιρέτου γνώμης ("not a matter for the law but for the independent mindset").[104]

The control of the passions is another aspect of the authority of the γνώμη. As with Chrysostom, Theodoret viewed the passions as natural, but because of mortality, irritating. In a passage explaining Romans 6:12, he launches into an expansion of an image contained in one of the terms used there by Paul:

> Kingship differs from tyranny in this way: tyranny is exercised against the will of its subjects, but kingship governs those who are willing. He [Paul] exhorts them, therefore, to observe no longer the lordship of sin, for our Lord, having put on human nature, brought that same lordship of sin to an end; and, inasmuch as humans still have a mortal body, the lawgiver frames laws commensurate with our weakness. Note that he does not say, 'Do not let sin tyrannise', but 'Do not let it hold kingly office', for the one is relevant only to sin, but the other to our mindset. This is because both the motion of the passions and the irritation they cause are naturally inborn, but the practice of those things forbidden has been made to depend upon our mindset.[105]

---

[99] Thdt., *Int. Pauli;* PG 82,249 35-37: Οἱ διδάσκαλοι τὰ θεῖα παιδεύουσιν, οἱ δὲ ἀκούοντες κατὰ τὸ τῆς γνώμης αὐθαίρετον τὸ πρακτέον αἱροῦνται.

[100] Thdt., *Int. Pauli;* PG 82,265 24-26: τὸ γὰρ αἱρεῖσθαι, ἢ ἀδικεῖσθαι, ἢ παρὰ τοῖς ὁμοπίστοις δοκιμάζεσθαι, τῆς αὐτῶν ἐξηρτᾶτο γνώμης.

[101] Thdt., *Int. Pauli;* PG 82,369 18-20.

[102] Thdt., *Int. Pauli;* PG 82,381 46-48: ...οὔτε ὀξυρρόπους ἔχω τὰς τῆς γνώμης μεταβολὰς, ὥστε νῦν μὲν τοῦτο, νῦν δὲ ἐκεῖνο αἱρεῖσθαι.

[103] Thdt., *Int. Pauli;* PG 82,524 23-24.

[104] Thdt., *Int. Pauli;* PG 82,524 27.

[105] Thdt., *Int. Pauli;* PG 82,108 33-44: Βασιλεία τυραννίδος διαφέρει ταύτῃ, τῷ τὴν μὲν τυραννίδα ἀκόντων γίνεσθαι τῶν ὑπηκόων, τὴν δὲ βασιλείαν βουλομένων τῶν ἀρχομένων.

It appears that the γνώμη was understood as keeping the passions under control, not standing in the way of those that are beneficial to express themselves in practice, but denying expression to those forbidden as detrimental to us. One cannot stop the passions from stirring, which is natural to us. It is the following steps where the γνώμη comes into play. The point Theodoret is making is that sin has been tipped out of office; its lordship no longer applies because of the work of Christ our Lord. Thus, the need is to keep it from usurping the kingly office by the proper disposition of our mindset. Further along in his exegesis he absolves the body of any blame when they were subject to sin; the γνώμη was the faculty worthy of accusation for ...ἡ τοῦτο [σῶμα] κακῶς ἄγουσα γνώμη ("...this [body] was evilly led away by the mindset").[106] Yet it was by the independent γνώμη under the power of spiritual instruction that the tyranny of sin was shaken off.[107] This indicates that Theodoret considered the γνώμη to retain its independence even when under the tyranny of sin. At all times it was responsible to keep the passions under control and not stray into sin.

As much as the γνώμη was seen to have power over the passions, it was also viewed as the responsible faculty for shutting out salvation. Theodoret's explanation of the spirit of slumber of Romans 11:8 is that it refers to τὴν ἀμετάβλητον γνώμην ("the unchangeable mindset").[108] The use of γνώμη here is to support his statement, "...that ít was not another that blinded them [Israelites], they shut their own eyes". As we have seen, γνώμη carries with it the sense of autonomy or independence, and any contemporary reader of Theodoret's era would immediately understand with whom the responsibility for their resistance rested. It certainly removed any liability from God. Theodoret continues to unpack the metaphor with the thought that like those enjoying slumber, "those who surrender completely to evil do not choose (αἱρεῖται) a change for the better".

Παραινεῖ τοίνυν, μηκέτι δυναστείᾳ τῆς ἁμαρτίας συντίθεσθαι· κατέλυσε γὰρ αὐτῆς τὴν βασιλείαν ὁ Δεσπότης ἐνανθρωπήσας· καὶ ἅτε δὴ θνητοῖς ἔτι καὶ παθητὸν ἔχουσι σῶμα νομοθετῶν, σύμμετρα τῇ ἀσθενείᾳ νομοθετεῖ. Καὶ οὐ λέγει, Μὴ τυραννείτω ἡ ἁμαρτία, ἀλλά, Μὴ βασιλευέτω. Τὸ μὲν γὰρ ἴδιον ἐκείνης, τὸ δὲ τῆς ἡμετέρας γνώμης. Ἡ μὲν γὰρ τῶν παθημάτων κίνησίς τε καὶ ἐνόχλησις κατὰ φύσιν ἡμῖν ἐγγίνεται· τῶν δὲ ἀπειρημένων ἡ πρᾶξις τῆς γνώμης ἐξήρτηται.

[106] Thdt., *Int. Pauli*; PG 82,112 18-19.

[107] Thdt., *Int. Pauli;* PG 82,112 2-5: Δοῦλοι γὰρ ἦτε, φησὶ, τῆς ἁμαρτίας, αὐθαιρέτῳ δὲ γνώμῃ τὴν ἐκείνης ἀπεσείσασθε δεσποτείαν, καὶ τὴν πνευματικὴν διδασκαλίαν ἠσπάσασθε.

[108] Thdt., *Int. Pauli*; PG 82,173 35-41: Οὐκ ἄλλος τοίνυν αὐτοὺς ἐτύφλωσεν, ἀλλ' αὐτοὶ τοὺς ὀφθαλμοὺς ἔμυσαν, καὶ τὸ φῶς ἰδεῖν οὐκ ἠθέλησαν. Πνεῦμα δὲ κατανύξεως τὴν ἀμετάβλητον ἐκάλεσε γνώμην. Ὥσπερ γὰρ ὁ τὴν ἐπαινουμένην ἔχων κατάνυξιν, τὴν ἐπὶ τὸ χεῖρον τροπὴν οὐκ εἰσδέχεται· οὕτως ὁ παντελῶς ἑαυτὸν ἐκδοὺς τῇ πονηρίᾳ, τὴν ἐπὶ τὸ κρεῖττον οὐχ αἱρεῖται μεταβολήν. Following references and citations in this paragraph are to or from this text.

Choice is dependent upon the γνώμη; if the γνώμη is in a state of sin-induced stupor, then choice or will is rendered inoperative as far as any move towards righteousness is concerned. The γνώμη is seen to be the determining factor of personal and corporate destiny.

If the essence of sin is the use of our God-given independence and freedom against, without, and in disdain of him, then, in the light of the previous discussion, the γνώμη qualifies well for the faculty in which sin finds its decisive hold. Thus, as with Chrysostom, it is not surprising to find that the γνώμη is connected with a range of sinful states as expressed in various epithets and substantives: θηιώδη (savage), ἀτεράμων (stubborn, hard unfeeling), φιλονείκος/ον (contentious), ῥαθυμία (indifference), μοχθηρία (wicked, depraved), πονηρά (evil, worthless), ἀβέβαιος/ον (unstable), ἀναίδεια (shamelessness, insolence), κούφη (unsubstantial, unstable), ὀξύρροπος/ον and ἀντιτυπός/ον (stubborn, obstinate, resistant).[109] There are the positives, such as ἀρίστη, noble.[110] The list of negatives is at least suggestive, but it is in those passages that speak of the workings of the γνώμη in relation to sin that the picture becomes defined and clear. His comment on σάρξ in Galatians 5:17 is enlightening: "Flesh is what he [Paul] calls the propensity of the mindset (γνώμη) towards the morally worse things, and Spirit he calls indwelling grace...".[111] It would appear that Theodoret understood the autonomous γνώμη, when left to itself in the absence of the grace of the Spirit of God, to be biased in the wrong direction. Further thought on this is found in Theodoret's comments on Romans 6:6 where he distinguishes our nature (φύσιν) from the παλαιὸν ἄνθρωπον ("old person"), which he defines as τὴν πονηρὰν γνώμην (the evil mindset).[112] The good news is that this evil mindset has been put to death by baptism so that the body and its members no longer need to respond to sinful passions. However, the γνώμη is not thereby eliminated. The discussion above on Romans 6:12 indicates that it continues to have a critical role, but now may operate with the aid of the indwelling grace of the Spirit. Sin lurks nearby but it need not reign. Theodoret makes a comment on Romans 8:3 relevant to the state of the γνώμη when explaining our Lord's incarnation:

> He did not say 'In the likeness of flesh', but, 'In the likeness of sinful flesh', for
> he took on human nature, but he did not take on human sin. Indeed, for the sake

---

[109] In the order given in the text: Thdt., *Int. Pauli*; PG 82,65 24; PG 82,68 45; PG 82,469 54; PG 82,553 9; PG 82,577 38; PG 82,105 41; PG 82,265 25; PG 82,557 38; PG 82,536 36 (twice); PG 82,712 5. Many on these lists occur numerous times in the commentary.

[110] Thdt., *Int. Pauli*; PG 82,153 53.

[111] Thdt., *Int. Pauli*; PG 82,496 51-497 1: Σάρκα λέγει τὴν ἐπὶ τὰ χείρω τῆς γνώμης ῥοπήν· πνεῦμα δὲ τὴν ἐνοικοῦσαν χάριν·

[112] Thdt., *Int. Pauli*; PG 82,105 41-42.

of this [condemning sin in the flesh], what he had taken was not the likeness of flesh but that he called the likeness of sinful flesh; he had the same nature as us but he did not have the same mindset.[113]

Analysing Theodoret's thought progression here suggests the following: (a) The statement that he took on human nature but he did not take on human sin, suggests that all other human nature was sinful. (b) The second statement qualifies this by using the term αὐτὴν ("same"). So the nature he took was the same as ours, which means that if his nature was devoid of sin then human nature *per se* is not sinful, a position adopted by all the Antiochenes. (c) What he did not take on was the same γνώμη as ours, which indicates that it was something to be avoided as of jeopardy to his mission. The obvious conclusion is that Theodoret understood that sin is situated with the γνώμη, which has been seen as having a propensity towards the worse things.[114]

It is evident that Theodoret had similar if not identical thought to Chrysostom concerning the place and role of the γνώμη in theological anthropology. I have no doubt a study across the whole of his corpus would not only confirm what has been discussed above but in all probability bring to light some further aspects that have not been touched upon in the above material. Though the Antiochenes did not agree on everything in the theological spectrum, there is nothing here that contradicts what has been presented from Chrysostom on the γνώμη.

---

[113] Thdt., *Int. Pauli*; PG 82,128 47-53: Οὐκ εἶπεν, Ἐν ὁμοιώματι σαρκός, ἀλλ᾽, Ἐν ὁμοιώματι σαρκὸς ἁμαρτίας. Φύσιν μὲν γὰρ ἀνθρωπείαν ἔλαβεν, ἁμαρτίαν δὲ ἀνθρωπείαν οὐκ ἔλαβε. Τούτου δὴ χάριν, τὸ ληφθὲν οὐχ ὁμοίωμα σαρκὸς, ἀλλ᾽ ὁμοίωμα σαρκὸς ἁμαρτίας ἐκάλεσε· τὴν γὰρ αὐτὴν ἔχων φύσιν ἡμῖν, τὴν αὐτὴν οὐκ ἔσχε ἡμῖν γνώμην.

[114] This raises some christological questions re Antiochene theology which are not the subject of this study: (a) did Jesus possess a γνώμη? (b) as γνώμη is ascribed by the Antiochenes to God, including our Lord in his incarnate form, he was understood as possessing a γνώμη, but not one derived from us. (c) It must have been without the propensity toward the worse things as previously discussed. (d) What then is the identity of his γνώμη: (i) the γνώμη of the Word? (ii) Or was his γνώμη completely new for his particular humanity? I consulted P.B. Clayton Jr., *The Christology of Theodoret of Cyrus: Antiochene Christology from the Council of Ephesus (431) to the Council of Chalcedon (451)*, OECS (Oxford–New York 2007), with the hope of finding some comment on Theodoret's exegesis of Rom. 8:3. I was disappointed to find that while he had dealt with all the other pertinent passages in *Int. Pauli*, for some reason he omitted this one, a strange oversight in what is otherwise a commendable study. He does not include γνώμη in his Glossary of Greek words in Appendix III, 255-259.

IV. Other Church Fathers

Originally, in my investigation of possible sources of Chrysostom's language and thought, I had written briefly on the usage of γνώμη in a few randomly selected church Fathers. Irenaeus and Justin Martyr were chosen from the second century, and Gregory of Nyssa from the fourth. The question in view concerned whether or not Chrysostom was part of a tradition that adopted a particular psychological language to explain critical implications of the Christian faith.[115] This survey, as far as it went, demonstrated that Chrysostom's employment of γνώμη was consistent with the usage of some of those who blazed the theological trail, and with that of a contemporary in his own time. The table below suggests limitations in that approach that could only be overcome by a much more concentrated and detailed investigation.[116]

Should we venture past Chrysostom into the seventh century, we find a fruitful field of relevant discussion in Maximus the Confessor. A good deal of work has been done on Maximus' theological anthropology by R.A. Gauthier, P. Sherwood, L. Thunberg, A. Louth, P. Christou and B. Neil.[117] Thunberg, summarising Maximus and critiquing Gauthier and Sherwood, defines γνώμη as "a disposition or *habitus* of will, such as a man as individual and as fallen creature may establish for himself".[118] Distinguishing γνώμη from nature and natural will, Thunberg refers to another defining passage in Maximus where it is explained as a "mode of

---

[115] R.J. Laird, "St John Chrysostom and the γνώμη: the critical faculty accountable for sin in his anthropology", diss. University of Sydney 2008, 198-207.

[116] I am indebted to Dr W. Mayer for the suggestion that a study of the other main Antiochenes would be more valuable to my purpose.

[117] See R.A. Gauthier, "Saint Maxime le Confesseur et la psychologie de 'acte humain'", *Recherches de théologie ancienne et médiévale* 21 (1954) 51-200; P. Sherwood (trans.), *The Earlier Ambigua of St Maximus the Confessor and His Refutation of Origenism*, Studia Anselmiana 36 (Rome 1955); Thunberg, *Microcosm and Mediator*; Nichols, *Byzantine Gospel*, 158-195; Christou, "Maximos the Confessor on the infinity of man", 261 -271; P. Allen and B. Neil, *Maximus the Confessor and his Companions: Documents from Exile*, OECT (Oxford 2002); B. Neil, "Two views on vice and virtue: Augustine of Hippo and Maximus the Confessor", in B. Neil, G.D. Dunn and L. Cross (eds), *Prayer and Spirituality in the Early Church* vol. 3: *Liturgy and Life*, (Strathfield 2003) 261-271; B. Neil, "The blessed passion of holy love: Maximus the Confessor's spiritual psychology", *Australian E-Journal of Theology* 2 (February 2004) np., http://dlibrary.acu.edu.au/research/theology/ejournal/aejt_2/bronwen_neil.htm; I.A. McFarland, "'Naturally and by grace': Maximus the Confessor on the operation of the will", *Scottish Journal of Theology* 58 (2005) 410-433.

[118] Thunberg, *Microcosm*, 226.

use (i.e. of the human faculty of willing) and not a principle of nature".[119] Expanding on this with various references to Maximus, Thunberg writes:

> It is a mode of life, i.e. a personal and individual disposition (διάθεσις) or *habitus* (ἕξις), acquired through free human acts of decision, though always changeable. It thus belongs to the field of personal existence (ὕπαρξις), though as such it stands in a constant relationship to the sphere of nature (φύσις).[120]

This is very much the way in which Chrysostom uses the term. In an extremely brief survey of the use of the term before Maximus, Thunberg gives little note to Chrysostom except to put him in with others as using it to denote "man's free consent" and a note including "opinion".[121] This, as I have demonstrated, is not the prime way in which Chrysostom uses the term. Thunberg attributes to Maximus the leading role in giving it a dominant position and a fixed use for later Byzantine theological anthropology.[122] In so doing, he overlooks the extensive use of the term by Chrysostom in his corpus.[123] It could well be that Maximus, who came from Constantinople, derived much of his perception of the term from the extant writings of the former patriarch of his home city. The difficulty in determining this lies in the enormity of the corpus and in the fact that Chrysostom, unlike Maximus, was not given to writing theological treatises. Although there appears to be some differences in details, it seems clear enough that Maximus' definition of γνώμη was anticipated by Chrysostom two centuries before.

A statistical survey of the use of γνώμη in the relevant Fathers shows the following:

---

[119] Thunberg, *Microcosm*, 229.

[120] Thunberg, *Microcosm*, 229-230.

[121] Thunberg, *Microcosm*, 227 and n. 3.

[122] Thunberg, *Microcosm*, 226.

[123] Thunberg acknowledges the assistance of one of the compilers of the very commendable LPGL for the use and frequency of the term in early Christian writers. I have not been privy to those notes, but Thunberg quotes only two references to Chrysostom. Those are two of the three ascribed to Chrysostom that appear in the lexicon. One of the two is from a homily on 1 Corinthians. I have noted sixty-seven occurrences in Chrysostom's homilies on that epistle; see my unpublished dissertation, "The Theology of Grace in the Thought of St John Chrysostom as Discerned in His Homilies on First Corinthians" diss., University of Newcastle. NSW 1989, 117, and Appendix, 168-175. There are over 1,400 uses of the term in Chrysostom's total corpus. I appreciate that a lexicon has to be selective, especially when it gives only a very limited treatment of a word, which it does in this case. Nevertheless, neither it, nor Thunberg, does justice to Chrysostom.

Irenaeus	2nd century	24 in seven works
Justin Martyr	2nd century	23 in four works
Basil of Caesarea	4th century	180 in seventy-one works
Gregory of Nazianzus	4th century	45 in sixty-one works
Gregory of Nyssa	4th century	106 in eighty works
John Chrysostom	4-5th century	Looking at occurrences in some individual works: 216 Genesis 120 Matthew 69 John 21 Acts 73 Romans 67 1 Corinthians 31 2 Corinthians 26 Galatians 75 Psalms 33 Paul's other epistles = 731 Total in these ten exegetical works. Overall in his corpus: 1423 in four hundred and eleven works, many of which are single occasional homilies, and many of these do not contain the term.
Diodore of Tarsus	4th century	29 in two works
Theodore of Mopsuestia	4-5th century	208 in twelve works
Theodoret of Cyrus	5th Century	492 in twenty-five works
Maximus the Confessor	7th century	125 in ten works
John of Damascus	7-8th century	168 in forty-seven works

This statistical survey of some of the Fathers indicates clearly the outstanding contribution of the Antiochenes in the usage of γνώμη. Diodore's extant works in Greek are so few, so his figures are significant even though the sample is small. Chrysostom's works, not only because there is a great number of them, but also since the incidence of γνώμη in the exegetical works is high, indicate that he is a rich source for exploring the use of the term in the patristic era. Theodore and Theodoret each have a high incidence in relation to the non-Antiochenes. The table also suggests that although Chrysostom did not write a treatise on theological anthropology, he contributed substantially to the patristic theological pool of anthropological thought in general, and to the significance of γνώμη in particular.

V. Conclusion

This survey of the Antiochene camaraderie reveals that Chrysostom by no means stood alone in his usage of γνώμη. Parallels are found in all three of his colleagues. Here again we encounter the γνώμη as the critical faculty of the psyche, controlling volition, responsible to manage the passions, and motivating both word and deed. In relationships with God, it is seen as determining the acceptability of offerings, the validity of prayers, and one's disposition toward him. It is claimed to be the focal point of conversion, divine judgement, divine grace, and the instruction that shapes it to God's desire. The γνώμη is said to be the very core of the person and the executive of their destiny. All three Antiochenes agree with Chrysostom in saying that God inspects the γνώμη.

There is the possibility that the Antiochenes were not alone in giving the γνώμη such a critical place in their anthropology. Precedents among the wider patristic context exist. From the seventh century onwards, the term comes into view in systematic theological discussion. From this point on its significance for human destiny is recognised, thus promoting attempts at definition and description. It may be too much to claim that Chrysostom led the way in defining the term. Certainly, as far as the patristic world was concerned, his frequent usage revealed the significance of the term for theology, helping to place it in the framework of both the psychology of the human soul and the workings of sin within the individual person.

The basis of Chrysostom's perception of the critical importance of the role of the γνώμη in the human psyche has been laid. Validation has been supplied that this was not an individual idiosyncrasy but a part of a Hellenistic heritage that was widely adapted to the exposition of the Christian faith. With this foundation in place, it is to the task of discerning Chrysostom's perception of the role of the γνώμη concerning sin that we now turn.

Chapter 10

Sin and the Γνώμη

It was noted in the introduction to this study that in the Eastern Orthodox theological tradition a doctrine of original sin and guilt as known in the West is absent. The emphasis in Orthodoxy is upon the consequences of the sin in our forebears in leaving mortality and death as the enemies against which the individual must struggle in the progress to be formed in God-likeness. It was also noted that Chrysostom stood tall in that tradition, and was claimed as a source for the position that is generally held in Orthodoxy. With the benefits of the study of Chrysostom's usage of γνώμη in his anthropology so far discerned, it is time to approach the problems that are raised by the Orthodox position concerning the operation and locus of sin in the human soul. This requires attention to the following: (a) sin and human nature, (b) sin and choice (προαίρεσις), (c) choice (προαίρεσις) and the γνώμη, (d) the critical role of the γνώμη, and (e) responsibility of the γνώμη for sin. Consideration of two other pertinent issues round off the discussion, (f) γνώμη and reason, and (g) original sin. A brief survey of the background to the emergence of the issue in the early part of the fifth century precedes the discussion of these matters and provides a framework to the various threads in Chrysostom's thought.

I. Background perspective

When, in 419, Julian of Eclanum (380-c. 455) claimed Chrysostom as an ally for what has been termed his Pelagian understanding of the human situation, little did he realise the extent of the debate that he was raising over Chrysostom's words.[1]

---

[1] For discussions of this debate and the issues arising: Stephens, *Saint John Chrysostom*, 397ff; Wenger, *Catéchèses baptismales*, 154, n. 2; Baur, *John Chrysostom and His Time*, vol. 1, 358-372; Kenny, "Was Chrysostom a semi-Pelagian?" 16-29; J. Quasten, Patrology vol. 3: *The Golden Age of Greek Literature: From the Council of Nicaea to the Council of Chalcedon* (Utrecht-Antwerp 1960) 478ff; Harkins, *Baptismal Instructions*, 232-233, n. 12; Altaner, "Augustinus und Johannes Chrysostomus", 302-311; Kelly, *Early Christian Doctrines*, 344-374; P.W. Harkins, "Chrysostom's *Sermo Ad Neophytos*", *SP* 10 (1970) 112-117; Rondet, *Original Sin*; Meyendorff, *Byzantine Theology*, 143-146; Hill, "A Pelagian commentator on the Psalms", 263-271; Donegan, "John Chrysostom's exegesis of Romans 5:12-21", 5-14; E. Pagels, *Adam, Eve, and the Serpent* (New York 1988); J. Heaney-Hunter, "Disobedience and curse or affection of the soul?", *Diakonia* 23 (1990) 21-42; J. Chryssavgis, "Sin and grace – an Orthodox

The debate had commenced some six years before when Pelagius (fl. 400) had claimed Chrysostom for support in his work *De Natura et gratia*. Augustine (354-430) replied at the time, but it was not until his correspondence with Julian that he considered in some detail the citations from Chrysostom.[2] Julian may have expected some reply from Augustine, but he could have had no idea that 1500 years later Chrysostom's words would still be under discussion. Julian, reading a deficient Latin translation of Chrysostom's *Ad Neophytos*, interpreted him as saying that infants are unstained by sin. In the text available to him, *peccato* (sin) was in the singular and thus appeared to fit the Pelagian theory that children of Christian parents do not inherit original sin or guilt.[3] Augustine replied by referring to the Greek text that has ἁμαρτήματα (sins) in the plural, that he appropriately translated as the Latin plural *peccata*. This, he asserted, must refer to actual sins rather than original sin and inserted *propria* (particular, personal) to clear away the mists of confusion.[4] Augustine also commented on an array of texts from Chrysostom to support his contention. Some modern commentators remain unconvinced that these texts prove what Augustine claimed: that Chrysostom taught that sin is hereditary. It is admitted by these writers that the texts teach that the consequences and penalties of Adam's sin affect all his descendants.[5] Stephens goes as far as to aver that they amount to a "doctrine of a universally inherited tendency to sin" but not to the inheritance of hereditary or original sin itself.[6]

---

perspective", *Colloquium* 26 (1994) 73-93; P.E. Papageorgiou, "Chrysostom and Augustine on the sin of Adam and its consequences", *St Vladimir's Theological Quarterly* 39 (1995) 316-378; I.R. Torrance, "'God the physician': ecclesiology, sin and forgiveness in the preaching of St. John Chrysostom", *Greek Orthodox Theological Review* 44 (1999) 163-176; M. Plested, "The influence of St John Chrysostom in the West", Symposium in honour of the 1600th anniversary of St John Chrysostom held under the aegis of the Ecumenical Patriarchate, Constantinople, 13-18th September 2007.

[2] Altaner, "Augustinus und Chrysostomus", 302-311, for a useful analysis of the texts available to Augustine at the time.

[3] Cited in Harkins, *Sermo*, 114; Altaner, "Augustinus und Chrysostomus", 305.

[4] Augustine, *Contra Iulianum*; PL 44,654-655.

[5] Quasten, *Patrology*, vol. 3, 478; Stephens, *Saint John Chrysostom*, 397; H. Berkhof, *Christian Faith: An Introduction to the Study of the Faith*, trans. S. Woudstra (Grand Rapids, MI 1979) 187-210, gives a useful survey of the various positions held by theologians on these issues pertaining to sin.

[6] Stephens, *Saint John Chrysostom*, 394-395. This is confusing. What is original sin? Many theologians of various persuasions agree that the term includes the thought of a "universally inherited tendency to sin". Is Stephens distinguishing between the tendency and the guilt attached to it? This appears unlikely for he thinks that Chrysostom allows for a "hereditary liability to the punishment of death", which means that somehow we are responsible for what happened.

In a French translation of the same passage, A. Wenger, a Benedictine scholar, comments on this issue. He is not convinced that Chrysostom meant anything less than the absence of original sin. He observes that *"la déliverance du péché* (deliverance from sin) is omitted from Chrysostom's list of the benefits of baptism".[7] Wenger proceeds to point to Chrysostom's comments on Cain, that his sin was greater than Adam's, and also to Enoch, that it was his perfection of virtue that enabled him to recover the immortality that Adam had lost, to demonstrate that Chrysostom possessed some erroneous elements in his teaching on this subject.[8] He feels that the matter is clinched by Chrysostom's assertion in homily twenty-eight on Matthew that the souls of children killed by sorcerers are in the hand of God along with the souls of the just, because those children of non-Christians also are without evil.[9] Wenger's argument carries some weight. Some of the material selected by Wenger may fall under the category of the preacher's hyperbole, but the suspicion remains that it does display Chrysostom's distaste for a concept of hereditary sin and guilt as understood in the western tradition.

Augustine's comment on the issue at the time was this: "Far be it from me to believe that John of Constantinople stands in opposition to such great fellow-bishops as Innocent, Cyprian, Basil, Hilary and Ambrose".[10] Chrysostom was certainly not as clear as his western counterparts, if for no other reason than that the Pelagian issue was not in contention in the East. Nevertheless, we do well to exercise caution about making hasty judgements based on a handful of lines from his vast output. J. Meyendorff claims that a consensus exists in Greek patristic and Byzantine traditions that identifies the inheritance of the Fall as mortality rather than sinfulness.[11] In those traditions, sinfulness is seen as a consequence of mortality, not vice-versa.[12] Chrysostom is cited as witness to this in a homily on Romans where he interprets the much-debated ἐφ' ᾧ in Romans 5:12 as causal,

---

[7] Wenger, *Catéchèses baptismales,* 154, n. 2; Harkins, *Sermo,* 114, n. 1, thinks that Wenger's concern is groundless. Harkins interprets Chrysostom as including deliverance from original sin in the benefits of baptism. The compound verb προστίθημι, he claims, includes this benefit and consequently translates as "that they may be given further gifts", further, that is, to the remission of original sin.

[8] The passages to which Wenger refers are *In Gen. hom.* 19; PG 53,162 6-7; *hom.* 21; PG 53,180 41-43.

[9] Wenger, *Catéchèses baptismales,* 154, n. 2, "Enfin, parlant dans un endroit des petits enfants assassiné par des sorciers (selon la croyance populaire ces âmes devenaient l'habitude d'un demon), Chrysostome dit, Cela n'est pas, car les âmes des justes, c'est aussi le cas des âmes de ces enfants, car elles non plus ne sont pas mauvais".

[10] Augustine, *Contra Iulianum*; PL 44,655. L.1.VI.21.

[11] Meyendorff, *Byzantine Theology,* 145.

[12] Cf. Thdt., *Interp. sancti Pauli*; PG 82,100.

223

and is claimed to explain that it is because of death that sin becomes inevitable.[13] Chrysostom does indeed see the universal inheritance of the Fall as mortality, but the inevitability of sin on that account is to read into Chrysostom more than his text asserts. All that Chrysostom says here is that humankind is subject to death because of Adam's sin. We have become mortal. If anything is inherited, it is mortality and not a nature biased toward sin. This is supported from his comment on verse nineteen, where he explains "sinners" as meaning in this text, no more than being liable to punishment and condemned to death.[14] There is, Meyendorf claims, no place in Chrysostom's anthropology for the concept of inherited guilt, or for a "sin of nature".[15] Meyendorff asserts that this position was common to the eastern Fathers. There is substance to his claim. Commenting on some extant fragments of the writings of the friend of Chrysostom, Theodore of Mopsuestia, H. Swete remarks that he "reiterates in effect it is only *nature* which can be inherited, not sin, which is the disobedience of the free and unrestrained will".[16] This appears to lend significant support to the claim that in Eastern Orthodox theological tradition there is no concept of original sin as understood in classical western tradition. Orthodoxy, it is suggested, prefers to talk about the sin of the forebears, and leave the individual free to progress and grow by struggling against death, the result of sin, as it affects us in its various forms.[17]

The question remains as to whether or not it is legitimate to claim Chrysostom in support of the Orthodox position. Theodoret of Cyrrhus, who was aware of Chrysostom and his friend Theodore, takes a similar position to Chrysostom's comment on Romans 5:12, but then follows the logic through to its conclusion. In a passage commenting on Psalm 51:5 he states that death comes from sin, corruption from the ensuing mortality and from corruption disordered passions. Corruptible parents give birth to corruptible children sharing their mortality and

---

[13] Meyendorff, *Byzantine Theology*, 144. See John Chrys., *In Rom. hom.* 10; PG 60,474 48-51: Τί δέ ἐστιν, Ἐφ' ᾧ πάντες ἥμαρτον; Ἐκείνου πεσόντος, καὶ οἱ μὴ φαγόντες ἀπὸ τοῦ ξύλου γεγόνασιν ἐξ ἐκείνου πάντες θνητοί ("What does 'Because all sinned' mean? That one (Adam) having fallen, all those from that one, who had not eaten from the tree, became mortal").

[14] *In Rom. hom.* 10; PG 60,477 51-52: Τί οὖν ἐστιν ἐνταῦθα τὸ, Ἁμαρτωλοί; Ἐμοὶ δοκεῖ τὸ ὑπεύθυνοι κολάσει καὶ καταδεδικασμένοι θανάτῳ. Chrysostom actually enumerates some of the benefits of mortality in the following passage.

[15] Meyendorff, *Byzantine Theology*, 143.

[16] H.B. Swete, *Theodore of Mopsuestia: Commentary on the Epistles of St Paul: Latin Version with Greek Fragments, Pecc. Orign.*, 2:332-7 (Cambridge1880-1882) cited in J. Pelikan, *The Christian Tradition: A History of the Development of Doctrine. The Emergence of the Catholic Tradition (100-600)* (Chicago–London 1971) vol. 1, 285.

[17] Chryssavgis, "Sin and grace", 80.

their struggle with disordered passions.[18] Was this part of the heritage he gained from Chrysostom? If so, then this appears to contradict Augustine's comments that Chrysostom did not hold a position on original sin contrary to the western bishops. However, the link between Theodoret and Chrysostom is tenuous. Even if Theodoret was influenced by Chrysostom, it is unlikely that he was a slavish follower of his illustrious predecessor. There is no hard evidence that he obtained his doctrine of sin from that source. The issue is complex, and if he did drink at the stream emanating from or through Chrysostom on this matter, he may have taken it further than Chrysostom was prepared to venture. Although Theodoret's text from the commentary on Psalms sounds very much like a doctrine of hereditary sin, it falls short in two ways: one, there is no mention of hereditary guilt. Each person is responsible for and punished only for their own sins. The other is that sinning is not inevitable. Nature may be weak, and resulting from that weakness it is inclined to stumble under the pressure of passions. There is no need to sin, as those passions may be overcome by the γνώμη. Furthermore, there is a contrary indication in Theodoret: like Chrysostom, he denies that the force of sin is part of nature.[19] In this, as with Chrysostom, he embraces a tension in his thought. Hill, in his translation of the Theodoret passage, comments on this point, and sees a distinction in Theodoret between nature and passions. The original balance in the human psyche has been upset by Adam's sin so that rebellion is of the passions and not of the nature.[20] If this interpretation of Theodoret is correct, then he does sound very much like Chrysostom.

J.N.D. Kelly gives a useful summary of the Greek Fathers, including Chrysostom, on this matter.[21] He asserts that they all possessed an appreciation of the mystical unity of humankind with Adam, and that, in some way his sin inflicted a wound on our moral nature. Some went as far as to claim that sinfulness has been transmitted from Adam to all humankind. Few, if any, held that Adam's guilt has been passed on to the race. All agreed that the freewill remains intact and that it is the culpable party in the issue of sin. Of particular note is Kelly's comment on the same passages referred to above from Theodore and Theodoret: "Both of them make the point, in almost exactly the same words, that the vitiation of human nature consists in a powerful bias (ῥοπή) towards sin, the implication

---

[18] Thdt., *Interp. in Psalmos*; PG 80,1244 39-1245 8.

[19] Thdt., *Interp. in Psalmos*; PG 80,1244 30-33.

[20] R.C. Hill (trans.), *Theodoret of Cyrus, Commentary on the Psalms*, FOTC 102 (Washington, DC 2000) 197, n. 9, suggests that Theodoret "steers a careful line between an Augustinian acceptance of the impairment of human nature and unwarranted Pelagian optimism: original sin (not his term) has upset a balance, and the resultant rebellion of the passions – not nature as such – is responsible for our sins".

[21] Kelly, *Early Christian Doctrines*, 348-352, 372-374.

being that men's actual sins are not inevitable and therefore deserve blame.".[22] In its bare form, this comment appears to contain a contradiction. Would not a powerful bias in our nature toward sin make sin inevitable? One would think so. If Adam, without such a bias, could not remain sinless, then there seems little hope that we might do so. How then is the contrary conclusion to be explained? In the discussion, Kelly is comparing with Augustine and thus has Augustine's bondage of the will in mind. He does distinguish between the full-blown Latin theory of original sin and that which he perceives to be held by the Greeks.[23] However, Kelly has left out a significant concept. He does not record the distinction that we have noted in these writers between nature and ψυχή (soul) and the passions. In their thought, sin is not inevitable because it is not a part of nature. It stems from our passions that become corrupted in the soul, and they are subject to control.

II. Nature (φύσις) and Sin

This distinction between nature and passions, with the consequence of freeing nature from responsibility for sin, leads to a consideration of this distinction in Chrysostom's anthropology. To begin with, it is important for understanding a basic element in his anthropology to note the distinction that he makes between φύσις, nature, and γνώμη. Attention was drawn in the introductory chapter of this study to this distinction in his exposition of the parable of the sower in Matthew's Gospel. There Chrysostom distinguishes between the basic nature of the land and the thing he calls the γνώμη. In explaining the analogy, he asserts that while the fault lies in the land, it is not, he says, in its basic nature (φύσις) but in the γνώμη.[24] In applying this parable, he declares that the failure of the word to become fruitful in people is attributed to their "corrupt γνώμη".[25]

---

[22] Kelly, *Early Christian Doctrines*, 373.

[23] Kelly, *Early Christian Doctrines*, 350-351.

[24] John Chrys., *In Matt. hom.* 44; PG 57,469 31: Ὁρᾷς οὐχὶ τὸν γεωργὸν αἴτιον ὄντα, οὐδὲ τὰ σπέρματα, ἀλλὰ τὴν δεχομένην γῆν· οὐ παρὰ τὴν φύσιν, ἀλλὰ παρὰ τὴν γνώμην ("You see that it is not the farmer who is to blame, or the seed, but the land that receives it, not arising from its nature, but from its mindset"). I have left γνώμη here as my usual 'mindset', since any English term used has to be anthropomorphic. Chrysostom did not believe that inanimate nature possessed γνώμη.

[25] John Chrys., *In Matt. hom.* 44; PG 57,469 10-12: Μὴ τοίνυν τὰ πράγματα αἰτιώμεθα, ἀλλὰ τὴν γνώμην τὴν διεφθαρμένην ("Therefore we should not accuse the things but the corrupt mindset").

In an explanation of Matthew 18:7, on the topic of offences, Chrysostom devotes a sizable portion of his homily to discussing the cause of good and evil.[26] His material may be summarised as follows:

(a) Virtue and vice are either of the mindset (γνώμη) or of nature (φύσις) (PG 58,576 14-17).

(b) God never deprives persons of the independence of their authority or the freedom of their moral choice (προαίρεσις), therefore offences are not of necessity but of moral choice (PG 58,574 41-44).

(c) We do not blame people for their natural physical features, therefore blame must refer to the moral choice (προαίρεσις) (PG 58,576 1-7).

(d) If virtue and vice are of nature (φύσις) they must be unchangeable because things of nature are unchangeable, but virtue and vice are not (PG 58,576 19-28).

(e) We have the proof that virtue and vice are changeable in our own lives: sometimes we exercise self restraint; other times we do not do so and sin. They are changeable, and therefore cannot be natural. It is plain that virtue and vice proceed from the mindset (γνώμη) and the moral choice (προαίρεσις) (PG 58,577 22-24).

(f) The presence of so much counsel and warning against offences would be superfluous if virtue and vice are inherent in human nature (PG 58,578 49-52).

(g) The concluding statement on the issue reads ...εὔδηλον ὅτι γνώμης ἡ πονηρία ("...it is clear that evil is of the mindset") (PG 58,578 52).

(h) Thus, nature is held to be unchangeable and exempt from blame. The responsibility belongs elsewhere, namely, in the γνώμη.

In a homily on Genesis, Chrysostom makes the same point in question form, "Do you see how deeds of virtue and evil do not originate in our nature (φύσις), but lie in the moral choice (προαίρεσις) of our γνώμη?".[27] In the context, a contrast is made between Abraham and Nachor. Nature is seen to be disposed toward virtue, but does not have the power to enact its virtuous leanings. That power belongs elsewhere in our beings. Chrysostom identifies that power as residing in the γνώμη that governs the προαίρεσις. These two men, Chrysostom asserts, were brothers in the order of nature but not so by προαίρεσις, the deliberated choice each one made. Chrysostom says much the same in a previous homily on Genesis. In speaking about Ham, he protects the essential incorruption of nature by making the point that the things of evil did not lie in the nature of Ham but in his γνώμη and his προαίρεσις.[28]

---

[26] John Chrys., *In Matt. hom.* 59; PG 58,574-578.

[27] John Chrys., *In Gen hom.* 3; PG 53,290 66: Εἶδες πῶς οὐκ ἐν τῇ φύσει, ἀλλ' ἐν τῇ προαιρέσει τῆς γνώμης τῆς ἡμετέρας κεῖται καὶ τὰ τῆς ἀρετῆς, καὶ τὰ τῆς κακίας;

[28] John Chrys., *In Gen. hom.* 29; PG 53,266 24-26: Ὅρα μοι ἐνταῦθα, ἀγαπητὲ, πῶς οὐκ ἐν τῇ φύσει τὰ τῆς κακίας ἔγκειται, ἀλλ' ἐν τῇ γνώμη καὶ ἐν τῇ προαιρέσει.

Chrysostom viewed nature as disposed toward virtue but limited in its capacity to bring about outcomes. This is confirmed in other passages in his works. For example, in a homily based on the text of Romans 11, he takes a moment to explain what the Apostle Paul meant, or did not mean, when he referred to the Gentiles being grafted into the original olive tree "contrary to nature".[29] This "nature", he asserts, does not refer to our own basic human nature but to the normal state of things, to the probable and improbable, so that "contrary to nature" refers simply to that which is out of the ordinary range of possibilities as the situation of the Gentiles was considered to be. This must be so he asserts, because our human nature is ἀκίνητον ("unchangeable"). Thus, he proceeds to say, "For good and evil are not automatically produced by our nature, but have their source and action in the mindset (γνώμη) and choice (προαίρεσις) alone.".[30] Our human nature (φύσις) cannot be held responsible. It does not produce anything involuntarily in the moral realm. We must look elsewhere for origin, responsibility and culpability.

Chrysostom appears to have held that our basic nature, though containing the knowledge of virtue, is, in fact, morally powerless. It does not have the power to produce such human actions directly. That function lies elsewhere. In his homily on the prayer of our Lord in Gethsemane, he makes some pertinent observations about human nature. There, in proving the full reality of Christ's humanity, he comments that it is amply demonstrated by this prayer of Christ's that τῇ φύσει γὰρ ἔγκειται τὸ φίλτρον τὸ περὶ τὰ παρόντα ("the love-spell of present affairs is implanted in human nature").[31] In the incarnation, he avers, we see the normal "weakness of human nature which does not bear up without pain when being broken away from this present life".[32] This affirms that Chrysostom's anthropology contained a view of human nature as constitutionally tied to the creation as an intrinsic part thereof. Under paradisiacal circumstances, this would not present a problem, but in a world blighted by the Fall, human nature groans in weakness along with the creation that it has corrupted and made subject to decay.[33] Here then is confirmation that Chrysostom, as did Theodoret and Theodore, held that the Fall had affected human nature, not by changing it but by making it subject to

---

[29] John Chrys., *In Rom. hom.* 19; PG 60,591 26-30: Παρὰ φύσιν δὲ καὶ κατὰ φύσιν ὅταν ἀκούσῃς αὐτοῦ συνεχῶς λέγοντος, μὴ τὴν ἀκίνητον ταύτην φύσιν νόμιζε λέγειν αὐτὸν, ἀλλὰ καὶ τὸ εἰκὸς καὶ τὸ ἀκόλουθον, καὶ τὸ ἀπεικὸς πάλιν τούτοις δηλοῦν τοῖς ὀνόμασιν.

[30] John Chrys., *In Rom. hom.* 19; PG 60,591 30-31: Οὐ γὰρ φυσικὰ τὰ καλὰ καὶ τὰ μὴ τοιαῦτα, ἀλλὰ γνώμης καὶ προαιρέσεως μόνης.

[31] John Chrys., *Poss.*; PG 51,38 18-19.

[32] John Chrys., *Poss.*; PG 51,38 12-13: καὶ τὴν ἀσθένειαν τῆς φύσεως τὴν οὐκ ἀνεχομένην ἀπαθῶς ἀπορραγῆναι τῆς παρούσης ζωῆς.

[33] See Chrysostom's discussion of Rom. 8:19-24, *In Rom. hom.* 14; PG 60,529-534.

the limitations imposed by the changed circumstances in which it now exists. In short, the boundary-marker, the pillar of mortality, relegated nature to aspirations without the inherent power to rise to them.

A significant discussion concerning sin and nature appears in a homily that comments on Romans 7:13. There Chrysostom sees sin as something not permanently attached to nature but as something that comes and goes with the evil action.[34] Sin is not, he says, δύναμιν τινα ἐνυπόστατον (some independent subsistent power) and is without existence or being, both before and after the actual deed. Indeed the things that are assigned to us with our nature, he asserts, are immovable or unalterable.[35] Legislators are aware of this and are not concerned about trying to alter what belongs to our natural state whatever that might be. It is outside of their province. All they are concerned with, all that their proclaimed laws attempt to do, is to restrain evil deeds whatever might be their source. In this vein, Chrysostom here limits sins to evil actions and separates them out from our nature. He constantly steers his hearers away from finding refuge from responsibility for sin behind the impregnable fortress of what he views as an imaginary corrupt nature. Everywhere he maintains the integrity and guiltlessness of nature. Consistently he ascribes sin to the twin culprits, γνώμη and προαίρεσις.

It is obvious from what has been considered that Chrysostom understood our nature to possess certain attributes. Its immutability, guiltlessness, and moral powerlessness have already been noted. Whilst Chrysostom viewed human nature, because of its limitations, in practice as virtually morally powerless, he also understood it as having nobility in that it possessed the knowledge of what and what not to do. In summarising his comments on Cain and Abel, he stated that although our nature may be powerless to effect action in one direction or another, God took care to implant within it the requisite knowledge of what is expected of us.[36] In another place, Chrysostom comments that the knowledge of virtue is

---

[34] John Chrys., *In Rom. hom.* 12; PG 60,503 24-36. Ἁμαρτίαν δὲ ὅταν ἀκούσης, μὴ δύναμίν τινα ἐνυπόστατον νομίσης, ἀλλὰ τὴν πρᾶξιν τὴν πονηράν, ἐπιγινομένην τε καὶ ἀπογινομένην ἀεί, καὶ οὔτε πρὸ τοῦ γενέσθαι οὖσαν, καὶ μετὰ τὸ γενέσθαι πάλιν ἀφανιζομένην ("Whenever you hear the term, sin, do not consider it to be some independent subsistent power, but an evil act both coming into being and always disappearing, neither existing before coming into existence nor after again becoming unseen").

[35] John Chrys., *In Rom. hom.* 20; PG 60,503 32-36: Τὰ γὰρ ἐκ ῥαθυμίας γινόμενα κακὰ ἀναστέλλουσι μόνον, οὐ τὰ τῇ φύσει συγκεκληρωμένα ἐπαγγέλλονται ἐκκόπτειν· οὐδὲ γὰρ δυνατόν. Τὰ γὰρ τῆς φύσεως ἀκίνητα μένει, ὃ πολλάκις πρὸς ὑμᾶς καὶ ἐν ἑτέραις εἴρηκα διαλέξεσι ("They [legislators] restrain only the evil things happening from indolence, and do not give orders to excise those that have been allotted with nature, for the things of nature are unalterable, as I have told you many times in other sermons").

[36] John Chrys., *In Gen. hom.* 20; PG 53,166 42-44: ὅπως ἔγκειται τῇ ἡμετέρᾳ φύσει ἡ γνῶσις τῶν πρακτέων καὶ τῶν μὴ πρακτέων.

inherent to our nature. It is ἐναποκειμένην, stored up in it. It is part of our innate nobility, and we would still have that knowledge as a conscious operating factor if we had not betrayed our natural nobility by an attitude of indifference in the desires we choose.[37] This affirms that, to Chrysostom, sin has everything to do with choices and the mindset behind those choices and not with nature. A pertinent practical example of this is found in a homily on Hebrews where he contends that the moral demands of scripture are addressed to all Christians in the city and not just to the monks.[38] They apply as much to the married as to the solitary. Marriage, Chrysostom argues, does not hinder anyone from the pursuit of virtue. Marriage is honourable; therefore, if anyone is hindered, it is not because of the institution but because of the choices made which have used marriage in a bad way. It is the same with wine. The wine is not to be blamed for drunkenness; rather, the blame belongs to the bad choice that sets no limits to its use.[39] Both marriage and wine, as natural to life, are wholesome in themselves, and neutral as regards virtue and evil. It is in the choices made in relation to their use that virtue and vice are to be found. It is the same with our nature, it is inherently noble but the choices we make will either affirm or betray that native nobility.

In a passage that addresses Romans 12:3 and discusses at length the value of humility or being lowly of mind (ταπεινοφρονεῖν), Chrysostom associates this virtue with the nobility of nature. He also contrasts it with ἀπόνοια (senselessness, recklessness or unreasonableness), as follows:

> In this way the soul also, whenever it makes void the essential dignity of its nature that is characterised by humility, it receives some weakening habit, becomes cowardly, arrogant and senseless, and eventually may fail to recognise itself.[40]

---

[37] John Chrys., *In Gen. hom.* 46; PG 54,571 32-36: Καὶ γὰρ ἕκαστος ἡμῶν ἐν αὐτῇ τῇ φύσει ἐναποκειμένην ἔχει τὴν γνῶσιν τῆς ἀρετῆς· καὶ εἰ μή τις βουληθῇ ἀπὸ ῥαθυμίας τὴν οἰκείαν προδοῦναι εὐγένειαν, οὐκ ἄν ποτε ταύτης ἀμοιρήσειε ("For each one of us has the knowledge of virtue that has been stored up in his/her nature; and if ever any one, should not choose from indifference to betray their natural nobility, then they will never lack a share in these benefits").

[38] John Chrys., *In Heb. hom.* 7; PG 63,67 10-11: οὐ γὰρ δὴ μοναχοῖς ταῦτα ἔγραφε μόνον, ἀλλὰ πᾶσι τοῖς οὖσιν ἐν ταῖς πόλεσι.

[39] John Chrys., *In Heb. hom.* 7; PG 63,68 10-14: Εἰ δέ τινες ἐνεποδίσθησαν ὑπὸ γάμου, ἰδέτωσαν ὅτι οὐχ ὁ γάμος ἐμπόδιον, ἀλλ' ἡ προαίρεσις ἡ κακῶς χρησαμένη τῷ γάμῳ· ἐπεὶ οὐδὲ ὁ οἶνος ποιεῖ τὴν μέθην, ἀλλ' ἡ κακὴ προαίρεσις, καὶ τὸ πέρα τοῦ μέτρου χρῆσθαι·

[40] John Chrys., *In Rom. hom.* 20; PG 60,600 57-61: οὕτω καὶ ἡ ψυχή, ἐπειδὰν τὸ μεγαλοφυὲς ἀπολέσῃ καὶ τὸ ταπεινοφρονεῖν, ἕξιν δεξαμένη τινὰ ἀσθενῆ, καὶ δειλὴ καὶ θρασεῖα καὶ ἀνόητος γίνεται, καὶ ἑαυτὴν ἀγνοήσει λοιπόν.

A senseless move toward ὑπερηφανία (arrogance) away from humility is a betrayal of nature and a fall from wisdom. Such a fall from wisdom results in weakness in the soul. The door is now open to habits of weakness to take root so that the soul ends up in ignorance of its own being, a recognised folly in the world of the Greek παιδεία. Chrysostom compares the soul's loss of its greatness of nature to the loss of condition in the body. The body out of condition becomes a prey to disease. It is the same with the soul. Thus, in Chrysostom's thought, the loss of the nobility of nature appears to be a loss to sight, consciousness or knowledge, and not one of essence. The innate knowledge of virtue and vice is still installed, but where the move to arrogance has been made, this natural nobility will no longer be displayed.

As suggested in the Romans' homily, another aspect of the nobility of nature that may be voided is rationality. This is made clear in a passage referring to Noah, where Chrysostom classifies those who do not practise virtue as not being truly human. They may "have the form of humanity, but have betrayed the nobility of their nature by the evil of their choice and thereby degenerated from their humanness to the irrationality of animals".[41] Our nature (φύσις), Chrysostom maintained, has an affinity with rationality so that it could be said that rationality (λογικότης) is not only an element of its inherent natural nobility, but also a distinctive mark of what it means to be human. Chrysostom, however, also equates rationality with virtue. A person conforms to or departs from their rationality, and thus their nobility, according to their moral choice (προαίρεσις) for virtue or vice.

A similar argument is used elsewhere by Chrysostom in a homily on John 1:1 where he calls his congregation to be attentive listeners and not irrational beasts, or worse still, like τέρας πολύμορφόν τι καὶ ποικίλον ("some protean monster").[42] This appalling distortion of human life is ascribed to the person "who, having cast away the rule of reason and fragmented off from God's model citizenship, yields him/herself to all the passions".[43] This fall from rationality leads to disaster. In assigning the cause of this tragic state of affairs, Chrysostom emphatically closes the door to anything but personal responsibility. Such a person, he says, "cannot

---

[41] John Chrys., *In Gen. hom.* 23; PG 53,201 57-202 1: ἀλλὰ μορφὴν μὲν ἔχοντες ἀνθρώπων, τῇ δὲ πονηρίᾳ τῆς προαιρέσεως τὴν εὐγένειαν τῆς φύσεως προδεδωκότες, καὶ ἀντὶ ἀνθρώπων πρὸς τὴν τῶν θηρίων ἀλογίαν ἐκπεσόντες.

[42] John Chrys., *In Joan. hom.* 2; PG 59,36 48-37 9, esp. 37 6-7.

[43] John Chrys., *In Joan. hom.* 2; PG 59,37 4-6: Καίτοι τὰ μὲν θηρία, ἓν ἕκαστον, ὡς εἰπεῖν, ἔχει πάθος, καὶ τοῦτο κατὰ φύσιν· ὁ δὲ ἄνθρωπος ὁ τῶν λογισμῶν τὴν ἀρχὴν ἐκβαλὼν καὶ τῆς κατὰ Θεὸν πολιτείας ἀπόρραγεὶς, πᾶσιν ἑαυτὸν ἐπιτρέπει τοῖς πάθεσι·

turn to his/her nature for an excuse, for all the evil comes from his/her choice (προαίρεσις) and mindset (γνώμη)".[44]

In places in his corpus, it could be thought that Chrysostom was distinguishing between the historic prelapsarian and postlapsarian situations as far as our nature is concerned, seeing nature as once innocent and guiltless but now as culpable. That this is not so is evident from the preceding comments in the homily on John 1:1. It is clear that Chrysostom would not allow sin and evil to be ascribed to the present state of human nature. It has been noted above, that in a discussion of the sin of Ham, Chrysostom draws the attention of his hearers to the obvious fact that evil deeds are not rooted in human nature. He makes his case by pointing to the sameness of the nature shared by the three sons of Noah. They had the same father, they came from the same maternal birth pains, and they experienced the same parental care.[45] One could not lay the blame at the feet of nature. The difference lay elsewhere. It is to be noted that with the sons of Noah we are in a postlapsarian situation. One thing appears certain, namely Chrysostom was convinced that Scripture taught that human nature after the Fall is not inherently sinful. Rather it is essentially noble, rational, appropriately humble and endowed with the knowledge of what and what not to do. What it does lack is the decisive ability to effect moral choice and human action. It remains as a voice crying out in the wilderness but, unlike John the Baptist, it is a voice without power to command hearing and decision.

III. Sin and Choice (προαίρεσις)

If nature is thus betrayed and deprived, and not depraved, then we must look elsewhere to discover where sin makes its lodging in the soul. The foregoing discussion points in the direction of the γνώμη and the προαίρεσις. That was expressly stated in the homily on John 1:1, and in the homily which was noted as addressing the sin of Ham; these two faculties are named as responsible for personal sin. The interaction between these faculties of the being in relation to sin is at the heart of Chrysostom's theological understanding of the human situation.

---

[44] John Chrys., *In Joan. hom.* 2; PG 59,37 8-9: καὶ οὐδὲ τὴν ἀπὸ τῆς φύσεως συγγνώμην ἔχει. Προαιρέσεως γὰρ καὶ γνώμης ἡ κακία πᾶσα.

[45] John Chrys., *In Gen. hom.* 29; PG 53,266 25-28: Ἰδοὺ γὰρ ἀμφότεροι τῆς αὐτῆς φύσεως, καὶ ἀδελφοί, τὸν αὐτὸν ἔσχον πατέρα, τῶν αὐτῶν ἀπήλαυσαν ὠδίνων, τῆς αὐτῆς ἐπιμελείας ἔτυχον, ἀλλ' οὐ τὴν αὐτὴν προαίρεσιν ἐπεδείξαντο·

Before examining this interaction, some attention will be given to the προαίρεσις.[46]

Evidence that Chrysostom saw the προαίρεσις as critical to human existence is found in a homily on Hebrews in which he demonstrates the wisdom of the Apostle Paul to whom he ascribes that epistle. He alleges that humans are harder to persuade than plants because humans have something plants do not, namely, the faculty of choice, προαίρεσις.[47] This must be, in his mind, a distinguishing feature of humankind. There is much evidence in his homilies to confirm that the προαίρεσις is given this critical place. In illustrating the intent of Romans 12:8 about giving with simplicity and showing mercy with cheerfulness, he points to the widow who gave her two mites. How may someone in extreme poverty eagerly give of his or her all? The widow shows the way. It is not poverty, he says, that makes for limitations; it is the προαίρεσις (deliberate choice) one makes.[48] This same example is used by Chrysostom in the homily on 2 Timothy where he discusses our liability for chastisement and thus the need to refrain from offending God. Most importantly, we must not be condemnatory of others. In the course of this exhortation, he makes the point that the size of a crime is not the issue. The critical thing is the will behind it. In making this point, Chrysostom changes from the negative to the positive by referring to our Lord's words on the widow's gift. She gave no less than those who gave gold because what is judged is not the size of the gift but the προαίρεσις to give it: Ἡ γὰρ προαίρεσις κρίνεται, καὶ οὐχ ἡ δόσις ("For he judges the choice and not the gift").[49]

It was noted above in this study that a significant observation is made by Chrysostom in a homily on 1 Timothy in which the προαίρεσις is given a critical role in the pathway of achieving God-likeness. What is of interest here, is that Chrysostom speaks of the person as being in two parts, οὐσία on the one hand and προαίρεσις on the other, with the προαίρεσις being equated with the "greater things" (τοῖς μείζοσι). Given the discussion above on nature (φύσις), the nobility of nature would belong to the οὐσία and the task given to it would be the formation of the person in harmony with our given nature by a continuous series

---

[46] This is additional material to that covered in the chapter on autonomy, as here the focus is on the role of the προαίρεσις in relation to sin.

[47] John Chrys., *In Heb. hom.* 12; PG 63,99 21-25: Ἐκεῖ μὲν γὰρ φύσις σωμάτων ἐστὶ καὶ γῆς, εἴκουσα ταῖς τῶν γηπόνων χερσίν· ἐνταῦθα δὲ προαίρεσις, πολλὰς δεχομένη μεταβολὰς, καὶ νῦν μὲν τοῦτο, νῦν δὲ ἐκεῖνο αἱρουμένη· ὀξύρρεπὴς γὰρ αὕτη πρὸς κακίαν.

[48] John Chrys., *In Rom. hom.* 21; PG 60,603 50-55: Καὶ πῶς ἔνι, φησὶ, πενία συζῶντα ἐσχάτῃ, καὶ πάντα κενοῦντα, μετὰ προθυμίας τοῦτο ποιεῖν; Ἐρώτησον τὴν χήραν, καὶ ἀκούσῃ τὸν τρόπον, καὶ εἴσῃ ὅτι οὐχ ἡ πενία ποιεῖ τὴν στενοχωρίαν, ἀλλ' ἡ προαίρεσις καὶ τοῦτο καὶ τοὐναντίον ἅπαν ἐργάζεται·

[49] John Chrys., *In 2 Tim. hom.* 3; PG 62,617 36.

of moral choices (προαίρεσις) of the virtuous and good. There is no doubt that this feature of moral choice was a constitutive element of the human person as far as Chrysostom was concerned. Along similar lines is the passage in a homily on Colossians 3:9-10 where Chrysostom, in discussing the old humanaity and the new humanity in the text, equates ἄνθρωπος with προαίρεσις, the power of moral choice. This is a determinative faculty in our being. This is a constituent part of the human person. In this vein, Chrysostom says:

> For the choice is more in control than the substance, and this [faculty of choice] is the person rather than that. For the substance does not cast a person into hell, nor does it lead one into the kingdom, but the moral choice (προαίρεσις) itself does...[50]

As persons, Chrysostom asserts, we end up being what we deliberately choose to be. We become the result of the moral choices we make. In the second homily on the devil, Chrysostom argues that even the devil is evil by choice and not by nature. He is evil by choice (προαίρεσις) and mindset (γνώμη).[51] Important here is the development of the argument to the point at which Chrysostom concludes that the things that happen and cease to happen, like slander, do not belong to the essence or nature of a thing. They are accidents, not part of the essential being.[52] As already seen, essential being, if anything, is disposed toward virtue but lacks potency. Evil, on the other hand, is attributed to the choice, a significant power of the soul.

This leads to further consideration of the freedom of the προαίρεσις as held by Chrysostom. It was noted in the passage on 1 Timothy that we have been created in control of our faculty of deliberate choice.[53] We are, he would say, truly free. An illuminating comment on this is made by him in an explanation of the sin of Adam. Asking his listeners to consider accurately and carefully the confession of Adam he comments, "There was no sense of necessity, no sense of force, but

---

[50] John Chrys., *In Col. hom.* 7; PG 62,352 54-353 4: Τῆς γὰρ οὐσίας ἡ προαίρεσις κυριωτέρα, καὶ τοῦτο μᾶλλον ἄνθρωπος, ἢ ἐκεῖνο. Οὐ γὰρ ἡ οὐσία ἐμβάλλει εἰς γέενναν, οὐδὲ εἰς βασιλείαν εἰσάγει, ἀλλ' αὐτὴ ἡ προαίρεσις...

[51] John Chrys., *De Diabolo hom.* 2; PG 49,259 41-43: Ἀφείσθω ὁ διάβολος ὁ σφόδρα πονηρὸς οὐ φύσει, ἀλλὰ προαιρέσει καὶ γνώμη· See *In Gen. hom.* 16; PG 53,126 51-52.

[52] John Chrys., *De Diabolo hom.* 2; PG 49,260.3-8:...τὸ διαβάλλειν δὲ καὶ μὴ διαβάλλειν οὐ φύσις ἐστίν, ἀλλὰ πρᾶγμα γιγνόμενον καὶ ἀπογιγνόμενον, συμβαῖνον καὶ ἀποσυμβαῖνον· τὰ δὲ τοιαῦτα οὐ φύσεως ἐπέχει τάξιν οὐδὲ οὐσίας. Οἶδα ὅτι πολλοῖς δυσκατάληπτος ὁ λόγος οὗτος ὁ περὶ τῆς οὐσίας καὶ τῶν συμβεβηκότων ("...but to slander and not to slander is not of nature, but matters that are coming and going, that are present and then absent; such things as these were not pouring out [from the Devil] as an array of nature or essence").

[53] John Chrys., *In 1 Tim. hom.* 15; PG 62,586, esp. line 19, Διὰ τί τῆς προαιρέσεώς ἐσμεν κύριοι;

choice and mindset. Only, she (Eve) gave; not that she constrained; not that she forced".[54] Here we get to the core of sinful action as understood by Chrysostom. When all else, such as force or necessity or persuasive argument or external constraint, is stripped away, what remains? – only these two powers of the soul, moral choice (προαίρεσις) and mindset (γνώμη). Chrysostom is emphatic about the absence of compulsion and force upon both Adam and Eve. If in Adam's case it was simply only choice and mindset, then it was the same for the woman; no compulsion was involved. She remained in possession of the power to choose one way or the other. She might plead that she was the victim of the serpents' deception, but Chrysostom will not hear it. "She was in control of being deceived or not being deceived."[55] What is set before us here is that our choices are not determined by external factors. Even God does not determine our choices. We are free to choose as we determine. Sin is to be understood as a deliberated moral choice.

Whilst Chrysostom is emphatic about the freedom of the προαίρεσις from external constraints, the same is not to be said about the internal situation of the human person. There is, he asserts, a problem with this faculty: it lacks stability and consistency, being "receptive of many changes, taking for itself now this, now that".[56] Even worse, it has some affinity with evil for it quickly turns to it. The term employed by Chrysostom, ὀξυρρεπής, "ready to change"[57] is well chosen, for it pictures a delicate balance that is easily moved in one direction or another. In the case of the προαίρεσις, the balance has been upset and this faculty has been inclined towards evil. There is a bias in choice and this bias must be sought within the psyche. It is to that search that we now turn.

IV. Choice (προαίρεσις) and Mindset (γνώμη)

It is evident that there is a very close relationship between προαίρεσις and γνώμη in Chrysostom's thinking. His comment on the Fall referred to in the

---

[54] John Chrys., *In Gen. hom.* 17; PG 53,140 31-33: Οὐδαμοῦ ἀνάγκη, οὐδαμοῦ βία, ἀλλὰ προαίρεσις καὶ γνώμη· ἔδωκε μόνον, οὐκ ἠνάγκασεν, οὐκ ἐβιάσατο.

[55] John Chrys., *In Gen. hom.* 17; PG 53,140 35-36: Ὁ ὄφις ἠνάγκασέ με, καὶ ἔφαγον. Ἀλλὰ τί; Ὁ ὄφις ἠπάτησέ με· τοῦ δὲ ἀπατηθῆναι, καὶ μὴ ἀπατηθῆναι κυρία ἦν.

[56] John Chrys., *In Heb. hom.* 12; PG 63,99 21-25. Ἐκεῖ μὲν γὰρ φύσις σωμάτων ἐστὶ καὶ γῆς, εἴκουσα ταῖς τῶν γηπόνων χερσίν· ἐνταῦθα δὲ προαίρεσις, πολλὰς δεχομένη μεταβολὰς, καὶ νῦν μὲν τοῦτο, νῦν δὲ ἐκεῖνο αἱρουμένη· ὀξύρρεπὴς γὰρ αὕτη πρὸς κακίαν ("For there [with plants] is a bodily nature and earth, compliant in the hand of the farmers; but here [in the human race] is moral choice, which is receptive to change, picking now this, and now that; for it is poised to change to evil").

[57] LPGL, 966 *s.v.*

paragraph above makes that clear. The Fall is the result of Adam's choice (προαίρεσις) and mindset (γνώμη). Another example is found in a homily on the virtue of Noah. There Chrysostom gives a number of illustrations from the Old Testament where people are likened to animals to show the extent of their fall from the nobility of their nature. At the beginning of the paragraph, this fall from rationality is ascribed to the evil choices (προαίρεσεις) that were made.[58] At the end of the paragraph, Chrysostom attributes their descent into bestial-like evil, their duplicity, to the mindset (γνώμη).[59] The choice may be the immediate cause, but behind it lies the mindset that determines it.

Reference has been made above to the προαίρεσις as somewhat balanced but being easily inclined towards evil. Why is this so? Chrysostom's answer is that the γνώμη is the distorted propelling force. Repeatedly, Chrysostom comes back to the γνώμη as governing the moral choice. This is made particularly clear in a passage discussing the actions of Cain and Abel. He prefaces his remarks by drawing attention to what he had already taught, namely, "that the Lord does not recognise any difference in outward appearances, but scrutinizing on the basis of their choice (προαίρεσις), rewards the mindset (γνώμη)".[60] The choice reveals the mindset behind it. There are a number of places in Chrysostom's works where it seems that these two terms are being used synonymously. This passage indicates that this is not the case. Rather, a distinction exists, for God appraises the mindset by which things are done by examining the considered choice. Then he rewards the person according to the mindset that oriented the will towards a particular choice. The moral choice (προαίρεσις) is disposed in a certain direction. The faculty that so orientates the προαίρεσις is designated the γνώμη. The inclination of the προαίρεσις is determined by the γνώμη.

A remarkable passage occurs in a homily in which the issue of God's grace and human responsibility is addressed. This is done in the context of election, or rather of election according to foreknowledge. Chrysostom paints a wonderful picture in his careful attempt at explanation:

---

[58] John Chrys., *In Gen. hom.* 23; PG 53,201 57-202 1, and n. 39 above.

[59] John Chrys., *In Gen. hom.* 23, PG 53,202 19: Εἶδες πῶς καὶ ἐνταῦθα τῆς γνώμης αὐτῶν τὸ δολερὸν ἀπὸ τῆς τοῦ θηρίου προσηγορίας ἠνίξατο; ("Do you see how here that from predicting/speaking darkly of the name of the beast, the deceit of their mindset?")

[60] John Chrys., *In Gen. hom.* 18; PG 53,154 37-40: ...ὅτι διαφορὰν προσώπων οὐκ οἶδεν ὁ Δεσπότης ὁ ἡμέτερος, ἀλλὰ ἐκ προαιρέσεως ἐξετάζων τὴν γνώμην στεφανοῖ. In this homily Chrysostom focuses on the γνώμη as being the crucial factor in God's dealings with Cain and Abel. God's concern is primarily for the γνώμη. There are a further sixteen references to γνώμη in the passage.

But he who knows the secret things, and being able to test and approve the fitness of the mind, knew the pearl lying in the mud. Passing by others and marvelling at the beauty of this one he elected it and, after adding grace from himself to the nobility of the choice (προαίρεσις), declared it as approved.[61]

All are immersed in the quagmire of sin. God is searching through the mud looking for a special pearl, one that had retained something of the nobility that is attached to the προαίρεσις. In some, that beauty of this power of the soul somehow has not become totally sullied by the mud. This means that the προαίρεσις has been endowed with nobility, probably the God-given freedom and authority that we have noted above. The moral choice, the προαίρεσις, represents, at least in part, the precious essence of the pearl lying in the mud. This also means that the corruption of the προαίρεσις may reach a stage where its bearer is passed by, which is both a tragedy and a crime noted of the Pharisees later in this section of the homily.[62] It is of note that the homily continues with illustrations from horse-breakers, judges of art, and analysers of and workers with gems, all of whom look for features that escape the ordinary onlooker, but which represent the essential value of the object. It is this way with God who searches, now Chrysostom says, not for one but for three things: a display of good works, nobility in the προαίρεσις, and a rightly disposed or rightminded γνώμη.[63] Good works are not a perfectly reliable guide, as these can be done with an unworthy γνώμη.[64] If, as I have argued, the operations of the προαίρεσις depend upon the state of the γνώμη, then the γνώμη determines response to God and is responsible for sin. In particular, the state of the γνώμη will determine either the continuing nobility of the προαίρεσις or its slide into irrecoverable corruption.

---

[61] John Chrys., *In Rom. hom.* 16; PG 60,557 27-33: Ἀλλ' ὁ τὰ ἀπόρρητα εἰδὼς, καὶ διανοίας ἐπιτηδειότητα δοκιμάσαι δυνάμενος, καὶ ἐν τῷ βορβόρῳ τὸν μαργαρίτην κείμενον ἔγνω, καὶ τοὺς ἄλλους παραδραμών, καὶ τούτου τὴν εὐμορφίαν θαυμάσας, αὐτὸν ἐξελέξατο, καὶ τῇ τῆς προαιρέσεως εὐγενείᾳ τὴν παρ' ἑαυτοῦ προσθεὶς χάριν, δόκιμον αὐτὸν ἀπέφηνεν.

[62] John Chrys., *In Rom. hom.* 16; PG 60,558 3-5: ὁ μέντοι Φαρισαῖος, οὐδὲν τούτων τολμήσας, ἀλλὰ καὶ ἐν ἄλλοις κομῶν ἀγαθοῖς, τῇ πονηρᾷ προαιρέσει πάντα ἀπώλεσε ("However, the Pharisee, who ventured on none of these effronteries, and showing care in other good qualities, ruined everything by his worthless choice").

[63] John Chrys., *In Rom. hom.* 16; PG 60,557 58-60: Οὐδὲ γὰρ ἔργων ἐπίδειξιν ζητεῖ μόνον ὁ Θεὸς, ἀλλὰ καὶ προαιρέσεως εὐγένειαν καὶ γνώμην εὐγνώμονα ("For God does not seek only for a display of works, but also for nobility in the moral choice and a rightminded mindset").

[64] John Chrys., *In Rom. hom.* 16; PG 60,557 64-66: ὥσπερ ὁ ταυτὶ διεφθαρμένος, κἂν ἀγαθόν τι δόξῃ ποιεῖν, ἀπολεῖται μετὰ πονηρᾶς τοῦτο ἐργαζόμενος γνώμης ("Just as this person has been corrupted, even if he/she seems to do some good thing, so he/she will perish because of performing this with an unworthy mindset").

Often in Chrysostom's corpus, we find the γνώμη being identified as the disposing faculty of our beings. In homily 20 on Genesis, in summarising his previous comments on Cain and Abel, he indicates that the disposing faculty is the γνώμη.[65] In the case of the widow who chose to give her all, Chrysostom, in the Romans homily, had asserted that behind the widow's choice there was a liberal γνώμη.[66] Indeed, he stated earlier in his comments on this verse that mercy must be shown with liberality and with a γνώμη that does not count giving mercy as painful.[67] He also explained that the Apostle's words to the Corinthians about sowing liberally were an attempt by the Apostle Paul to correct (διορθούμενος,) their γνώμη on this matter.[68] It seems clear enough that while the choice made is critical, it is determined by the mindset, the προαίρεσις by the γνώμη. In a homily on Titus, he described heretics as those who were distorted and προηρημένος μεταθέσθαι τὴν γνώμην, "having preferred not to change their γνώμη".[69] At first glance, this could suggest that the γνώμη is subject to change by means of a deliberate choice. In some instances, this may be the case, but only under certain circumstances. The word used here, προηρημένος, which I have translated as "having preferred", is the perfect middle participle of προαιρέω. In its middle form, it bears the meaning of having determined for oneself, for one's own advantage.[70] Thus, a simple "chose" is too bland. It does not bring out enough the nuance that the choice is made because of its perceived benefit to the one who is choosing. If, as indicated above, the προαίρεσις (from the same verb) is governed by the γνώμη, then instinctively the preference and choice of the heretics would be not to change their mindset. The γνώμη of the heretics had settled in its distorted state so that the choice, the προαίρεσις, would follow the γνώμη and not act contrary to it. In this sense the NPNF translation, "predetermined", is to the point, though for the reasons stated above I think "preferred" is better.[71] The relationship between these two powers of the soul is made quite evident.

---

[65] John Chrys., *In Gen. hom.* 20; PG 53,166 43: καὶ ὅτι αὐτεξουσίους ἡμᾶς εἰργάσατο ὁ τῶν ἀπάντων δημιουργὸς, καὶ πανταχοῦ ἀπὸ τῆς γνώμης τῆς ἡμετέρας ἢ κατακρίνει ("...and that the creator of all has made us autonomous, and always judges us for our mindset...").

[66] John Chrys., *In Rom. hom.* 21; PG 60,603 48-50: Οὕτω καὶ ἡ χήρα πολλὰ τάλαντα ὑπερηκόντισε διὰ δύολεπτῶν· δαψιλὴς γὰρ ἦν ἡ γνώμη ("In this way the widow went way beyond many talents through her two small coins; for her mindset was liberal").

[67] John Chrys., *In Rom. hom.* 21; PG 60,603 17-18: Οὐ γὰρ ἀρκεῖ τὸ ἐλεῆσαι, ἀλλὰ καὶ μετὰ δαψιλείας καὶ γνώμης ἀλύπου τοῦτο δεῖ ποιεῖν ("It is not sufficient to show mercy, but this must be done from a liberal and spontaneous mindset").

[68] John Chrys., *In Rom. hom.* 21; PG 60,603 25-26.

[69] John Chrys., *In Titum hom.* 6; PG 62,696 26.

[70] LSJ, 1467 *s.v.* II.

[71] John Chrys., *John Chrys., Titus;* J. Tweed, in P. Schaff (ed.), NPNF Series 1, vol. 13, 540.

A significant passage on the interaction of the προαίρεσις and the γνώμη is found in a homily on the devil where there is an extended argument placing the problem of sin upon the choice of the person. In a comprehensive sweep, Chrysostom looks at creation, Jesus, the Cross, salvation, Paul's words, the apostles, the members of our bodies (eyes, hands, feet) and comments that the morally strong are advantaged, the weak are hindered. He then sums up by saying, Πανταχοῦ γὰρ ἡ προαίρεσις αἰτία, πανταχοῦ ἡ γνώμη κυρία ("Always the choice is responsible, always the mindset is the master").[72] Actions are determined by choices and mindsets. These could be synonymous terms, and thus be a simple duplication that is employed to direct attention away from the outward to the inward. From what has been discussed above, it is more likely that a distinction is being made. Whilst choice is seen to be the immediate cause, it is the mindset behind the choice that is the controlling factor, the master. The προαίρεσις is the servant that implements, the γνώμη the master that directs. Together they are culpable.

V. The Accountability of the Γνώμη

It is evident from the above that in Chrysostom's anthropology the γνώμη plays a critical role. This applies to a person's perspectives on life and all its circumstances, issues, relationships, and particularly to the issue of sin in a person's being. Thus far, it has been argued that of the two powers of the psyche that Chrysostom understood to be crucial in this matter, the γνώμη had precedence over the προαίρεσις. Although Chrysostom often used γνώμη in a positive role in human-divine relationships, the negative aspects have been the main concern of this study. With that in mind, this section examines the place given to the γνώμη in the matter of personal accountability and responsibility. It is clearly stated that the γνώμη is the faculty of the soul that is held accountable by God for all attitudes and actions. Nothing either external or internal to the person, no gift of God, no circumstance of life, no privileged position, no other inner capacity or any other thing can release the γνώμη from its liability before the Creator. These features will now be considered.

Chrysostom calls for the right disposition of the γνώμη in a wide range of situations. Examples of this have already been considered above. It is constructive, however, to examine what he considered is an extremely difficult situation, perhaps the most challenging of all. In the call not only to weep with others when

---

[72] John Chrys., *De Diabolo hom.* 2; PG 49,261 59-61.

they weep, but also to rejoice with them when they rejoice, Chrysostom deems the latter thing is, for reasons which he enumerates, far more difficult than the former. Standing by someone in danger is simply, he avers, a matter of toil and sweat; doing so when another is honoured is the more difficult matter of προαίρεσις and γνώμη.[73] This has to deal with the tyranny of jealousy and therefore is in need of a γνώμη marked by its philosophy (φιλοσόφου γνώμης), that is, by Christian teaching and discipline.[74] As A.-M. Malingrey has pointed out in her study on usage of certain terms in fourth-century Christianity, φιλοσοφία in Chrysostom's usage has a range of nuances, but when used in this sense of the orientation of a person's being, refers to the authentic praxis of the Christian life as lived in the everyday world.[75] The requirement then is a mindset that is appropriately educated in and committed to true Christian thought and behaviour in everyday living. Chrysostom held that in every situation the unique Christianised γνώμη should be expressed through the προαίρεσις into the appropriate action. The γνώμη is the responsible faculty.

It is from this perspective that Chrysostom argues that there are no circumstances that provide a legitimate excuse for personal sinful acts. He observed that more often than not, blame is shifted to something external, to those things Chrysostom considered as being included in the gifts of God. He points out that in the case of Judas it was not the fact that he was entrusted with the moneybag that was the cause of his sin. The circumstances in which he was placed were not to blame. The problem lay within himself, the state of his γνώμη.[76] In similar vein, the tree of Eden cannot be blamed as the cause of Adam's sin.[77] Likewise, those who were entrusted with the Law of Moses, a vehicle that was designed to suppress sin, cannot blame that Law or any other external factor for their sin. He claims, "the total accusation, is against their γνώμη that has been corrupted beyond all hope".[78] For the sake of explanation, he draws a comparison by likening the Law to a medicine prescribed by a doctor for a patient who then

---

[73] John Chrys., *In Rom. hom.* 7; PG 60,447 62-64: Τοσαύτη ἡ τῆς βασκανίας τυραννίς. Καίτοι τὸ μὲν πόνων καὶ ἰδρώτων, τοῦτο δὲ προαιρέσεως καὶ γνώμης μόνον ("So great is the tyranny of jealousy. Yet the one is of labours and sweat; but this one is of the choice and mindset alone").

[74] John Chrys., *In Rom. hom.* 7; PG 60,447 52: σφόδρα μέντοι μέγα ἐστὶ καὶ φιλοσόφου δεόμενον γνώμης ("However, it is extremely great and stands in need of a disciplined mindset").

[75] Malingrey, "*Philosophia*", 263-288, for a perceptive discussion of John Chrysostom's usage.

[76] John Chrys., *In Rom. hom.* 12; PG 60,500 44-46: ἀλλ' οὐ τὸ πιστευθῆναι τὸ γλωσσόκομον αὐτὸν τοῦτο εἰργάσατο, ἀλλ' ἡ τῆς γνώμης πονηρία. ("…but it was not that he was entrusted with the purse that caused this, but the bad state of his mindset").

[77] John Chrys., *In Rom. hom.* 12; PG 60,500 47-48.

[78] John Chrys., *In Rom. hom.* 12; PG 60,501 54-58: …ἀλλὰ πᾶσα ἡ κατηγορία τῆς ἐκείνων γνώμης ἐστὶ παρ' ἐλπίδα πᾶσαν διαφθαρείσης.

makes wrong use of it. The fault lies not with the medicine but with the patient. The Law would quench lust, but there is something in the patient that uses the Law's medicine to inflame lust and thus negate the intended cure. That something, Chrysostom asserts, is "sin, that is your own indolence and your worthless mindset (γνώμη)".[79] Likewise, troubles and afflictions cannot be blamed, especially as they are often, if not always, intended to teach us dependence upon God. Here again, Chrysostom uses the medical image: in the case of someone with a weak stomach who cannot take a particular medicine because it would only make things worse, the medicine is not the problem. So, he concludes, neither are the troubles the real problem. It is in the moral passivity of the γνώμη that the fault lies.[80] There is no doubting where Chrysostom understood the accountability for sin to be laid. There is no valid alibi that may be used wherewith to shift the responsibility to any external cause.

Similarly, Chrysostom taught that there is no privileged position that may serve to release the γνώμη from its accountability to God. The special case of the Jews is addressed in Homily 19 where Chrysostom takes up the issue of Israel's blindness as presented in Romans 11. His opening comments include the charge that Jewish inconsistency in not accepting the righteousness for which they sought was a matter of their own insolence or wrong-mindedness (ἀγνωμοσύνη).[81] That a condition or disposition of the γνώμη is in view is made clear in the approach he takes of closing off any loophole for excuse, such as an appeal to nature, by explicitly applying the blame to "the γνώμη of those persons".[82] Their spiritual

---

[79] John Chrys., *In Rom. hom.* 12; PG 60,500 28-30: ἡ δὲ ἁμαρτία, τουτέστιν, ἡ ῥαθυμία ἡ σὴ καὶ ἡ γνώμη ἡ πονηρά, τῷ καλῷ πρὸς τὸ ἐναντίον ἐχρήσατο ("but sin, that is to say, your own indolence and worthless mindset used the good [Law] for the opposite [purpose]").

[80] John Chrys., *In Rom. hom.* 9; PG 60,473 11-15: οὐ τὸ φάρμακον αἰτιασόμεθα, ἀλλὰ τὴν ἀρρωστίαν τοῦ μέλους, ὥσπερ οὖν καὶ ἐνταῦθα τὴν εὐκολίαν τῆς γνώμης ("...we may not blame the medicine, but the weakness of the member [stomach], just as in this case, therefore, we should blame the passivity of the mindset"). The term, εὐκολία, contentedness, *s.v.* LSJ 718, and pliability/docility s.v. LPGL 566, suggests that Chrysostom had ῥαθυμία, indolence/ indifference, his favourite term for failing to obey, lurking in his mind. Hence, I use passivity here in translation, allowable for εὐκολία as the essence of its signification, and in line with Chrysostom's theology of concurrence in the divine-human relationship.

[81] John Chrys., *In Rom. hom.* 19; PG 60,583 25-30: Εἶτα ἀποστερῶν αὐτοὺς πάλιν συγγνώμης, ἀπὸ τῶν εἰληφότων δείκνυσιν αὐτῶν τὴν ἀγνωμοσύνην, οὕτω λέγων· Ἡ γὰρ ἐκλογὴ ἐπέτυχε. Κἀκεῖνοι τούτους κατακρινοῦσι ("Then, depriving them of excuse, he demonstrates their insolence/wrong-mindedness from those Jews who have accepted it [righteousness], by saying, 'The election has found it.' Those who have accepted condemn these who have not"). For my analysis of ἀγνωμοσύνη, see discussion on Genesis Homily 27, Chapter 3 above.

[82] John Chrys., *In Rom. hom.* 19; PG 60,583 33-35: Ἵνα γὰρ μηδεὶς τῇ τοῦ πράγματος φύσει ἐγκαλῇ, ἀλλὰ τῇ ἐκείνων γνώμῃ, δείκνυσι καὶ τοὺς ἐπιτυχόντας ("So that nobody may accuse

blindness was the result of their ἀκαίρου φιλονεικίας ("untimely love of contention").[83] Thus, when the prophet referred to the blindness of their eyes and the deafness of their ears, Chrysostom asserts that God was blaming "nothing other than their contention-loving γνώμη (mindset)".[84] This theme is also found in Homily 18 where it is applied both negatively and positively. For Israel, it was τῆς γνώμης αὐτῶν τὴν ἀπώλειαν γενομένην ("of their γνώμη that ruin came upon them").[85] On the other hand, the drawing in of the Gentiles was not only a matter of God's grace, ἀλλὰ καὶ τῆς γνώμης τῶν προσελθόντων ("but also of the mindset of those who came").[86] Here, though, Chrysostom is quick to crush any thought of Gentile superiority by putting all the initiative back on God. The Gentiles were powerless to draw God to them,...τὴν αὐτοῦ χάριν τὸ πᾶν ἐργασαμένην... "it was his grace that worked the whole thing".[87] Nevertheless, Chrysostom was consistent in holding people responsible, privileged in position or not so, with the responsible faculty being, in his thinking, the γνώμη.

Chrysostom makes a very interesting comment in a homily on Romans that bears upon this critical role of the γνώμη. There he says that our Lord is called "a stone of stumbling and a rock of offence from the mindset (γνώμη) and end of those who do not believe".[88] This indicates that in his estimation the state or disposition of the γνώμη determines how people, events, circumstances and, indeed, all things affect us in our inner being. This general principle Chrysostom applied to Providence.[89] The issue here in this Romans' homily is that it is the state of the γνώμη that is critical in a person's relationship with God and his revelation in Christ. The γνώμη has the capacity to shut out that revelation and to distort its intended effect upon us. Awareness of this critical role of the γνώμη in receiving or rejecting revelation is applied by Chrysostom in his exposition of Romans 9:20. There he discusses the Apostle Paul's technique in answering objections. Before he introduced his answer, he prepared the hearer by καταστείλῃ

---

nature of the matter, but the mindset of those persons, he points out those [Jews among them] who had who found [faith]").

[83] John Chrys., *In Rom. hom.* 19; PG 60,583 55.

[84] John Chrys., *In Rom. hom.* 19; PG 60,583 55-58: Ὅταν γὰρ εἴπῃ, Ὀφθαλμοὺς τοῦ μὴ βλέπειν, καὶ ὦτα τοῦ μὴ ἀκούειν, οὐδὲν ἕτερον ἢ τὴν γνώμην αὐτῶν τὴν φιλόνεικον διαβάλλει.

[85] John Chrys., *In Rom. hom.* 18, PG 60,575 57-576 1.

[86] John Chrys., *In Rom. hom.* 18; PG 60,575 30-33.

[87] John Chrys., *In Rom. hom.* 18; PG 60,575 47-50.

[88] John Chrys., *In Rom. hom.* 16; PG 60,564 32-34: Προσκόμματος δὲ λίθον καὶ πέτραν σκανδάλου φησὶν ἀπὸ τῆς γνώμης καὶ τοῦ τέλους τῶν μὴ πιστευσάντων.

[89] John Chrys., *Scand.* 13.6, where Chrysostom states that Abraham maintained the same γνώμη of radiant faith throughout all events.

καὶ λεάνη τὴν γνώμην ("restraining and softening his γνώμη").[90] This, Chrysostom says, made Paul's words εὐπαράδεκτον ("easily received").[91] It is apparent from this that in Chrysostom's view, the faculty to be appropriately conditioned in order to receive revelation, at least in the usual mediated manner, is the γνώμη. It stands at the gateway to the inner workings of the mind and soul.

In commenting on Romans 10:6-9, Chrysostom speaks of the enemies against acceptance of the concept of righteousness by faith. Just as listlessness (ῥαθυμία) opposes the virtue displayed in works, so there are "reasonings that stridently confuse and outrage the intellects of most persons".[92] This calls for a νεανικωτέρας ψυχῆς ("a more vigorous soul"). Illustrating from Abraham, who did not stagger in unbelief, the point is made that to embrace faith in the face of such opposition calls for a lofty soul, a disciplined and wise intellect, and a great and heavenly mindset.[93] There is obvious interaction and perhaps overlap in the terms used. The latter epithetical phrase here "heavenly and great", or more literally "heaven-reaching" is probably an allusion in this patriarchal context to Jacob at Bethel with his dream of the ladder reaching to heaven and communication being made through the angels using it. The call is for a mindset that is focused on that which is ὑπὲρ φύσιν ("above nature"),[94] and which through the power of God is able to cast "the weakness of reasonings" away. Much then is laid upon the state of the mindset. It is critical in the conflict involved in the life of faith.

VI. The Esoteric Responsibility

While it is clear that nothing of an external nature could be used to move accountability from the γνώμη, it might be asked if, of the inner faculties of the

---

[90] John Chrys., *In Rom. hom.* 16; PG 60,558 50-51.

[91] John Chrys., *In Rom. hom.* 16; PG 60,558 52-53.

[92] John Chrys., *In Rom. hom.* 17; PG 60,566 39-42: οὕτω καὶ ὅταν πιστεῦσαι δέοι, εἰσὶ λογισμοὶ θορυβοῦντες καὶ λυμαινόμενοι τὴν τῶν πολλῶν διάνοιαν, καὶ δεῖ νεανικωτέρας ψυχῆς, ὥστε αὐτοὺς διακρούσασθαι.

[93] John Chrys., *In Rom. hom.* 17; PG 60,566 56-61: Καὶ ἔδειξεν, ὅτι καὶ δυνάμεως χρεία καὶ ψυχῆς ὑψηλῆς τὰ ὑπὲρ ἐλπίδα δεχομένης, καὶ μὴ προσπταιούσης τοῖς ὁρωμένοις. Τοῦτο τοίνυν καὶ ἐνταῦθα ποιεῖ, καὶ δείκνυσιν ὅτι φιλοσόφου διανοίας χρεία καὶ γνώμης οὐρανομήκους τινὸς καὶ μεγάλης ("He pointed out that there is need of power and of a lofty soul for receiving the things beyond hope, and of not stumbling at things that are seen. This therefore he does, and points out that there is need of a disciplined and wise intellect and of a heavenly mindset, something even great").

[94] John Chrys., *In Rom. hom.* 17; PG 60,566 66.

person, the γνώμη alone carried the burden of responsibility. Chrysostom asserted that the Greeks, by which he meant the Greek philosophers, could not blame the gift of reason (λόγος) they received from God for any failure on their part. The gift was intended to lead them to the Creator but was misused by them. The blame for this misuse and sin is placed on their γνώμη.[95]

In a comment on Romans 7:13 Chrysostom gives us a description, if not a definition, of sin. In so doing, he lists the γνώμη among four faculties that together comprise the sinful act.[96] It is pertinent to note that reason is not included. First, he mentions ἡ ῥάθυμος προαίρεσις (the indolent choice), the choice that, in this condition, is frivolous or listless, that is careless in that it lacks discipline and fire, is without backbone, lacking moral strength and allows itself to be steered toward the evil that it will make happen. Then he refers to ἡ ἐπὶ τὸ χεῖρον ὁρμή (the impulse toward what is worse). Here is the strong inclination, which having overcome or having been released from the restraints imposed upon it by other faculties, rushes towards action. Here, Chrysostom notes, it is rushing in the morally wrong direction. The next item is αὐτὴ δὲ ἡ πρᾶξις (the act itself), the end product, for which no epithet is required because it is patently evil. With his final phrase, ἡ διεφθαρμένη γνώμη (the mindset that has been corrupted or made morally bankrupt), he appears to go back to the root. We may ask where the driving force of sin is in this description of the various elements involved. Obviously, it is not the action, for that is the result. Equally clearly, it is not the προαίρεσις, as it does not have the moral strength, it is servant not master. That leaves us with ὁρμή and γνώμη. If ὁρμή is the initial impulse that overcomes inertia then it is a good candidate. However, in another place Chrysostom shows that the ὁρμή is activated by the passions: "Cain, moved by jealousy, rushed impulsively to the murder of his brother".[97] A more instructive insight into Chrysostom's understanding of the motivation of actions is found in Homily 27 of the Genesis material. There Chrysostom exhorts his listeners to pursue eagerly a healthy

---

[95] John Chrys., *In Rom. hom.* 12; PG 60,501 16-19: Ἀλλ' οὐ δήπου διὰ τοῦτο κατηγορήσομεν τῶν εὐεργεσιῶν τοῦ Θεοῦ, ἀλλὰ ταύτας μὲν θαυμασόμεθα μειζόνως καὶ μετὰ ταῦτα, τὴν δὲ γνώμην τῶν εἰς τἀναντία τοῖς ἀγαθοῖς κεχρημένων διαβαλοῦμεν ("But doubtless, we shall not denounce God's acts of kindness, but we shall admire these all the greater, and after this we shall accuse the mindset of those who have used the good things for opposite purposes").

[96] John Chrys., *In Rom. hom.* 12; PG 60,502 58-61: Τουτέστιν, ἵνα δειχθῇ ὅσον κακὸν ἡ ἁμαρτία, ἡ ῥάθυμος προαίρεσις καὶ ἡ ἐπὶ τὸ χεῖρον ὁρμή, καὶ αὐτὴ δὲ ἡ πρᾶξις καὶ ἡ διεφθαρμένη γνώμη· τοῦτο γὰρ πάντων αἴτιον τῶν κακῶν ("This means, so that sin may be shown as so great an evil, there is the indolent moral choice, and the impulse to what is worse, and the deed itself, and the mindset that has been corrupted; this is responsible for all evils").

[97] John Chrys., *In Gen. hom.* 20; PG 53,167 46-47: καὶ ὅτι ἐντεῦθεν ὑπὸ βασκανίας κινηθεὶς ὁ Κάϊν ἐπὶ τὸν τοῦ ἀδελφοῦ φόνον ὥρμησε,

γνώμη, because, he claims, it is the cause of all good things we do.[98] There we see that the originating impulse to our deeds is connected with our intellect or thinking (διάνοια).[99] The initiating impulse may arise from the passions or the intellect and is not autonomous.[100] It is controlled by the γνώμη to which the διάνοια is vitally connected.[101] Thus, as always with Chrysostom, deeds are assessed on the basis of the condition of the mindset from which the impulse to do them flows. Like the προαίρεσις, the ὁρμή is servant rather than master. This leaves the γνώμη, the mindset, as the accountable factor. The passage referring to Cain actually makes this explicit. There Chrysostom says,...καὶ πανταχοῦ ἀπὸ τῆς γνώμης τῆς ἡμετέρας ἢ κατακρίνει ("he [God] judges invariably on the basis of our mindset").[102] Sin then is ascribed to the mindset. It is in the γνώμη that sin makes its home and turns it into a citadel of rebellion and resistance to the will of God.

This conclusion is supported by another passage in the same Romans' homily, notably Chrysostom's comments on verses Romans 7:19-20. There he argues that Paul clears the substance (οὐσία) of both the body and the soul of any culpability for sin. The offence is tied up with the substance (οὐσία) or motion (κίνησις) of the προαίρεσις. Indeed, he asserts, there are two kinds of desire or willing (βούλησις): one a natural God-given desire; the other our own creation originating in the γνώμη. This latter desire or willing that originates in the γνώμη is identified as the προαίρεσις.[103] It is plain from this explanation that the deliberate moral

---

[98] John Chrys., *In Gen. hom.* 27; PG 53,243 36: Πανταχοῦ τοίνυν σπουδάζωμεν, παρακαλῶ, γνώμην ὑγιῆ ἐπιδείκνυσθαι. Αὕτη γὰρ αἰτία γίνεται πάντων τῶν ἀγαθῶν ("Therefore, let us be eager, I encourage you, to display a healthy mindset, for this is responsible for all our good works").

[99] John Chrys., *In Gen. hom.* 27; PG 53,243 38-41: Ὁ γὰρ ἀγαθὸς Δεσπότης οὐ τοῖς παρ' ἡμῶν γινομένοις προσέχειν εἴωθεν ὡς τῇ ἔνδοθεν διανοίᾳ, ἀφ' ἧς ὁρμώμενοι ταῦτα διαπραττόμεθα, καὶ πρὸς ἐκείνην βλέπων ἢ προσίεται τὰ ὑφ' ἡμῶν γινόμενα, ἢ ἀποστρέφεται ("For the good Lord is not in the habit of taking notice of the things done from our own contribution than as from our inner purpose, from which we bring about the initial impulse to these things, and to that he looks either to approve or disapprove our own deeds").

[100] LSJ, 1253 *s.v.*, refers to Stoic philosophy where it is defined as appetition, including reasoned choice and irrational impulse; Sorabji, *Emotion*, 42-47, dislikes "impulse" as a translation and leans toward "conation", and "desire".

[101] In this passage γνώμη is identified with τῇ ἔδοθεν διανοίᾳ, the inner purpose.

[102] John Chrys., *In Gen. hom.* 20; PG 53,166 43-44.

[103] John Chrys., *In Rom. hom.* 13; PG 60,510 25-29: Οὐ γὰρ ταυτὸν ψυχῆς οὐσία καὶ σώματος καὶ προαιρέσεως, ἀλλὰ τὰ μέν ἐστιν ἔργα Θεοῦ, τὸ δὲ ἐξ ἡμῶν αὐτῶν γινομένη κίνησις, πρὸς ὅπερ ἂν αὐτὴν βουληθῶμεν ἀγαγεῖν. Ἡ μὲν γὰρ βούλησις, ἔμφυτον καὶ παρὰ Θεοῦ· ἡ δὲ τοιάδε βούλησις, ἡμέτερον καὶ τῆς γνώμης ἡμῶν ("For the substance of the body and of the soul and of the moral choice are not the same, but the first two are works of God, and the other is a motion coming from ourselves towards whatever we may desire it to go. For, on one hand, the desire is natural and from God; but this kind of desire is ours and of our mindset").

choices made by a person are determined by the state of the γνώμη. The γνώμη, then, is the locus of responsibility for sin in the psyche.

This responsibility of the γνώμη for making evil choices on one hand, and of responding to grace on the other, is spoken of in a homily on Cain and Abel that opens with a discussion, under the image of incurable wounds, of the soul affected by sin.[104] Here the relevant powers of the soul come into view in their interaction. The soul does not respond to any remedy whatsoever, the problem being not a lack of ability but a lack of will or desire (βούλησις) towards a particular object or goal. The προαίρεσις, the faculty of choice, which is not permanently stationary but can change, needs to play its part. Thus, God exhorts and advises us in the depth of our intellect (διάνοια), but the γνώμη is the determining faculty. Everything rests upon it.[105] Cain, however, directed by his mindset, made an evil choice thus adding further wounds to his condition. He damages his γνώμη even more with the result that it becomes further entrenched in its sinful condition.

It is now possible to discern Chrysostom's conception of the locus of sin in the human psyche. Nature (φύσις), our essential being (οὐσία), is noble, rational, and unchangeable as far as its basic moral knowledge and goodness are concerned. Therefore, nature cannot be the locus of sin. The intent of God is that we, by appropriate moral choices, adorn it, beautify it and truly conform it to the character of God. The problem arises in that the faculty of deliberate choice, the προαίρεσις, is very much involved in the sinful act. Often our choices are inappropriate rather than what is morally required. However, this particular power of the soul, though a partner with the γνώμη in autonomy, is viewed as servant rather than master. The master is the γνώμη that Chrysostom perceives as the seat of autonomy in the soul and to which, often in concert with the προαίρεσις, he invariably charges the responsibility for sin. Further support for this is found in a passage in a Genesis homily where Chrysostom launches into a vivid and powerful condemnation of the murder of Abel. To capture the full force of the condemnation requires a reading of this whole passage of his rhetorical art, but sufficient for this analysis is the following extract:

> Fearful is the deed, dangerous is the brazen act, loathsome is the attack, unpardonable is the sin; it is the mindset (γνώμη) of a bestialised soul...O bloody hand! O miserable salute! Rather, the hand must not be called miserable and bloody, but the mindset (γνώμη), that to which the hand rendered service. So let

---

[104] John Chrys., *In Gen. hom.* 19: PG 53,158-160.

[105] John Chrys., *In Gen. hom.* 19; PG 53,159 4-5: οὐ μὴν ἀνάγκην ἐπιτίθησιν, ἀλλὰ τὰ φάρμακα κατάλληλα ἐπιθεὶς, ἀφίησιν ἐν τῇ γνώμῃ τοῦ κάμνοντος κεῖσθαι τὸ πᾶν ("Truly, no necessity is placed upon us, but in applying the appropriate medicines, everything is left to rest in the mindset of the one who is sick").

us say it this way: O brazen, bloody, wretched mindset! Whatever one may say, nothing can say it worthily enough to describe it.[106]

With all the passion of his being, Chrysostom lays the blame at the feet of the γνώμη. He then follows this up with a series of rhetorical questions to press home the enormity of the crime. Among them are two that are germane to this discussion: "How is that he did not change course and alter his mindset (γνώμη)? How is it that he did not take cognizance of his nature (φύσις)?"[107] First, γνώμη is set over against φύσις. Had Cain considered his fundamental nature with its inherent nobility, he could never have committed this murder. As it says in the passage, it is a wonder that his hand was not paralysed, that his sword was not immobilised, that his soul did not discard his body. Chrysostom presses home the utter abhorrence of nature to such a crime. Contrary to nature, Cain's γνώμη was of a different character and did not shrink back from the awful crime. Φύσις said one thing, γνώμη the opposite, and it prevailed. Nature is essentially virtuous; mindset, in this case, was terribly distorted. This signals the second matter that arises from the text: the action was determined by the γνώμη, not by φύσις nature. The mindset pushed nature aside, if it took any notice at all of nature, and moved Cain into his sinful act. As usual with Chrysostom, responsibility for sin, to reflect the text of Genesis 5:7, is laid at the door of the γνώμη.

VII. Γνώμη and Reason

This leaves the extent of the corruption of the γνώμη to be considered. Is it merely an individual matter or is it universal. Is damage only experienced from a personal Fall, or is there permanent damage that has occurred to the race? There is much in Chrysostom, in his emphasis upon individual responsibility, that may be construed as suggestive of the former being the total picture. However, in chapter 3 above, the case was argued for a universal innate experience. It has been noted that in

---

[106] John Chrys., *In Gen. hom.* 19: PG 53,160 5,8-9: Φοβερὰ ἡ πρᾶξις, ἐπικίνδυνον τὸ τόλμημα, μυσαρὰ ἡ ἐπιχείρησις, ἀσύγγνωστον τὸ ἁμάρτημα, τεθηριωμένης ψυχῆς ἡ γνώμη...Ὦ μιαρᾶς χειρός· ὦ δεξιᾶς ἐλεεινῆς· μᾶλλον δὲ οὐ τὴν χεῖρα ἐλεεινὴν δεῖ καλεῖν καὶ μιαρὰν, ἀλλὰ τὴν γνώμην, ἢ καὶ τὸ μέλος ὑπηρετήσατο. Εἴπωμεν τοίνυν οὕτως· ὦ γνώμης τολμηρᾶς, καὶ μιαρᾶς, καὶ ἐλεεινῆς, καὶ ὅπερ ἂν εἴποι τις, οὐδὲν ἄξιον ἐρεῖ.

[107] John Chrys., *In Gen. hom.* 19; PG 53,160 14-15: πῶς οὐκ ἐπεκάμφθη, καὶ μετέβαλε τὴν γνώμην; πῶς οὐκ ἔλαβεν ἔννοιαν τῆς φύσεως;

Chrysostom's anthropology γνώμη is closely connected to διάνοια, intellect or theoretical reasoning. This seems logical, as γνώμη has emerged in this study as a practical reason, combining elements of both intellect and emotions. To appreciate Chrysostom's position on the extent of the corruption of the γνώμη, it is necessary to discuss his thought on λογισμός, reason.

In a passage commenting on 1 Corinthians 1:18-21, Chrysostom argues that faith is superior over reason and human wisdom for the knowledge of God and humankind. He spells out the role assigned to λογισμός (reason) and σοφία (wisdom) prior to the incarnation and concludes,

> This is to say, that in the past, to reason that the one who founded such a so very great world is a God similar to someone who has irresistible and ineffable power, and that through these means to comprehend him, was the function of human wisdom; but now, there is no longer the need for reasonings, but for faith alone.[108]

The picture is clear and sharp. The faculty of comprehension or intellect, the διάνοια, takes the evidence presented to it in general revelation in the world and by the faculty of reasoning, the λογισμός, comes to the discovery of divine reality. One thing is missing: Chrysostom is adamant that humans, in matters divine, could not reason correctly by themselves alone. The soul needed help, and that was available in the presence of the Spirit of God. The soul must not trust to its own unaided powers in its reasonings. It must depend on God. If it attempts to see without the divine aid of the Spirit of God, it becomes a hindrance to itself.[109] Chrysostom maintains that this is what happened.[110] "The sceptre of knowledge was placed in the hand of independent reasonings",[111] rather than in the hand of the Spirit. The soul became πανταχοῦ ἄτονος ("absolutely unstrung"),[112] and

---

[108] John Chrys., *In 1 Cor. hom.* 4; PG 61,32 42-46: Τὸ μὲν γὰρ εἰπεῖν, ὅτι τὸν κτίσαντα τὸν κόσμον τὸν τοσοῦτον καὶ οὕτω μέγαν, Θεὸν εἶναι εἰκὸς δύναμιν ἀμήχανόν τινα ἔχοντα καὶ ἀπόρρητον, σοφίας ἀνθρωπίνης λογίζεσθαι ἦν, καὶ διὰ τούτων αὐτὸν καταλαμβάνειν· νῦν δὲ οὐκέτι λογισμῶν, ἀλλὰ πίστεως δεῖ μόνης.

[109] John Chrys., *In 1 Cor. hom.* 7; PG 61,60 29-31: Οὕτω τοίνυν καὶ ψυχὴ, ἐὰν βουληθῇ χωρὶς Πνεύματος βλέπειν, καὶ ἐμπόδιον ἑαυτῇ γίνεται ("Even so, therefore, if a soul should desire to see apart from the Spirit, he/she becomes even an obstacle to his/her self").

[110] John Chrys., *In 1 Cor. hom.* 7; PG 61,58 57-59 3: Ἡ δὲ ἔξωθεν τοὐναντίον ἐποίησεν· οὐ μόνον οὐκ ἐπαίδευσεν, ἀλλὰ καὶ ἐκώλυσε καὶ διετείχισε, καὶ μετὰ τὸ γενέσθαι ἐπεσκίαζε τοῖς γεγενημένοις, τὸν σταυρὸν κενοῦσα ("For the pagan wisdom did the opposite. It not only did not educate, but also hindered and put up a wall, and after the event, overshadowed the things that had been done [concerning the Lord Jesus], thus voiding the Cross").

[111] John Chrys., *In 1 Cor. hom.* 7; PG 61,60 36-37:...λογισμοῖς τὰ σκῆπτρα τῆς γνώσεως ἐγχειρίσαντες...

[112] John Chrys., *In 1 Cor. hom.* 7; PG 61,60 57-58.

opened itself to receive τοῖς σφόδρα ἀτόποις ("extreme absurdities").[113] Chrysostom uses various metaphors to explain this fall and the limitations that came upon reason as a result. One is the image of a metalworker drawing a piece of hardened metal out of the fire with fire tongs. He suggests that if anyone did this with their hand without tongs they would be voted against for their τὴν ἐσχάταν ἄνοιαν ("extreme foolishness").[114] Likewise are the philosophers who commit to their unaided reason things that cannot be found except by faith. He has already noted their σφόδρα μωροὶ ("extreme stupidity") and their ἐσχάτην ἀπόνοιαν ("uttermost senselessness").[115] Two things are of significance in this analogy. Quite explicit is the point that the philosophers by counting themselves wise, τὴν πίστιν ἠτίμασαν ("disdained faith").[116] They cast aside the specially designed tongs as worthless. This is madness enough. Then, implicit in the image is the glaring fact that the instrument, not being designed for the task, must be extensively damaged. Λογισμός, διάνοια, and σύνεσις, all part of the reasoning processes, have been so damaged that they no longer can function as was intended. Chrysostom notes that the διάνοια or σύνεσις, the faculty of comprehension that functions as τῶν τῆς ψυχῆς ὄψεων ("the eyes of the soul"),[117] due to its consequent ἀσθενείας ("weakness") and εὐτέλειαν ("poor quality") has its range severely limited, so that the divine is well beyond it.

Chrysostom does not leave us stumbling around feeble and short-sighted. He shows instead the effect of the grace of God upon the soul, particularly in baptism. In this sacrament, grace grabs hold of the soul, he declares, and plucks out sin by the roots.[118] Changing the metaphor, he asserts that the soul is melted down and recast in the smelting furnace of baptism, sins are consumed and the soul is prepared to shine more brightly than pure gold.[119] The process of the grace of παλλιγενέσις (regeneration) in baptism restores the soul to its pristine powers; the rational faculty is made whole. However, proper use must be made of the renewed reason and other faculties. Chrysostom is aware that struggle and conflict is the order of the day for the renewed soul.

With this background in place, the relation between γνώμη and διάνοια and

---

[113] John Chrys., *In 1 Cor. hom.* 7; PG 61,60 41.

[114] John Chrys., *In 1 Cor. hom.* 5; PG 61,40 20-21.

[115] John Chrys., *In 1 Cor. hom.* 5; PG 61,40 15-16.

[116] John Chrys., *In 1 Cor. hom.* 5; PG 61,40 23.

[117] John Chrys., *In 1 Cor. hom.* 7; PG 61,61 29-41. The items cited are at lines 36, 35 and 41.

[118] John Chrys., *In 1 Cor. hom.* 40; PG 61,349 8-12: Θεὸς γὰρ μόνος τοῦτο ποιεῖ. Ὃ δὴ καὶ ἐν τῷ λουτρῷ τῆς παλιγγενεσίας ἐργάζεται· αὐτῆς γὰρ ἅπτεται τῆς ψυχῆς ἡ χάρις, κἀκεῖθεν πρόρριζον ἀνασπᾷ τὴν ἁμαρτίαν ("God alone does this. He works it in the laver of regeneration; for grace grabs the soul itself and pulls up sin with the roots from that place").

[119] John Chrys., *In 1 Cor. hom.* 40; PG 6,349 13-23.

λογισμός may be clarified. Chrysostom, in commenting on 1 Corinthians 4:3-4, where he probes the motives behind the quality of good deeds as a basis for self justification, draws attention to the possibility of their being done from a satanic γνώμη. In doing this, he links the satanic γνώμη to the corrupted διάνοια.[120] The διάνοια as the faculty of comprehension, theoretical reasoning, and intention, involves reason, so that reason also becomes controlled by the γνώμη. Chrysostom, in an extended discussion, relates how the διάνοια has been corrupted.[121] Darkness has come into it. The ruling principle, the light of λογισμός was burning in it, but this light has been extinguished by the strong blast of the spirit of fornication or some other improper love or desire. Control passes from reason to the improper reasonings fuelled by of one or other of these improper appetites. How does this affect the γνώμη? This study has shown that Chrysostom describes various feelings or emotional attitudes as arising from the γνώμη, or at least, being mediated by it. When all is in order with enlightened λογισμός acting as the ἡγεμονικόν (ruling principle) in the soul, the γνώμη is subject to right reason, the διάνοια regains its true sight, and the desires are under control of a ὀρθὴ γνώμη (right mindset). Then right κρισεῖς (judgments) are then able to be made, and the προαίρεσις makes right moral choices. When the desires are allowed their rein, this order is thrown into confusion. Right reason is dethroned and a corrupted γνώμη takes its place as the ruling principle in the soul. Reason is not able to function as intended with the result that all judgments suffer from the distortion imparted to them by a corrupted γνώμη in which the desires or passions are often allowed to dominate.

A pattern or prototype is discernable in Chrysostom's treatment of sin that incorporates these faculties of the ψυχή. This is well illustrated by Chrysostom's adaptation of the charioteer image from his studies in Plato. In discussing the value of mortality, he addresses the common objection that the mortal body is the cause of sin, the reason for the passions being out of control.[122] On the contrary, Chrysostom claims that the mortality of the body is a positive blessing. It is an agent of self control, and accomplishes great things in us. He continues on to specify how this is so, but there is no need to elaborate further except to note that in his application of the charioteer metaphor the body is likened to the reins or bridle by which the horses are controlled. The body, if we permit it, may be used to hold down the wild surges of the soul, to subdue madness and folly, to check

---

[120] John Chrys., *In 1 Cor. hom.* 11; PG 61,91 47-48: ἡ δὲ διάνοια διεφθαρμένη· ἀπὸ σαταννικῆς γὰρ γίνεται γνώμης.
[121] John Chrys., *In 1 Cor. hom.* 11; PG 61,91 21-52.
[122] John Chrys., *In 1 Cor. hom.* 17; PG 61,144-146. The following analysis is based on this passage.

boastfulness, and to serve us in the attainment of the greatest morally perfect and absolutely right deeds. This is a far cry from the Greek philosophers' view of the body as a hindrance to the attainment of perfect deeds and of the progress of the soul upward to its goal. In Plato's *Phaedrus* the body is at best neutral, although Plato does give it a negative connotation by referring to it as a living tomb in which the soul is imprisoned like an oyster in its shell.[123] In Chrysostom, the body is an ally to reason: the body is the bridle by which the charioteer, the λογισμός, reason, reigns in the passions of the ψυχή. The negative is made positive, the hindrance becomes a help, the weakness becomes the strength. Therefore, in the event of sin when the passions have surged out of control, Chrysostom, like Plato, argues that the charioteer is the responsible party. The reins, in this case the body, are not to blame, but rather the charioteer, λογισμος that has failed to hold them properly. In the exposition he introduces each of the faculties we have noted. The first to bear the blame is the προαίρεσις.[124] The choice is not quite the end product, but the immediate cause of the sinful action. Then he fixes on the λογισμός as the ἡγεμονικόν,[125] and our διεφθαρμένη γνώμη ("corrupted mindset")[126] as the objects of blame. Then he turns to accuse our πονηρᾶς διανοίας ("worthless comprehension"),[127] before finally coming back to the διεφθαρμένη γνώμη.[128] The λογισμός, γνώμη, διάνοια, and προαίρεσις are in close connection, affecting each other in their condition and their operation. All the elements of a prototype noted above are here. The corrupt γνώμη directs the contest. The διάνοια cannot see properly to comprehend the situation in relation to God. Thus the λογισμός, reasoning that is based upon the comprehension, is crippled, and the γνώμη releases the passions through the damaged λογισμός so that the προαίρεσις makes the evil choice. It is to be noted that Chrysostom suggests the cure: Σωφρονῶμεν ("Let us be soundminded/soberminded"),[129] and πρὸς τὸν Θεὸν τὸ ὄμμα τῆς διανοίας τείνατε ("stretch the eye of your faculty of comprehension towards God").[130] The verb, τείνω, to stretch/pull tight, such as for a bow, a sail or reins, signifies the making of something or someone effective.[131] The διάνοια was unstrung; it required tensioning, so that it would be effective as an instrument for reception from God of understanding and discernment.

---

[123] Plato, *Phaedrus* 250c, 5-6.
[124] John Chrys., *In 1 Cor. hom.* 17; PG 61,144 23, 39.
[125] John Chrys., *In 1 Cor. hom.* 17; PG 61,144 53, 64.
[126] John Chrys., *In 1 Cor. hom.* 17; PG 61,144 63.
[127] John Chrys., *In 1 Cor. hom.* 17; PG 61,145 4.
[128] John Chrys., *In 1 Cor. hom.* 17; PG 61,145 6.
[129] John Chrys., *In 1 Cor. hom.* 17; PG 61,145 1.
[130] John Chrys., *In 1 Cor. hom.* 17; PG 61,146 1.
[131] LSJ 1766 *s.v.*

VIII. Original Sin

It might be objected that Chrysostom presents the above scenario in the context of the post-baptismal struggle against sin. This may be so, but there is cause to think that he is applying the prototype of how damage results universally, a prototype experienced at and derived from the story of the Fall; one that he may have experienced himself, and that he had observed time and again during his ministry. There are several reasons to apply this prototype in this way. These are the testimony of baptism, the polemic against wisdom as practised by the Greek philosophers, the polemic against the Jews, and his general treatment of unbelievers in his homilies.

If baptism is required to restore our damaged faculties, then it must follow that the damage is universal. There is no other way of restoration but by the grace of παλλιγγενέσις (regeneration), therefore all must have been affected by the Fall in a substantial way that led to personal sins. So, although Chrysostom was at pains to guard φύσις from the Fall, and insist upon its continuing native nobility, he does not hesitate to speak of universal damage to the ψυχή and its various faculties. The passions rage, reason attempts to assert its independence, the intellect is in darkness, the γνώμη is unstrung and becomes a hotbed of distortion, and the moral choice runs wild under the control of the γνώμη. Although φύσις is unchanged, not so the ψυχή; it is viewed by Chrysostom as needing the wholesale renewal and renovation that the Spirit conveys in baptism.

Chrysostom's extensive polemic against the Greek philosophers and their wisdom emphasises the general picture of human weakness. In the Graeco-Roman world of Chrysostom's day, the philosophers and their legacy represented the highest achievements of human aspiration. The sage had a revered place in society. Chrysostom's broadside targeted their σοφία, their λογισμός, their διάνοια, their γνώμη, plus their morals and thus their προαίρεσις. Again, it is seen that the critical faculties of the ψυχή are in a distorted state and not functioning as God intended. One might ask that if the best citizens of society are in such a state, what of the rest? There is cause to think that Chrysostom's polemic was so intense and extensive for this very reason.

His polemic against the Jews is probably of the same order as that against the philosophers. In the Jews, the best of religious faith as compared with others, stands the enigma of their rejection of the Christ. When commenting on 2 Corinthians 3:14, he says this should be no surprise, for it has been their history. The veil on Moses face that hid the glory of God in the Law was indicative of their inability to perceive the Law gifted to them. Chrysostom described the hardness of heart demonstrated in this incident as γνώμης ἐστὶν ἀναισθήτου καὶ ἀγνώμονος ("...of an insensate and insolent mindset").[132] Some lines later, he attributes this hardness to διὰ τὴν τούτων παχύτητα καὶ σαρκικὴν γνώμην ("...on account of their dullness and carnal mindset").[133] The same problems occur as in the Greeks and in the passages previously analysed; the eyes of the soul are darkened, and the passions are unchecked, because of the disposition of the γνώμη. Again, there is a people with a damaged ψυχή.

Chrysostom speaks of the unbelieving in terms that has them alienated from God with the faculties of their souls terribly distorted. To take but one example, the approach he says is needed when preaching to them. In commenting on 1 Corinthians 1:17, "I was not sent to baptise but to preach the gospel", he compares and contrasts the labour required in the ministry of the latter with that of the former. Baptising is relatively easy, the candidates are convinced and at the point of initiation.[134] Just the opposite applies to preaching the Gospel to unbelievers. Great changes are required in the ψυχή. The προαίρεσις must be persuaded to change, no easy task. Then the γνώμη must be transposed, turned right around, the task of undoing years of shaping the γνώμη by experience and education, and to do this in a comparatively short time. Then, some serious surgery is required as error is to be pulled up by the roots and truth planted in its place. The labour required is intense and earnest. Great wisdom is required. The διάνοια and the λογισμός are clearly involved in this process. In Chrysostom's theological anthropology, the non-Christian lives with a damaged soul. All the faculties that are involved in the prototypic fall and the typical regeneration are seen to be in need of the power of grace.

Much more could be marshalled along these lines, but sufficient has been considered in some detail to conclude that Chrysostom held the opinion that a damaged ψυχή and its faculties has been the normal experience of all humankind from the time of the Fall. From consideration of some of the material in his corpus, it is difficult not to conclude that this is innate. If it is not, it is held to be inevitable for all. At the same time, each person is culpable for their personal sins,

---

[132] John Chrys., *In 2 Cor. hom.* 7; PG 61,445 42-43.

[133] John Chrys., *In 2 Cor. hom.* 7; PG 61,446 55-56.

[134] John Chrys., *In 1 Cor. hom.* 3; PG 61,26 18-23: Ἐκεῖ μὲν γὰρ τὸ πᾶν γέγονε, καὶ πέπεισται ὁ μυσταγωγεῖσθαι μέλλων, καὶ οὐδὲν μέγα, πεισθέντα βαπτίσαι· ἐνταῦθα δὲ πολὺς ὁ πόνος ὥστε μεταπεῖσαι προαίρεσιν, καὶ μεταθεῖναι γνώμην, καὶ ἀναμοχλεῦσαι πλάνην, καὶ καταφυτεῦσαι τὴν ἀλήθειαν ("In the former [the one being baptised] the lot has been done, and the one who is going to be initiated has been convinced, and it is no great thing to baptise a convinced person. But the latter (convincing an unbeliever) the labour to persuade change in the moral choice, to turn the mindset around, to pull up error by the roots, and to plant the truth in its place, is great").

irrespective of this damage, because they are autonomous beings who retain this feature of the freedom to choose according to their desires, or even against them, as seen in some circumstances. Thus, damage to the ψυχή is inevitable and universal. Sinning is not so, a difficult concept to comprehend given the presence of damage in the ψυχή.

Wherein does this differ from the traditional typical doctrine of original sin in western Christianity? There is certainly no bondage of the will. There is no hereditary guilt. There is no sin of nature. There is no bias toward sin coming from the φύσις. Yet, Phan, after surveying Chrysostom's Genesis homilies, 19, 67 and 68, and eight baptismal instructions, Matthew homily 8, and Romans homily 10, concludes: "In brief, then, though falling short of Augustinianism, there was here an outline of a doctrine of original sin which would be elaborated in greater detail by Augustine, especially in his struggle against Pelagius and his disciples".[135] It is doubtful if Chrysostom would have been happy with this, although there are some statements in his corpus that, considered in isolation, could lead to such a conclusion. More pertinently, I do not think enough consideration has been given to Chrysostom's distinction between φύσις and ψυχή. On one hand, φύσις lies undamaged in its native nobility. On the other, ψυχή has been devastated, especially in its capacity to plumb the divine. Therein lies a problem. It constitutes a tension in Chrysostom's anthropology. Perhaps, therein lies an answer. What is evident is that the γνώμη has suffered damage, so that it needs an initial renewal in regeneration and a lifetime of careful attention for it to fulfil its critical function as was intended in the purposes of God. The citation from R. Hill in n. 20 in the opening section of this chapter about Theodoret, has some affinity to the above findings from Chrysostom, but there are issues to be raised. To repeat, Hill writes that Theodoret,

> steers a careful line between an Augustinian acceptance of the impairment of human nature and unwarranted Pelagian optimism: original sin (not his term) has upset a balance, and the resultant rebellion of the passions – not nature as such – is responsible for our sins.[136]

As seen in this study, Chrysostom varies from this in some significant ways. There is no impairment of human nature in his theology, and indeed in all Antiochene theology. As discussed above in chapter 9, Theodoret viewed the unregenerate γνώμη as having a propensity towards moral evil, and is one with Chrysostom in situating sin in the γνώμη. There also, it was seen that Theodoret viewed the passions as natural but irritating, and not the responsible cause of sin; the γνώμη is

---

[135] Phan, *Grace and the Human* Condition, 197-203 at 203.
[136] Hill, *Theodoret of Cyrus, Commentary on the Psalms*, 197, n. 9.

the cause. This, too, is in agreement with Chrysostom. A significant addition is made by Chrysostom: he names the entity that has been unbalanced, and it is not primarily the passions. The ψυχή has suffered the damage, and that is where the equilibrium in the person has been upset. This touches all the faculties of the soul, and none more so than the γνώμη, which controls the passions, and which has had the burden of human destiny thrust upon it. Therefore, Chrysostom sails close to the Augustinian acceptance of impairment, not of nature, but of the soul, the ψυχή. As far as the other part of Hill's observation, perhaps Chrysostom should not have been as optimistic as he is supposed to have been. Even on his figures of those who attained perfection, perhaps Enoch and Noah, and very few more, his general perception of humankind is that a damaged γνώμη got the better of them.

IX. Conclusion

Chrysostom regarded our human nature as noble, rational, humble and endowed with the knowledge of what is good and what is evil. Indeed, he was at pains to guard and preserve the concept of the essential dignity of humankind.[137] This has not been changed by the Fall. Thus, unlike many in the western tradition, he does not hold that the nature of humankind is inherently sinful. However, it suffers what appears to be a great weakness, the lack of decisive ability to effect moral human action. It stands as a testimony to God's purpose for us to be conformed to his character, but it cannot effect such an outcome. Nevertheless, it is not responsible for sin.

The Fall is presented as a fall from nature rather than a fall of nature. The problem is found in the powers or faculties of the soul or psyche. The passions may have been unleashed by Adam, but they are subject to other faculties and may be used for good. They are not inherently evil. Two powers of the soul are invariably charged with responsibility by Chrysostom for sin. One is the προαίρεσις, the deliberate moral choice, which he understood as autonomous, that is, free from external restraints. It is marked by instability, and is easily inclined toward evil. It is dependent upon another faculty for its operation. The other power of the soul held responsible for sin, the γνώμη, is the faculty that controls the προαίρεσις. It is presented by Chrysostom as charged with ordering the passions, impulses and desires of the soul, and of directing the προαίρεσις in its choices. It

---

[137] See G.C. Morgan, *God's Last Word to Man: Studies in Hebrews* (London–Edinburgh 1948) 26, where I read fifty years ago in his delightful expositions this comment on Heb 2:9-11, "It may be said that one phase of the terrible malady from which humanity suffers is that he thinks of himself more meanly than God thinks of him." Chrysostom would say, Amen.

determines settled attitudes to external factors and is responsible as to how these are experienced and used. It is presented as being corrupted since the Fall, and shares in the damage that the Fall either visited upon the soul and its faculties, or opened the way for that damage to occur in a universal manner. Undoubtedly, in Chrysostom's anthropology, this faculty bears ultimate responsibility for sin. The autonomy and authority of the γνώμη leave it and its masters without excuse before God. Individuals control their own γνώμη, and are responsible for its state, and therefore for their destiny. Chrysostom was so convinced of its importance in the soul of the human person that he thought neglect of it was tantamount to spiritual suicide.[138]

---

[138] John Chrys., *In Rom. hom.* 9; PG 60,472.

Chapter 11

Conclusion

The question basic to this investigation is: in Chrysostom's anthropology, or more specifically his psychology, what faculty of the soul is held responsible for sin? This question, formulated against the background of the differences in understanding of original sin between the Eastern Orthodox and the traditional western position, has led to an examination of the γνώμη, which I interpret to refer to the mindset and its various functions. In my reading of Chrysostom's homilies, γνώμη occurred so often at critical points that it became clear that not only did it have a major role in the functioning of the psyche, but bore a great deal of responsibility for the determination of life and conduct. This examination of the functions and role of γνώμη in Chrysostom's homilies has confirmed those suspicions, and has also provided a coherent picture of his understanding of the process of sin.

The examination of the γνώμη in Chrysostom's usage may be summed up under the following categories: constitution, functions, health, sin and change. Starting with the constitution first, it was observed that he understood the γνώμη to be a faculty or power of the ψυχή (soul), possessing both rational and emotional elements and features. It is described as being the locus of personal autonomy with a consequent authority in the soul. It is identified as the set habit of the soul, and thus the seat of personality.

Its functions are presented as interacting with a number of faculties and a vast panorama of operations. These may be divided into ruling and deliberation. As far as ruling is concerned, we find that the γνώμη has authority over desire, passions, impulse, intellect, moral choice, conscience and, in its distorted state, even reasoning (λογισμός), the true ἡγεμονικόν of the soul, an office that the γνώμη has usurped on account of its fall. Perhaps, one or more of the other faculties may suffer in the same way. Under the function of deliberation, there is discernment, evaluation, agenda-setting, purpose, decision and choice, policy determination and steerage in its implementation, motive resolution and motivation, establishment of settled desires, focusing of intention, commitment, consecration, and arbitration of good and evil.

Health is a vital aspect of the γνώμη because Chrysostom indicates that the state or condition of the γνώμη is of utmost importance to God. He evaluates it for the purpose of rewards and condemnation. He accepts or rejects prayers, deeds, and offerings because of its state. Chrysostom asserts that a person is responsible to God for the disposition of the γνώμη, using the Stoic metaphor of tension to measure its condition, that is, whether it is well strung or unstrung, either rightminded or insolent.

Sin is presented as the result of a distorted γνώμη. It is flawed by a propensity toward evil since the Fall. It is asserted to be the source of rebellion, a citadel shrouded in darkness and set in a distorted state, often referred to as indolence (ῥαθυμία), and depravity (μοχθηία). A survey of the Antiochene camaraderie demonstrated that Chrysostom stood well within a tradition of common understanding of the significance, role and operation of the γνώμη in Antiochene theological anthropology. They shared a common pool of knowledge about nature, sin, and the γνώμη with very little individual difference. Chrysostom, in tune with his Antiochene comrades, did not hold to a doctrine of original sin as traditionally accepted in the West. There is no hereditary sin of nature, although, along with his comrades he believed in the universal damage of the soul. Chrysostom and his colleagues understood our human nature to be noble, rational, humble, and endowed with the knowledge of what is good and what is evil. Although it lacks the decisive ability to effect human action, it is not inherently sinful and not responsible for sin. Chrysostom constantly charged the προαίρεσις and the γνώμη with responsibility for sin. The προαίρεσις, though sharing in God-given autonomy, is marked by instability and is easily inclined toward evil, and is dependent upon the γνώμη for its operation. The γνώμη is the faculty presented by Chrysostom as charged with ordering the passions, impulses and desires of the soul, and of directing the προαίρεσις in its choices. It is the faculty that bears ultimate responsibility for sin. As the usage of γνώμη by the Antiochenes is high compared with the few other patristic theologians that I randomly and rather cursorily surveyed, it may be that this was a feature derived from Diodore's anthropology, which, with his education and experience, would be sourced in the Greek παιδεία. Diodore's influence in this respect would have supplemented and intensified Chrysostom's education in the παιδεία, especially from his time under Libanius. Diodore in his ἀσκητήριον may have encouraged its use in his exegesis of the Scriptures.

The capacity for change is presented as a major feature of the γνώμη except when it becomes hardened in a settled state. Normally, it is unstable and subject to change, usually in the wrong direction. It is subject to shaping through education, experience, and circumstances either for good or for evil. Thus, Chrysostom, discerning a need for change towards God in the γνώμη, spent his life attempting to make that happen in the course of his ministry. Conversion takes place in the γνώμη, so that is the faculty targeted in the preaching of the Gospel. Regeneration in the process of baptism effects an initial transformative change in the γνώμη. This initial change needs to be followed up by a continuing program of instruction and personal discipline.

The significance of the γνώμη in Chrysosotom's anthropology has been little recognised, even in Orthodox theology. It has been noted in this study that Maximus the Confessor was the first to write anything substantial about γνώμη in treatise form. Orthodoxy has largely followed Maximus, and while there has been some recognition of γνώμη in Orthodox theology, it has usually been in terms of will, gnomic will. This is not the main way in which Chrysostom used the term, and for the most part προαίρεσις has been given prominence over γνώμη. This, as, amply demonstrated in this study, is the opposite order to Chrysostom, both in numerical usage and in linguistic and theological signification. Researchers on Maximus have not recognised any dependence upon Chrysostom, and without any discussion from that quarter, it is difficult to ascertain to what extent it may have occurred. As noted above, Maximus dwelt in Constantinople and would have had access to Chrysostom's works. There are some hints in Maximus that he was aware of a fuller significance of γνώμη, but apart from the few exceptions referred to in this study, much of that appears to have been lost or forgotten.

Without doubt, the γνώμη is of great significance in Chrysostom's anthropology. From what has been discussed here, there is no hesitation in describing Chrysostom as the theologian of the mindset. This is said against the common background in patristics that Chrysostom has little to offer in the way of theology. For example, I was quite surprised, when researching on Antiochene christology for purposes other than this work, that Mcleod, gave little value to Chrysostom in this regard.[1] This surely, is an issue of methodology. In a massive corpus of a special category of literature such as Chrysostom's, it cannot be expected that his theology should be nicely laid out on a plate. As argued in Chapter 1 above, there is an underlying theology, and in this case an underlying anthropology, which can only be discerned by examining his terminology in context consistently across his corpus. Arduous sifting and searching is required to unearth the rich vein of coherent theological acumen that is there. The treasure is worth the toil, and I trust that this study demonstrates this to be so. There is much more mining waiting to be done. It should be added that Chrysostom uses the term δόγμα in his corpus over 400 times, which suggests that he had some interest in theology.

It hardly seems necessary to remind those engaged in historical theology that texts must be interpreted in relation to their cultural backgrounds. This includes among other things, psychological, societal, educational, professional, and the

---

[1] McLeod, *The Image of God,* 117-120, esp. 119 n. 14.

religious. This I have endeavoured to do, especially by tracing his sources in the Greek παιδεία. Sometimes the task looked overwhelming, but in order to light up the text it had to be done. No doubt, I will be told if I have failed in some aspect or another. Nevertheless, I have enjoyed the attempt, and a bygone world that I knew to some extent has come much more alive to me in the course of this study. I trust that proves true for the reader.

Related to that aspect of this exercise is a reminder that for communication to be effective, it must be couched in terms and forms that are endemic to the target culture, or subculture, as the case may be. Implicit in that is the need for professional communicators to be diligent in studying the culture they wish to persuade.

As indicated above, Chrysostom's vocation may be defined as educating the γνώμη. He understood that it was dependent upon experience and education for its formation, a process that eventually sets the γνώμη so that it becomes a store of attitudes, inclinations, aspirations, and policy. It was this understanding of the γνώμη as a work in progress that made Chrysostom such a great educator of the church. It explains his methodology of careful exposition, and his confidence in the power of the Christian Scriptures and the sacraments of the church to transform people. It lay behind his conviction of the efficacy of preaching. If anything of practical spiritual worth may be learned from this study, this feature must figure near the top. In an age when the long proved disciplines of the faith have been brushed aside in favour of instant bliss and short term remedies, this voice from the past is both a timely warning and a wise guide. Chrysostom delves below the surface to expose the workings of the psyche, and thus points us again to the supreme importance of the inner springs of our lives. He challenges us about our responsibility to tend to their health. These two things make this study of value in respect to spirituality. Here again, many patristic commentators label Chrysostom as being concerned almost solely with little more than outward morality. This study demonstrates that such a view cannot be sustained. More than sufficient has been presented to reveal both his and his Lord's concern with motive over deed.

Chrysostom understood the γνώμη to be the centre of responsibility of the person. Its accountability extended to all areas of life. All circumstances, all relationships, all attitudes, all decisions, all actions, and all the operations of the soul, come under the jurisdiction of the γνώμη, and it bears the responsibility for all. Chrysostom does not hesitate to apply this to sin. Repeatedly in his homilies, the γνώμη is held responsible for sin, not only in action, but in thought and intention as well. With the role of the γνώμη thus made plain, the issue of sin becomes clear. The γνώμη is the power of the soul ultimately responsible for sin. It evaluates impulses, passions and thoughts, and then directs the προαίρεσις, the moral choice, towards the end to which it, the γνώμη, inclines. Indeed, one may go a step further: if the γνώμη is a store of attitudes and inclinations, then it is not only responsible for sin but is the very lodging-place of sin in the soul, that is, it harbours the pervasive propensity of selfishness and insolence that blights human life. Chrysostom, holding our nature to be unchangeable, found in the γνώμη a faculty of the soul distinct from nature, a citadel of sin needing to be overcome by the power of the Gospel. When the γνώμη is thereby transformed from its ugliness, then the soul, and the person, with a renewed and duly shaped γνώμη, is on the path to be conformed to the beauty of the image of Christ.

BIBLIOGRAPHY

Primary Sources

Texts of John Chrysostom

Migne, J.-P., (ed.), *PG* 47-64.

Field, F., *Joannis Chrysostomi homiliae in Matthaeum*, 3 vols (Cambridge 1838-1839).

—, *Joannis Chrysostomi Interpretatio Omnium Epistularum Paulinarum* I-VII (Oxford 1854-1862).

Malingrey, A.-M., *Jean Chrysostome. Sur la providence de Dieu*, SC 79 (Paris 1961).

—, *Jean Chrysostome. Sur le sacerdoce*, SC 272 (Paris 1980).

Wenger, A., *Jean Chrysostome: Huit catéchèses baptismales inédites*, SC 50 (Paris 1957, 1970²).

Translations of John Chrysostom

Christo, G.G. (trans.), *St John Chrysostom: On Repentance and Almsgiving*, FOTC 96 (Washington, DC 1998).

Hall, C.A., *"John Chrysostom's 'On Providence': a translation and theological interpretation"*, diss., Drew University 1991.

Harkins, P.W. (trans.), *Demonstration Against the Pagans that Christ is God*, in M.A. Schatkin and P.W. Harkins (eds), *Saint John Chrysostom: Apologist*, FOTC 73 (Washington D.C. 1985) 153-262.

—, *Baptismal Instructions*, ACW 31 (Westminster, MD–London 1963).

—, *Discourses Against Judaizing Christians*, FOTC 68 (Washington, DC 1979).

—, *On the Incomprehensible Nature of God*, FOTC 72 (Washington, DC 1982).

—, *Demonstration Against the Pagans that Christ is God*, 153-262, FOTC 73 (Washington, DC 1985).

Hill, R.C. (trans.), *Saint John Chrysostom: Homilies on Genesis 1-17*, FOTC 74 (Washington, DC 1985).

—, *Saint John Chrysostom: Homilies on Genesis 18-45*, FOTC 82 (Washington, DC 1990).

—, *Saint John Chrysostom: Homilies on Genesis 46-67*, FOTC 87 (Washington, DC 1992).

—, *St. John Chrysostom: Eight Sermons on the Book of Genesis* (Boston, MA 2004).

Hunter, D.G. (trans.), *A Comparison Between a King and a Monk*; *Against the Opponents of the Monastic Life*: *Two Treatises by John Chrysostom*, SBEC 13 (New York 1988).

Laistner, M.L.W., *Christianity and Pagan Culture in the Later Roman Empire together with an English Translation of John Chrysostom's "Address on Vainglory and the Right Way for Parents to Bring Up Their Children"* (Ithaca, NY–London 1951; paperback edn 1967, 1978).

Mayer, W. and Allen, P. *John Chrysostom*, ECF (London–New York 2000)

Schaff, P. (ed.), *A Select Library of Nicence and Post Nicene Fathers of the Christian Church,* Series 1, vols 9-14, (New York, 1886-1890; repr. Grand Rapids, MI 1975, 1988).

Schatkin, M.A. (trans.), *Discourse on Blessed Babylas and Against the Greeks*, in M.A. Schatkin and P.W. Harkins (eds), *Saint John Chrysostom: Apologist*, FOTC 73 (Washington, DC 1985) 1-152.

Schatkin, M.A., and Harkins, P.W. (eds), *Saint John Chrysostom: Apologist*, FOTC 73 (Washington, DC 1985).

Texts of Other Ancient Writers

Alexander of Aphrodisias
De fato
Bruns, I., *Alexander Aphrodisiensis praetor commentaria scripto minora (Commentaria I Aristotelem Graeca)*, supp. 2.2 (Berlin 1892) 164-212.

Aristotle
Bywater, I., *Aristotolis ethica Nicomachea* (Oxford 1894; repr. 1962).
Ross, W. D., *Aristotelis ars rhetorica* (Oxford 1959; repr. 1964).

Augustine
Contra Iulianum haeresis Pelagianae defensorem libri sex
Migne, J.-P. (ed.), PL 44,654-655.

Basil of Caesarea
Epistulae
Courtonne, Y., *Saint Basile, Lettres*, vol. 3 (Paris 1966).

Diodore
Olivier, J.M. (ed.), *Diodore of Tarsus: Commentarii in Psalmos. I, Commentarii in Psalmos I-L*, CCSG 6 (Turnhout 1980).

Epictetus
Dissertationes
Schenkel, H., *Epicteti dissertationes ab Arriano digestae* (Leipzig 1916; repr. 1965) 7-454.

Enchiridion
Schenkel, H., *Epicteti dissertationes ab Arriano digestae* (Leipzig 1916; repr. 1965) 5-38.

Herodotus
Historiae
Legrand, Ph.-E., *Hérodote, Histoires*, 9 vols (Paris 1932-1954).

Libanius
Foerster, R., *Orationes 1-64, Libanii opera*, vols 1-4 (Leipzig 1903-1908; repr. Hildesheim 1997).
—, *Declamationes 1-51, Libanii opera*, vols 5-7 (Leipzig 1909-1913; repr. Hildesheim 1997).
—, *Epistulae 1-1544, Libanii opera*, vols 10-11 (Leipzig 1921-1922; repr. Hildesheim 1997).

Plato
Republica in J. Burnett, *Platonis opera*, vol. 14 (Oxford 1902, repr.1968) STII 327a-621d.
Phaedrus, in J. Burnett, *Platonis opera*, vol. 2 (Oxford 1901, repr. 1967) ST III 227a 279c.

Plutarch
Plutarch, *Demosthenes*, in K. Ziegler (ed.), *Plutarchi vitae parallelae*, 2 vols (Leipzig 1964³) 312-368.

Plotinus
Enneades
Henry, P. and Schwyzer, H.-R., *Plotini Opera*, vol. 3 (Leiden 1973).

Theodore of Mopsuestia

Fragmenta in epistulam ad Romanos (in catenis) in K. Staab (ed.), *Pauluskommentar aus der griechischen Kirche aus Katenenhandschriften gesammelt* (Münster 1933) 83-112.

Devreese, R. (ed.), *Commentarii in Joannem (e catenis)*, in R. Devreese, *Essai sur Théodore de Mopsueste*, Studi e Testi 141 (Rome 1948) 301-409.

Mingana, A. (ed.), *Commentary of Theodore of Mopsuestia on the Nicene Creed*, Woodbrooke Studies 5 (Cambridge 1932).

Sprenger, H.N. (ed.), *Theodori Mopsuesteni Commentarius in XII Prophetas*, Biblica et Patristica 1 (Wiesbaden 1977).

Swete, H.B. (ed.), *Theodori Episcopi Mopsuesteni, In Epistolas B. Pauli: Commentarii, The Latin Version with the Greek Fragments with an Introduction, Notes and Indices*, 2 vols (Cambridge 1880, 1882).

Theodoret

Minge, J.P. (ed.), *Interpretatio in xiv epistula snacti Pauli*; PG 82 36-877.

Migne, J.P. (ed.), *Interpretatio in Psalmos*; PG 80 857-1997.

Migne, J.P. (ed.), *De providentia orationes decem*; PG 83 556-773.

Canivet, P., *Théodoret de Cyr.Thérapeutique des maladies helléniques*, 2 vols, SC 57 (Paris 1975). [*Graecarum affectionum curatio*].

Ettlinger, G.H., *Theodoret of Cyrus: Eranistes* (Oxford 1975).

Migne, J.P. (ed.), *Haereticarum fabularum compendium*; PG 83 336-556.

Papadopoulos-Kerameus, A., *Quaestiones et responsiones ad orthodoxos.* θεοδωήτου ἐπισκόπου πόλεως Κύρρου πρὸς τὰς ἐπενεχθείσας αὐτῷ ἐπερωτήσεις παρά τινος τὸν ἐξ Αἰγύπτου ἐπίσκοπον ἀποκρίσεις (St Petersberg 1895).

Thucydides

Historiae

Jones, H. S. and Powell, J.E. (eds), *Thucydidis historiae*, 2 vols (Oxford 1942^2).

Translations of Other Ancient Writers

Allen, P. and Neil, B., *Maximus the Confessor and His Companions: Documents from Exile*, OECT (Oxford 2002).

Bers, V. (trans.), *Demosthenes Speeches 50-59*, Orators of Classical Greece 6 (Austin, TX 2003).

Bradbury, S. (trans.), *Libanius: Selected Letters of Libanius: from the Age of Constantius and Julian*, TTH 41 (Liverpool 2004).

Crawley, R. (trans.) and Feetham, R. (rev.), *Thucydides: The Peloponnesian War*, GBWW 6 (Chicago–London–Toronto–Geneva 1952 repr.)

Deferrari, R.J. and McGuire, M.R.P. (trans.), *Basil*, vol. 4, *Letters 249-368. Address to Young Men on Greek literature*, LCL 270 (Cambridge, MA 1934).

Ellis, J.R., and Milns, R D., *The Spectre of Philip: Demosthenes'* First Philippic, Olynthiacs, *and* Speech On the Peace: *A Study in Historical Evidence*, Sources in Ancient History 1 (Sydney 1970).

Gibson, C. (trans.), "Libanius' *Hypotheses* to the Orations of Demosthenes", in C. Blackwell (ed.), *Dēmos: Classical Athenian Democracy*, at A.M. Mahoney and R. Scaife (eds), *The Stoa: A Consortium for Electronic Publication in the Humanities*, [www.stoa.org], 2003.

Halton, T. (trans.), *Theodoret of Cyrus: On Divine Providence (De Providentia orationes decem)*, ACW 49 (New York—Mahwah, NJ 1998).

Hill, R.C. (trans.), *Theodoret of Cyrus: Commentary on the Psalms*, FOTC 102 (Washington, DC 2000).

—, *Theodoret of Cyrus: Commentary on the Letters of St Paul*, 2 vols (Brookline, MA 2001).

—, *Theodore of Mopsuestia: Commentary on the Twelve Prophets*, FOC 108 (Washington, DC 2004).

—, *Diodore of Tarsus: Commentary on Psalms 1-51*, WGRW 9 (Atlanta, GA 2005).

Hornblower, S., *A Commentary on Thucydides,* vol. 1 (Oxford 1997).

Kalantzis, G. (trans.), *Theodore of Mopsuestia: Commentary on the Gospel of John*, ECS 7 (Strathfield 2004).

Macan, R.W. (trans.), *Herodotus: The Seventh, Eighth, and Ninth Books with Introduction and Commentary*, 2 vols (Edinburgh 1907).

MacDowell, D.M. (trans.), *Demosthenes Speeches 27-38,* The Oratory of Classical Greek (Austin, TX 2004).

Norman, A.F. (trans.), *Libanius: Selected Orations*, 2 vols, LCL 451-452 (Cambridge, MA–London 1969-1977).

—, *Libanius: Autobiography and Selected Letters*, 2 vols, LCL 478, 479 (Cambridge, MA–London 1992).

Rackham, H. (trans.), *Aristotle: Nicomachean Ethics*, LCL 19 (Cambridge, MA 1934).

Rawlinson, G. (trans.), *The History of Herodotus*, GBWW 6 (Chicago 1952).

Roberts, A. and Rambaut, W.H. (trans.), in A. Roberts and J. Donaldson (eds), *The Writings of Irenaeus* vol. 1, ANF 5 (Edinburgh–London–Dublin 1867).

Roberts, W.R. (trans.), *Aristotle: Rhetoric*, GBWW 9 (Chicago 1952) 593-675.

Rolfe, J.C. (trans.), *Ammianus Marcellinus: Roman History*, 3 vols LCL 300, 315, 331 (Cambridge, MA 1935-1939; repr. 1971-1972).

Ross, W.D. (trans.), *Aristotle: Nicomachean Ethics*, GBWW 9 (Chicago 1952) 335-436.

Russell, D. A. (trans.), *Libanius, Imaginary Speeches: A Selection of Declamations* (London 1996).

Schaff, P. and Wace, H. (eds), *A Select Library of Nicence and Post Nicene Fathers of the Christian Church,* Series 2, vols 3, 5, and 8 (New York 1890-1900; repr. Grand Rapids. MI 1975).

Sherwood, P. (trans.), *The Earlier Ambigua of St. Maximus the Confessor and his Refutation of Origenism,* Studia Anselmiana 36 (Rome 1955).

—, *St. Maximus the Confessor: The Ascetic Life; The Four Centuries on Charity*, ACW 21 (New York–Ramsey, NJ 1955).

Stevenson, J. (ed.), *Creeds, Councils, and Controversies: Documents Illustrative of the History of the Church A.D.337-46* (London 1966) 160-161.

Warner, R. (trans.), *Thucydides: History of the Peloponesian War*, Penguin Classics (Harmondsworth 1972[2]).

Wooten, C., *A Commentary on Demosthenes' Philippica I: With Rhetorical Analyses of Philippica II and Philippica III* (New York 2008).

Reference Works

Aland, K. et al (eds), *The Greek New Testament* (Stuttgart 1994[4]).

Aldama, J.A. de, *Repertorium pseudochrysostomicum,* Documents, études et répertoires publiés par l'Institut de Recherche et d'Histoire des Textes (Paris 1965).

Geerard, M. (ed.), *Clavis Patrum Graecorum. II. Ab Athanasio ad Chrysostomum,* Corpus Christianorum (Turnhout 1974).

Geerard, M. and Noret, J. (eds), *Clavis Patrum Graecorum. Supplementum*, Corpus Christianorum (Turnhout 1998).

Howatson, M.C. (ed.), *The Oxford Companion to Classical Literature* (Oxford 1989).

Moulton, J.H. and Milligan, G. (eds), *The Vocabulary of thre Greek New Testament: Illustrated from the Papyri and Other Non-Literary Sources* (Grand Rapids, MI 1930; repr. 1980).

Rahlfs, A. (ed.), *Septuaginta*, 2 vols (Stuttgart 1935[9]; repr. 1971).

BIBLIOGRAPHY
Secondary Sources

Aland, B., "Trustworthy preaching: reflections on John Chrysostom's interpretation of Romans 8", in S.K. Soderlund and N.T. Wright (eds), *Romans and the People of God: Essays in Honor of Gordon D. Fee on the Occasion of his 65th Birthday* (Grand Rapids–Cambridge 1999) 271-280.

Allen, P., "The homilist and the congregation: a case-study of Chrysostom's Homilies on Hebrews", *Augustinianum* 36 (1996) 397-421.

Allen, P. and Neil, B., *Maximus the Confessor and His Companions: Documents from Exile*, OECT (Oxford 2002).

Altaner, B., "Augustinus und Johannes Chrysostomus. Quellenkritische Untersuchungen", *Kleine Patristiche Schriften herausgegeben von Günter Glockmann* (Berlin 1967) 302-311, repr. from *Zeitschrift für neutestamntliche Wissenschaft* 44 (1952-1953) 76-84.

Amand, D., *Fatalisme and liberté dans l'Antiquité grecque* (Louvain 1945).

Ameringer, T.E., *A Study in Greek Rhetoric: The Stylistic Influence of the Second Sophistic on the Panegyrical Sermons of St John Chrysostom*, Patristic Studies of the CUA 5 (Washington, DC 1921) 102.

Amirav, H., "Exegetical models and Chrysostomian homiletics: the example of Gen. 6.2", *SP* 37 (1999) 311-325.

—, *Rhetoric and Tradition: John Chrysostom on Noah and the Flood*, TEG 12 (Leuven 2003).

Anderson, G., *The Second Sophistic: A Cultural Phenomenon in the Roman Empire* (New York 1993).

Attrep, A., "The Teacher and his teachings: Chrysostom's homiletic approach as seen in the commentaries on the Gospel of John", *St Vladimir's Theological Quarterly* 38 (1994) 293-301.

Bardenhewer, O., *Patrology: The Lives and Works of the Fathers of the Church*, trans. T.J. Shahan (Freiburg–St Louis, MO 1908).

Barkhuizen, J.H., "John Chrysostom on the parables in the Gospel of Matthew: a study in Antiochean exegesis", *Ekklesiastikos Pharos* 80 (1998) 160-178.

Barr, J., *The Semantics of Biblical Language* (London 1961).

Baur, C., *John Chrysostom and His Time*, 2 vols, trans. M. Gonzaga (London–Glasgow 1959-1960²).

Benin, S.D., "The 'cunning of God' and divine accommodation", *Journal of the History of Ideas* 45 (1984) 179-191.

—, *The Footprints of God: Divine Accommodation in Jewish and Christian Thought* (Albany, NY 1993).

—, "Sacrifice as education in Augustine and Chrysostom", *Church History* 52 (1983) 7-20.

Berkhof, H., *Christian Faith: An Introduction to the Study of the Faith*, trans. S. Woudstra (Grand Rapids 1979).

Blass, F., *Die attische Beredsamkeit*, 3 vols (Leipzig 1887-1898²).

Bobzien, S., *Determinism and Freedom in Stoic Philosophy* (Oxford 1998).

Boularand, E., "La nécessité de la grâce pour arriver à la foi d'après Saint Jean Chrysostome", *Gregorianum* 19 (1938) 514-542.

Bouyer, L., *The Spirituality of the New Testament and the Fathers,* trans. M.P. Ryan, A History of Christian Spirituality 1 (London 1963).

Brändle, R., "Jean Chrysostom: l'importance de Matth. 25.31-46 pour son éthique" *Vigiliae Christianae* 31 (1977) 47-52.

—, "*Sunkatabasis* als hermeneutisches und ethisches Prinzip in der Paulusauslegung des Johannes Chrysostomus", in G. Schöllgen and C. Schölten (eds.), *Stimuli: Exegese und ihre Hermeneutik in Antike und Christentum. Festschrift für Ernst Dassmann* (Münster 1996) 297-307.

—, "Johannes Chrysostomus I.", in E. von Dassmann et al. (eds), *RAC* 17 (Stuttgart 1998) cols 426-503.

—, *Johannes Chrysostomus: Bischof – Reformer – Märtyr* (Stuttgart–Berlin–Cologne 1999).

—, *John Chrysostom: Bishop – Reformer – Martyr*, trans. J. Cawte and S. Trzcionka, with rev. notes by W. Mayer, ECS 8 (Strathfield 2004).

—, "Synergismus als Phänomen der Frömmigkeitsgeschichte, dargestellt an den Predigten des Johannes Chrysostomus", in F. von Lilienfeld and E. Mühlenberg (eds.), *Gnadenwahl und Entscheidungsfreiheit in der Theologie der Alten Kirche. Vorträge gehalten auf der Patristischen Arbeitsgemeinschaft, 3-5. Januar 1979 in Bethel*, Oikonomia 9 (Erlangen 1980) 69-89 and 113-121.

Brennan, T., "Stoic moral psychology", in B. Inwood (ed.), *The Cambridge Companion to the Stoics* (Cambridge 2003) 257-294.

Brundage, J.A., *Law, Sex and Christian Society in Medieval Europe* (Chicago 1987).

Brunner, E., *The Christian Doctrine of Creation and Redemption: Dogmatics*, vol. 2, trans. O. Wyon (London 1952).

Campenhausen, H. von, *The Fathers of the Greek Church* (London 1963).

Carey, C., "Rhetorical means of persuasion", in I. Worthington (ed.), *Persuasion: Greek Rhetoric in Action* (New York 1994) 26-45.

Carter, R.E., "The future of Chrysostom studies: theology and Nachleben", in P. Christou (ed.), *ΣΥΜΠΟΣΙΟΝ: Studies on St John Chrysostom*, Analecta Vlatadon 18 (Thessaloniki 1973) www.myriobiblos.gr/texts/English/

carter_future.html.

—, "St John Chrysostom's rhetorical use of the Socratic distinction between kingship and tyranny", *Traditio* 14 (1958) 367-371.

Cassel, D., "Key principles in Cyril of Alexandria's exegesis", *SP* 37 (2001) 411-420.

Chadwick, H., "Freedom and necessity in early Christian thought about God", *Concilium* 166 (1983) 8-13.

Chase, F.H., *Chrysostom, A Study in the History of Biblical Interpretation* (Cambridge 1887).

Chirban, J.T. (ed.), *Personhood: Orthodox Christianity and the Connection between Body, Mind, and Soul* (Westport, CT–London 1996).

Christou, P., "Maximos the Confessor on the infinity of man," in F. Heinzer and C. Schönborn (eds), *Actes du Symposium sur Maxime le Confesseur* (Fribourg 1982) 261-271.

Chryssavgis, J., "Sin and grace – an Orthodox perspective", *Colloquium* 26 (1994) 73-93.

Clark, E.A., *Reading Renunciation: Asceticism and Scripture in Early Christianity* (Princeton, NJ 1999).

Clayton Jr, P.B., *The Christology of Theodoret of Cyrus: Antiochene Christology from the Council of Ephesus (431) to the Council of Chalcedon (451)*, OECS (Oxford–New York 2007).

Collett, B., "A Benedictine scholar and Greek patristic thought in pre-Tridentine Italy: a monastic commentary of 1538 on Chrysostom", *JEH* 36 (1985) 66-81.

Constantelos, D., "Hellenic paedeia and church fathers – educational principles and cultural heritage," Greek Orthodox Archdiocese of America art. 8 (New York 2003). http://www.goarch.org/print/en/ourfaith/article8143.asp.

—, "John Chrysostom's Greek Classical education and its importance to us today", *Greek Orthodox Review* 36 (1991) 109-129.

Crane, G.R. (ed.), Perseus Digital Library Project, Greek and Roman Collections, Word Frequency Information, at www.perseus.tufts.edu/hopper

Cribiore, R., *Gymnasts of the Mind: Greek Education in Hellenistic and Roman Egypt* (Princeton–Oxford 2005).

—, "Lucian, Libanius, and the short road to rhetoric", *GRBS* 47 (2007) 71-86.

—, *The School of Libanius in Late Antique Antioch* (Princeton, NJ 2007).

Cudwood, R., *A Treatise Concerning Eternal and Immutable Morality; with a Treatise of Freewill*, S. Hutton (ed.), Cambridge Texts in the History of Philosophy (Cambridge–New York 1996).

Cunningham, M.B. and Allen, P. (eds), *Preacher and Audience: Studies in Early*

Christian and Byzantine Homiletics, A New History of the Sermon 1 (Leiden–Boston–Cologne 1998).

Dewart, J.McW., *The Theology of Grace of Theodore of Mopsuestia,* Studies in Christian Antiquity 16 (Washington, DC 1971).

Dobbin, R., "Προαίρεσις in Epictetus", *Ancient Philosophy* 11 (1991) 111-135.

Donegan, S., "John Chrysostom's exegesis of Romans 5:12-21: does it support a doctrine of original sin?", *Diakonia* 22 (1988-1989) 5-14.

Downey, G., *Antioch in the Age of Theodosius the Great,* The Centers of Civilization Series (Norman, OK 1962).

Easterling, P.E. and Kenny, E.J. (eds), *The Cambridge History of Classical Literature,* vol. 1 (Cambridge 1985).

Edmunds, L., *Chance and Intelligence in Thucydides,* Loeb Classical Monographs (Cambridge MA 1975).

Edwards, M., "Pagan and Christian monotheism in the age of Constantine", in S. Swain and M. Edwards (eds), *Approaching Late Antiquity: The Transformation from Early to Late Empire* (New York 2004) 211-234.

Fabbi, F., "La 'condescendenza divina nell'inspirazione biblica secondo s. Giovanni Crisostomo", *Biblica* 14 (1933) 330-347.

Fabricius, C., *Zu den Jugendschriften des Johannes Chrysostomos: Untersuchungen zum Klassizismus des vierten Jahrhunderts* (Lund 1962).

Fairweather, J., "The Epistle to the Galatians and Classical rhetoric: parts 1 and 2", *Tyndale Bulletin* 45 (1994) 1-38.

Fee, G.D., *To What End Exegesis? Essays Textual, Exegetical and Theological* (Grand Rapids, MI–Cambridge 2001).

Festugière, A.-J., *Antioche païenne et chrétienne: Libanius, Chrysostome et les moines de Syrie* (Paris 1959).

Fisher, N.R.E., "*Hybris* and dishonour: I", *Greece and Rome* 23 (1976) 177-193.

—, "*Hybris* and dishonour: II", *Greece and Rome* 26 (1979) 32-47.

Flanagan, M.H., *St. John Chrysostom's Doctrine of Condescension and Accuracy in the Scriptures: Being an Extract from an Essay having the above title which was Presented to the Theological Faculty of St. Patrick's College, Maynooth, as a Thesis for the Degree of Doctor* (N.Z. 1948).

Foxhalk, L. and Lewis, A.D.E. (eds), *Greek Law in its Political Setting: Justifications not Justice* (Oxford 1996).

Frede, D., "Stoic determinism", in B. Inwood (ed.), *The Cambridge Companion to the Stoics* (Cambridge 2003) 179-205.

Gargarin, M., "Probability and persuasion: Plato and early Greek rhetoric", in I. Worthington (ed.), *Persuasion: Greek Rhetoric in Action* (New York 1994).

Gauthier, R.A., "Saint Maxime le Confesseur et la psychologie de 'acte humain'",

Recherches de théologie ancienne et médiévale 21 (1954) 51-200.

Gill, C., "The school in the Roman imperial period", in B. Inwood (ed.), *The Cambridge Companion to the Stoics* (Cambridge 2003) 33-58.

Gilson, E., *The Spirit of Medieval Philosophy*, trans. A.H.C. Downes, Gifford Lectures 1931-1932 (London 1936).

Gorday, P., *Principles of Patristic Exegesis: Romans 9-11 in Origen, John Chrysostom and Augustine*, SBEC 4 (New York–Toronto 1983).

Greer, R.A., *Theodore of Mopsuestia: Exegete and Theologian* (Westminster 1961).

Griffith, M., "'Public' and 'private' in early Greek institutions of education", in Yun Lee Too (ed.), *Education in Greek and Roman Antiquity* (Boston 2001) 23-84.

Hall, C.A., "John Chrysostom's 'On Providence': a translation and theological interpretation", diss. Drew University 1991.

—, *Learning Theology with the Church Fathers* (Downers Grove 2002).

—, "Nature wild and tame in St John Chrysostom's 'On the Providence of God'", in K. Tanner and C.A. Hall (eds), *Ancient and Postmodern Christianity* (Downers Grove 2002) 23-37.

Hall, M.D., "Even dogs have Erinyes: sanctions in Athenian practice and thinking", in L. Foxhalk and A.D.E. Lewis (eds), *Greek Law in Its Political Setting: Justifications not Justice* (Oxford 1996) 73-89

Halliwell, S., "Philosophy and rhetoric", in I. Worthington (ed.), *Persuasion: Greek Rhetoric in Action* (New York 1994) 222-243.

Hansen, M.H., *The Athenian Ecclesia II: A Collection of Articles 1983-1989*, (Copenhagen 1989).

—, "The numbers of rhetores in the Athenian ecclesia 355-322 BC", *GRBS* 24 (1984) 123-155.

Harkins, P.W., "Chrysostom's *Sermo Ad Neophytos*", *SP* 10 (1970) 112-117.

Hartney, A., "Men, women and money: John Chrysostom and the transformation of the city", *SP* 37 (1999) 527-534.

—, *John Chrysostom and the Transformation of the City* (London 2004).

Heaney-Hunter, J.-A., "Disobedience and curse or affection of the soul?", *Diakonia* 23 (1990) 21-42.

Heath, M., "John Chrysostom, rhetoric and Galatians", *Biblical Interpretation* 12 (2004) 369-400.

Hill, R.C., "*Akribeia*: a principle of Chrysostom's Exegesis," *Colloquium* 14 (1981) 32-36.

—, "On looking again at *synkatabasis*", *Prudentia* 13 (1981) 3-11.

—, "Chrysostom's terminology for the inspired Word", *EB* 41 (1983) 367-373.

—, "Chrysostom as Old Testament commentator", *EB* 46 (1988) 61-77.

—, "A Pelagian commentator on the Psalms", *ITQ* 63 (1988) 263-271.

—, "The spirituality of Chrysostom's *Commentary on the Psalms*", *JECS* 5 (1997) 569-579.

—, "Chrysostom, interpreter of the Psalms", *EB* 56 (1998) 61-74.

—, *Reading the Old Testament in Antioch,* Bible in Ancient Christianity 5 (Leiden–Boston 2005.

—, "Theodoret's commentary on Paul," *EB* 58 (2000) 1-21.

How, W.W. and Wells, J., *A Commentary on Herodotus*, vol. 2 (Oxford 1928).

Huart, P., *Le Vocabulaire de l'analyse psychologique dans l'œuvre de Thucydide*, Études et Commentaires 69 (Paris 1968).

—, *Γνώμη chez Thucydide et ses contemporains (Sophocle – Euripide – Antiphon – Andocide –Aristophane)*, Études et Commentaires 81 (Paris 1973).

Hunter, D.G., "Borrowings from Libanius in the *Comparatio regis et monachi* of St John Chrysostom", *Journal of Theological Studies* n.s. 39 (1988) 525-531.

—, "Libanius and John Chrysostom: new thoughts on an old problem", *SP* 22 (1989) 129-135.

—, "Preaching and propaganda in fourth-century Antioch: John Chrysostom's *Homilies on the Statues*", in D.G. Hunter (ed.), *Preaching in the Patristic Age: Studies in Honor of Walter J. Burghardt* (New York–Mahwah, NJ 1989) 119-138.

Inwood, B., *Ethics and Human Action in Early Stoicism* (Oxford 1985).

Jaeger, W., *Early Christianity and the Greek Paideia* (Cambridge, MA 1965).

—, *The Greek Paideia*, 3 vols trans. G. Highet (New York 1943-1945).

Johnson, A.P., "Approaching late antiquity: the transformation from early to late empire", Review article, *Theological Studies* 66 (2005) 891-892.

Jones, A.H.M., "St John Chrysostom's parentage and education", *HTR* 46 (1953) 171-173.

Karavites, P., "*Gnome's* nuances: from its beginning to the end of the fifth century", *Classical Bulletin* 66 (1990) 9-34.

Kelly, J.N.D., *Early Christian Doctrines* (London 1968[4]).

—, *Golden Mouth: The Story of John Chrysostom – Ascetic, Preacher. Bishop* (New York 1995).

Kennedy, G.A., *A New History of Classical Rhetoric* (Princeton, NJ 1994).

Kenny, A., "Was Chrysostom a semi-Pelagian?", *Irish Quarterly Review* 27 (1960) 16-29.

—, *Reason and Religion: Essays in Philosophical Theology* (Oxford 1987).

Kinzig, W., "The Greek Christian writers", in S.E. Porter (ed.), *Handbook of Classical Rhetoric in the Hellenistic Period 330 BC – AD 400* (Boston–Leiden 2001) 645-670.

Laird, R.J., "The theology of grace in the thought of St John Chrysostom as discerned in his Homilies on first Corinthians", diss., University of Newcastle, NSW 1989.

—, "St John Chrysostom and the γνώμη: the critical faculty accountable for sin in his anthropology", diss., University of Sydney 2008.

Laistner, M.L.W., *Christianity and Pagan Culture in the Later Roman Empire together with an English translation of John Chrysostom's "Address on Vainglory and the Right Way for Parents to Bring Up Their Children"* (Ithaca, NY–London 1951).

Lakoff, G. and Johnson, M., *Metaphors We Live By* (Chicago–London 1980).

Leyerle, B., "John Chrysostom on almsgiving and the use of money", *HTR* 87 (1994) 29-47.

Liebescheutz, J.H.W.G., *Barbarians and Bishops: Army, Church, and State in the Age of Arcadius and Chrysostom* (Oxford–New York 1991).

Locke, J., *An Essay Concerning Human Understanding*, GBWW 35 (Chicago–London–Toronto–Geneva 1952) 85-395.

Long, A.A., *Epictetus: A Stoic and Socratic Guide to Life* (Oxford 2002).

Lossky, V., *The Mystical Theology of the Eastern Church* (Crestwood, NY 1976).

Louth, A., "Dogma and spirituality in St Maximus the Confessor", P. Allen et al. (eds), *Prayer and Spirituality in the Early Church* (Everton Park 1998) 197-208.

—, *Maximus the Confessor,* ECF (London–New York 1996).

Luginbill, R.D., *Thucydides on War and National Character* (Boulder, CO 1999).

McCormick, A.S., "John Chrysostom's Homily 50 as an example of the Antiochene exegetical tradition", *Patristic and Byzantine Review* 12 (1993) 65-82.

McFague, S., *Metaphorical Theology: Models of God in Religious Language* (London 1982).

McFarland, I.A., "'Naturally and by grace': Maximus the Confessor on the operation of the will'', *Scottish Journal of Theology* 58 (2005) 410-433.

McLeod, F.G., *The Image of God in the Antiochene Tradition* (Washington, DC 1999).

—, Theodore of Mopsuestia revisited", *Theological Studies* 61 (2000) 447-480.

Malingrey, A-M., *"Philosophia"*: *Étude d'un groupe de mots dans la littérature grecque, des Présocratiques au IVe siècle après J.-C.*, Études et Commentaires 40 (Paris 1961).

Martin, E., "Golden mouths and speaking bodies: St John Chrysostom's depiction of Christian martyrs", *eSharp* 8 (Autumn 2006) 1-20.

Martin, R.P., "Gnomes in poems: wisdom performance on the Athenian stage", Princeton–Stanford Working Papers in Classics (May 2005) 1-25.

Maxwell, J.L., *Christianization and Communication in Late Antiquity: John Chrysostom and His Congregation in Antioch* (Cambridge 2006).

—, "Lay piety in the sermons of John Chrysostom", in D. Krueger (ed.), *Byzantine Christianity*, A People's History of Christianity 3 (Minneapolis, MN 2006) 19-38.

Mayer, W., "John Chrysostom: extraordinary preacher, ordinary audience" in M.B. Cunningham and P. Allen (eds), *Preacher and Audience: Studies in Early Christian and Byzantine Homiletics,* A New History of the Sermon 1 (Leiden–Boston–Cologne 1998) 105-137.

—, "Poverty and society in the world of John Chrysostom", in L. Lavan, W. Bowden, A. Gutteridge and C. Kachado (eds), *Social and Political Archaeology in Late Antiquity*, Late Antique Archaeology 3 (Leiden 2006) 465-484.

Meyendorff, J., *Byzantine Theology: Historical Trends and Doctrinal Themes* (New York 1979²).

Meyer, L., "Liberté et moralisme chrétien dans la doctrine spirituelle de Saint Jean Chrysostome", *Recherches de science religieuse* 23 (1933) 283-305.

—, *Saint Jean Chrysostome, maître de perfection chrétienne*, Études de théologie historique 19 (Paris 1933).

Mitchell, M.M., *The Heavenly Trumpet: John Chrysostom and the Art of Pauline Interpretation* (Louisville, KY–Westminster, MD 2002).

Morgan, G.C., *God's Last Word to Man: Studies in Hebrews* (London–Edinburgh 1948).

Mühlenberg, E., "From early Christian morality to theological ethics", *SP* 19 (1987) 203-215.

Murphy, F.X., "The moral doctrine of St John Chrysostom", *SP* 11/ 2 (1967) 52-64.

Murphy, N., *Beyond Liberalism and Fundamentalism: How Modern and Postmodern Philosophy Set the Theological Agenda* (Valley Forge, PA 1996).

Murray, G., *A History of Ancient Greek Literature* (New York 1897).

Muto, S., "The Syrian origin of the divine condescension as the key to biblical interpretation", *The Harp* 20 (2006) 249-261.

Naegele, A., "Johannes Chrysostomus und sein Verhältnis zum Hellenismus", *Byzantinische Zeitschrift* 13 (1904) 73-113.

Nash, H.S., "The exegesis of the School of Antioch", *JBL* 11 (1892) 22-37.

Nassif, B., "The 'spiritual exegesis' of Scripture: the school of Antioch revisited", *Anglican Theological Review* 75 (1993) 437-470.

—, "Antiochene in John Chrysostom's exegesis", in K. Tanner and C.A. Hall (eds), *Ancient Modern Christianity* (Downers Grove, IL 2002) 23-37.

Neil, B., "The blessed passion of holy love: Maximus the Confessor's spiritual psychology", *Australian E-Journal of Theology* 2 (February 2004) np. http://dlibrary.acu.edu.au/research/theology/ejournal/aejt_2/bronwen_neil.htm.

—, "Two views on vice and virtue: Augustine of Hippo and Maximus the Confessor", in B. Neil, G.D. Dunn and L. Cross (eds), *Prayer and Spirituality in the Early Church* vol. 3: *Liturgy and Life* (Strathfield 2003) 261-271.

Nichols, A., *Byzantine Gospel: Maximus the Confessor in Modern Scholarship* (Edinburgh 1993).

Norman, A.F., "The book trade in fourth-century Antioch", *JHS* 80 (1960) 122-126.

Norris, R.A., *Manhood and Christ: A Study in the Christology of Theodore of Mopsuestia* (Oxford 1963).

Nowak, E., *Le Chrétien devant la souffrance. Étude sur la pensée de Jean Chrysostome,* Théologie Historique 19 (Paris 1972).

Ober, J., *Mass and Elite in Democratic Athens: Rhetoric, Ideology, and the Power of the People* (Princeton, NJ 1989).

O'Keefe, J.J., "Sin, ἀπάθεια, and freedom of the will in Gregory of Nyssa", *SP* 22 (1989) 52-59.

Olivar, A., "Reflections on problems raised by early Christian preaching", trans. J. Munitiz, in M.B. Cunningham and P. Allen (eds), *Preacher and Audience: Studies in Early Christian and Byzantine Homiletics,* A New History of the Sermon 1 (Leiden–Boston–Cologne 1998) 21-32.

Osborn, E., *Ethical Patterns in Early Christian Thought* (London–New York–Melbourne 1976).

Pagels, E., *Adam, Eve, and the Serpent* (New York 1988).

Papageorgiou, P.E., "Chrysostom and Augustine on the sin of Adam and its consequences", *St Vladimir's Theological Quarterly* 39 (1995) 316-378.

Pelikan, J., *The Christian Tradition: A History of the Development of Doctrine. The Emergence of the Catholic Tradition (100-600),* vol. 1 (Chicago–London 1971).

Perusek, G., "Strategy and changing moods in Thucydides", *Poroi* 3.2 (December 2004). http://inpress.lib.uiowa.edu/poroi/papers/perusek041001.html.

Petit, P., *Les Étudiants de Libanius* (Paris 1956).

Phan, P.C., *Grace and the Human Condition,* MFC 15 (Wilmington, DE 1988).

Pink, T. and Stone, M.W. (eds), *The Will and Human Action: From Antiquity to the Present Day* (New York 2003).

Plested, M., "The Influence of St John Chrysostom in the West", Symposium in honour of the 1600th anniversary of St John Chrysostom held under the aegis of the Ecumenical Patriarchate, Constantinople, 13-18 September

2007. http://www.iocs.cam.ac.uk/resources/texts/st_john_chrysostom_in_the_west. pdf. Accessed 30.06.11.

Pollard, T.E., "The origins of Christian exegesis", *JRH* 1 (1961) 138-147.

Porter, S.E., *Handbook of Classical Rhetoric in the Hellenistic Period 330 BC-AD 400* (Boston–Leiden 2001).

Price, A.W., "Aristotle, the Stoics and the will", in T. Pink and M.W.F. Stone (eds), *The Will and Human Action: From Antiquity to the Present Day* (New York 2003) 29-52.

Price, J.J., *Thucydides and Internal War* (Cambridge 2001).

Quasten, J., *Patrology*, vol. 3: *The Golden Age of Greek Literature: From the Council of Nicaea to the Council of Chalcedon* (Utrecht–Antwerp 1960).

Quiroga, A., "From Sophistopolis to Episcopolis. The case for a Third Sophistic", *Journal for Late Antique Religion and Culture* 1 (2007) 31-42.

Reuling, H., *After Eden: Church Fathers and Rabbis on Genesis 3:16-21* (Leiden 2006).

Romeny, R.B. ter Haar, "Eusebius of Emesa's Commentary on Genesis and the origins of the Antiochene school", in J. Frishman and L. Van Rompay (eds), *The Book of Genesis in Jewish and Oriental Christian Interpretation: A Collection of Essays*, TEG 5 (Leuven 1997).

Rondet, H., *Original Sin: The Patristic and Theological Background*, trans. C. Finnegan (New York 1972).

Rood, T., Review article of Robert D. Luginbill, *Thucydides on War and National Character*, *Bryn Mawr Classical Review* (1999) http://ccat. sas.upenn.edu/bmcr/200/2000.02.20.html.

Rupprecht, A., "Die demosthenische Prooemiensammlung", *Philologos* 82 (A27) 365-432.

Rylaarsdam, D., "Painful preaching: John Chrysostom and the philosophical tradition of feeding souls," *SP* 41 (2006) 463-468.

—, "The adaptability of divine pedagogy: *sunkatabasis* in the theology and rhetoric of John Chrysostom", diss., University of Notre Dame 1999.

Sandwell, I., "Outlawing magic or outlawing religion?: Libanius and the Theodosian Code as evidence for legislation against pagan practices in the fourth century AD", in W.V. Harris (ed.), *Understanding the Spread of Christianity in the First Four Centuries: Essays in Explanation*, Columbia Studies in the Classical Tradition 27 (Leiden–Boston 2005) 87-124.

—, *Religious Identity in Late Antiquity: Greeks, Jews and Christians in Antioch* (Cambridge 2007).

Schäublin, C., *Untersuchungen zu Methode und Herkunft der antiochenischen*

Exegese, Theophaneia: Beiträge zur Religions- und Kirchengeschichte des Altertums 23 (Cologne–Bonn 1974).

—, "Diodor von Tarsus", *TRE* 8 (1981) 763-767.

Schor, A., "Theodoret on the 'school of Antioch': a network approach", *JECS* 15 (2007) 517-562.

Schouler, B., *La Tradition Héllenique chez Libanios* (Lille–Paris 1984).

Shatkin, M.A., *John Chrysostom as Apologist, with Special Reference to* De incomprehensibili, Quod nemo laeditur, Ad eos qui scandalizati sunt, *and* Adversus oppugantores vitae monasticae, Analecta Vlatadon 50 (Thessaloniki 1987).

Simonetti, M., *Biblical Interpretation in the Early Church: An Historical Introduction to Patristic Exegesis*, trans. J.A. Hughes (Edinburgh 1994).

Sorabji, R., *Emotion and Peace of Mind: From Stoic Agitation to Christian Temptation* (Oxford-New York 2000).

—, "The concept of will from Plato to Maximus the Confessor" in T. Pink and M.W.F. Stone (eds), *The Will and Human Action: From Antiquity to the Present Day* (New York 2003) 6-28.

—, *The Philosophy of the Commentators 200-600 AD: A Sourcebook*, vol. 2: *Physics*, (Ithaca, NY 2005).

Soskice, J., *Metaphor and Religious Language* (Oxford 1985).

Stavropoulos, C., "Partakers of the divine nature" in D.B. Glendenin (ed.), *Eastern Orthodoxy: A Contemporary Reader* (Grand Rapids 1965) 183-192.

Stephens, W.R.W., *Saint John Chrysostom; His Life and Times: A Sketch of the Church and the Empire in the Fourth Century* (London 1883[3]).

Stiver, D.R., *Theology after Ricoeur: New Directions in Hermeneutical Theology* (Louisville, KY 2001).

Stockton, D., *The Classical Athenian Democracy* (New York 1990).

Swain, S. and Edwards, M. (eds), *Approaching Late Antiquity: The Transformation from Early to Late Empire* (New York 2004).

Tanner, R.G., "Chrysostom's exegesis of Romans", *SP* 17 (1982) 1185-1197.

Thonnard, F.J., "Saint Jean Chrysostome et Saint Augustin dans la controverse pélagienne", *Revue des Études Byzantines* 25 (1967) 189-218.

Thunberg, L., *Man and the Cosmos: The Vision of St Maximus the Confessor* (Crestwood, NY 1985).

—, *Microcosm and Mediator: The Theological Anthropology of Maximus the Confessor*, trans. A.M. Allchin (Chicago 1995[2]).

Thurén, L., "John Chrysostom as a rhetorical critic: the hermeneutics of an early Father", *Biblical Interpretation* 9 (2001) 180-218.

Torrance, I.R., "'God the physician': ecclesiology, sin and forgiveness in the preaching of St. John Chrysostom," *Greek Orthodox Theological Review* 44 (1999) 163-176.

Trakatellis, D., "Being transformed: Chrysostom's exegesis of the Epistle to the Romans", *Greek Orthodox Theological Review* 36 (1991) 211-229.

—, *Being Transformed: Chrysostom's Exegesis of the Epistle to the Romans* (Brookline, MA 1992).

Tse, M.W., "*Synkatabasis* and *akribeia* – the warp and woof of Chrysostom's hermeneutic: a study based on Chrysostom's Genesis homilies", *Jian Dao* 15 (2001) 1-17.

Tyng, D., "Theodore of Mopsuestia as an interpreter of the Old Testament", *JBL* 50 (1931) 298-303.

Usher, S.A., *Greek Oratory: Tradition and Originality* (New York 1999).

Walden, J.W.H., *The Universities of Ancient Greece* (New York 1909).

Wallace, R.W., "The power to speak—and not to listen—in ancient Athens", in I. Sluiter and R.M. Rosen (eds), *Free Speech in Classical Antiquity*, Mnemosyne Suppl. 254 (Leiden 2004) 221-232.

Wallace-Hadrill, D.S., *Christian Antioch: A Study of Early Christian Thought in the East* (Cambridge 1982).

Ware, K., "In the image and likeness: the uniqueness of the human person" in J.T. Chirban, (ed.), *Personhood: Orthodox Christianity and the Connection between Body, Mind, and Soul* (Westport, CT–London 1996) 1-13.

Wilken, R.L., "Defence of allegory", *Modern Theology* 14 (1998) 198-212.

—, "Biblical humanism: the patristic convictions" in R. Lints, M.S. Horton and M.R. Talbot (eds), *Personal Identity in Theological Perspective* (Grand Rapids,MI–Cambridge 2006) 13-28.

Wilson, P., *The Athenian Institution of the Khoregia* (Cambridge 2000).

Wittgenstein, L., *Philosophische Untersuchungen: Bi-lingual Edition*, trans. G.E.M. Anscombe (London 1958[2]).

Wood, J., *Epistemology: Becoming Intellectually Virtuous* (Leicester 1998).

Wooten, C., *A Commentary on Demosthenes' Philippica I: with Rhetorical Analyses of Philippica II and Philippica III* (New York 2008).

Worthington, I., *Persuasion: Greek Rhetoric in Action* (New York 1994).

Yazigi, P.I., "Human freedom and eschatology: freedom and fall", and "the eschatological pedagogy (παιδεία): the 'Good'", Cambridge University Institute of Orthodox Christian Studies, November 2006.

—, "Fleshy, psychic and spiritual man: flesh's and soul's warfare according to the Apostle Paul and St John Chrysostom", (www.balamand.edu.lb/theology/Hawliyat/vol4-5/hawlia.1fr.pdf).

Young, F., *From Nicaea to Chalcedon: A Guide to the Literature and its Background*

(London 1983).

—, "Exegetical method and scriptural proof: the Bible in doctrinal debate", *SP* 19 (1988) 290-304.

—, "The rhetorical schools and their influence on patristic exegesis" in R. Williams (ed.), *The Making of Orthodoxy: Essays in Honour of Henry Chadwick* (Cambridge 1989) 182-199.

—, "Paideia and the myth of static dogma", in S. Coakley and D.A. Pallin (eds), *The Making and Remaking of Christian Doctrine: Essays in Honour of Maurice Wiles* (Oxford 1993) 265-282.

—, *Biblical Exegesis and the Formation of Christian Culture*, Cambridge 1997.

Yunis, H., *Taming Democracy: Models of Political Rhetoric in Classical Athens* (Ithaca, NY 1996).

General Index

Ancient Authors Index

Modern Authors Index

Scripture Index

CPSIA information can be obtained
at www.ICGtesting.com
Printed in the USA
LVHW021930190720
661002LV00015B/607